Texte und Studien zum Antiken Judentum

herausgegeben von
Martin Hengel und Peter Schäfer

40

Die Deutsche Bibliothek – CIP-Einheitsaufnahme

Wilson, Walter T.:
The mysteries of righteousness: the literary composition and genre of the
sentence of Pseudo-Phocylides / bei Walter T. Wilson. – Tübingen: Mohr, 1994
   (Texte und Studien zum antiken Judentum; 40)
   ISBN 3–16–146211–4
NE: GT

The book was typeset by M. Fischer in Tübingen using Times typeface, printed by Gulde-Druck in Tübingen on acid-free paper from Papierfabrik Buhl in Ettlingen and bound by Heinr. Koch in Tübingen.

ISSN 0721–8753

The Mysteries of Righteousness

The Literary Composition and Genre
of the *Sentences* of Pseudo-Phocylides

by

Walter T. Wilson

To Dieter,
With warm regards–
–Walter

J.C.B. Mohr (Paul Siebeck) Tübingen

For Beth

οὐ μὲν γὰρ τοῦ γε κρεῖσσον καὶ ἄρειον,
ἢ ὅθ᾿ ὁμοφρονέοντε νοήμασιν οἶκον ἔχητον
ἀνὴρ ἠδὲ γυνή· πόλλ᾿ ἄλγεα δυσμενέεσσι,
χάρματα δ᾿ εὐμενέτῃσι, μάλιστα δέ τ᾿ ἔκλυον αὐτοί.

For there is nothing greater or more splendid
than when man and wife dwell in their home
with one heart and mind, a grief to their foes
and a joy to their friends; but they themselves know it best.

Homer, *Odyssey* VI.182–185

Acknowledgments

It is a pleasure to acknowledge here those friends and colleagues who have generously assisted with the preparation and publication of this investigation of the literary composition and genre of Pseudo-Phocylides' *Sentences*. I owe a special debt of gratitude to Professor Hans Dieter Betz (University of Chicago), who read every draft of the text and offered numerous helpful suggestions. Professor Betz also kindly allowed me access to the manuscript version of his forthcoming commentary on the Sermon on the Mount / Sermon on the Plain for the *Hermeneia* series, from which I benefited significantly. Professor Edward N. O'Neil (University of Southern California) provided expert advice on the translation of the poem, and on a number of occasions (as indicated in the footnotes) I have simply borrowed his proposals, deeming them better than anything I could offer. Many thanks also go to Professor John J. Collins (University of Chicago), who critiqued an early draft of the book (with special attention to Chapter Six), and to Professors Martin Hengel and Peter Schäfer for accepting the volume for the *Texte und Studien zum Antiken Judentum* series. Here at Yale University, Professors David R. Bartlett and Wayne A. Meeks generously assisted with the thankless job of reading the final proofs. The research specialists who assisted with the preparation of the bibliography and indices were Ms. Jerry Anne Dickel and Mr. Warren Smith. To all I express my sincere thanks.

New Haven, Christmas, 1993   Walter T. Wilson

Table of Contents

Abbreviations

The abbreviations used for this study are taken from the "Instructions for Contributors," *JBL* 107 (1988) 579–596 and from Siegfried Schwertner, *IATG: Internationales Abkürzungs-verzeichnis für Theologie und Grenzgebiete* (Berlin and New York: de Gruyter, 1974).

AARSBLA	*American Academy of Religion / Society of Biblical Literature Abstracts*
AB	Anchor Bible
ABAW	*Abhandlungen der bayerischen Akademie der Wissenschaften*
ABD	*Anchor Bible Dictionary*
AGJU	Arbeiten zur Geschichte des antiken Judentums und des Urchristentums
AHAW.PH	Abhandlungen der Heidelberger Akademie der Wissenschaften; Philo-sophisch-historische Klasse
AISP	*Archivio Italiano per la Storia della Pietà*
AJP	*American Journal of Philology*
AKG	Arbeiten zur Kirchengeschichte
AnBib	Analecta Biblica
AnOr	*Analecta Orientalia*
ANRW	*Aufstieg und Niedergang der römischen Welt*
AOS	American Oriental Series
APA	American Philological Association
ASGW.PH	Abhandlungen der (königlichen) sächsischen Gesellschaft der Wissenschaften; Philologisch-historische Klasse
BAGD	Bauer, Arndt, Gingrich, and Danker, *Greek-English Lexicon of the New Testament*
BASOR	*Bulletin of the American Schools of Oriental Research*
BBB	Bonner biblische Beiträge
BEFAR	Bibliothèque des Ecoles Françaises d'Athènes et de Rome
BETL	Bibliotheca Ephemeridum Theologicarum Lovaniensium
BGBE	Beiträge zur Geschichte der biblischen Exegese
BGBH	Beiträge zur Geschichte der biblischen Hermeneutik
BHT	Beiträge zur historischen Theologie
BJS	Brown Judaic Studies
BT	Bibliotheca Teubneriana
BZ	*Biblische Zeitschrift*
BZAW	Beihefte zur ZAW
BZNW	Beihefte zur ZNW
CBQ	*Catholic Biblical Quarterly*
CBQMS	Catholic Biblical Quarterly Monograph Series
ConBNT	Coniectanea Biblica, New Testament
CP	*Classical Philology*
CQ	*Classical Quarterly*
CR	*Classical Review*
CRINT	Compendia Rerum Iudaicarum ad Novum Testamentum
CSCP	Cornell Studies in Classical Philology

DBSup	*Dictionnaire de la Bible, Supplément*
DSp	*Dictionnaire de Spiritualité, Ascétique et Mystique*
EBib	Etudes Bibliques
EDNT	*Exegetical Dictionary of the New Testament*
EncJud	*Encyclopaedia Judaica*
EPRO	Etudes Préliminaires aux Religions Orientales dans l'Empire Romain
EWNT	*Exegetisches Wörterbuch zum Neuen Testament*
FB	Forschung zur Bibel
FF	Forum Fascicles
FKGG	Forschungen zur Kirchen- und Geistesgeschichte
FRLANT	Forschungen zur Religion und Literatur des Alten und Neuen Testaments
GBLS	Greifswalder Beiträge zur Literatur- und Stilforschung
HAT	Handbuch zum Alten Testament
HAW	Handbuch des Altertumswissenschaft
HKAT	Handkommentar zum Alten Testament
HKATSup	Handkommentar zum Alten Testament Supplement Series
HR	*History of Religions*
HSCP	*Harvard Studies in Classical Philology*
HTKNT	Herders theologischer Kommentar zum Neuen Testament
HTS	Harvard Theological Studies
HUCA	*Hebrew Union College Annual*
Int	*Interpretation*
JBL	*Journal of Biblical Literature*
JCPhSup	*Jahrbücher für classische Philologie Supplementband*
JHP	*Journal of the History of Philosophy*
JJS	*Journal of Jewish Studies*
JR	*Journal of Religion*
JRS	*Journal of Roman Studies*
JSHRZ	Jüdische Schriften aus hellenistisch-römischer Zeit
JSJ	*Journal for the Study of Judaism in the Persian, Hellenistic and Roman Period*
JSNT	*Journal for the Study of the New Testament*
JSNTSup	Journal for the Study of the New Testament Supplement Series
JSOT	*Journal for the Study of the Old Testament*
JSOTSup	Journal for the Study of the Old Testament Supplement Series
JSP	*Journal for the Study of the Pseudepigrapha*
JTS	*Journal of Theological Studies*
KP	*Der Kleine Pauly: Lexikon der Antike*
KPS	Klassisch-philologische Studien
LÄ	*Lexikon der Ägyptologie*
LCC	Library of Christian Classics
LCL	Loeb Classical Library
LEC	Library of Early Christianity
LSJ	Liddell, Scott, and Jones, *Greek-English Lexicon*
LUÅ	*Lunds Universitets Årsskrift*
MBPF	Münchener Beiträge zur Papyrusforschung und antiken Rechtsgeschichte
NIDNTT	*New International Dictionary of New Testament Theology*
NovT	*Novum Testamentum*
NTAbh	Neutestamentliche Abhandlungen
NTOA	Novum Testamentum et Orbis Antiquus
NTS	*New Testament Studies*
OBO	Orbis Biblicus et Orientalis
OCD	*Oxford Classical Dictionary*

OCT	Bibliotheca Oxoniensis (Oxford Classical Texts)
OTL	Old Testament Library
OTS	*Oudtestamentische Studiën*
PCPS	Proceedings of the Cambridge Philological Society
PFLUS	Publications de la Faculté des Lettres de l'Université de Strasbourg
PG	J. Migne, ed., *Patrologia Graeca*
PPR	*Philosophy and Phenomenological Research*
PVTG	Pseudepigrapha Veteris Testamenti Graece
PW	Pauly-Wissowa, *Real-encyclopädie der classischen Altertumswissenschaft*
PWSup	Supplement to *PW*
QD	Quaestiones Disputatae
RAC	*Reallexikon für Antike und Christentum*
RB	*Revue Biblique*
REG	*Revue des Etudes Grecques*
REJ	*Revue des Etudes Juives*
RGG	*Religion in Geschichte und Gegenwart*
RMP	*Rheinisches Museum für Philologie*
RSPT	*Revue des Sciences Philosophiques et Théologiques*
RSR	*Recherches de Science Religieuse*
RTL	*Revue Théologique de Louvain*
SBL	Society of Biblical Literature
SBLBMI	SBL The Bible and its Modern Interpreters
SBLDS	SBL Dissertation Series
SBLMS	SBL Monograph Series
SBLSCS	SBL Septuagint and Cognate Studies
SBLSP	*SBL Seminar Papers*
SBLTT	SBL Texts and Translations
SBS	Stuttgarter Bibelstudien
SBT	Studies in Biblical Theology
SCHNT	Studia ad Corpus Hellenisticum Novi Testamenti
SD	Studies and Documents
SHAW.PH	Sitzungsberichte der Heidelberger Akademie der Wissenschaften; Philosophisch-historische Klasse
SJ	Studia Judaica
SJLA	Studies in Judaism in Late Antiquity
SJT	*Scottish Journal of Theology*
SNTSMS	Society for New Testament Studies Monograph Series
SNVAO	Skrifter utgitt av det Norske Videnskaps-Akademi i Oslo
SPB	Studia Postbiblica
ST	*Studia Theologica*
Str-B	H. Strack and P. Billerbeck, *Kommentar zum Neuen Testament*
SUNT	Studien zur Umwelt des Neuen Testaments
Sup.	Supplement(s)
SVTP	Studia in Veteris Testamenti Pseudepigrapha
TBAW	Tübinger Beiträge zur Altertumswissenschaft
TDNT	*Theological Dictionary of the New Testament*
ThA	Theologische Arbeiten
TRE	*Theologische Realenzyklopädie*
TSAJ	Texte und Studien zum Antiken Judentum
TU	Texte und Untersuchungen zur Geschichte der altchristlichen Literatur
TZ	*Theologische Zeitschrift*
UaLG	Untersuchungen zur antiken Literatur und Geschichte
VCSup	Vigiliae Christianae Supplement Series

Part One

Literary Presuppositions

Introduction

The task of clarifying the role played by the sapiential traditions of Second Temple Judaism and early Christianity in the theological and ethical development of these formative religious movements, while by no means new, has enjoyed something of a revival in recent years.[1] One witness to this tradition, the *Sentences*, or *Sententiae*, of Pseudo-Phocylides, a didactic poem of about 230 lines written in Greek, has attracted a fair amount of current scholarly interest, both as an important source for investigating the literature and thought of Hellenistic-Jewish wisdom and as evidence for the milieu in which early Christian wisdom and ethics evolved.[2] Proof of this interest can be found in a number of recent publications, including the full-scale commentary of Pieter van der Horst for the *Studia in Veteris Testamenti Pseudepigrapha* series,[3] the translation with notes and introduction for the *Jüdische Schriften aus hellenistisch-römischer Zeit* series by Nikolaus Walter,[4] and Pascale Derron's critical edition of the text prepared for the *Budé* series.[5] Mention should also be made at this point of the important critical studies by Max Küchler, Karl-

---

[1] For literature see the recent surveys by Max Küchler, *Frühjüdische Weisheitstraditionen: Zum Fortgang weisheitlichen Denkens im Bereich des frühjüdischen Jahweglaubens* (OBO 26; Freiburg [Schweiz]: Universitätsverlag; Göttingen: Vandenhoeck & Ruprecht, 1979) and Hermann von Lips, *Weisheitliche Traditionen im Neuen Testament* (WMANT 64; Neukirchen-Vluyn: Neukirchener Verlag, 1990); cf. Robert L. Wilken, ed., *Aspects of Wisdom in Judaism and Early Christianity* (University of Notre Dame Center for the Study of Judaism and Christianity in Antiquity 1; Notre Dame and London: University of Notre Dame Press, 1975); John D. Crossan, ed., *Semeia 17: Gnomic Wisdom* (Chico, CA: Scholars Press, 1980).

[2] For a survey of scholarship on the *Sentences* before 1976, see Pieter W. van der Horst, *The Sentences of Pseudo-Phocylides, with Introduction and Commentary* (SVTP 4; Leiden: E.J. Brill, 1978) 3–54; for literature between 1976 and 1987 see idem, "Pseudo-Phocylides Revisited," *JSP* 3 (1988) 3–30.

[3] Van der Horst, *Sentences*; cf. idem, "Pseudo-Phocylides and the New Testament," *ZNW* 69 (1978) 187–202; idem, trans., "Pseudo-Phocylides (First Century B.C. – First Century A.D.)," *The Old Testament Pseudepigrapha* (ed. James H. Charlesworth; 2 vols.; Garden City, New York: Doubleday, 1983, 1985) 2.565–582; idem, "Pseudo-Phocylides Revisited," 3–30; idem, "Phocylides, Pseudo-," *ABD* 5 (1992) 347–348.

[4] Nikolaus Walter, *Poetische Schriften* (JSHRZ 4.3; Gütersloh: Mohn, 1983) 182–216.

[5] Pascale Derron, *Pseudo-Phocylide: Sentences* (Budé; Paris: Société d'Edition 'Les Belles Lettres', 1986); cf. idem, "Inventaire des Manuscrits du Pseudo-Phocylide," *Revue d'Histoire des Textes* 10 (1980) 237–247.

Wilhelm Niebuhr, and Johannes Thomas.[6] Besides the general wealth of background information and parallels from contemporaneous sources that they provide for the exegetical task, these books have made noteworthy strides in formulating modern consensus on a number of historical-critical and literary issues that are pertinent to our interpretation of the poem. It follows that the present state of research as represented by such studies constitutes an essential starting-point for any investigation of this text.[7]

As these scholars (and others before them) have demonstrated, it is apparent that our poem could not have been written by the putative author, the famous gnomic poet Phocylides of Miletus, who lived during the sixth century B.C.[8] Rather, it was penned by an anonymous Hellenistic-Jewish author, either during the first century B.C. or the first century A.D., residing perhaps in Alexandria. The poem itself, composed with rough dactylic hexameters in the old Ionic dialect, consists chiefly of lengthy sequences of monostichic sayings. Because many of these sayings are practical in their orientation, addressing issues of ethical conduct and decision-making in the form of gnomic sentences, critics normally treat the text as part of the sapiential corpus of ancient

---

[6] Küchler, *Frühjüdische Weisheitstraditionen*, especially 236–302; Karl-Wilhelm Niebuhr, *Gesetz und Paränese: Katechismusartige Weisungsreihen in der frühjüdischen Literatur* (WUNT 2.28; Tübingen: J.C.B. Mohr [Paul Siebeck], 1987) especially 5–72; Johannes Thomas, *Der jüdische Phokylides: Formgeschichtliche Zugänge zu Pseudo-Phokylides und Vergleich mit der neutestamentlichen Paränese* (NTOA 23; Freiburg [Schweiz]: Universitätsverlag; Göttingen: Vandenhoeck & Ruprecht, 1992).

[7] The various introductory surveys on Second Temple Judaism provide general information on the authorship, date, provenance, and significance of the *Sentences* of Pseudo-Phocylides; see Albert-Marie Denis, *Introduction aux Pseudépigraphes Grecs d'Ancien Testament* (SVTP 1; Leiden: E.J. Brill, 1970) 215–219; James H. Charlesworth, *The Pseudepigrapha and Modern Research, with a Supplement* (SBLSCS 7; 2nd ed.; Ann Arbor, MI: Scholars Press, 1981) 173–175, 298–299; Maurice Gilbert, "Wisdom Literature," *Jewish Writings of the Second Temple Period* (ed. Michael E. Stone; CRINT 2.2; Assen: van Gorcum; Philadelphia: Fortress, 1984) 313–316; Emil Schürer, et al., *The History of the Jewish People in the Age of Jesus Christ*, Volume 3, Part 1 (2nd ed.; Edinburgh: T. & T. Clark, 1986) 687–692; Burton L. Mack and Roland E. Murphy, "Wisdom Literature," *Early Judaism and its Modern Interpreters* (ed. Robert A. Kraft and George W. E. Nickelsburg; SBLBMI 2; Philadelphia: Fortress; Atlanta: Scholars Press, 1986) 395–396; Nikolaus Walter, "Jewish-Greek Literature of the Greek Period," *The Cambridge History of Judaism*, Volume Two: *The Hellenistic Age* (ed. W. D. Davies and Louis Finkelstein; Cambridge: Cambridge University Press, 1989) 394–396.

[8] On the popularity of Phocylides of Miletus in antiquity see van der Horst, *Sentences*, 59–63; also Karl Bielohlawek, *Hypotheke und Gnome: Untersuchungen über die griechische Weisheitsdichtung der vorhellenistischen Zeit* (Philolog. Sup. 32.3; Leipzig: Dieterich'sche Verlagsbuchhandlung, 1940) 14–20; P. Ahlert and Wilhelm Kroll, "Phokylides," *PW* 20.1 (1941) 503–510; Rudolf Keydell, "Phokylides," *KP* 4 (1971) 298–299. For text and translation of the extant fragments see J. M. Edmonds, trans., *Elegy and Iambus* (LCL; 2 vols.; London: Heinemann; New York: G. P. Putnam's Sons, 1931) 1.172–181; Bruno Gentili and Carolus Prato, eds., *Poetarum Elegiacorum Testimonia et Fragmenta* (BT; 2 vols.; Leipzig: Teubner, 1979, 1985) 1.135–140.

Judaism and for this reason have frequently held it up for comparison with other wisdom documents such as Proverbs, Qohelet, Ben Sira, and the Wisdom of Solomon. It should also be underscored that, in terms of both content and mode of composition, the *Sentences* is analogous to certain early Christian sapiential materials as well, including the synoptic sayings source Q,[9] the epistle of James, the *Gospel of Thomas*,[10] the *Teachings of Silvanus*,[11] and the *Sentences of Sextus*,[12] though these parallels have not been extensively studied.[13]

Perhaps the most remarkable feature of our text – and a characteristic that somewhat distinguishes it from other Jewish sapiential writings – is the degree and manner in which Pseudo-Phocylides has integrated Greek and Jewish moral concepts and perspectives, leaving very little that could be called distinctively Jewish. Indeed, the author seems to have gone to some lengths in concealing his Jewish identity and his commitment to any practices or beliefs unique to his faith. One special strength of recent publications on the *Sententiae* is the thoroughness and erudition they have exhibited in documenting the text's connections with the Greek and Roman ethical traditions; in this way they have elucidated both its multicultural nature and the complexity of its literary and material background. Notwithstanding its international qualities, though, it should be emphasized that the poem relies extensively on the Torah for its material and that the author's stance towards ethical issues is fundamentally Jewish in nature. In this regard, certain sections of the Pentateuch, specifically Exodus 20–23, Leviticus 18–20, and Deuteronomy 5 and 27, appear to have enjoyed a prominent place in his thinking.[14] This is significant inasmuch as, in the opinion of some Jews of the Second Temple period, these chapters (or portions of them) were understood to recount in condensed form the essential points of the Torah, especially as it pertained to ethical matters.[15] These facts have suggested to some critics that our author intended to create a sort of compendium or summary of the moral teachings of the Law (including other Jewish and non-Jewish sources interpreted to be consistent with its teachings) for a thoroughly Hellenized Jewish community that was grappling

---

[9] See below, p 40.

[10] See below, p. 16, n. 4.

[11] See below, p. 36, n. 83.

[12] See below, pp. 30–31.

[13] See especially van der Horst, "Pseudo-Phocylides and the New Testament," 187–202; Thomas, *Der jüdische Phokylides*, 365–453.

[14] According to Niebuhr's reckoning of the *Sentences'* LXX parallels (see his chart on p. 10 of *Gesetz und Paränese*), the poem exhibits 131 parallels with the Pentateuch, 162 with the wisdom literature (mostly Proverbs and Ben Sira), and 27 with other books of the LXX. While one could dispute the exact numbers and their distribution, Niebuhr's statistics provide an adequate picture of the extent and nature of Pseudo-Phocylides' dependence on the Torah; cf. Thomas, *Der jüdische Phokylides*, 35–49, 57–89, 147–149, 161–179.

[15] Luke T. Johnson, "The Use of Leviticus 19 in the Letter of James," *JBL* 101 (1982) 391–401; Niebuhr, *Gesetz und Paränese*, 5–72.

with the various problems posed by living in a pluralistic and cosmopolitan society while simultaneously maintaining something of its distinctive religious identity and purpose. Thus the choice of a Greek pseudonym and the avoidance of peculiarly Jewish features should not of themselves lead to the conclusion that the author was a "God-fearer" or that the intended audience was pagan. Rather, as Eduard Lohse puts it, the author "placed these sentences in the mouth of a Greek thinker who lived centuries earlier in order to show that already in ancient times the wisdom of the Greeks was influenced by the spirit of Moses, with the result that Jewish Torah and Greek ethics were thoroughly in agreement."[16] Consequently, Pseudo-Phocylides' principle of selection in drawing from the Torah exhibits a preference for those moral rules that would gain wide approval with a Hellenistic readership. On the other hand, he integrates into the poem precepts of originally non-Jewish provenance that stand side-by-side with Jewish directives, all presented without distinction as "resolutions of God" revealed through "divine judgments" (verses 1–2).

Determining the exact *Sitz im Leben* of such a summary remains something of an open question, especially in light of the absence in the work itself of any explicit indications of its intended audience or function. One fairly attractive theory, suggested by van der Horst, proposes that Pseudo-Phocylides intended to compose a schoolbook for educational purposes. Such a function would fit with what we know about the role that gnomic texts could play in Greco-Roman education, where gnomic primers, frequently in verse, served as instruction in pronunciation, orthography, spelling, and grammar, as well as a means of exposing students to material of special literary, cultural, and ethical merit.[17] It would also be consistent with what can be surmised about the operation of wisdom 'schools' in ancient Near Eastern societies, including those of Judaism.[18] As van der Horst puts it, "one could imagine that, as a Jewish

---

[16] Eduard Lohse, *Theological Ethics of the New Testament* (Minneapolis: Fortress, 1991) [originally, *Theologische Ethik des Neuen Testaments* (Stuttgart: W. Kohlhammer, 1988)] 22–23.

[17] Van der Horst, *Sentences*, 72–73, 79–80 (with references); cf. Derron, *Sentences*, vii–xxxi; Walter T. Wilson, *Love Without Pretense: Romans 12.9–21 and Hellenistic-Jewish Wisdom Literature* (WUNT 2.46; Tübingen: J.C.B. Mohr [Paul Siebeck], 1991) 77–81; Thomas, *Der jüdische Phokylides*, 355–361.

[18] See, for example, P. A. Munch, "Die jüdischen 'Weisheitspsalmen' und ihr Platz im Leben," *AnOr* 15 (1937) 112–140; R. B. Y. Scott, "Solomon and the Beginnings of Wisdom in Israel," *Wisdom in Israel and in the Ancient Near East: Presented to Professor Harold Henry Rowley* (ed. Martin Noth and D. Winton Thomas; VTSup 3; Leiden: E.J. Brill, 1955) 262–279 [reprint, James L. Crenshaw, ed., *Studies in Ancient Israelite Wisdom* (Library of Biblical Studies; New York: KTAV, 1976) 84–101]; Wolfgang Richter, *Recht und Ethos: Versuch einer Ortung des weisheitlichen Mahnspruches* (SANT 15; München: Kösel, 1966) 147–189, and s.v. Schule; Hans-Jürgen Hermisson, *Studien zur israelitischen Spruchweisheit* (WMANT 28; Neukirchen-Vlyun: Neukirchener Verlag, 1968) 97–136; Walther Zimmerli, "Das Buch Kohelet- Traktat oder Sentenzensammlung?" *VT* 24 (1974) 221–230; Bernhard Lang, "Schule und Unterricht im alten Israel," *La Sagesse de l'Ancient Testament*

writer, he tried to provide a 'pagan' text that could be used safely in Jewish schools to satisfy Jewish parents who wanted their children to be trained in the classical pagan authors."[19] The nature of the poem's teaching (including directives on sexual conduct, for instance) suggests that it was aimed at more advanced, mature students; and there is no reason according to this proposal that the text could not have been of some interest or educational value for Jewish adults as well.

In light of these comments, it comes as no surprise that one of the more intriguing problems raised by the investigation of Pseudo-Phocylides' *Sententiae* is the question of its sources and the manner in which they have been manipulated. Indeed, most of the poem appears to be indebted in some fashion or another to a fairly wide pool of previous texts or traditions.[20] This is true of verses 175–227, for instance, a block of material whose general framework resembles that of some of the so-called *Haustafeln* known from the New Testament and Hellenistic Judaism as well as from certain Greco-Roman writings, Stoic sources in particular.[21] Ever since the appearance of Paul Wendland's seminal essay in 1896, scholars have focused their attention on the similarities between these verses in the *Sentences* and comparable Jewish 'codes' found in Josephus' *Contra Apionem* 2.190–219 and Philo's *Hypothetica* 8.7.1–20 (preserved in Eusebius' *Praeparatio Evangelica*).[22] The par-

---

(ed. Maurice Gilbert; BETL 51; Leuven: Leuven University Press; Gembloux: Duculot, 1979) 186–201; James L. Crenshaw, *Old Testament Wisdom: An Introduction* (Atlanta: John Knox, 1981) s.v. School.

[19] Van der Horst, "Pseudo-Phocylides Revisited," 16.

[20] Parallels that Pseudo-Phocylides' *Sentences* exhibits with the Sibylline Oracles and the Didache also figure in the analysis of its sources; in addition to the works cited below see Alfred Seeberg, *Die beiden Wege und das Aposteldekret* (Leipzig: A. Deichert, 1906) 24 ff.; Gottlieb Klein, *Der älteste christliche Katechismus und die jüdische Propagandaliteratur* (Berlin: Reimer, 1909) 143–153; Anton Kurfuss, "Das Mahngedicht des sogenannten Phokylides im zweiten Buch der Oracula Sybyllina," *ZNW* 38 (1939) 171–181. Also, Derron (*Sentences*, 35–54) offers a chart that catalogues the more important sources and parallels for the *Sentences*.

[21] The literature on the *Haustafeln* is extensive; see, for example, Klaus Berger, "Hellenistische Gattungen im Neuen Testament," *ANRW* II.25.2 (1984) 1078–1086; idem, *Formgeschichte des Neuen Testaments* (Heidelberg: Quelle & Meyer, 1984) 135–141; Karl-Heinrich Bieritz and Christoph Kähler, "Haus III," *TRE* 14 (1985) 478–492; Peter Fiedler, "Haustafel," *RAC* 13 (1986) 1063–1073; Marlis Gielen, *Tradition und Theologie neutestamentlicher Haustafelethik: Ein Beitrag zur Frage einer christlichen Auseinandersetzung mit gesellschaftlichen Normen* (BBB 75; Frankfurt am Main: Hain, 1990); also see the references in the next note. See below, pp. 120 ff. and 134 ff. As David L. Balch and others have argued, the New Testament codes are also related to Hellenistic discussions περὶ οἰκονομίας, especially as outlined in Aristotle's *Politica* 1.2.1–2; for a summary see idem, "Household Codes," *Greco-Roman Literature and the New Testament* (ed. David E. Aune; Atlanta: Scholars Press, 1988) 25–50, with references.

[22] Paul Wendland, "Die Therapeuten und die philonische Schrift vom beschaulichen Leben," *JCPhSup* 22 (1896) 693–772, especially 709 ff.; cf. Klein, *Der älteste christliche*

allels between Pseudo-Phocylides' poem and these texts pertain not only to specific ideas and commands but extend also to matters of basic presentation and general moral outlook. These facts have raised in the minds of many critics the possibility that the three authors may have independently borrowed from a common source of Hellenistic-Jewish ethical instruction. Of course describing the nature of this 'source' in specific terms remains as yet an unresolved issue, and it may be more accurate at this point to speak of a common ethical tradition rather than a particular written text. Van der Horst's comment regarding the literary relationship of these three documents is representative:[23]

> Though seemingly presented as a summary of Jewish laws, the material offered goes in so many instances beyond the injunctions of the Torah that one must explain the similarities between these three authors by assuming that they drew upon a common source in which the universally valid principles of the Torah were amalgamated with a Stoic καθήκοντα-scheme into which, in turn, several Greek so-called ἄγραφοι νόμοι, unwritten laws, had been incorporated.

He concludes by observing that, "it is an established fact that Pseudo-Phocylides drew upon a source which was also used by Philo and Josephus, and that writings like those of these three authors were, in turn, sources for some New Testament authors."[24]

Besides the implications that findings like these have for our interpretation of the poem's textual history and ethical orientation, they also have an important bearing on the current analysis of the nature of its literary design. Because critics understand Pseudo-Phocylides as relying extensively on an assortment of texts for his poem, they often assume that as a rule it is only within the blocks of earlier, appropriated material that we may expect to uncover any signs of careful composition or argumentation; elsewhere only a minimal structure is detectable, as the author links together his various sources. In this sense, then, we may better characterize our 'author' as an editor – and certainly not as a poet in the ordinary or modern sense of the term. Van der Horst's views of the *Sentences* on this issue are again representative. He identifies the section in verses 175–227 as one of only two coherent blocks in the text, the other being the exhortation on labor in verses 153–174, which immediately precedes.[25] The

---

Katechismus, 143–153; James E. Crouch, *The Origin and Intention of the Colossian Haustafel* (FRLANT 2.109; Göttingen: Vandenhoeck & Ruprecht, 1972) 74–101; Küchler, *Frühjüdische Weisheitstraditionen*, 207–235, 281–283; Niebuhr, *Gesetz und Paränese*, 5–72; George P. Carras, "Philo's Hypothetica, Josephus' Contra Apionem and the Question of Sources," *SBLSP* 29 (ed. David J. Lull; Atlanta: Scholars Press, 1990) 431–450.

[23] Van der Horst, "Pseudo-Phocylides and the New Testament," 197; on the 'unwritten laws' see below, pp. 68–69.

[24] Van der Horst, "Pseudo-Phocylides and the New Testament," 197.

[25] This section itself is largely based on sources, especially LXX Proverbs 6.6–8; cf. van der Horst, *Sentences*, 216; idem, "Pseudo-Phocylides," in Charlesworth, *Pseudepigrapha*, 579.

employment of the *Haustafel*-scheme (women-children-slaves) as an organizing principle for the sayings in verses 175–227 stands in contrast to the bulk of the poem, where he sees no comparable principles at work. Thus, according to this interpretation, Pseudo-Phocylides has not applied in a consistent or thoughtful fashion any literary framework or argumentative strategy to the text as a whole. Instead, in his commentary van der Horst groups the verses of the poem into thirteen rather vague topical units (plus a prologue and epilogue), though he does not attempt to explain the organization of sayings within these units or how the units are related to one another:[26]

1–2	Prologue
3–8	Summary of the Decalogue
9–21	Exhortations to Justice
22–41	Admonitions to Mercy
42–47	Love of Money and its Consequences
48–58	Honesty, Modesty and Self-Control
59–69	Moderation in All Things
70–96	The Danger of Envy and Other Vices
97–115	Death and After-Life
116–121	The Instability of Life
122–131	Speech and Wisdom, Man's Distinction
132–152	Avoidance of Wickedness and Virtuous Life
153–174	The Usefulness of Labour
175–227	Marriage, Chastity and Family Life
228–230	Epilogue

Subsequent investigations of Pseudo-Phocylides' *Sententiae* have for the most part implicitly endorsed van der Horst's basic interpretation of the poem's literary genre and compositional mode, though the outlines provided by other authors do entail certain refinements. Such summaries are important for the present study particularly in so far as they represent the closest attempts to a compositional analysis of the text presently available.

In his translation for the *Jüdische Schriften aus hellenistisch-römischer Zeit* series, Nikolaus Walter subdivides the poem as follows:[27]

1–2	Proömium
3–8	Summe der Gebote
9–12	Dem Recht die Palme!
13–17	Üb immer Treu und Redlichkeit!
18–21	Redlichkeit zumal gegen den Armen
22–31	Übe Barmherzigkeit an Bedürftigen
32–34	Gewalttat löst keine Probleme
35–38	Achte Acker und Feldfrucht des Nächsten!

---

[26] Van der Horst, *Sentences*, 106 and passim; the outline he provides in Charlesworth, *Pseudepigrapha*, 574–582, is somewhat different; cf. Küchler, *Weisheitstraditionen*, 273, n. 18; van der Horst, "Pseudo-Phocylides Revisited," 16, 29, n. 4; Thomas, *Der jüdische Phokylides*, 317–327.

[27] Walter, *Poetische Schriften*, 197–216.

Clearly, Walter's outline exhibits more meticulousness in identifying the number and the extent of the topical clusters and in describing their contents; however, as a consequence we tend to lose sight of some of the larger material connections and developments within the poem. Like van der Horst, he sets the blocks of sayings in the *Sententiae* side-by-side in a long sequence, apparently seeing each unit on an equal footing with regard to its literary character and argumentative contribution to the text as a whole.

Pascale Derron's summary of the contents of the *Sentences* for the *Budé* edition makes use of thematic divisions and titles similar to those employed by van der Horst:[28]

---

[28] Derron, *Sentences*, xxvi–xxvii.

9–21	περὶ δικαιοσύνης
22–41	περὶ φιλανθρωπίας
42–47	séquence traditionelle περὶ πλούτου
48–58	περὶ φρονήσεως
59–69	περὶ μετριότητος
70–75	περὶ φθόνου
76–96	περὶ σωφροσύνης
97–115	περὶ θανάτου καὶ ψυχῆς
116–121	περὶ τύχης
122–131	περὶ λόγου καὶ σοφίας
132–152	περὶ ἀρετῆς καὶ κακίας
153–174	περὶ ἐργασίας
175–206	περὶ γάμου
207–222	περὶ παίδων καὶ γονέων
223–227	περὶ δεσποτῶν καὶ οἰκετῶν
228–230	épilogue

While Derron's subdivisions suffer from the same sort of indefiniteness as van der Horst's, her employment of Greek titles in the outline reflects the more sustained effort she puts forth in relating the topics of the different paragraphs within the poem to those familiar from contemporaneous Greek literature. As she observes in her introduction and notes to the poem, many of these topics would have been at home in the moral literature of the time, particularly gnomic literature.[29] This should not occasion any surprise, since the gnomic style that Pseudo-Phocylides employs represented a nearly universal phenomenon in the ancient world, exhibiting many cross-cultural features with respect to content, form, and purpose. To the extent that our author has shaped his material in accordance with certain literary conventions familiar from such sources, it behooves us to investigate the poem's structural and topical units against the background of relevant comparative texts in order to describe better their compositional and material characteristics.

The recent work of van der Horst, Walter, and Derron, as reflected in the outlines above, evidences an important trend in the interpretation of the literary composition of the *Sentences*. To a significant extent, the scholarly consensus that they represent corresponds also with prevailing presuppositions in the matter of the generic identification of the poem. While not all modern critics have explicitly designated it as such, it seems safe to conclude that, judging from the exegetical assumptions and arguments that they make in the course of analyzing the text, they understand the *Sentences* primarily as a gnomologium, or gnomic anthology.[30] As a gnomologium, the poem would

---

[29] Derron, *Sentences*, vii–xxxi and passim.

[30] Van der Horst, *Sentences*, 77–80; Küchler, *Weisheitstraditionen*, 258–274, cf. 236 ff.; Walter, *Poetische Schriften*, 188–190; Derron, *Sentences*, xxvi–xxvii; Thomas, *Der jüdische Phokylides*, 239–272. See below, pp. 25 ff.

be expected to exhibit virtually no comprehensive formal design or palpable argument, only loosely connected clusters of sayings interspersed among long sequences of largely independent wisdom sayings with little mutual connection or coherence. While scholars have entertained other generic possibilities for the document, such as wisdom poem or didactic poem, they have not vigorously pursued such alternatives through comparative literary analysis. Consequently, contemporary exegesis of the *Sentences* focuses on its micro-level, the interpretation of specific verses, their content and material relationship with other sources, at the expense of the macro-level, the study of the overall design and argument of the text. In this regard, the observations of John J. Collins in his review of van der Horst's commentary are insightful. After noting how van der Horst simultaneously classifies the *Sentences* as a wisdom poem, a didactic poem, and a gnomology, he writes, "[h]is comments on genre are perhaps the least satisfactory part of the introduction. He does not consider that the different classifications may refer to different levels of the work. Generic presuppositions may be more instructive for the commentary than van der Horst allows ..."[31]

Taking its cue from Collins' remarks, the present study will critically address this question of the poem's composition and genre in order to help clarify its literary, rhetorical, and ideational character. By way of preliminaries, we should note that the same recent studies that have tended to atomize the interpretation of the text have also made a number of fundamental observations touching upon the literary coherency of the *Sententiae*, observations that do not necessarily support the identification of the poem as a gnomic anthology and that may in fact suggest the validity of generic designations other than or in addition to gnomologium. First, it is obvious that the author has affixed a coordinated prologue (verses 1–2) and epilogue (verses 228–230) to the body of the text as a framing device.[32] Second, there are signs that the author has organized the maxims throughout the document into various thematic clusters and paragraphs, though, as we saw above, modern opinions differ as to the number, character, and significance of these subdivisions. Third, critics have depicted at least some of these clusters and paragraphs in the poem as constituting coherent blocks of material, for example, verses 153–174 and verses 175–227. Finally, many of the topics of these different units are familiar from

---

[31] *JBL* 100 (1981) 479–480; for other significant reviews see A. S. van der Woude in *JSJ* 9 (1978) 224–225; Sebastian Brock in *JJS* 30 (1979) 246–247; H. J. de Jonge in *Nederlands Theologisch Tijdschrift* 33 (1979) 246–247; M. L. West in *CR* 30 (1980) 136–137; Eduard Lohse in *Mnemosyne* 35 (1982) 179–181.

[32] See below, pp. 150–151.

those of other ancient sapiential sources, including many sources that are not gnomologia. This indicates that at least to some degree the author has molded his material in order to meet certain prevalent expectations regarding the structure of moral exhortation in general. For this reason, any analysis of the poem must take into account the affinities it exhibits with contemporaneous materials not only with respect to the content of its individual lines but also with respect to its overall literary design and the argumentation of its larger constituent elements.

The presence of these formal characteristics in the *Sentences* as recognized by modern scholars serves as a point of departure for our study of its literary composition and genre. As indications that Pseudo-Phocylides has made some effort to impose order upon his material, these observations raise the more fundamental question of whether the poem exhibits any comprehensive literary plan and, if so, what organizational principles have contributed to its design. If such a plan is at work in the text, its investigation will be of value in unearthing the ethical, religious, and philosophical arguments that undergird the poet's exhortation at the presuppositional level and in demonstrating how these arguments inform the content and function of the *Sententiae*. Such an investigation should also be of use in evaluating the historical and literary matrix of the poem, clarifying how it relates to various literary, rhetorical, and hermeneutical categories of the Hellenistic era.

Before analyzing the text directly, however, it will be necessary to discuss in an introductory fashion two prior topics pertaining to ancient literature on the whole whose investigation will have some important bearing on the answers offered to the questions posed above. The first involves a survey of the chief gnomic genres of antiquity – chreiae collections, gnomic poetry, gnomologia, and wisdom instruction (Chapter One). The second topic concerns the use of the so-called Canon of Cardinal Virtues, namely, justice, moderation, courage, and wisdom, in ancient ethical and philosophical texts (Chapter Two). The next three chapters of our study (Chapters Three, Four, and Five) will investigate the literary composition and argument of the three major subdivisions of the body of the *Sentences* itself (verses 3–8, 9–131, and 132–227, respectively), while Chapter Six will analyze the poem's title, prologue, and epilogue. I will conclude by arguing that, on the basis of the compositional analysis in Chapters Three through Six, as well as other considerations, the *Sentences* is best understood generically as a gnomic poem that epitomizes the ethical teachings of the Torah, incorporating certain non-biblical materials considered to be consistent with these teachings and of value for Hellenized Jews. As part of this epitomizing activity, the internal structure of the poem benefits from literary structures informed by the Canon of Cardinal Virtues (in verses 9–131) and by the different types of moral relationships or areas of life in which one lives, in a manner akin to the ancient discussions of ethical 'duties' (in verses 132–227). As I will attempt to demonstrate through the analysis of the *Sentences* below, the identification of these generic and compositional features has important implications for our interpretation of the text's original meaning and purpose.

Chapter One

The Ancient Genres of Gnomic Wisdom

In order to classify and analyze the literary composition and particularly the genre of the *Sentences* of Pseudo-Phocylides, it is important at least in a preliminary way to distinguish and describe the basic features of the different ancient genres that were, like the *Sentences*, characterized by the gnomic style, taking into account their morphology, function, setting, and intended hermeneutic. An improved appreciation for the complexities of some of the issues involved in this task will provide us with a framework against which to categorize the poem generically. As an additional consequence of a more nuanced understanding of how he participates in the generic and literary conventions of his time, we will also be in a better position to interpret the author's message and intentions within the context of his own literary and intellectual milieu. The purpose of this chapter, though, is not to answer the question of the poem's genre directly, but rather to survey what appear to be the most viable options. As we will see, coming to grips with the issue of a text's literary composition is a critical prerequisite to classifying it generically. For this reason, it will be necessary to postpone direct discussion of the genre of the *Sentences* until Chapter Seven, after the analysis of the text's literary composition has been completed in Chapters Three through Six.

Even a cursory inspection of ancient literature leads to the observation that a whole spectrum of types of texts could effectively employ wise sayings in one manner or another. It occasions no surprise that the authors of various genres – among them letters, orations, diatribes, and different paraenetic genres – took advantage of gnomic forms and themes since they were of use in achieving their broader instructional or exhortatory objectives. We should take note, however, that most of these genres are not necessarily characterized by the employment of maxims and so are not strictly speaking gnomic. By contrast, in the extant literature we can isolate a much more restricted corpus for which the utilization of the gnomic style constitutes an essential generic feature; within this corpus it is possible to identify at least four types of modalities for the collection and presentation of γνῶμαι: chreiae collections, gnomic poetry, gnomic anthologies, and wisdom instruction. While a number of gnomic texts appear to be somehow 'mixed' or ambiguous with respect to genre, most can be classified satisfactorily according to this four-fold scheme.

Chreiae Collections

As for the generic description of the *Sentences* of Pseudo-Phocylides, the first
item on the list of possible candidates can be disposed of fairly quickly. As its
name suggests, a chreiae collection assembles in some fashion a number of
χρεῖαι, brief, self-contained narratives of a practical or instructional nature.[1]
Typically, a χρεία relates some edifying episode from the life of a noteworthy
historical figure, whose climactic saying or action normally brings the story to
a close. Some of these concluding sayings may also be designated as maxims,
yet these differ from wisdom sayings as they are employed in other gnomic
genres because they are situated in narrative frameworks that tend to fix their
meaning and application. In conjunction with this, and in contrast to a simple
maxim, a chreia betrays a biographical interest alongside the didactic one.[2]

A chreiae collection brings together a group of such stories, which are usu-
ally ascribed to a single person, often a philosopher. Among the important
Hellenistic representatives of this genre, mention can be made of Lucian's
Demonax, The Sayings of Secundus,[3] the *Gospel of Thomas*,[4] *Pirke 'Avot*,[5] the

---

[1] On the chreia and its relationship with the maxim see Konstantin Horna, "Gnome,
Gnomendichtung, Gnomologien," *PWSup* 6 (1935) 75–76 (with additional notes by Kurt
von Fritz, 87–89); Theodor Klauser, "Apophthegma," *RAC* 1 (1950) 545–550; Heinrich
Lausberg, *Handbuch der literarischen Rhetorik* (2nd ed.; München: Hueber, 1973) §§ 1117–
1120; Berger, "Hellenistische Gattungen," 1074, 1092–1110; idem, *Formgeschichte*, 80–93;
Robert C. Tannehill, "Types and Functions of Apophthegms in the Synoptic Gospels,"
ANRW II.25.2 (1984) 1792–1829; cf. the series of essays in Daniel Patte, ed., *Semeia 29.
Kingdom and Children: Aphorism, Chreia, Structure* (Chico, CA: Scholars Press, 1983).
Many authors note the imprecision of terminology in the ancient texts; for instance, the τῶν
ἑπτὰ σοφῶν ἀποφθέγματα (text: Hermann Diels and Walter Kranz, eds., *Die Fragmente der
Vorsokratiker* [6th ed.; 3 vols.; Berlin: Weidmann, 1952] 1.62–66) is formally closer to the
gnomologium than the chreiae collection.
[2] The comments in Nicolaus of Myra's *Progymnasmata* (text: Ronald F. Hock and
Edward N. O'Neil, *The Chreia in Ancient Rhetoric*, Volume 1: *The Progymnasmata*
[SBLTT 27, Graeco-Roman Religion Series 9; Atlanta: Scholars Press, 1986] 262–265) are
representative; he observes that the maxim differs from the chreia in that 1) it has only a
saying and never an action, 2) it is never attributed to someone, 3) it is general advice and
not composed on the basis of some set circumstances, 4) it is always ethical, while the
chreia is also employed for the sake of wit. For further references to the progymnasmata,
see Benjamin Fiore, *The Function of Personal Example in the Socratic and Pastoral Epistles* (AnBib 105; Rome: Biblical Institute Press, 1986) 42.
[3] See Ben E. Perry, ed., *Secundus the Silent Philosopher* (APA Philological Monographs; Ithaca: Cornell University Press, 1964).
[4] The literature is extensive; see, for example, Stevan L. Davies, *The Gospel of Thomas
and Christian Wisdom* (New York: Seabury, 1983); F. T. Fallon and Ron Cameron, "The
Gospel of Thomas: A Forschungsbericht and Analysis," *ANRW* II.25.6 (1988) 4195–4251;
Michael Fieger, *Das Thomasevangelium: Einleitung, Kommentar, und Systematik* (NTAbh
22; Münster: Aschendorff, 1991); Marvin W. Meyer, *The Gospel of Thomas: The Hidden
Sayings of Jesus* (San Francisco: Harper & Row, 1992).
[5] See especially M. B. Lerner, "The Tractate Avot," *The Literature of the Sages*, First
Part: *Oral Tora, Halakha, Mishna, Tosefta, Talmud, External Tractates* (ed. Shmuel Safrai;

'Avot de Rabbi Nathan,[6] and the several collections incorporated by Diogenes Laertius into his *Vitae Philosophorum*. As this list suggests, the genre was primarily Greek in provenance, though we find examples in the literature of Judaism and Christianity as well. As a whole, the extant collections admit of considerable variation, both in the types of chreiae utilized and in the types of gnomic sayings enveloped within them. Additionally, we discover little sustained or consistent effort to organize the constituent elements according to any literary or argumentative plan. At most, the editors of these collections link together small clusters of chreiae here and there by means of catchword, formal analogy, or topic.

It seems that the majority of the chreiae collections functioned within philosophical 'schools' of one sort or another. It follows that the contents of the respective collections generally bear the mark of their tradents' characteristic presuppositions, outlook, and agenda. Those editing the χρεῖαι of a certain philosophical figure apparently presented them in such form as a means both of handing down the master's noteworthy teachings and of preserving the memory of his personal example for educational purposes. This was done with a view to the assimilation and propagation of the philosophy's doctrines and way of life by the students of a particular school.[7]

It is clear, even without a close reading, that Pseudo-Phocylides' *Sentences* does not conform to the genre of chreiae collection. While our text contains many gnomic sayings, none of them have been incorporated into chreiae and, indeed, the author seldom has recourse to narrative devices of any kind (though see the discussion of verses 164–170 and 198–206 below). There is, additionally, no evidence for poetic chreiae collections nor any indication that such compilations circulated among Greek-speaking Jewish communities. It

---

CRINT 2.3.1; Assen, Maastricht: van Gorcum; Philadelphia: Fortress, 1987) 262–281; also Louis Finkelstein, "Introductory Study to Pirke Aboth," *JBL* 57 (1938) 13–50 [reprint, idem, *Pharisaism in the Making* (New York: KTAV, 1972) 121–158]; Jacob Neusner, "Types and Forms of Ancient Jewish Literature: Some Comparisons," *HR* 11 (1971–72) 354–390; Henry A. Fischel, "The Transformation of Wisdom in the World of Midrash," in Wilken, *Aspects of Wisdom*, 67–101; Küchler, *Weisheitstraditionen*, 176–198, cf. 199–206; Dieter Zeller, *Die weisheitlichen Mahnsprüche bei den Synoptikern* (FB 17; 2nd ed.; Würzburg: Echter Verlag, 1983) 42–46.

[6] Judah Goldin, *The Fathers according to Rabbi Nathan* (New Haven: Yale University Press, 1955); Anthony J. Saldarini, *The Fathers According to Rabbi Nathan (Abot de Rabbi Nathan): Version B* (SJLA 11; Leiden: E. J. Brill, 1975); idem, *Scholastic Rabbinism: A Literary Study of the Fathers According to Rabbi Nathan* (BJS 14; Chico, CA: Scholars Press, 1982); Küchler, *Weisheitstraditionen*, 176–198, cf. 199–206; M. B. Lerner, "Avot de-R. Natan," in Safrai, *The Literature of the Sages*, 369–379.

[7] In addition to the references in notes 1 and 2 above see Gunnar Rudberg, "Zur Diogenes-Tradition," *Symbolae Osloenses* 14 (1935) 22–43; John S. Kloppenborg, *The Formation of Q: Trajectories in Ancient Wisdom Collections* (Studies in Antiquity and Christianity; Philadelphia: Fortress, 1987) 290–292, 306–316, 340–341.

appears that the most germane comparative materials, then, will come from those gnomic genres that consist largely or entirely of sayings material, and it is to these we now turn with a somewhat more extended treatment.

Gnomic Poetry

We may begin our discussion of gnomic poetry by taking note of the several features that distinguish the genre. First, as the name of this category implies, the gnomic saying constitutes a vital component for any gnomic poem, though the types of sayings employed and the extent to which they are applied can vary considerably. Second, the genre typically manifests the same sorts of ethical themes and instructional stance familiar from γνῶμαι. Thus among the issues encountered in gnomic poems are appropriate personal conduct, familial and civic responsibilities, and various ethical problems. Third, the representatives of the genre are, by definition, poetic or hymnic in composition. In Greek gnomic poems the dactylic hexameter and the elegiac couplet were apparently the standard rhythms, though gnomic poets had recourse to iambic, choliambic, trochaic, anapaestic, and other meters as well.[8] It should be noted, too, that a number of Greek texts in this category represent 'prose hymns' that do not scan according to the regular meters. This includes in particular Jewish pieces in Greek that have been translated from originally Hebrew poems. Although the translators do not make use of Greek meters, it is often possible to detect other poetic devices at work as they attempt to capture something of the original's aesthetic impact. Fourth, gnomic poems are for the most part short, being only a paragraph or two in length, though a number of them, such as Hesiod's *Opera et Dies*, the *Comparatio Menandri et Philistionis*, the *Theognidea* (which is actually an anthology of gnomic poetry), and Gregory of Nazianzus' *Carmina Moralia* (which is also anthological in nature), extend to many lines and address a number of topics. Finally, some common theme or outlook unifies the contents of a gnomic poem in one fashion or another. For this reason it is possible to discern in a given poem an overall structure and argument. It is this final characteristic that is most crucial for distinguishing a gnomic poem from a gnomologium.

Within the Hebrew Bible and the literature of Hellenistic Judaism modern scholars have identified a number of gnomic poems, which they often refer to as 'didactic poems' or 'wisdom hymns'.[9] Compositions of this sort, most of

---

[8] Gustav A. Gerhard, *Phoinix von Kolophon: Texte und Untersuchungen* (Leipzig: Teubner, 1909) 253–255; Horna, "Gnome," 76–78.

[9] W. Baumgartner, "Die literarischen Gattungen in der Weisheit des Jesus Sirach," *ZAW* 34 (1914) 161–198; H. Ludin Jansen, *Die spätjüdische Psalmendichtung. Ihr Entstehungskreis und ihr "Sitz im Leben": Eine literaturgeschichtlich-soziologische Untersuchung*

which are located in wisdom books such as Proverbs, Ben Sira, and the Wisdom of Solomon, do not themselves constitute a separate genre but rather are to be compared with similar texts from non-wisdom literature, especially the Psalms. Their morphology, therefore, is familiar from Hebrew hymns, thanksgivings, prayers, and laments, though their themes are sapiential and their tone is exhortatory. Accordingly, most of these wisdom texts take advantage of hymnic features such as the participial style and the praise of God as creator and redeemer, even while including sapiential components such as maxims, rhetorical questions, and concluding warnings. Mention can also be made at this point of the exhortatory sections incorporated in the Odes of Solomon,[10] the Pseudo-Orphica,[11] and the fragments of Hellenistic-Jewish pseudepigraphical philosophical and poetic texts,[12] all of which exhibit comparable material, compositional, and generic characteristics. In analyzing the features of these and other materials of the Second Temple period, James H. Charlesworth correctly observes that although wisdom motifs are fairly dominant in later hymns and prayers (such as the wisdom hymn preserved in

---

(SNVAO 2.3; Oslo: Jacob Dybwad, 1937) 55–94; Frank Crüsemann, *Studien zur Formgeschichte von Hymnus und Danklied in Israel* (WMANT 32; Neukirchen-Vlyun: Neukirchener Verlag, 1969) 115–121; Gerhard von Rad, *Wisdom in Israel* (trans. James D. Martin; London: SCM, 1972) 38–40, 206–226; James L. Crenshaw, "Wisdom," *Old Testament Form Criticism* (ed. John H. Hayes; Trinity University Monograph Series in Religion; San Antonio: Trinity University Press, 1974) 247–248; cf. Eduard Norden, *Agnostos Theos: Untersuchungen zur Formengeschichte religiöser Rede* (Leipzig and Berlin: Teubner, 1913) [reprint, Darmstadt: Wissenschaftliche Buchgesellschaft, 1956] 177–207.

[10] Regarding the Odes of Solomon, the comments of James H. Charlesworth ("Odes of Solomon [Late First to Early Second Century A.D.]," in Charlesworth, *Old Testament Pseudepigrapha*, 2.730, cf. 725–771) are insightful: "An aspect of the the Odist's thought that has remained not only unexamined but almost unseen is the ethical exhortations that appear in no less than fourteen Odes. These exhortations are certainly dissimilar to brilliant and perceptive philosophical discussions like those found in Aristotle's *Nicomachean Ethics*; they are more similar to the injunctions found in Pseudo-Phocylides and are especially similar to the exhortations preserved in the Testaments of the Twelve Patriarchs." For literature see the bibliography provided on p. 734, to which add Majella Franzmann, *The Odes of Solomon: An Analysis of the Poetical Structure and Form* (NTOA 20; Freiburg [Schweiz]: Universitätsverlag; Göttingen: Vandenhoeck & Ruprecht, 1991).

[11] Anton Elter, *Gnomologiorum Graecorum Historia Atque Origine* (9 parts plus 2-part supplement; Bonn: C. George, 1893–1897) 154–184; Nikolaus Walter, *Der Thoraausleger Aristobulos* (TU 86; Berlin: Akademie-Verlag, 1964) 103–115, 202–261; idem, *Poetische Schriften*, 217–243; Denis, *Introduction*, 223–238; M. Lafargue, trans., "Orphica (Second Century B.C. – First Century A.D.)," in Charlesworth, *Old Testament Pseudepigrapha*, 2.795–801; Schürer, *History of the Jewish People*, 3.1.661–667.

[12] Walter, *Aristobulos*, 172–201; idem, *Poetische Schriften*, 244–276; Denis, *Introduction*, 223–238; Harold W. Attridge, trans., "Fragments of Pseudo-Greek Poets (Third to Second Century B.C.)," in Charlesworth, *Old Testament Pseudepigrapha*, 2.821–830; Schürer, *History of the Jewish People*, 3.1.656–671; Niebuhr, *Gesetz und Paränese*, 227–231.

Baruch 3.9–4.4), modern scholarship has yet to clarify precisely why and to what extent this is the case.[13]

Standing somewhat apart from these poems is a series of hymns in praise of personified Wisdom, particularly as God's mediator in creation; both Egyptian wisdom and Jewish prophecy have substantially influenced their distinctive content and composition.[14] In Proverbs 8, to take an example, Wisdom, poised at the entrance to the holy city, exhorts its citizens to heed her appeal. In this highly artistic composition, the poet depicts Wisdom's primacy in creation and enumerates the benefits realized by those who love her, including not only prudence but also prosperity, virtue, and justice.[15] Modern critics have argued that on account of their special subject matter and form this and similar hymns constitute a separate genre.[16]

Within the Psalter there is also a small number of 'wisdom psalms', though their identification remains rather problematic.[17] These poems apparently

---

[13] James H. Charlesworth, "Jewish Hymns, Odes, and Prayers (ca. 167 BCE–135 CE)," in Kraft and Nickelsburg, *Early Judaism and its Modern Interpreters*, 422, cf. 411–436; also Michael Lattke, *Hymnus: Materialien zu einer Geschichte der antiken Hymnologie* (NTOA 19; Freiburg [Schweiz]: Universitätsverlag; Göttingen: Vandenhoeck & Ruprecht, 1991) 97–103, 110–118. On the relationship between the *Teachings of Silvanus*, an early Christian sapiential text, and Hellenistic hymns see William R. Schoedel, "Jewish Wisdom and the Formation of the Christian Ascetic," in Wilken, *Aspects of Wisdom*, 190–193. On Baruch 3.9–4.4 see below, pp.159–160.

[14] Christa Kayatz, *Studien zu Proverbien 1–9: Eine form- und motivgeschichtliche Untersuchung unter Einbeziehung ägyptischen Vergleichsmaterials* (WMANT 22; Neukirchen-Vluyn: Neukirchener Verlag, 1966) 76–134; Johann Marböck, *Weisheit im Wandel: Untersuchungen zur Weisheitstheologie bei Ben Sira* (BBB 37; Bonn: Hanstein, 1971) 17–96; Crenshaw, "Wisdom," 248–249; Hans-Jürgen Hermisson, "Observations on the Creation Theology in Wisdom," *Israelite Wisdom: Theological and Literary Essays in Honor of Samuel Terrien* (ed. John G. Gammie, Walter A. Brueggemann, W. Lee Humphreys, and James M. Ward; New York: Union Theological Seminary; Missoula: Scholars Press, 1978) 43–57.

[15] On Proverbs 8 see R. N. Whybray, "Proverbs 8.22–31 and its Supposed Prototypes," *VT* 15 (1965) 504–514 [reprint, Crenshaw, *Studies*, 390–400]; Kayatz, *Studien zu Proverbien 1–9*, 76–119; von Rad, *Wisdom in Israel*, 149–157; Maurice Gilbert, "Le Discours de la Sagesse en Proverbes 8: Structure et Cohérence," *La Sagesse de l'Ancien Testament* (ed. idem; BETL 51; Leuven: Leuven University Press; Gembloux: Duculot, 1979) 202–218; Patrick W. Skehan, "Structures in Poems on Wisdom: Proverbs 8 and Sirach 24," *CBQ* 41 (1979) 365–379.

[16] There is a special set of problems regarding the Wisdom of Solomon with respect to its hymnic features; see Chrysostome Larcher, *Le Livre de la Sagesse ou la Sagesse de Salomon* (EBib 1, 3, 5; 3 vols.; Paris: Gabalda, 1983–1985) 2.561–605; Reese, *Hellenistic Influence*, 42–50, 105–109; Burton L. Mack, *Logos und Sophia: Untersuchungen zur Weisheitstheologie im hellenistischen Judentum* (SUNT 10; Göttingen: Vandenhoeck & Ruprecht, 1973) 63–78. Also, some of the hymns of the New Testament exhibit sapiential features, see, for example, Elisabeth Schüssler Fiorenza, "Wisdom Mythology and the Christological Hymns of the New Testament," in Wilken, *Aspects of Wisdom*, 14–41, with further references.

[17] Hermann Gunkel and Joachim Begrich, *Einleitung in die Psalmen: Die Gattungen der religiösen Lyrik Israels* (HKATSup 2.19; Göttingen: Vandenhoeck & Ruprecht, 1933) 381–

served in cultic as well as instructional capacities.[18] Following Roland Murphy, we may list the following with some confidence: 1, 32, 34, 37, 49, 112, 128 (= LXX 1, 31, 33, 36, 48, 111, 127); Murphy also describes a number of other psalms that incorporate sapiential elements or themes.[19] Formally, these wisdom psalms have much in common with their non-wisdom neighbors, though they also exhibit special characteristics, including the use of maxims (especially beatitudes, 'better' sayings, and numerical sayings), an address of a father or teacher to his 'son', rhetorical questions, and the loose, sometimes anthologized, organization of independent sayings, as well as acrostic arrangement. The practical scope and didactic tone of the wisdom psalms are familiar from Jewish sapiential texts; we discover also numerous common themes and motifs, including the two ways, the contrast of the sage and the fool, the fear of the Lord, and the rendering of practical moral advice.

In Greek literature, gnomic poetry flourished almost from the very beginning; many of the earliest poems enjoyed long careers and exercised considerable influence on later poets as models of form and style, not to mention their use as convenient sources of 'quotations'. Foremost among these were Hesiod's *Opera et Dies* and the poems of Theognis and Phocylides,[20] though other notable authors, such as Solon, Pindar, Aeschylus, Sophocles, Euripides, and Menander, indulged in the gnomic style and assimilated gnomic themes and forms into their works.[21]

During the Hellenistic era, gnomic poetry continued as a mode of ethical instruction, though paraenetic prose, or prose interspersed with verse, began to

---

397; Jansen, *Psalmendichtung*, 8–55; Munch, "Die jüdischen 'Weisheitspsalmen'," 112–140; Sigmund Mowinckel, "Psalms and Wisdom," in Noth and Thomas, *Wisdom in Israel*, 205–224; idem, *The Psalms in Israel's Worship* (2 vols.; Nashville: Abingdon, 1962) 2.104–125; von Rad, *Wisdom in Israel*, 195–206; Crenshaw, "Wisdom," 249–252; idem, *Old Testament Wisdom*, 180–189; Erhard Gerstenberger, "Psalms," in Hayes, *Form Criticism*, 218–221.

[18] On the scholastic setting and didactic tone of these psalms see especially Munch, "Weisheitspsalmen," 112–140; cf. Jansen, *Psalmendichtung*, 95–133; Mowinckel, *Psalms*, 2.104–125; Gerstenberger, "Psalms," 218–221.

[19] Roland E. Murphy, "A Consideration of the Classification 'Wisdom Psalms'," *VTSup* 9 (1962) 156–167 [reprint, Crenshaw, *Studies*, 456–467].

[20] Isocrates, in *Ad Nicoclem* 43–44 (cf. 2.3), suggests the prominence of these authors; for some of the larger questions concerning their literature see Alois Rzach, "Hesiodos," *PW* 8.1 (1912) 1167–1240; P. Friedländer, "ΥΠΟΘΗΚΑΙ," *Hermes* 48 (1913) 558–616; Wolfgang Aly, "Theognis," *PW* 5.A2 (1934) 1972–1984; Aurelio Peretti, *Teognide nella Tradizione Gnomolica* (Classici e Orientali 4; Pisa: Libreria Goliardiea, 1953); idem, "Calchi Gnomici nella Silloge Teognidea," *Maia* 8 (1956) 197–217; Martin L. West, *Hesiod: Works and Days* (Oxford: Clarendon, 1978); Thomas J. Figueira and Gregory Nagy, eds., *Theognis of Megara: Poetry and the Polis* (Baltimore and London: Johns Hopkins University Press, 1985). On Phocylides of Miletus see above, p. 4, n. 8.

[21] Besides the standard works on these authors see Horna, "Gnome," 76–78; Ernst Ahrens, *Gnomen in griechischer Dichtung: Homer, Hesiod, Aeschylus* (Würzburg: Triltsch, 1937); Heinrich Bischoff, *Gnomen Pindars* (Würzburg: Triltsch, 1938); Bielohlawek,

overshadow the earlier genre in importance. Another significant trend was the co-optation of the genre by philosophers, who both cited the poets as evidence and composed verses of their own. As Donald R. Dudley observes, the Cynics were instrumental in this process: "The great quantity of moralizing verse which characterizes the Hellenistic age cannot all be put down to the account of the Cynics, though it is safe to say that Cynic influence gave the first impetus to that literature. And it is noteworthy that this gnomic poetry exhibits the same features as the moralizing prose of the diatribe, the χρεία, and the ἀπομνημονεύμα (sic)."[22] As Dudley's comments suggest, the Cynic style and themes became distinctive features of the genre. But of the Cynics themselves, only the poems of Crates of Thebes[23] and Cercidas of Megalopolis[24] survive in substantial quantities.

Other gnomic poets, though not Cynics, were influenced by the movement, or at least their writings manifest Cynic themes. Among these writers mention may be made of Leonidas of Tarentum,[25] Sotades of Maroneia,[26] Chares,[27] and

---

Hypotheke und Gnome, passim; Woldemar Görler, *Menandrou Gnomai* (Berlin: Freie Universität Berlin, 1963).

[22] Donald R. Dudley, *A History of Cynicism* (London: Methuen, 1937) [reprint, Hildesheim: Olms, 1967] 113; cf. the references below in note 67. Of related interest are the poets discussed by Ewen L. Bowie, "Greek Sophists and Greek Poetry in the Second Sophistic," *ANRW* II.33.1 (1989) 209–258.

[23] Crates propagated Cynicism in epics and tragedies, as well as in elegiac epigrams called ΠΑΙΓΝΙΑΙ; for texts see Hermann Diels, *Poetarum Philosophorum Fragmenta* (Berlin: Weidmann, 1901) 207–223; Ernst Diehl, *Anthologia Lyrica Graeca* (3rd ed.; Leipzig: Teubner, 1958) 1.120–126. Like most Cynic writings, the poems are characterized by biting satire, striking images, and pedestrian language. Among their themes are attacks on wealth and hypocrisy, often coupled with praise of the difficult though virtuous Cynic way of life; cf. Gerhard, *Phoinix*, 237–238; Dudley, *Cynicism*, 42–53, 56–58; Heinrich Dörrie, "Krates 2," *KP* 3 (1969) 327–328.

[24] The lyrical ΜΕΛΙΑΜΒΟΙ of Cercidas convey ethical concepts and argumentative energy comparable to that of Crates. They consist largely of the regular stock of Cynic topics, including an autobiographical contemplation of prudence and discipline in the face of impending death. Text and translation: A. D. Knox, trans., *Herodes, Cercidas, and the Greek Choliambic Poets* (LCL; Cambridge: Harvard University Press; London: Heinemann, 1967) 189–221, with the *Cercidea*, 228–239; cf. Gerhard, *Phoinix*, 237; J. U. Powell and E. A. Barber, *New Chapters in the History of Greek Literature* (Oxford: Clarendon, 1921) 2–12; Dudley, *Cynicism*, 74–84, 93–94; Knox, *Herodes*, xvii–xix, 222–227.

[25] Leonidas was a popular epigrammatist of the third century B.C. whose works are noteworthy for their clash of elaborate style and diction with mundane subject matter. Some of his poems exhibit gnomic features, and the themes of these and other epigrams attest to the influence of Cynic ideas, for example, *Anthologia Graeca* 6.302, 7.67, 452, 472, 648, 660, 665, 726, 731, 736, 9.99, 335; text: Andrew S. F. Gow and Denys L. Page, eds., *The Greek Anthology: Hellenistic Epigrams* (2 vols.; Cambridge: Cambridge University Press, 1965) 1.107–139; cf. Gerhard, *Phoinix*, 240, 242; Dudley, *Cynicism*, 114–115; Gow and Page, *Hellenistic Epigrams*, 2.307–398; Rudolf Keydell, "Leonidas 9," *KP* 3 (1969) 567–568.

[26] Sotades was an ethical critic and satirist of the third century B.C.; cf. Gerhard, *Phoinix*, 243–244, 266, 277; Dudley, *Cynicism*, 114.

[27] See Douglas Young, ed., *Theognis* (BT; 2nd ed.; Leipzig: Teubner, 1971) 113–118; cf.

Phoenix of Colophon.[28] Several scholars have also speculated as to the Cynic background of some of the gnomic poems incorporated in the *Theognidea*.[29]

While a great deal of Hellenistic gnomic poetry may be attributed, directly or indirectly, to the Cynics, the philosophers associated with this movement by no means exercised a monopoly on the continuation and development of the genre. In fact, writers connected with virtually every philosophical school, as well as some apparently connected with no school at all, took advantage of this medium of ethical expression and instruction. Such widespread use during the Hellenistic period testifies to the genre's popularity and flexibility, suggesting also its widespread employment in the context of philosophical education, not to mention in moral training that took place outside the auspices of the 'established' schools. Among the poets of this type we may mention Timon of Phlius,[30] Cleanthes of Assos,[31] and Philodemus of Gadara;[32] the Pythagorean *Carmen Aureum* also belongs to this category.[33]

Gnomic poetry also enjoyed a rigorous life outside the realm of philosophy. The *Mimes* of Herodes, for instance, depict short, colorful scenes of daily life in choliambic verse. These poems, which may have been originally intended

---

Siegfried Jaekel, ed., *Menandri Sententiae* (BT; Leipzig: Teubner, 1964) 26–30; also Gerhard, *Phoinix*, 264; idem, ΧΑΡΗΤΟΣ ΓΝΩΜΑΙ (SHAW.PH 3.13; Heidelberg: Carl Winter, 1912); Otto Hense, "Chares und Verwandtes," *RMP* 72 (1917–18) 14–34; Powell and Barber, *New Chapters*, 18; Dudley, *Cynicism*, 114.

[28] See Gerhard, *Phoinix*, passim; also Powell and Barber, *New Chapters*, 12–16; Dudley, *Cynicism*, 89, 114; Knox, *Herodes*, xvi–xvii, 242–263.

[29] For example vv. 83–86, 731–752, 1135–1150, 1191–1194; Gerhard, *Phoinix*, 257–264; Dudley, *Cynicism*, 113–114; cf. Martin L. West, *Studies in Greek Elegy and Iambus* (Berlin and New York: de Gruyter, 1974) 40–64; Gregory Nagy, "Theognis and Megara: A Poet's Vision of his City," in Figueira and Nagy, *Theognis*, 46–51.

[30] The works of Timon (c. 320–230 B.C.) have some affinity with Cynicism, though the author's true allegiance belonged to Pyrrho of Elis, the forerunner of Skepticism. While Timon was reputed to have published in a wide range of prose and poetic forms, the extant fragments are predominantly from two works, the ΣΙΛΛΟΙ in hexameters, and the ΙΝΔΑΛΜΟΙ in elegiacs. Text: Diels, *Poetarum Philosophorum Fragmenta*, 173–206; cf. Gerhard, *Phoinix*, 242–243, 250–251; Dudley, *Cynicism*, 107–108, 114; Heinrich Dörrie, "Timon 3," *KP* 5 (1975) 847; A. A. Long, "Timon of Phlius: Pyrrhonist and Satirist," *PCPS* 204 (1978) 68–91.

[31] Of the surviving nine poems of Cleanthes (died 232 B.C.), the best-known is the *Hymn to Zeus*, an eloquent Stoic statement of theology and ethics composed in dactylic hexameters. This composition draws upon much traditional poetic language and its thought is indebted to the (largely gnomic) philosophy of Heraclitus. Text: Hans F. A. von Arnim, ed., *Stoicorum Veterum Fragmenta* (4 vols.; Leipzig: Teubner, 1905–1924) 1.121–123 (# 537); text and translation: A. A. Long and D. N. Sedley, *The Hellenistic Philosophers* (2 vols.; Cambridge: Cambridge University Press, 1987) 1.326–327, 2.326–327; cf. below, p. 149, n. 8.

[32] Text and translation: Andrew S. F. Gow and Denys L. Page, eds., *The Greek Anthology: The Garland of Philip and Some Contemporary Epigrams* (2 vols.; Cambridge: Cambridge University Press, 1968) 1.351–369, cf. 2.371–400; Elizabeth Asmis, "Philodemus' Epicureanism," *ANRW* II.36.4 (1990) 2369–2406, with references.

[33] See below, pp. 52–54.

for dramatic production, employ popular language, maxims, and proverbial expressions to amuse and entertain the audience, as well as to make some serious ethical points.[34] Fables, with their joint aims of entertainment and instruction, might also be considered a type of gnomic poetry. In the first century A.D., Babrius compiled an anthology of Aesopic fables, ΜΥΘΙΑΜΒΟΙ, rewriting them into choliambic verse.[35] Many of the fables conclude with a maxim that encapsulates the moral of the story.[36] Finally, mention should be made of the vast *Carmina Moralia* of Gregory of Nazianzus.[37] This is an anthology of ethical poems and maxims, including several gnomologia[38] and an alphabetic acrostic of gnomic verses.[39] While it appears that Gregory himself is responsible for the composition of the poems in the *Carmina Moralia*, he draws extensively from the works of well-known poets such as Theognis, Euripides, and Callimachus, as well as from the available fund of proverbial lore and popular philosophy.[40]

Generally speaking, gnomic poems became an effective and popular genre in the ancient world largely because they joined ethical instruction with the aesthetic pleasure associated with reading or hearing a work of poetry. The potential of poetic expression enabled authors to lend a certain dignity to their subject matter and to make their messages more striking and memorable. The prologue to the *Comparatio Menandri et Philistionis II* illuminates the ethos of the genre:

ʽΟ πᾶσιν ἀρέσας ἐν σοφοῖς ποιήμασιν
ὁ τοῦ βίου τὴν πρᾶξιν ἐπιδείξας σοφοῖς,
Μένανδρος ὁ σοφὸς νῦν πάλιν παραινέσω,
χαίρειν προ{σ}τάξας τοῖς ἀκούουσιν νέοις,
ὅπως ἕκαστος ἀκούων μου μανθάνῃ
τὴν τοῦ βίου εὐθεῖαν, ἥν ὑμῖν φράσω,

---

[34] Text: I. C. Cunningham, ed., *Herodae Mimiambi* (BT; Leipzig: Teubner, 1987); text and translation: Knox, *Herodes*, 80–175; also see Powell and Barber, *New Chapters*, 112–123; Rudolf Keydell, "Herodas," *KP* 2 (1967) 1090; Knox, *Herodes*, xix–xxiv, 74–79, 177–185.

[35] Text and translation: Otto Crusius, ed., *Babrii Fabulae Aesopeae* (BT; Leipzig: Teubner, 1897); Ben Edwin Perry, trans., *Babrius and Phaedrus* (LCL; Cambridge: Harvard University Press; London: Heinemann, 1984); also see Gerhard, *Phoinix*, 246–247, 267–269.

[36] For example, *Mythiamboi* 5, 6, 13, 14, 18, 20–22, 24, 29, 31, 33, 37, 44, 47, 50, 52, 56, 58, 59, 64–67, 69, 71, 79, 81–85, 87, 92, 94, 96, 98, 103, 111, 112, 116, 119, 127; cf. Perry, *Babrius*, xiv–xvi.

[37] Text: *PG* 37.521–968.

[38] *PG* 37.910–915, 916–927, 927–945.

[39] *PG* 37.908–910.

[40] Gerhard, *Phoinix*, 255, 275; Vetschera, *Paränese*, 27–29; Henry Chadwick, "Florilegium," *RAC* 7 (1969) 1145–1146; D. A. Sykes, "The Poemata Arcana of St. Gregory Nazianzen: Some Literary Questions," *Byzantinische Zeitschrift* 72 (1979) 6–15; idem, "Gregory Nazianzen as Didactic Poet," *Studia Patristica* 16 (1985) 433–437; Bernhard Wyß, "Gregor II (Gregor von Nazianz)," *RAC* 12 (1983) 793–863, especially 808–814, 839–859.

παρηγορῶν ἕκαστον ἐς τὸ συμφέρον,
ἔχων ἀγῶνα πρὸς Φιλιστίωνα νῦν,
τὸν τερπνὸν καὶ φιλητὸν καὶ βιωφελῆ,
ἐκ τῶν κατὰ μέρος ἐκλεγέντων πραγμάτων.

He who pleases all with wise poems,
and displays the praxis of life to the wise,
I, Menander the wise, shall once more prescribe
instructions to delight the youth who listen,
so that each, hearing me, will learn
the straight way of life, which I will recommend to you,
exhorting each to what is useful,
now holding a contest against Philistion,
the pleasant and beloved and beneficent,
on chosen issues, each in turn.[41]

The introduction to this fairly substantial work (over 200 lines in length) expresses the implicit connection often made between learning and pleasure in gnomic poems. In verses 1–3, Menander associates his exhortations with wisdom literature as well as with traditional paraenesis. Hence his recommendations are wise, practical, and useful, especially in so far as they teach "the straight way of life" (verse 6) to young people, suggesting for the text some sort of connection with moral education. At the same time, these verses aim to please and delight the reader, and the whole atmosphere of the ἀγών seems as playful as it is studious. Following the prologue to the *Comparatio* we find a series of instructional paragraphs in meter and organized according to moral topics on which Menander and Philistion offer their wise counsel. The poem includes, for example, paragraphs περὶ τύχης, περὶ γήρους, περὶ πλούτου, περὶ θανάτου, and so forth. In form, substance, and perspective the entire poem (as well as these constituent sections) is representative of the genre.

Gnomologia

The need to preserve and collect well-known, useful, or artistic sayings, verses, quotations, and so forth must have been felt from almost the beginning of human literary activity. Ancient florilegia, of which Stobaeus' *Anthologium* is an example, gathered material on a wide range of themes and from a wide range of sources, including gnomic sources.[42] A special manifestation of this

---

[41] Text: Jaekel, *Sententiae*, 102; my translation; cf. Wilhelm Meyer, "Die athenische Spruchrede des Menander und Philistion," *ABAW* 19 (1891) 227–295; Gerhard, *Phoinix*, 264–267, 274–275, 280.

[42] Kurt Wachsmuth, *Studien zu den griechischen Florilegien* (Berlin: Weidmann, 1882); Henri-Marie Rochaise, "Florilèges Latins," *DSp* 5 (1964) 435–460; Philippe Delhaye, "Florilèges Mediévaux d'Ethique," *DSp* 5 (1964) 460–475; Marcel Richard, "Florilèges Grecs," *DSp* 5 (1964) 475–512; Chadwick, "Florilegium," 1131–1160.

activity is the gnomologium, an anthology or collection composed entirely (or almost entirely) of gnomic sayings. Such texts demonstrate little logical or material means of comprehensive organization; they ordinarily consist of a series of largely unconnected entries without any overarching order or plan. Thus a gnomologium lacks a 'macro-argument', as it were, though it may contain any number of 'micro-arguments', relatively short sequences of related sayings loosely strung together.

While the term gnomologia refers principally to anthologies of Greek provenance, similar collections were clearly important in ancient Near Eastern societies as well.[43] The Hebrew Bible, for instance, preserves an anthology of gnomic verses in Proverbs 10.1 ff.[44] Like other ancient gnomologia, this collection represents a multiplicity of sayings spanning the intellectual activity of several centuries and incorporating the experiential insights of different social groups. The maxims here counsel and admonish the reader, but chiefly they provide illustrations of various types of behavior and their consequences. Although explicit concepts appear only infrequently, Proverbs 10.1 ff. betrays a thoroughly Jewish ethos, and for its authors conformity to the order of creation appears to be consistent with the will of God.

Sometime during the first century B.C., perhaps in Alexandria, translators rendered the Hebrew book of Proverbs into Greek.[45] Significantly, this rendi-

---

[43] For examples see: E. I. Gorden and T. Jacobsen, *Sumerian Proverbs* (Philadelphia: University Museum of the University of Pennsylvania, 1959); W. G. Lambert, *Babylonian Wisdom Literature* (Oxford: Clarendon, 1960) 92–117, 213–282; James B. Pritchard, ed., *Ancient Near Eastern Texts Relating to the Old Testament* (3rd ed.; Princeton: Princeton University Press, 1969) 425–427, 593–594; William McKane, *Proverbs: A New Approach* (OTL; Philadelphia: Westminster, 1970) 183–208; Brendt Alster, *Studies in Sumerian Proverbs* (Copenhagen: Akademisk Forlag, 1975); Miriam Lichtheim, *Late Egyptian Wisdom Literature in the International Context: A Study of Demotic Instructions* (OBO 52; Freiburg [Schweiz]: Universitätsverlag; Göttingen: Vandenhoeck & Ruprecht, 1983) 7–10; cf. Küchler, *Weisheitstraditionen*, 167–175; Waltrand Guglielmi, "Sprichwort," *LÄ* 5 (1984) 1219–1222.

[44] There are a host of complex and unresolved problems regarding the content, background, purpose, and setting of the book of Proverbs; see, for instance, Udo Skladny, *Die ältesten Spruchsammlungen in Israel* (Göttingen: Vandenhoeck & Ruprecht, 1962); Berend Gemser, *Sprüche Salomos* (HAT 1.16; 2nd ed.; Tübingen: J.C.B. Mohr [Paul Siebeck], 1963); R. N. Whybray, *Wisdom in Proverbs: The Concept of Wisdom in Proverbs 1–9* (SBT 45; Naperville: Allenson; London: SCM, 1965); McKane, *Proverbs*, 1–47, 262 ff.; von Rad, *Wisdom in Israel*, 74–96; Roland E. Murphy, *The Forms of the Old Testament Literature*, Volume 13: *Wisdom Literature* (Grand Rapids: Eerdmans, 1981) 47–82; Claus Westermann, *Wurzeln der Weisheit: Die ältesten Sprüche Israels und anderer Völker* (Göttingen: Vandenhoeck & Ruprecht, 1990) 9–114.

[45] Gillis Gerleman, "The Septuagint Proverbs as a Hellenistic Document," *OTS* 8 (1950) 15–27; idem, "Studies in the Septuagint: Religion and Ethics in the LXX Proverbs," *LUÅ* 1.52.3 (1956) 36–63; McKane, *Proverbs*, 33–47; Emanuel Tov, "Jewish Greek Scriptures," in Kraft and Nickelsburg, *Early Judaism and its Modern Interpreters*, 221–237; idem, "The Septuagint," *Mikra: Text, Translation, Reading, and Interpretation of the Hebrew Bible in*

tion exhibits considerable Hellenization and deviates from its original more than any other document of the Septuagint, as Sidney Jellicoe observes: "To a still greater extent (than the translator of Job) the translator of Proverbs adapts his original to its new environment. Maxims of purely Greek origin are incorporated and 'tags of rough hexameters and iambics abound'. Greek rather than Hebrew standards determine the style."[46] The translators of the LXX Proverbs felt free to replace Hebrew sayings with their Greek equivalents, and they often had recourse to poetic and other literary methods familiar from Greek gnomologia, particularly the Greek paroemiographia, such as the ΕΠΙΤΟΜΗ of Zenobius (second century A.D., but based on earlier collections).[47] This suggests that those who originally used the LXX Proverbs understood their gnomic collection in the same terms as those familiar to them from Greek sources and intended their translation to stand together with comparable gnomologia. So while the LXX Proverbs possesses distinct formal and material qualities, this is also true of other gnomic collections, and there are sufficient similarities for it to be considered in the basic investigation of ancient gnomologia.

In Greece, anthologies of this type were compiled beginning at least as early as the fourth century B.C. and endured as a vital though peripheral genre in education, literature, ethics, and philosophy throughout antiquity and beyond. The compilations normally consisted of sayings excerpted from the works of one or more sages, poets, or philosophers.[48] As Dimitri Gutas observes, the gnomologial corpus possessed two distinct yet complementary social identities: "The gnomologia were popular in the true sense of the term: they were designed for public consumption, and as such were on the border line between folk literature, like proverbs, tales, etc., which is mostly oral, and scholarly

---

Ancient Judaism and Early Christianity (ed. Martin J. Mulder; CRINT 2.1; Assen, Maastricht: van Gorcum; Philadelphia: Fortress, 1988) 159–188; John G. Gammie, "The Septuagint of Job: Its Poetic Style and Relationship to the Septuagint of Proverbs," *CBQ* 49 (1987) 14–31; von Lips, *Weisheitliche Traditionen*, 103–105.

[46] Sidney Jellicoe, *The Septuagint and Modern Study* (Oxford: Clarendon, 1968) 317–318.

[47] H. J. Thackeray, "The Poetry of the Greek Book of Proverbs," *JTS* 13 (1911–12) 46–66; regarding Zenobius consult the articles by Otto Crusius in volume 3 of *Corpus Paroemiographorum Graecorum* (ed. Ernst L. Leutsch and F. G. Schneidewin; 2 vols.; Göttingen: Vandenhoeck & Ruprecht, 1839–1851) [reprint with vol. 3, Hildesheim: Olms, 1958]; cf. Jürgen Werner's review of Winfried Bühler, ed., *Griechische Sprichwörter: Zenobii Athoi Proverbia* (4 vols.; Göttingen: Vandenhoeck & Ruprecht, 1982) in *Göttingische Gelehrte Anzeigen* 240 (1988) 92–96; also Karl Rupprecht, "Paroimiographoi," *PW* 18.4 (1949) 1735–1778.

[48] For general comments on the Greek gnomologia see Horna, "Gnome," 78–82; J. Barnes, "A New Gnomologium, with Some Remarks on Gnomic Anthologies," *CQ* 44 (1950) 126–137 and 45 (1951) 1–19; Spoerri, "Gnome," 825–829; Chadwick, "Florilegium," especially 1152–1156; Dimitri Gutas, *Greek Wisdom Literature in Arabic Translation: A Study of the Graeco-Arabic Gnomologia* (AOS 60; New Haven: American Oriental Society, 1975); Küchler, *Weisheitstraditionen*, 236–302, cf. 157–235, 303–414; Kloppenborg, *The Formation of Q*, 289–306, 337–341.

philosophical and ethical literature. On the one hand they commanded greater respect than folk literature because the sayings and anecdotes were ascribed to venerable figures, and on the other they were not as forbidding as philosophical treatises because their contents were simple, easily understood and memorized."[49] On account of this 'border line' existence, the gnomic anthologies as a whole manifest considerable range with regard to their traditional content, philosophical inclination, and literary character.

Gnomic collections carry with them, like any other genre, a host of philological and literary problems. Along with the usual questions of authorship, date, provenance, and the status of the text, special complications arise concerning gnomologia in matters of the analysis of sources, textual history, original purpose, and subsequent functions. While the anthologies are normally ascribed to particular historical figures and may preserve some authentic sayings, their contents are by and large pseudepigraphical. We should bear in mind that most ancient gnomologia enjoyed constant circulation and use. Thus over the course of centuries any number of additions, abridgments, or rearrangements could be made to a collection, all at the hands of anonymous writers and editors according to their particular needs.[50] With the notable exception of Anton Elter's investigations, the modern analysis of these formidable complexities has been limited in scope and quality.[51]

One reason for the difficulty in studying gnomologia is the remarkable diversity they exhibit in form, content, and function. Their morphology, to begin with, may be described with respect to two rudimentary characteristics: the types of sayings that occur in a collection and the means utilized by an author or editor to organize the sayings.

Evidence suggests that the earliest gnomologia were in verse; this no doubt reflects the poetic inclinations of the first gnomic authors.[52] Yet while several of the surviving anthologies contain largely metrical sayings, most are in prose. The majority of gnomologia consist solely of a sequence of independent maxims; these may be predominantly either indicative or imperative sentences, though typically it is a fair mixture of both.[53] A small number of col-

---

[49] Gutas, *Greek Wisdom Literature*, 1–2.

[50] Horna, "Gnome," 82–84; Gutas, *Greek Wisdom Literature*, 1–5, 9–35, 436–438; Küchler, *Weisheitstraditionen*, 258–261. The various gnomic collections attributed to Menander are typical of this phenomenon, see Görler, *Menandrou Gnomai*, 102 ff.

[51] Anton Elter, *Gnomologiorum Graecorum Historia Atque Origine* (9 parts plus 2-part supplement; Bonn: C. George, 1893–1897); idem, *Gnomica Homoeomata* (5 parts; Bonn: C. George, 1900–1904). A recent gnomologial study of interest is Alessandra B. Malgarini, "ΑΡΧΑΙΩΝ ΦΙΛΟΣΟΦΩΝ ΓΝΩΜΑΙ ΚΑΙ ΑΠΟΦΘΕΓΜΑΤΑ in un Manoscritto di Patmos," *Elenchos* 5 (1984) 153–200.

[52] Horna, "Gnome," 76–78; Barnes, "Gnomologium," 132–137; Spoerri, "Gnome," 824; Chadwick, "Florilegium," 1131–1136.

[53] Cf. Kloppenborg, *The Formation of Q*, 298–299.

lections, for instance the *Gnomologium Vaticanum* and the *Gnomologium Epictetum*, may supplement particular entries with explanations, illustrations, or supporting arguments, and so might be better understood as collections of enthymemes rather than gnomologia in the ordinary sense. Perhaps the specialized nature of these collections precipitated the need for such expansions. A related practice is to combine several related maxims together with motive clauses or examples according to various criteria in order to produce discrete thematic units.

Gnomologia ordinarily display little argumentative or material organization with respect to their overall structure. The sequence from one maxim to the next often appears to be illogical or inconsistent, and sayings with differing literary structures, subject matter, and ethical viewpoints are situated side-by-side. Because normally anticipated connections and transitions are absent, individual sayings stand more or less in isolation and their application seems arbitrary and impersonal. Thus maxims in this sort of setting lack ordinary contexts and their projected meanings and functions are obscure or indeterminate. It remains for the user of the anthology to remove these ambiguities by contextualizing individual sayings in specific situations or by imposing some sense of rational order on the collection as it stands. By construing meaning in this way, the readers become more self-conscious of the hermeneutical principles involved in their understanding of the text, and there is a greater than normal risk of individualized or idiosyncratic interpretations.[54] A related phenomenon is the 'antilogical' tendency at work in some gnomologia; occasionally editors would juxtapose maxims conveying opposing points of view on the same subject. Plutarch suggests one rationale for this procedure in *Moralia* 20C–22A: the contrast of differing views helps formulate a more balanced judgment, sharpens the critical faculties, and serves as preparation for future argument and debate.[55]

---

[54] These comments apply sometimes to other types of gnomic wisdom as well. For more see Nigel Barley, "A Structural Approach to the Proverb and Maxim with Special Reference to the Anglo-Saxon Corpus," *Proverbium* 20 (1972) 737–750; Philip E. Lewis, "The Discourse of the Maxim," *Diacritics* 2 (1972) 41–48; Paul Requadt, "Das Aphoristische Denken," *Der Aphorismus: Zur Geschichte, zu den Formen und Möglichkeiten einer literarischen Gattung* (ed. Gerhard Neumann; WdF 356; Darmstadt: Wissenschaftliche Buchgesellschaft, 1976) 331–377; Jonathan Barnes, "Aphorism and Argument," *Language and Thought in Early Greek Philosophy* (ed. Kevin Robb; La Salle, IL: Hegeler Institute, 1983) 91–109; Arvo Krikmann, "On Denotative Indefiniteness of Proverbs," *Proverbium: Yearbook of International Proverb Scholarship* 1 (1984) 47–91.

[55] The title of the treatise is *Quomodo Adolescens Poetas Audire Debeat*. For text and translation see Frank Cole Babbitt, et al., trans., *Plutarch's Moralia* (LCL; 15 vols.; Cambridge: Harvard University Press; London: Heinemann, 1927–69) 1.71–197. As Barnes observes ("Gnomologium," 2–4), this sort of reasoning from both sides of an issue bears some resemblance to sophistic argumentation, and he in fact argues that the sophistic movement made use of such gnomologia.

This is not to say, however, that the constituent elements of a gnomic anthology necessarily lack arrangement and order altogether. Inspection of the texts suggests that editors could employ two types of methods for organizing sayings in a gnomologium. First, sometimes they consistently utilize an arbitrary system such as alphabetization in order to serialize all the maxims in a given text. Second, they may deploy various literary devices in order to link small clusters of sayings together; these devices include catchword, linkword, inclusio, ring composition, formal analogy, and arrangement by topic.[56] While these features are extremely common they only rarely unite substantial portions of text and editors never apply them consistently throughout an anthology. In addition, some gnomologia exhibit a high degree of formal consistency in their sayings beyond any metrical requirements, for example, Proverbs 10–15, a collection of mostly antithetically formulated sayings, and the prologue to the *Dicta Catonis*, a collection of mostly two- and three-word sayings.[57] Significantly, the patterns of arrangement characteristic of gnomologia are often based upon certain concrete verbal qualities of the sayings, such as their morphology or language. This is hardly unexpected, given the maxim's deliberate and artistic literary style, and the presence of such patterns underscores the form-intensive nature of gnomic wisdom.

Some typical examples of the sorts of organizational structures and devices that gnomologia characteristically deploy can be found in verses 414–425 of the *Sententiae* of Sextus, a Christian gnomologium of the second century A.D.:[58]

χαίρειν ἔθιζέ σου τὴν ψυχὴν ἐφ' οἷς καλὸν χαίρειν.
415 a　ψυχὴ χαίρουσα ἐπὶ μικροῖς ἄτιμος παρὰ θεῷ.
415 b　σοφοῦ ψυχὴ ἀκούει θεοῦ.

---

[56] By *catchword* I mean the connection of a saying with the one that immediately precedes it by means of the repetition of a word or short phrase; *linkword* refers to a similar connection of three or more sayings which are not necessarily contiguous; *inclusio* is the use of the same term, phrase, or concept, at or near both the beginning and the end of a passage; *ring composition* is the sustained chiastic structure of a passage, for example, A B C B' A', where the correspondence of structural pairs can depend on such things as wording, topic, formal analogy, and so forth. Cf. Horna, "Gnome," 79; Küchler, *Weisheitstraditionen*, 260–261, cf. 265–274; Patrick W. Skehan and Alexander A. DiLella, *The Wisdom of Ben Sira: A New Translation with Notes* (AB 39; Garden City, New York: Doubleday, 1987) s.v. mot crochet, chiastic patterns; Kloppenborg, *The Formation of Q*, 299; Wilson, *Love Without Pretense*, s.v. catchword, inclusio, ring composition.

[57] Text and translation: J. Wight Duff and Arnold M. Duff, trans., *Minor Latin Poets* (LCL; 2nd ed.; Cambridge: Harvard University Press; London: Heinemann, 1935) 592–629; cf. Otto Skutsch, "Dicta Catonis," *PW* 5.1 (1903) 358–370.

[58] Cf. Robert L. Wilken, "Wisdom and Philosophy in Early Christianity," in idem, *Aspects of Wisdom*, 143–168; Frederik Wisse, "Die Sextus-Sprüche und das Problem der gnostischen Ethik," *Zum Hellenismus in den Schriften von Nag Hammadi* (ed. Alexander Böhlig and Frederick Wisse; Göttinger Orientforschungen 6.2; Wiesbaden: Otto Harrassowitz, 1975) 55–86.

σοφοῦ ψυχὴ ἁρμόζεται πρὸς θεὸν ὑπὸ θεοῦ.
σοφοῦ ψυχὴ ἀεὶ θεὸν ὁρᾷ.
ψυχὴ σοφοῦ σύνεστιν ἀεὶ θεῷ.
καρδία θεοφιλοῦς ἐν χειρὶ θεοῦ ἵδρυται.

420 ψυχῆς ἄνοδος πρὸς θεὸν διὰ λόγου θεοῦ.
σοφὸς ἕπεται θεῷ καὶ ὁ θεὸς ψυχῇ σοφοῦ.
χαίρει τῷ ἀρχομένῳ τὸ ἄρχον, καὶ ὁ θεὸς οὖν σοφῷ χαίρει.
ἀχώριστόν ἐστιν τοῦ ἀρχομένου τὸ ἄρχον, καὶ θεὸς οὖν τοῦ σοφοῦ προνοεῖ καὶ κήδεται.
ἐπιτροπεύεται σοφὸς ἀνὴρ ὑπὸ θεοῦ, διὰ τοῦτο καὶ μακάριος.

425 ψυχὴ σοφοῦ δοκιμάζεται διὰ σώματος ὑπὸ θεοῦ.

Accustom your soul to rejoice in those things in which it is good to rejoice.
415a A soul rejoicing in trivial matters is dishonored before God.
415b The soul of a sage hears God.
The soul of a sage is joined to God by God.
The soul of a sage always sees God.
The soul of a sage always attends to God.
The heart of one dear to God lies in God's hand.
420 The ascent of the soul to God is through God's word.
A sage follows God and God follows the soul of a sage.
That which rules rejoices in what is ruled, and so God rejoices in a sage.
That which rules is inseparable from what is ruled, and so God takes thought for a sage and cares about him.
A wise man is governed by God and for this reason is blessed.
425 The soul of a sage is tested by God through the body.[59]

While these maxims are united to a certain degree by theme and perspective, we detect in the passage no real progression of thought from beginning to end; the passage also lacks a clear material or formal connection with what immediately precedes or follows in the *Sententiae*. The unit in verses 414–425 itself has been organized by means of a number of interlocking, inconsistently applied devices, including catchword,[60] linkword,[61] anaphora,[62] and inclusio,[63] as well as an apparent attempt to arrange sayings according to length.

The subject matter, provenance, and intended audience of the gnomological genre, like its morphology, is wanting for consistency. A number of largely overlapping functions may be identified. In their preservational and referential function, the maxims of a gnomologium represent noteworthy excerpts culled

---

[59] Text: Henry Chadwick, ed., *The Sentences of Sextus: A Contribution to the Early Christian History of Ethics* (TextsS 5; Cambridge: Cambridge University Press, 1959) 58, 60; my translation; cf. Richard A. Edwards and Robert A. Wild, eds., *The Sentences of Sextus* (SBLTT 22; Chico, CA: Scholars Press, 1981) 66–69.

[60] χαίρειν (v. 414) and χαίρουσα (v. 415a); ἀεί (vv. 417 and 418); τῷ ἀρχομένῳ τὸ ἄρχον (v. 422) and τοῦ ἀρχομένου τὸ ἄρχον (v. 423); καὶ ὁ θεὸς οὖν (v. 422) and καὶ θεὸς οὖν (v. 423).

[61] ψυχή: vv. 414–418, 420–421, 425; σοφοῦ ψυχή: vv. 415b–418, 421, 425; θεός: vv. 415a–425; σοφός: vv. 421–425.

[62] σοφοῦ ψυχή begins vv. 415b–417.

[63] χαίρ- appears at the beginning and end of vv. 414 and 422; also ψυχὴ σοφοῦ ... θεῷ (v. 418) and ψυχὴ σοφοῦ ... θεοῦ (v. 425).

from earlier literary works, quotations of famous figures, or the apt observations of a wise sage. It is in their capacity as repositories of edifying as well as accessible sayings that the use of gnomic anthologies in elementary education is best understood. For younger pupils, the anthologies served as copy-books or primers for instruction in reading and writing. For more advanced students, compilations were made with an eye to their ethical, literary, or didactic content, and were frequently arranged topically. Because the study of maxims facilitated the development of cultural awareness and the process of social initiation in such ways, gnomologia often became a basis of moral education in the ancient world. The gnomic anthologies embodied fundamental social norms and ethical attitudes, enabling them to be transmitted to different cultures and subsequent generations.[64]

The philosophical schools provided the decisive impetus for the growing use of gnomologia in the Hellenistic era. This was particularly true of the Stoics and the Cynics, though the Epicureans, the Pythagoreans, and other groups employed such anthologies as well.[65] Within the schools it is possible to identify two broad and overlapping motives for the anthologizing activities. First, philosophers would compile collections of sayings from previous authors, especially the well-known poets, for use in their own compositions. Sextus Empiricus articulates the motives behind this practice, reporting the common opinion that, "the best and character-forming philosophy had its original roots in the gnomic sayings of the poets, and on this account the philosophers, when giving exhortations, always stamped, as it were, their injunctions with phrases from the poets."[66] The Cynic tradition, beginning apparently from the earliest stages of its development, also participated in compiling gnomologia.[67] These stores of maxims provided them with a resource that was amenable to their message, style, and audience. Apropos of the collections and their relationship with philosophical movements, J. Barnes writes, "[w]e may assume that they

---

[64] Horna, "Gnome," 78; Henri I. Marrou, *A History of Education in Antiquity* (New York: Sheed and Ward, 1956) 150–159, 234–235; Barnes, "Gnomologium," 132–137, 5–8; Chadwick, "Florilegium," 1131–1133; Gutas, *Greek Wisdom Literature*, 451; Kloppenborg, *The Formation of Q*, 295, 299; cf. Quintilian, *Institutio Oratoria* 1.9.3–4; Abraham J. Malherbe, *Social Aspects of Early Christianity* (2nd ed.; Philadelphia: Fortress, 1983) 41–45.

[65] On the connection between gnomologia and philosophy see Horna, "Gnome," 79–82; Barnes, "Gnomologium," 4–14; Chadwick, "Florilegium," 1136–1143; Spoerri, "Gnome," 825–826; Wilken, "Wisdom and Philosophy," 158–164; Küchler, *Weisheitstraditionen*, 250–261; Gutas, *Greek Wisdom Literature*, 451–457, cf. 9–35.

[66] Sextus Empiricus, *Adversus Mathematicos* 1.271; text and translation: R. G. Bury, trans., *Sextus Empiricus* (LCL; 4 vols.; Cambridge: Harvard University Press; London: Heinemann, 1933–1949) 3.152–153.

[67] Zeph Stewart, "Democritus and the Cynics," *HSCP* 63 (1958) 179–191; Gutas, *Greek Wisdom Literature*, 453–457, and s.v. Cynicism; cf. Kurt von Fritz's additions to Horna, "Gnome," 87–89; Dudley, *Cynicism*, 110–116; Jan F. Kindstrand, "The Cynics and Heraclitus," *Eranos* 82 (1984) 149–178.

were approved or used by philosophers who set a high value upon literary education and inquiry and were tolerant of, or actively interested in, *rhetoric* from Antisthenes onwards. In fact it is difficult to see how the writers of diatribes (for instance) would have fared without such assistance as a gnomologium, compiled beforehand either by themselves or by others, could afford."[68] Thus gnomic anthologies served as a medium through which Greek literature and rhetoric influenced the development of Hellenistic philosophy.[69]

The students and followers of the philosophers participated in the second area of anthologizing activity, as they culled the treatises of their masters for precepts that characterized the ethical system of their philosophical school. Collections such as the *Gnomologium Vaticanum* and the *Gnomologium Epictetum* contributed to the process of individual indoctrination and training within their respective communities. In so far as their contents were less intimidating and more easily remembered than full-blown philosophical tractates, texts such as these expedited efforts to attract and instruct new students. They also represented a means of preserving and transmitting the master's teachings, adding stability and continuity to the school.[70] Most of these collections, because of their more restricted pool of sources and more focused audience, bear the distinctive stamp of their particular philosophical movement or founder. Thus correct interpretation is often contingent upon knowledge of the philosophical doctrines, or at least a familiarity with the maxims' original context and function. Yet at the same time, some of the schools, particularly those associated with the Cynic movement, preserved not only the sayings of their own teachers but anything they deemed useful or adaptable to their purposes. Thus a philosophical gnomologium may exhibit a broader and more elementary outlook than the philosophical treatises from which it draws.

Wisdom Instruction

Near Eastern wisdom instructions constituted a stable and influential genre beginning as early as the third millennium B.C. They offered practical guidance

---

[68] Barnes, "Gnomologium," 9 (his italics).

[69] The progymnasmata also offer evidence that maxims played a part in rhetorical training. Students were expected to memorize sayings of the poets and then to write their own explanations and elaborations of the sayings. They may also have been required to compile their own gnomic collections as part of their preparation. See Fiore, *Personal Example*, 42–44; Horna, "Gnome," 75, 79; Barnes, "Gnomologium," 9–14. Also see the prologue to the gnomic anthology of Epicharmus; text and translation: Denys L. Page, trans., *Select Papyri III: Literary Papyri and Poetry* (LCL; Cambridge: Harvard University Press, 1970) 440–443.

[70] Cf. Kloppenborg, *The Formation of Q*, 300–301; Gutas, *Greek Wisdom Literature*, 451–457.

and ethical advice in the form of an authoritative speech, ostensibly given by a
father to his son. The setting of the literature is clearly didactic, and there is a
stress on order and tradition, as well as on prudential behavior, proper discretion, and intellectual discipline. Instruction in its earliest form was intended for
a political and intellectual elite – future rulers, scribes, and statesmen. Thus
many of the texts are ascribed to kings and other famous figures. However,
some, particularly later, instructions have a wider audience in view, and so they
address matters of daily life and conduct more than affairs of the court.[71] While
in some respects they represent a counterpart to gnomologia, wisdom instructions differ from the anthologies in at least four important respects: 1) their
chief provenance is the Near East, particularly Egypt, and not the Greek-speaking world; 2) their morphology and function remain comparatively stable
through the centuries; 3) the authors of these texts normally make a more con-
certed effort to provide a coherent structure for their material; 4) while maxims
may comprise a significant portion of an instructional text, they never account
for the document in its entirety but instead are employed in conjunction with
complementary and non-sapiential forms and constructions as well.

The typical morphology of wisdom instruction may be sketched as follows.[72] For the most part, instructions open with a title, ascribing the speech to
an authoritative figure. A prologue often follows, frequently with some narrative description of the setting or occasion, which calls upon the reader to pay
heed and promises benefits to the obedient. In some instructional texts the
author may raise similar themes again in an epilogue.[73] The body of the docu-

---

[71] On the content, setting, and purpose of Near Eastern instructions see Kayatz, *Studien
zu Proverbien 1–9*, 76–134; Helmut Brunner, *Altägyptische Erziehung* (Wiesbaden: Otto
Harrassowitz, 1957); idem, "Erziehung," *LÄ* 2 (1977) 22–27; idem, "Lehren," *LÄ* 3 (1980)
964–968; idem, *Altägyptische Weisheit: Lehren für das Leben* (Die Bibliothek der Alten
Welt; Zürich and München: Artemis, 1988); McKane, *Proverbs*, 51–182; Bernhard Lang,
Die weisheitliche Lehrrede: Eine Untersuchung von Sprüche 1–7 (SBS 54; Stuttgart: KBW,
1972) especially 27–60; Kenneth A. Kitchen, "Basic Literary Forms and Formulations of
Ancient Instructional Writing in Egypt and Western Asia," *Studien zu altägyptischen
Lebenslehren* (ed. Erik Hornung and Othmar Keel; OBO 28; Freiburg [Schweiz]:
Universitätsverlag; Göttingen: Vandenhoeck & Ruprecht, 1979) 235–282; Leo G. Perdue,
"Liminality as the Social Setting of Wisdom Instructions," *ZAW* 93 (1981) 114–126;
Kloppenborg, *The Formation of Q*, 264–289, 329–336.

[72] On the literary structure of instructions see Kayatz, *Studien zu Proverbien 1–9*, passim;
Hans H. Schmid, *Wesen und Geschichte der Weisheit: Eine Untersuchung zur altorientalischen und israelitischen Weisheitsliteratur* (BZAW 101; Berlin: Töpelmann,
1966) 8–84; Brunner, "Die Lehren," 113–139; idem, *Weisheit*, 75–87; McKane, *Proverbs*,
51–182; Kitchen, "Literary Forms," 249–279; Kloppenborg, *The Formation of Q*, 265–272,
276–282.

[73] The Instruction of Any has an unusual epilogue in which father and son debate the utility of the text's contents; translation: Miriam Lichtheim, *Ancient Egyptian Literature: A
Book of Readings* (3 vols.; Berkeley, Los Angeles, London: University of California Press,
1975–1980) 2.135–146; cf. Brunner, *Altägyptische Weisheit*, 196–214.

ment consists of a sequence of instructional units or paragraphs, composed and arranged in a more or less careful manner according to subject matter.[74] The length of each of these units varies from, say, five to fifty lines. The topical and structural divisions evident may be especially pronounced, as in Amenemope and *Papyrus Insinger*, whose authors organize their material according to numbered 'chapters', but are normally somewhat more relaxed and may occasionally disappear altogether.

The rigor with which authors arrange the instructional units in a text varies considerably. In Amenemope and *Papyrus Insinger*, for instance, the topical units are logically integrated, and we can discern in these writings a clear progression of thought from beginning to end.[75] Other texts, such as Ptahhotep and Ben Sira, display some overall plan, but it appears to be rather loose and may break down in places.[76] Some authors, like Shuruppak, have organized substantial passages, but the structure has not been sustained throughout the entire document.[77] Perhaps the rabbinic tractates *Derek Eretz Rabbah* and *Derek Eretz Zuta* fall within the parameters of this category of instructional texts as well, though we should note that there are a number of special issues involved in the classification and description of these documents.[78] The instructional paragraphs of a final group, which includes the *Sayings* of Ahiqar, are apparently serialized with little regard to any plan.[79] Such loose structure

---

[74] Lichtheim (*Late Egyptian Wisdom*, 6–7) observes that virtually all pre-Demotic instructions consist of integrated speeches of varying length, composed of maxims and other kinds of sentences.

[75] "The style of Amenemope is rich in similes and metaphors which are sustained at length and with skill. The work as a whole is carefully composed and unified, both through the device of thirty numbered chapters and through concentration on two basic themes: first, the depiction of the ideal man, the 'silent man', and his adversary, the 'heated man'; second, the exhortation to honesty and warnings against dishonesty." Lichtheim, *Ancient Egyptian Literature*, 2.147 (with a translation of the text on pp. 148–163); cf. McKane, *Proverbs*, 102–117; Brunner, *Altägyptische Weisheit*, 234–256; Irene Grumach-Shirun, "Lehre des Amenemope," *LÄ* 3 (1980) 971–974. On *Papyrus Insinger*: Lichtheim, *Late Egyptian Wisdom*, 109–116 (with a translation of the text on pp. 197–234); cf. idem, "Observations on Papyrus Insinger," in Hornung and Keel, *Studien*, 284–305; Karl-Theodor Zauzich, "Pap. Dem. Insinger," *LÄ* 4 (1982) 898–899; Brunner, *Altägyptische Weisheit*, 295–349.

[76] On the literary composition of Ben Sira see Wolfgang Roth, "On the Gnomic-Discursive Wisdom of Jesus Ben-Sirach," *Semeia* 17 (1980) 59–79; Kloppenborg, *The Formation of Q*, 281–282.

[77] Cf. Brendt Alster, *The Instructions of Shuruppak: A Sumerian Proverb Collection* (Copenhagen: Akademisk Forlag, 1974).

[78] Text and translation: M. Ginsberg, trans., *Hebrew-English Edition of the Babylonian Talmud: Minor Tractates* (ed. Abraham Cohen; London: Soncino, 1984) 55b–59a; cf. M.B. Lerner, "The Tractates Derekh Erets," in Safrai, *The Literature of the Sages*, 379–389, with bibliography; also Zeller, *Mahnsprüche*, 46–47. See below, p. 185, n. 15.

[79] Cf. Frederick C. Conybeare, J. R. Harris, A. S. Lewis, *The Story of Ahikar from Aramaic, Syriac, Arabic, Ethiopic, Old Turkish, Greek and Slavonic Versions* (2nd ed.; Cam-

suggests the potential for rearranging instructional units or for removing them to be deployed in new contexts.

As for the thematic units themselves, it often appears that instructional writers gave considerable care to their literary composition and rhetorical impact. The binary wisdom admonition predominates, either standing on its own or in conjunction with other admonitions that may be linked logically or by formal devices such as catchword. Authors may also combine the admonitions with conditional, motive, and final clauses, as well as with explanations, illustrations, and extended motivations, in order to create complex arguments. Wisdom sentences, particularly in the later writings, may be employed independently or as a means of buttressing the admonitions. Non-instructional materials, such as narrative descriptions, hymns, or autobiographical elements may also be incorporated.[80] We also find on occasion programmatic or concluding statements, and even repeating formulae, which may be applied as framing devices for the paragraphs within a text. Another feature common to most instructions is the propensity to cite or rework sayings from earlier sources of wisdom, sources that were no doubt familiar to their original audiences. This is especially clear in representatives of the genre like Ankhsheshonqy, *Papyrus Insinger*,[81] Ben Sira,[82] and the *Teachings of Silvanus*,[83] which draw not only from their own sapiential traditions, but from the corpus of Greek wisdom as well.

Many of the same types of linguistic and literary devices mentioned above in the discussion of gnomologia (catchword, anaphora, inclusio, ring composition, and so forth) are at work also in the genre of wisdom instruction, though the authors of these documents customarily apply them in a more sophisticated

---

bridge: Cambridge University Press, 1913); McKane, *Proverbs*, 156–182; Küchler, *Weisheitstraditionen*, 319–413; James M. Lindenberger, *The Aramaic Proverbs of Ahiqar* (Baltimore and London: Johns Hopkins University Press, 1983); idem, trans., "Ahiqar (Seventh to Sixth Century B.C.)," in Charlesworth, *Old Testament Pseudepigrapha*, 2.479–507.

[80] See, for example, Brunner, *Altägyptische Weisheit*, 81–87.

[81] On Ankhsheshonqy and *Papyrus Insinger*: Lichtheim, *Late Egyptian Wisdom*, 28–37, 43–52, 65, 112–169, 184–196; cf. Heinz-Josef Thissen, "Lehre des Anch-Scheschonqi," *LÄ* 3 (1980) 974–975.

[82] Jack T. Sanders, *Ben Sira and Demotic Wisdom* (SBLMS 28; Chico, CA: Scholars Press, 1983); Skehan and DiLella, *Ben Sira*, 40–50, and passim; cf. E. G. Bauckmann, "Die Proverbien und die Sprüche des Jesus Sirach: Eine Untersuchung zum Strukturwandel der Israelitischen Weisheitslehre," *ZAW* 72 (1960) 33–63.

[83] Malcolm L. Peel and Jan Zandee, "The Teachings of Silvanus from the Library of Nag Hammadi," *NovT* 14 (1972) 294–311; idem, "The Teachings of Silvanus (VII, 4)," *The Nag Hammadi Library in English* (ed. James M. Robinson; 3rd ed.; San Francisco: Harper & Row, 1988) 346–361; Schoedel, "Jewish Wisdom," 169–199; Jan Zandee, "The Teachings of Silvanus (NHC VII, 4) and Jewish Christianity," *Studies in Gnosticism and Hellenistic Religions Presented to Gilles Quispel on the Occasion of his 65th Birthday* (ed. R. van den Broek and Maarten J. Vermaseren; EPRO 91; Leiden: E.J. Brill, 1981) 498–584.

and consistent manner. For an illustration of a typical instructional paragraph we may turn to *Papyrus Insinger* 26.18–27.1:[84]

26.18 Do not alter your word when spending, do not cheat at the time of sealing (a contract).
26.19 A wise man who is trusted, his pledge is in one's hand.
26.20 His word in a matter is a pledge without an oath.
26.21 Do not set a due date for someone while another (date) is in your heart.
26.22 What is in the heart of the wise man is what one finds on his tongue.
26.23 Do not draw back from what you have said except from a lawless wrong.
26.24 The honor of the true and wise scribe is in his words.
27.1   Do not cheat when you are questioned, there being a witness behind you.

This segment constitutes a coherent paragraph composed of gnomic sayings that address the themes of trust and honesty in the reader's dealings with other people, particularly in what appear to be public and commercial matters. The author's command "do not cheat" in the opening line (26.18) is repeated in the concluding line (27.1), producing an inclusio that establishes the segment's formal boundaries and helps drive home a main point. As for its internal structure, we discern in the paragraph a rather carefully planned alternation between direct commands, all of which are cast in the form of negative prohibitions (26.18, 21, 23, 27.1), and declarative statements offered by way of support, all of which extol the wise man (or scribe) as an ethical model for the audience to emulate (26.19–20, 22, 24). This alternation of command and statement creates a certain rhythm that contributes to the paragraph's literary style and unity. Lastly, the repetition of certain key terms ("word" in 26.18, 20, and 24; "wise" in 26.19, 22, and 24; "pledge" in 26.19 and 20; "heart" in 26.21 and 22) also contributes to the overall literary construction as it helps bind the sentences to one another.

As concerns the nature and level of its literary style, it should be underscored that the instructional genre is not poetic and that none of the surviving texts are in verse. This is one important feature that helps to distinguish wisdom instruction from gnomic poetry as well as from a number of gnomologia. However, Miriam Lichtheim has argued that although the genre is not technically poetry, it also defies classification as prose. The sayings portions of the instructions (as opposed to the prologues or narrative sections) are written in a "third style" that she describes as "orational," a term suggestive of their oral qualities.[85] These writers achieve rhythm and poetic effect in ways other than by meter, mainly by parallelism, balance, and economy of language. Other literary devices commonly utilized in the instructional sayings include rhyme, alliteration, asso-

---

[84] Translation: Lichtheim, *Late Egyptian Wisdom*, 224.

[85] Lichtheim, *Ancient Egyptian Literature*, 1.5–12; cf. Kevin Robb, "Preliterate Ages and the Linguistic Art of Heraclitus," in idem, *Language and Thought*, especially 174–179. On prose rhythm in the Wisdom of Solomon see Chrysostome Larcher, *Etudes sur le Livre de la Sagesse* (Paris: Gabalda, 1969) 1.88–89.

nance, word play, and chiasmus. As Lichtheim observes, the orational style observable in wisdom instruction is closely akin to that which characterizes the Hebrew Bible's Book of Proverbs.[86]

These literary features of the instructions indicate that they were originally designed to be recited and memorized as part of their pedagogical function. But, as with gnomic anthologies, the success of a particular instructional text depended largely upon the development of certain skills and abilities beyond a knowledge of the contents of the text itself. As William McKane observes in his discussion of the Instructions of Ptahhotep, "[t]he educational process goes much deeper than the memorizing of the principles, and whoever would model himself on those who have succeeded best in life must assimilate the spirit of their approach to statesmanship and acquire the insight, discipline and precision which brought them their success."[87] So the instructions were not intended solely as a step-by-step guide to proper conduct in specific situations or as a blueprint for a prosperous life. Rather, they afford the reader some essential glimpses of the "process" and "insight" of the exemplary speaker, who represents not only the experience and authority of a father or ruler but also the time-tested wisdom of many generations. The conclusion to the Instructions of Amenemope (chapter 30) summarizes these and some other cardinal aspects of the genre's ethos:

> Mark for yourself these thirty chapters:
>   They please, they instruct,
> They are the foremost of all books;
>   They teach the ignorant.
> If they are read to an ignorant man,
>   He will be purified through them.
> Seize them; put them in your mind
>   And have men interpret them, explaining them as a teacher.
> As a scribe who is experienced in his position,
>   He will find himself worthy of being a courtier.[88]

The conclusion to Amenemope resembles the prologue to the *Comparatio Menandri et Philistionis II* (cited above) in that its author understands the contents of his manual as possessing both instructional and aesthetic functions, and that he intends these functions to work in tandem. Significantly, the text projects itself as being employed in a didactic, perhaps scholastic, setting; its sayings are meant to be studied, interpreted, and explained with the assistance of others who serve as teachers. Students who successfully appropriate and

---

[86] Cf. above, pp. 26–27.

[87] McKane, *Proverbs*, 60, cf. 51–65; also cf. Helmut Brunner, "Lehre des Ptahhotep," *LÄ* 3 (1980) 989–991; idem, *Altägyptische Weisheit*, 104–109.

[88] Translation: William K. Simpson, trans., *The Literature of Ancient Egypt: An Anthology of Stories, Instructions, and Poetry* (2nd ed.; New Haven and London: Yale University Press, 1973) 265; cf. Pritchard, *Ancient Near Eastern Texts*, 424.

apply these instructions can expect professional advancement, personal enrichment, and improvements in social stature and respect. Most interestingly, the author associates his work with the 'purification' of the ignorant: Amenemope's object is apparently not just the acquisition of information per se, but a qualitative change in the moral character and perspective of the serious student.[89]

By way of conclusion, we should note that in categorizing some ancient materials it is often difficult to make formal distinctions between gnomic poetry, gnomic anthologies, and wisdom instructions. This is particularly true of late texts such as the Demotic Ankhsheshonqy, whose author (or editor) was influenced by the compositional techniques of both the Greek gnomologial and the Near Eastern instructional genres.[90] Ankhsheshonqy contains a preponderance of wisdom sentences and independent, linear maxims; further, it exhibits no overall structure and only a few thematic units. Yet, though it betrays these traits of the gnomologial style, the document is still technically wisdom instruction and refers to itself as such. Thus it is possible to speak of a number of ambiguous or 'mixed' forms. Pseudo-Isocrates' *Ad Demonicum* represents another hybrid example. As various modern critics have observed, this writing is not a gnomologium but rather a moral treatise or instructional speech whose composition has been substantially influenced by the popularity of gnomologia.[91] The treatise includes an extended introduction and conclusion specifying its occasion and purpose that create a frame for a lengthy anthology of prose maxims organized by topic. Although the structure within and among the topical units is weak, Pseudo-Isocrates has composed some of the paragraphs in a thoughtful manner and it is possible to detect a basic arrangement of the units. This treatise, then, provides evidence that at least some texts of Greek provenance exhibit material and compositional features comparable with Near Eastern wisdom instructions.

Such descriptive complications are symptomatic of the underlying similarities of the three sapiential genres discussed above. It is possible to identify a

---

[89] Cf. Kloppenborg, *The Formation of Q*, 284–287; also below, pp. 173–176.

[90] Lichtheim, "Papyrus Insinger," 284–305; idem, *Late Egyptian Wisdom*, 13–65; Kloppenborg, *The Formation of Q*, 269–271; cf. Berend Gemser, "The Instructions of 'Onchsheshonqy' and Biblical Wisdom Literature," *VTSup* 7 (1960) 102–128 [reprint, Crenshaw, *Studies*, 134–160]; McKane, *Proverbs*, 117–150.

[91] On the contents and composition of *Ad Demonicum* see Kurt Emminger, "Ps-Isokrates πρὸς Δημόνιχον," *Jahrbücher für Philologie und Pädagogik* B 27 (1902) 373–442; Paul Wendland, *Anaximenes von Lampsakos: Studien zur ältesten Geschichte der Rhetorik* (Berlin: Weidmann, 1905) 81–101; Carl Wefelmeier, *Die Sentenzensammlung der Demonicea* (Athens: Rossolatos, 1962) 65–81; Bernhard Rosenkranz, "Die Struktur der Pseudo-Isokrateischen Demonicea," *Emerita* 34 (1966) 95–129; Küchler, *Weisheitstraditionen*, 248–250; Fiore, *Personal Example*, 56–67; Lichtheim, *Late Egyptian Wisdom*, 25; Berger, "Hellenistische Gattungen," 1068–1069.

number of ways in which they resemble one another. First, the three appear to draw from approximately the same pool of ideas and topics; the focus on such themes as practical conduct, proper social behavior, and correct self-understanding constitutes a regular feature of the three genres. Second, most of these texts envision for themselves a didactic or educational setting; consequently they possess a decidedly persuasive or pedagogical tone. In connection with this, each genre strives to join its ethical and didactic aims with aesthetic or artistic features in order to make the ethical concepts more striking and memorable. Third, a significant number of these authors draw from preexisting sapiential materials; consequently, the effectiveness of their compositions relies in part upon the readers' familiarity with those materials and their ability to perceive how they have been manipulated. Fourth, in light of the first three similarities it follows that maxims figure as basic components in the composition of each of these three modes of sapiential discourse. Finally, we should note that the logical and literary structures of these texts are often based upon distinct thematic sections of a paragraph or so in length. This is true of many gnomic poems per se as well as the individual units of wisdom instructions, and even in gnomologia it is sometimes possible to detect comparable topical sequences here and there. We will need to bear in mind such overlapping characteristics as we examine in the chapters that follow the literary composition of Pseudo-Phocylides' *Sentences* and consider its literary genre.

These formal and functional similarities no doubt abetted the employment of two or more of these sapiential genres in the same text. The Book of Proverbs, for instance, begins with a prologue consisting of wisdom instructions and gnomic poems (chapters 1–9) followed by a gnomic collection (chapters 10 ff.). It was also possible for ancient authors to join one or more of these genres with non-wisdom literary forms. Thus in Ben Sira, for example, the author has appended the encomiastic Hymn in Praise of the Fathers (chapters 44–50) to the wisdom instructions and gnomic poems that make up the bulk of the book (chapters 1–43).[92] Instructional or gnomic paragraphs could be incorporated into larger non-sapiential genres as well. Tobit 4.3–20, for example, constitutes a wisdom passage embedded in a narrative folktale.[93] Similar integrations occur in the literature of early Christianity. As John Kloppenborg has argued, the formative literary structure of Q was a series of wisdom instructions;[94] these

---

[92] Thomas R. Lee (*Studies in the Form of Sirach 44–50* [SBLDS 75; Atlanta: Scholars Press, 1986]) argues that the hymn is consciously patterned after the Hellenistic encomium; cf. Burton L. Mack, *Wisdom and the Hebrew Epic: Ben Sira's Hymn in Praise of the Fathers* (Chicago Studies in the History of Judaism; Chicago and London: University of Chicago Press, 1985); Skehan and DiLella, *Ben Sira*, 497–555.

[93] Cf. Paul Deselaers, *Das Buch Tobit: Studien zu seiner Entstehung, Komposition und Theologie* (OBO 43; Göttingen: Vandenhoeck & Ruprecht, 1982) 374–425.

[94] Kloppenborg (*The Formation of Q*, 171–245) identifies six "sapiential speeches": Q 6.20b–49; 9.57–62, 10.2–11, 16; 11.2–4, 9–13; 12.2–7, 11–12; 12.22–31, 33–34; 13.24,

were later supplemented with biographical elements and eventually incorporated into the Gospels of Matthew and Luke. Another early Christian text, the Letter of James, embodies a number of gnomic paragraphs on coherent themes within an epistolary framework.[95] To these examples we may also add Didache 1.1–6.2 and the Epistle of Barnabas 18.1–21.1, both of which utilize a relatively large number of gnomic sayings within the context of Jewish-Christian teaching on the 'Two Ways'.[96] Illustrations such as these indicate both the prevalence and the adaptability of gnomic forms in the moral literature of Hellenistic Judaism and early Christianity.

14.26, 27, 17.33. Numerous other studies have focused on the gnomic features of the synoptic tradition, for instance, Rudolf Bultmann, *The History of the Synoptic Tradition* (trans. John Marsh; 2nd ed.; Oxford: Blackwell, 1968) 69–108; James M. Robinson, "LOGOI SOPHON: On the Gattung of Q," *Trajectories through Early Christianity* (ed. idem and Helmut Koester; Philadelphia: Fortress, 1971) 71–113 [= *The Future of Our Religious Past: Essays in Honor of Rudolf Bultmann* (ed. idem; New York, Evanston, San Francisco: Harper & Row, 1971) 84–130]; Zeller, *Mahnsprüche*, passim; Ronald A. Piper, *Wisdom in the Q-Tradition: The Aphoristic Teaching of Jesus* (SNTSMS 61; Cambridge: Cambridge University Press, 1989); Alan P. Winton, *The Proverbs of Jesus: Issues of History and Rhetoric* (JSNTSup 35; Sheffield: JSOT, 1990); von Lips, *Weisheitliche Traditionen*, 197–227. A. E. Harvey (*Strenuous Commands: The Ethic of Jesus* [London: SCM; Philadelphia: Trinity Press International, 1990]) emphasizes the role played by gnomic wisdom in the ethic of Jesus as presented in the gospels.

[95] See, for instance, Ulrich Luck, "Die Theologie des Jakobusbriefes," *ZTK* 81 (1984) 1–30; Martin Dibelius, *James: A Commentary on the Epistle of James* (rev. Heinrich Greeven; Hermeneia; Philadelphia: Fortress, 1975); Franz Mußner, *Der Jakobusbrief* (HTKNT 13.1; 3rd ed.; Freiburg, Basel, Wien: Herder, 1975) especially 168–175; Rudolf Hoppe, *Der theologische Hintergrund des Jakobusbriefes* (FB 28; Würzburg: Echter Verlag, 1977) 39–71, 146–148; Ernst Baasland, "Der Jakobusbrief als neutestamentliche Weisheitsschrift," *ST* 36 (1982) 119–139; idem, "Literarische Form, Thematik und geschichtliche Einordnung des Jakobusbriefes," *ANRW* II.25.5 (1988) 3646–3684; Peter H. Davids, "The Epistle of James in Modern Discussion," *ANRW* II.25.5 (1988) 3621–3645; von Lips, *Weisheitliche Traditionen*, 409–437.

[96] See below, p. 185, n. 14; cf. Michael Mees, "Die Bedeutung der Sentenzen und ihrer auxesis für die Formung der Jesus-worte nach Didaché 1,3b–2,1," *Vetera Christianorum* 8 (1971) 55–76; Küchler, *Weisheitstraditionen*, 567–571; Kurt Niederwimmer, *Die Didache* (Kommentar zu den Apostolischen Vätern 1; Göttingen: Vandenhoeck & Ruprecht, 1989) 48–64, 83–157.

Chapter Two

The Canon of Cardinal Virtues in Antiquity

In the course of surveying in Chapter One the most likely candidates for identifying the literary genre of the *Sentences*, it has become clear that coming to grips with the question of the poem's compositional principles and internal design will be essential for any generic evaluation. In order to do so, however, we need to address some additional preliminary issues, this time dealing with how ancient exhortatory and moral materials, gnomic and otherwise, were structured, and how the presence of these structures in a given text reveals something about its message, argumentative strategies, and purpose. While there were certainly many different types of structures to choose from, the following discussion focuses on a particular literary and ethical convention of antiquity that appears to be central for explaining the internal composition and genre of the *Sentences*. This is the so-called Canon of Cardinal Virtues, which plays a significant role in many writings of the Greco-Roman period. It could function either on an explicit level, in philosophical debates over the nature of virtue and which were the primary virtues, or on an implicit level, as an organizational technique in formulating moral exhortations. While texts that employ the canon in such ways vary considerably in form, substance, and style, one feature that they consistently exhibit is the presence (at least at the presuppositional level) of some effort to portray virtue as a concept that is unified but at the same time encompasses a multiplicity of human excellences and positive moral aspirations. The use of the canon as a means of enumerating the foremost virtues betrays a clear practical side as well, either as writers articulate certain agendas for moral thought and action or as they strive to enact specific objectives that are informed by a grasp of the larger ethical issues involved. Of course, any account of the place of ἀρετή in ancient thought or of the meaning and significance of the individual virtues embraced by the canon for different ancient authors extends well beyond the scope of the present study. My point, instead, is to demonstrate by way of example the basic characteristics and functions of this four-fold scheme and to examine some of the ways that it could condition the structure and argument of various literary compositions. The analysis that follows is not at all comprehensive in this regard; rather it will focus on those aspects of the canon that will best inform our investigation of the *Sentences* of Pseudo-Phocylides, particularly in Chapter Four. Consequently, many of the texts examined below are predominantly gnomic in nature, such as those types of materials already inspected in Chapter One.

While a shifting alignment of four or five primary virtues had been known earlier,[1] it was Plato who exercised the most influence in 'defining' the canon, particularly in Book IV of his *Republic*. Although the identification and description of the virtues there remain somewhat provisional and he offers different versions of the canon elsewhere, in the *Republic* Plato includes σοφία, δικαιοσύνη, σωφροσύνη, and ἀνδρεία as the primary virtues. In this instance, Plato's account of the virtues derives from his psychological analysis of the tripartite structure of the human self. Each faculty, or aspect, of the soul possesses its own particular virtue: wisdom in the rational faculty, courage in the spirited aspect, and moderation in the appetitive part. Additionally, both moderation and justice work simultaneously to maintain harmony among the three faculties of the soul. Plato then links these same virtues, mutatis mutandis, to the class structure of his ideal community. Thus, in the Platonic tradition, the canon signifies the various forms of moral excellence as they may be manifested both in the human personality and in the interactions of human society. The list of four virtues employed in the *Republic*, usually referred to as the 'Platonic' or 'Stoic' canon by modern writers, came the nearest to a standardized formulation of the canon in the Hellenistic era and it is the one we encounter most often in subsequent treatments.[2]

At the same time, it should be emphasized that the number, identity, hierarchy, and meaning of the virtues in the canon were subject to a considerable amount of variation throughout antiquity, depending upon the differing views or objectives of particular individuals or philosophical systems. A fair amount

---

[1] Some examples: Pindar, *Isthmian Ode* 8.24–28; Aeschylus, *Septem Contra Thebas* 610; Euripides, *Fragmenta* 282.23–28; Aeschines, *In Ctesiphontem* 168; cf. Helen North, "Pindar, Isthmian, 8, 24–28," *AJP* 69 (1948) 304–308. On the origins of the canon see Otto Kunsemüller, *Die Herkunft der platonischen Kardinaltugenden* (Erlangen: Gutenberg, 1935).

[2] F. M. Cornford, "Psychology and Social Structure in the Republic of Plato," *CQ* 6 (1912) 246–265; John Ferguson, *Moral Values in the Ancient World* (London: Methuen, 1958) 24–52, especially 28–30; Arthur W. H. Adkins, *Merit and Responsibility: A Study in Greek Values* (Oxford: Oxford University Press, 1960) [reprint, Midway Reprints; Chicago: University of Chicago Press, 1975] 283–299; Helen North, *Sophrosyne: Self-Knowledge and Self-Restraint in Greek Literature* (CSCP 35; Ithaca: Cornell University Press, 1966) 151, 169–176, and s.v. Canon of cardinal virtues; idem, "Canons and Hierarchies of the Cardinal Virtues in Greek and Latin Literature," *The Classical Tradition: Literary and Historical Studies in Honor of Harry Caplan* (ed. Luitpold Wallach; Ithaca: Cornell University Press, 1966) 165–183, especially 167, 172–174; T. M. Robinson, *Plato's Psychology* (Phoenix Sup. 8; Toronto: University of Toronto Press, 1970) 34–58; Terence Irwin, *Plato's Moral Theory: The Early and Middle Dialogues* (Oxford: Clarendon, 1977) 191–204; Gilbert C. Meilaender, *The Theory and Practice of Virtue* (Notre Dame: Notre Dame University Press, 1984) 45–74.

of diversity emerges in the kinds of applications to which the canon could be applied as well.

Substitutions in the precise terms employed for one or more elements in the canon, for example, were quite common. Thus φρόνησις could stand in place of σοφία, or ἐγκράτεια for σωφροσύνη, or καρτερία for ἀνδρεία, and so forth.[3] Consistency was not always observed with respect to the number of virtues in the canon either. Authors frequently added piety (εὐσέβεια or ὁσιότης) as a fifth element; it could also substitute for one of the usual four.[4] In the *De Virtutibus et Vitiis* (perhaps first-century B.C.), Pseudo-Aristotle expands the list to include eight virtues, contrasting each of them with a corresponding vice.[5] Considerable disagreement also arose over the hierarchy of the virtues within the canon. Plato, for instance, tended to view wisdom as the foremost of the virtues, encompassing the other three.[6] In the *Nicocles*, by comparison, Isocrates, probably representing the more popular opinion, describes justice and moderation as the most beneficial. Cicero exhibits a great deal of flexibility in his evaluation of the virtues, sometimes ranking either justice, moderation, or wisdom at the top.[7] All three of these writers, like many others, would often relegate courage to the bottom of the scale or make some effort to 'spiritualize' the virtue.[8]

---

[3] For example, Plato, *Leges* 631C–D; Isocrates, *Nicocles* 44, *Panathenaicus* 197; Xenophon, *Cyropaedia* 3.1.16, *Memorabilia* 1.5.4, 3.9.1–5, 4.8.11; Aristotle, *Ethica Nicomachea* 7.2, 8; Diogenes Laertius, *Vitae Philosophorum* 3.80; cf. Ferguson, *Moral Values*, 30–32; North, "Cardinal Virtues," 175.

[4] For example, Pindar, *Isthmian Ode* 8.24–28; Aeschylus, *Septem Contra Thebas* 610; Plato, *Gorgias* 507C, *Laches* 199D, *Protagoras* 349B; Xenophon, *Memorabilia* 4.6.1–12, 4.8.11, *Agesilaus* 3.1–5; Isocrates, *De Pace* 63; Philo, *De Mutatione Nominum* 197, *De Praemiis et Poenis* 160, *De Vita Mosis* 2.216, *Quod Deterius Potiori Insidiari Soleat* 18; cf. Stephen C. Mott, "Greek Ethics and Christian Conversion: The Philonic Background of Titus 2.10–14 and 3.3–7," *NovT* 20 (1978) 23–26.

[5] For text and translation see H. Rackham, trans., *Aristotle: The Athenian Constitution, The Eudemian Ethics, On Virtues and Vices* (LCL; Cambridge: Harvard University Press; London: Heinemann, 1961) 484–503. The virtues listed here are φρόνησις, πραότης, ἀνδρεία, σωφροσύνη, ἐγκράτεια, δικαιοσύνη, ἐλευθεριότης, and μεγαλοψυχία; the corresponding vices are ἀφροσύνη, ὀργιλότης, δειλία, ἀκολασία, ἀκρασία, ἀδικία, ἀνελευθερία, and μικροψυχία.

[6] For example, *Leges* 631C, though, as Ferguson (*Moral Values*, 28), notes, Plato's thinking on this matter was by no means standardized; cf. Adkins, *Merit and Responsibility*, 283–299; North, *Sophrosyne*, 187, 192; Irwin, *Plato's Moral Theory*, 18–36, 204–217.

[7] As North observes ("Cardinal Virtues," 175–177), no Latin author makes greater use of the canon of virtues than Cicero, who utilizes it in his speeches as well as in his philosophical treatises.

[8] But cf. Aristotle, *Rhetorica* 1.9.6–8; see below, pp. 103 ff.; also Ferguson, *Moral Values*, 40–42; North, *Sophrosyne*, s.v. andreia; idem, "Cardinal Virtues," 170–174.

Although present in the writings of other philosophical schools,[9] the Stoics made the most extensive and significant use of the canon during the Hellenistic era and most every major Stoic thinker delved into the issue, though here again the sources evidence numerous disagreements and variations.[10] On account of the wide-ranging influence of the Stoic analyses of virtue and the canon of virtues, it is worthwhile to discuss briefly some of the essential points. Generally speaking, we might say that the Stoics conceived of virtue as a uniform "disposition" (διάθεσις) of the human soul by which one rationally chooses what is morally good and rejects what is morally evil. This idea of a consistent disposition was important for the Stoics in so far as it underscored the stability of character and fixity of purpose that was to accompany the possession of virtue throughout life. Also basic to their doctrine was the belief that the moral agent must arrive at the choices associated with virtuous activity rationally; thus virtue is measured by the state of mind of the doer, and not only by what is done. In connection with this, some Stoic philosophers defined the different virtues as kinds of knowledge and in this manner argued for the unity of virtue. Of course, the Stoic virtues did not represent merely the potentiality or capability to make correct moral decisions, but necessarily entailed the power and the inclination to act virtuously at all times as well. The importance attached by the Stoics to the practical component of virtue helps explain the development of the canon of virtues within their philosophical system, since for them the virtues embodied both the concrete manifestations of virtue in the human self as well as the different areas of human life in which virtue is potentially actualized and experienced. The canon afforded the Stoics a means of depicting the range and the balance necessary in the personal character and specific moral actions of the possessor of virtue.[11]

---

[9] On the function of the canon in Neo-Platonism, for example, see North, *Sophrosyne*, 237–242; idem, "Cardinal Virtues," 178–180. On its employment by Epicurean philosophers see Cicero, *De Finibus* 1.42–54.

[10] See, for example, von Arnim, *Stoicorum Veterum Fragmenta*, 1.201, 374, 563, 3.95, 255, 256, 262, 263, 264, 265, 266, 275, 280. Cf. North, *Sophrosyne*, 213–231; idem, "Cardinal Virtues," 174–178.

[11] Max Pohlenz, *Die Stoa: Geschichte einer geistigen Bewegung* (2nd ed.; 2 vols.; Göttingen: Vandenhoeck & Ruprecht, 1959) 123–131; Ludwig Edelstein, *The Meaning of Stoicism* (Martin Classical Lectures 21; Cambridge: Harvard University Press, 1966) 71–98; John M. Rist, *Stoic Philosophy* (Cambridge: Cambridge University Press, 1969) 1–21, 192–197; F. H. Sandbach, *The Stoics* (Ancient Culture and Society; New York: W. W. Norton & Co., 1975) 28–68; I. G. Kidd, "Moral Actions and Rules in Stoic Ethics," *The Stoics* (ed. John M. Rist; Berkeley and Los Angeles: University of California Press, 1978) 247–258; Maximilian Forschner, *Die stoische Ethik: Über den Zusammenhang von Natur-, Sprach- und Moralphilosophie im altstoischen System* (Stuttgart: Klett-Cotta, 1981) 64–66, 174–182, 212–226; A. A. Long, *Hellenistic Philosophy: Stoics, Epicureans, Sceptics* (2nd ed.; New York: Scribner's, 1986) 199–206.

In light of these observations, it comes as no surprise that another feature that typified Stoic evaluations of the canon was the propensity to divide the individual virtues into a number of more specific or limited subordinate virtues. The different components, or species, of δικαιοσύνη, for example, are at one point identified as εὐσέβεια ("piety"), χρηστότης ("honesty"), εὐκοινωνησία ("sociability"), and εὐσυναλλαξία ("affability").[12] The utilization of these subdivisions enabled Stoic philosophers to describe on a more concrete level the ethical attributes or elements of each of the primary virtues, and to relate an array of particular virtues to the canon in a more-or-less systematic fashion. No doubt these efforts at refinement also abetted the actual practice of virtue by articulating ethical concepts that were more graspable and ethical objectives that were more attainable for participants of the philosophical school.

Book I of Cicero's *De Officiis*, which relies extensively on the ethical theories of Panaetius of Rhodes, provides us with an excellent example of a Stoic exposition of the canon written approximately the same time (about 45 B.C.) as the *Sententiae* of Pseudo-Phocylides.[13] Cicero here conducts his discussion of moral duties (Greek: καθήκοντα) in terms of the cardinal virtues, and he has organized the main body of the treatise according to the canon. In an introductory section of the work he explains the rationale for his procedure (1.5.15):[14]

> Sed omne, quod est honestum, id quattuor partium oritur ex aliqua: aut enim in perspicientia veri sollertiaque versatur aut in hominum societate tuenda tribuendoque suum cuique et rerum contractarum fide aut in animi excelsi atque invicti magnitudine ac robore aut in omnium, quae fiunt quaeque dicunter, ordine et modo, in quo inest

---

[12] Von Arnim, *Stoicorum Veterum Fragmenta*, 3.264.24–25, cf. 3.264.40–43. Further, Ferguson, *Moral Values*, 43–47; Andrew Erskine, *The Hellenistic Stoa: Political Thought and Action* (Ithaca: Cornell University Press, 1990) 114–115; cf. Cicero, *De Inventione* 2.53.159–2.54.165; Plutarch, *De Stoicorum Repugnantiis* 7; Diogenes Laertius, *Vitae Philosophorum* 7.92–93, 126; Stobaeus, *Anthologium* 2.7.5.

[13] On the *De Officiis* see Gred Ibscher, *Der Begriff des Sittlichen in der Pflichtenlehre des Panaitios: Ein Beitrag zur Erkenntnis der mittleren Stoa* (München: R. Oldenbourg, 1934); Max Pohlenz, *Antikes Führertum: Cicero De Officiis und das Lebensideal des Panaitios* (Neue Wege zur Antike 2.3; Leipzig and Berlin: Teubner, 1934) [reprint, Amsterdam: Adolf M. Hakkert, 1967] 2–90; Olof Gigon, "Bemerkungen zu Cicero De Officiis," *Politeia und Respublica: Beiträge zum Verständnis von Politik, Recht und Staat in der Antike. Dem Andenken Rudolf Starks gewidmet* (ed. Peter Steinmetz; Palingensia 4; Wiesbaden: Franz Steiner, 1969) 267–278; Paolo Fedeli, "Il 'De Officiis' di Cicerone: Problemi e Atteggiamenti della Critica Moderna," *ANRW* 1.4 (1973) 357–427; A. R. Dyck, "The Plan of Panaetius' ΠΕΡΙ ΤΟΥ ΚΑΘΗΚΟΝΤΟΣ," *AJP* 100 (1979) 408–416; idem, "Notes on the Composition, Text and Sources of Cicero's De Officiis," *Hermes* 112 (1984) 215–227; Willibald Heilmann, *Ethische Reflexion und römische Lebenswirklichkeit in Ciceros Schrift De Officiis: Ein literatursoziologischer Versuch* (Palingensia 17; Wiesbaden: Franz Steiner, 1982) 1–28, 49–58, 74–88, 119–125.

[14] Text and translation: Walter Miller, trans., *Cicero: De Officiis* (LCL; Cambridge: Harvard University Press; London: Heinemann, 1961) 16–17; cf. Ibscher, *Der Begriff des Sittlichen*, 141–148; Heilmann, *Ethische Reflexion*, 78–80.

modestia et temperantia. Quae quattuor quamquam inter se colligata atque implicata sunt, tamen ex singulis certa officiorum genera nascuntur ...

But all that is morally right rises from some one of four sources: it is concerned either (1) with the full perception and intelligent development of the true; or (2) with the conservation of organized society, with rendering to every man his due, and with the faithful discharge of obligations assumed; or (3) with the greatness and strength of a noble and invincible spirit; or (4) with the orderliness and moderation of everything that is said and done, wherein consist temperance and self-control. Although these four are connected and interwoven, still it is in each one considered singly that certain definite kinds of moral duties have their origin ...

Cicero proceeds to show how each of the cardinal virtues individually generates different moral responsibilities within the framework of his philosophical system: he discusses first wisdom briefly (1.6.18–19), then justice (1.7.20–1.18.60), fortitude (1.18.61–1.26.92), and finally temperance (1.27.93–1.42.151). His closing remarks address the question of the hierarchy of the virtues, suggesting that one's obligations to observe justice outweigh those that pertain to the other virtues, except in certain extreme cases (1.43.152–1.45.161). Taken as a whole, the analysis in *De Officiis* Book I demonstrates one possible way for grounding the recognition and performance of one's moral duties in a thoroughgoing concern both for the development of the virtues in the fulfillment of an individual's moral potential and for realizing the noble objectives that these same virtues represent for society. In doing so, Cicero delineates the practical and goal-oriented aspects of virtue itself, demonstrating a keen interest in the content of virtuous action. In asking what is the appropriate relationship of each virtue to the other virtues and to the fundamental appropriation of virtue per se, Cicero also perceives the need for a harmonious and well-ordered arrangement for the various aspects of moral life as they pertain to the recognition of ethical choices and obligations.

The canon also enjoyed a vigorous life in Greek and Roman oratory, and discussion of the cardinal virtues represents an important point at which the fields of philosophy and rhetoric converged during the Hellenistic era. In the *Ars Rhetorica*, Aristotle recommends that his students bring the canon to bear in composing their epideictic speeches, though here, as elsewhere, he lists more than the usual four virtues.[15] The author of the *Rhetorica ad Herennium* and

---

[15] μέρη δὲ ἀρετῆς δικαιοσύνη, ἀνδρεία, σωφροσύνη, μεγαλοπρέπεια, μεγαλοψυχία, ἐλευθεριότης, πραότης, φρόνησις, σοφία. Aristotle, *Rhetorica* 1.9.5; text: Rudolf Kassel, ed., *Aristotelis: Ars Rhetorica* (Berlin and New York: de Gruyter, 1976) 41; cf. William M. A. Grimaldi, *Aristotle, Rhetoric I: A Commentary* (New York: Fordham University Press, 1980) 194–199; also cf. Pseudo-Aristotle, *Rhetorica ad Alexandrum* 35. Ordinarily, Aristotle did not employ the Platonic tetrad, though it is evident in his *Protrepticus*; see Ingemar Düring, *Aristotle's Protrepticus: An Attempt at Reconstruction* (Studia Graeca et Latina Gothoburgensia 12; Göteborg: Elanders Boktryckeri Aktiebolag, 1961) 206 (*Fragmenta* 40); North, *Sophrosyne*, 198; cf. Adkins, *Merit and Responsibility*, 332–354; also cf. Aristotle, *Politica* 7.1.2, 7.13.18.

Cicero, in Book II of *De Inventione*, express a later and perhaps more representative view when they confine themselves to the Platonic tetrad while extending its application to deliberative as well as epideictic speechmaking.[16]

Within the epideictic branch of oratory, we often discover the canon as an organizing device in encomia, and especially in what is sometimes termed the βασιλικὸς λόγος, the formal encomium of someone in a position of authority.[17] The largest section of such a speech would ordinarily deal with the subject's πράξεις, frequently including, among other topics, a consideration of how his deeds or character exhibited each of the cardinal virtues. As D. A. Russell and N. G. Wilson have noted in their study of Menander of Laodicea's ΠΕΡΙ ΕΠΙΔΕΙΚΤΙΚΩΝ, by the Hellenistic era the scheme of the four cardinal virtues had evidently become part of the traditional way of praising great men.[18]

Related to the βασιλικὸς λόγος are a number of more general exhortatory treatises περὶ βασιλείας, which stipulate the various responsibilities of a person of authority.[19] Typical of the genre are the four essays of Dio Chrysostom (first century A.D.) addressed to the emperor Trajan.[20] Although ostensibly intended for a ruler, speeches such as these ordinarily possess a fairly broad moral and rhetorical scope, exhibiting protreptic as well as epideictic functions. As A. C. van Geytenbeek observes, treatises of this type frequently

---

[16] Pseudo-Cicero, *Rhetorica ad Herennium* 3.2.3–3.3.6, 3.6.10; Cicero, *De Inventione* 2.53.159–2.54.165; cf. Wilhelm Kroll, "Rhetorica V," *Philologus* 90 (1935) 206–215.

[17] For the term see especially Menander of Laodicea, ΠΕΡΙ ΕΠΙΔΕΙΚΤΙΚΩΝ 368–377, and D. A. Russell and N. G. Wilson, *Menander Rhetor* (Oxford: Clarendon, 1981) 76–95, 271–281; Theodore Burgess, "Epideictic Literature," *University of Chicago Studies in Classical Philology* 3 (1902) 113–136, and s.v. βασιλικὸς λόγος.

[18] Menander of Laodicea, ΠΕΡΙ ΕΠΙΔΕΙΚΤΙΚΩΝ 373–376, and Russell and Wilson, *Menander*, xiv–xxxii, 84–93, 277–280; Burgess, "Epideictic Literature," 113–136. Some examples: Isocrates, *Evagoras*, passim; Xenophon, *Agesilaus* 3.1–9.7, 11.1–16; Julian, *Orationes* 1.41B-49A; Plato parodies the encomiastic style in *Symposium* 194E–197E.

[19] Burgess, "Epideictic Literature," 136–138, 228–229, and s.v. περὶ βασιλείας. Cf. W. Schubart, "Das Königsbild des Hellenismus," *Die Antike* 13 (1937) 272–288; Johannes A. Straub, *Vom Herrscherideal in der Spätantike* (FKGG 18; Stuttgart: W. Kohlhammer, 1939) especially 146–159; Moses Hadas, *Aristeas to Philocrates (Letter of Aristeas)* (Jewish Apocryphal Literature, Dropsie College Edition, volume 17; New York: Harper and Brothers, 1951) 40–45; Pierre Hadot, "Fürstenspiegel," *RAC* 8 (1972) 555–632; Claire Préaux, "L'Image du Roi de l'Epoque Hellenistique," *Images of Man in Ancient and Medieval Thought: Studia Gerardo Verbeke ab Amicis et Collegis Dicata* (ed. Fernand Bossier, et al.; Symbolae, Facultatis Litterarum et Philosophiae Lovaniensis A.1; Leuven: Leuven University Press, 1976) 53–76.

[20] George A. Kennedy, *The Art of Rhetoric in the Roman World* (History of Rhetoric 2; Princeton: University of Princeton Press, 1972) 566–582; P. A. Brunt, "Aspects of the Social Thought of Dio Chrysostom and the Stoics," *PCPS* 19 (1973) 9–34; Christopher P. Jones, *The Roman World of Dio Chrysostom* (Loeb Classical Monographs; Cambridge and London: Harvard University Press, 1978) 115–123.

"enumerate the king's duties in systematically arranged lists of virtues."[21] The application of such schemes enables authors of treatises περὶ βασιλείας to link the performance of the specific obligations that they prescribe to the pursuit of loftier moral objectives and the overall character development of the recipient. By deploying the canon in an artful manner, the orator could highlight the range and scope of moral responsibilities that the reader must accept and in this fashion indicate the balance necessary in developing an agenda for ethical action.

One illustration of this genre, the *Ad Nicoclem* of Isocrates (c. 370 B.C.), which exemplifies "a kind of gnomic oratory,"[22] is of interest for our investigation on account of its generic and material similarities with Pseudo-Phocylides' *Sententiae*.[23] While a thorough inspection of this treatise cannot be undertaken in this context, the results of my analysis of the text may at least be indicated by way of an outline:

1–9	I.	Introduction
1–2		A. Prologue: the discourse as a gift (compare § 54)
3–6a		B. On the education of a monarch
6b–8		C. Plan and objectives for the discourse
9		D. The central issue of the discourse: what is the ἔργον of the monarch?
10–39	II.	Gnomic exhortation structured according to the Canon of Cardinal Virtues
10–14		A. Relating to the topic of wisdom
10–11		1. The successful king must surpass others in virtue
12–14		2. Instruction on pursuing wisdom
15–29a		B. Relating to the topic of justice
15–16a		1. Basic principles concerning justice and φιλανθρωπία
16b–19		2. Advice on civic matters and institutions
16b–18		a. Legal matters
19		b. Fiscal management
20–29a		3. Advice on treating different types of referents fairly
20		a. The gods
21a		b. Friends and family
21b–22a		c. The citizens
22b		d. Foreigners

---

[21] A. C. van Geytenbeek, *Musonius Rufus and Greek Diatribe* (Wijsgerige Teksten en Studies 8; Assen: van Gorcum, 1962) 126, cf. 124–129 (on *Fragmenta* 8: OTI ΦΙΛΟΣΟΦΗΤΕΟΝ ΚΑΙ ΤΟΙΣ ΒΑΣΙΛΕΥΣΙΝ, "That Kings Also Should Study Philosophy").

[22] George A. Kennedy, *The Art of Persuasion in Greece* (History of Rhetoric 1; Princeton: Princeton University Press, 1963) 190; he classifies the speech under the category of epideictic rhetoric. For text and translation see George Norlin, trans., *Isocrates* (LCL; 2 vols.; Cambridge: Harvard University Press; London: Heinemann, 1928, 1929) 1.40–71; cf. Stephen Usher, *Isocrates: Panegyricus and To Nicocles* (Greek Orators 3; Warminster: Aris & Phillips, 1990) 117–148, 202–216.

[23] On the generic identification of the *Ad Nicoclem* see Burgess, "Epideictic Literature," 136; while the *Ad Nicoclem* has received little attention with regard to its literary composition, there have been several such studies of the similar *Ad Demonicum* of Pseudo-Isocrates; see above, p. 39, n. 91; cf. Thomas, *Der jüdische Phokylides*, 273–286.

The *Ad Nicoclem* consists of three major formal sections, §§ 1–9, 10–39, and 40–54. At either end of the discourse we find the Introduction (§§ 1–9), which specifies the author's occasion and purpose for writing, and an expanded Conclusion (§§ 40–54), which summarizes the text's objectives and links these with an interesting digression of a more general nature on the character and function of didactic literature (§§ 42–50). In the body of the speech, §§ 10–39, it appears that Isocrates, like Cicero in Book I of the *De Officiis*, benefits substantially from the Canon of Cardinal Virtues as an organizational device in discussing ethical responsibilities, though the style here is far less systematic and more plainly practical and exhortatory, as befits the gnomic character of the treatise. Isocrates' employment of the tetrad in this manner is consistent with the central purpose of the oration as stated in 8.5–6, namely, to provide the reader with the moral guidelines necessary "to turn to virtue" (ἐπ' ἀρετὴν προτρέπειν).[24] It is important to note that he does not always identify the individual virtues by name (no doubt the canon was familiar enough to his intended audience) and the fashion in which he depicts each of the virtues is for the most part as much highly selective as it is oriented towards its rhetorical impact. The treatment of the virtues typically includes both the formulation of basic principles for ethical conduct and the rendering of advice on specific

---

[24] Cf. 11.6–12.1. The use of this verb may imply some connection with the objectives familiar from philosophical protreptic literature; see the references below, p. 194, n. 36.

types of issues or on particular types of moral referents, often as a means of elucidating the general principles. In keeping with Isocrates' focus on the practical and societal aspects of the pursuit of virtue, the topic of justice (§§ 15–29 a) enjoys the longest and most involved discussion, while he accords wisdom (§§ 10–14) and courage (§§ 35 b–39) relatively cursory treatment.

The *Ad Nicoclem* was by no means the only exhortatory or gnomic text to utilize the canon as a means of structuring its ethical topics. The Stoic Musonius Rufus (first century A.D.), for instance, frequently organized his diatribe-style lectures around the four primary virtues.[25] The *Theognidea*, an anthology of Greek gnomic poems, also makes use of different versions of the canon, for example, in verses 1135–1150.[26] The *Sententiae* of Sextus both refers to a canon of virtues[27] and utilizes the canon as a compositional pattern for arranging some of its clusters of sayings, for example, verses 167–182, which can be outlined as follows:

167–169	On wisdom and truth
170	On faith and courage
171–173	On moderation:
171	– be reserved in speaking
172	– do not be fond of pleasure
173	– be reserved in speaking
174–176	Ignorance vs. wisdom
177–183	On justice:
177	– avoid hypocrisy
178	– do not even intend misdeeds
179	– a version of the golden rule
180	– do not compel others to sin
181	– remove sin from your thoughts
182	– remember God when dealing with others

As in other gnomic texts that employ the canon as an organizational device, we detect here a certain amount of unevenness and repetition in the presentation of the virtues, and the individual maxims serve more as paradigms or illus-

---

[25] See, for example, *Fragmenta* 3 (ΟΤΙ ΚΑΙ ΓΥΝΑΙΞΙ ΦΙΛΟΣΟΦΗΤΕΟΝ, "That Women Too Should Study Philosophy"); text and translation: Cora E. Lutz, *Musonius Rufus: 'The Roman Socrates'* (YCS 10; New York: Yale University Press, 1942) 39–43, cf. 27; also the translation and comments of Abraham J. Malherbe, *Moral Exhortation: A Greco-Roman Sourcebook* (LEC 4; Philadelphia: Westminster, 1986) 132–134; van Geytenbeek, *Musonius Rufus*, 25–28, 51–53.

[26] In these verses the poet laments that gone from the earth are πίστις, σωφροσύνη, and the Χάριτες, with only ἐλπίς remaining. For text see M. L. West, ed., *Iambi et Elegi Graeci* (2nd ed.; 2 vols.; Oxford: Clarendon, 1989) 1.228.

[27] For example v. 399: οὐκ ἔστιν κατὰ θεὸν ζῆν ἄνευ τοῦ σωφρόνως καὶ καλῶς καὶ δικαίως πράττειν. For text see Chadwick, *The Sentences of Sextus*, 58; cf. Edwards and Wild, *The Sentences of Sextus*, 66–67; cf. Cleitarchus, *Sententiae* 123. Perhaps it is significant that this line is immediately preceded by a version of the Delphic maxim 'know thyself' in v. 398. On καλός as a virtue cf. Isocrates, *Evagoras* 22; Xenophon, *Memorabilia* 1.1.16. On the use of three virtues as representative of the canon cf. Mott, "Greek Ethics," 26–29.

trations of the sorts of ethical behavior associated with each of the virtues than as parts of a systematic analysis or an exhaustive list of duties. Like Isocrates in the *Ad Nicoclem*, Sextus devotes more lines to the topic of justice than to any of the other virtues, with the section on courage occupying only one verse.[28]

Another example comes from the Pythagorean *Carmen Aureum*, a gnomic poem of the Hellenistic era that in many respects parallels Pseudo-Phocylides' *Sentences* materially and formally. As Johan C. Thom has demonstrated, an important introductory section of the poem treats the four virtues in summary fashion.[29] This passage, verses 9–20, is short enough to cite in full:[30]

> ταῦτα μὲν οὕτως ἴσθι, κρατεῖν δ' εἰθίζεο τῶνδε·
> 10 γαστρὸς μὲν πρώτιστα καὶ ὕπνου λαγνείης τε
>   καὶ θυμοῦ. πρήξῃς δ' αἰσχρόν ποτε μήτε μετ' ἄλλου
>   μήτ' ἰδίῃ· πάντων δὲ μάλιστ' αἰσχύνεο σαυτόν.
>   εἶτα δικαιοσύνην ἀσκεῖν ἔργῳ τε λόγῳ τε
>   μηδ' ἀλογίστως σαυτὸν ἔχειν περὶ μηδὲν ἔθιζε,
> 15 ἀλλὰ γνῶθι μέν, ὡς θανέειν πέπρωται ἅπασιν,
>   χρήματα δ' ἄλλοτε μὲν κτᾶσθαι φιλεῖ, ἄλλοτ' ὀλέσθαι.
>   ὅσσα δὲ δαιμονίαισι τύχαις βροτοὶ ἄλγε' ἔχουσιν,
>   ἣν ἂν μοῖραν ἔχῃς, ταύτην φέρε μὴ δ' ἀγανάκτει.
>   ἰᾶσθαι δὲ πρέπει καθ' ὅσον δύνῃ, ὧδε δὲ φράζευ·
> 20 οὐ πάνυ τοῖς ἀγαθοῖς τούτων πολὺ Μοῖρα δίδωσιν.

> Know the above, then, and accustom yourself to be master of the following:
> 10 first of all, of your stomach, of sleep, of lust,
>   and of anger. Never do anything shameful, neither with somebody else,
>   nor on your own. Feel shame before yourself most of all.
>   Furthermore, practice justice both in deed and in word,
>   and accustom yourself not to be thoughtless about anything,
> 15 but know that death has been destined for all,
>   and that property is wont to be acquired now, tomorrow lost.
>   But whatever pains mortals suffer through the divine workings of fate,
>   whatever lot you have, bear it and do not be angry.
>   You have to be healed as far as possible, and say to yourself as follows:
> 20 Fate does not give very many of these sufferings to the good.

Thom's analysis of this passage according to the scheme of the Platonic canon is corroborated by observations made about the poem in some of the ancient

---

[28] For text and translation see Edwards and Wild, *The Sentences of Sextus*, 36–37; cf. Chadwick, *The Sentences of Sextus*, 32, 170–171.

[29] Johan C. Thom, *The Golden Verses of Pythagoras: Its Literary Composition and Religio-Historical Significance* (Ph.D. Dissertation, University of Chicago, 1990) 63–64, 105–127. Further on this poem see Mario Meunier, *Pythagore: Les Vers d'Or. Hiéroclès: Commentaire sur les Vers d'Or des Pythagoriciens. Traduction Nouvelle avec Prolégomènes et Notes* (Paris: L'Artisan du Livre, 1925) especially 23–31; P. C. van der Horst, *Les Vers D'Or Pythagoriciens: Etudes avec une Introduction et un Commentaire* (Leiden: E.J. Brill, 1932) especially xxv–xxxiii; Küchler, *Weisheitstraditionen*, 251–252, 271–272; Kloppenborg, *The Formation of Q*, 300.

[30] Text and translation: Thom, *Golden Verses*, 71–72, 77; cf. Douglas Young, ed., *Theognis* (BT; 2nd ed.; Leipzig: Teubner, 1971) 87–88.

commentaries, particularly Hierocles of Alexandria, *In Aureum Pythagoreorum Carmen Commentarius* 10.1.[31] Thom's outline of the section, which he labels "The Cardinal Virtues", is as follows:[32]

9	A. Summary commands concerning
9a	1. The previous precepts: know them
9b	2. The following precepts: master them
10–12	B. Precepts concerning σωφροσύνη
10–11a	1. ἐγκράτεια regarding pleasures and passions
10a	a. Qualification: first of all
10a–11a	b. Enumeration of pleasures and passions:
10a	i. Eating
10b	ii. Sleep
10c	iii. Sex
11a	iv. Anger
11b–12	2. αἰδώς
11b–12a	a. Negative precept to avoid shameful deeds
11c–12a	i. Circumstances
11c	α. In public
12a	β. In private
12b–c	b. Positive precept on the criterion of self-respect
12b	i. Qualification: most of all
13	C. Precept concerning δικαιοσύνη
13b	1. In deed
13c	2. In word
14–16	D. Precepts concerning φρόνησις
14	1. Negative precept to avoid thoughtlessness
	a. Qualification: in any way
15–16	2. Positive precept to have insight into
15b	a. Gnomic truth concerning the universality of death
16	b. Gnomic truth concerning the instability of property
17–20	E. Precepts concerning ἀνδρεία
17–18b	1. Positive precept to practice καρτερία regarding
17	a. Sufferings
	i. Reason: they are due to the divine workings of fate
18a	b. One's lot in general
18c	2. Negative precept entailing a warning against resentment
19a	3. Positive precept to heal the self
	a. Qualification: as far as possible
19b–20	4. Positive precept to have the following insight
20	5. Gnomic truth concerning the limitation of suffering
	a. Qualification: regarding the good

Looking first at the poem in its entirety, we see that the author has divided his instruction into two large blocks of material, differentiated by their function.

---

[31] As Thom observes (*Golden Verses*, 8) this commentary is not only an invaluable witness to the understanding of the *Carmen Aureum* in late antiquity but also a useful resource for contemporary interpretation. On p. 105, n. 126, he notes that Hierocles explicitly employs the terms σωφροσύνη, δικαιοσύνη, φρόνησις, and ἀνδρεία when analyzing this section of the poem.

[32] Thom, *Golden Verses*, 63–64, cf. 105–127.

The opening section (verses 1–49), which consists chiefly of gnomic precepts to be mastered, recommends a specific philosophical way of life to the audience. The second part (verses 50–71) buttresses the first by pointing to the ultimate goals of this way of life and by promising insight and benefits to the obedient. As Thom argues, the first section focuses on the cultivation of virtue. The passage cited above, verses 9–20, serves to introduce this subject, establishing a material and pedagogical foundation for the more specific prescriptions to virtue in verses 21–49 a, which concentrate on the development of the readers' moral deliberation and reflection. In verses 9–20, as elsewhere in gnomic sources that resort to the canon, most of the virtues are left unnamed (only δικαιοσύνη [verse 13] is mentioned), and the nature of the exhortation is fairly condensed and paradigmatic. The author fixes his attention on specific aspects of the virtues, issuing special commands that are of use in illustrating the virtues rather than formulating definitions or extended descriptions of their ideal character. In exhorting the recipient to pursue a particular virtue, the author often alternates negative and positive commands as he explores both sides of an ethical issue; the text thus balances protreptic and apotreptic strategies in delineating its ethical program. Also noteworthy is the manner in which the author divides the treatment of some of the virtues into ancillary sub-sections that deal with more specific or subordinate characteristics of the virtue in question. We can see this most clearly in section B (on moderation), which consists of paraenesis on ἐγκράτεια (verses 10–11 a) and on αἰδώς (verses 11 b–12).

Attention to the canon of virtues as a means for organizing a constructive exposition of philosophical and ethical doctrines appears in other Pythagorean contexts as well, for example, the *De Vita Pythagorica* of Iamblichus. As John Dillon and Jackson Hershbell observe, this text constitutes a systematic presentation of the life and thought of Pythagoras that concentrates on the teaching of individual and social virtues. It can, moreover, be understood as "a kind of protreptic summation of the whole ethical tradition of Greek philosophy, a tradition in which all the major schools agreed, that philosophy was not simply a set of doctrines, but a whole way of life."[33] Thus we can detect a certain protreptic interest alongside the biographical one. A chief section of the work, chapters 28–33, surveys the six Pythagorean virtues, which include piety and friendship alongside the regular Platonic-Stoic tetrad. This survey apparently contributes in a fundamental way to the text's pedagogical objective, contribut-

---

[33] John Dillon and Jackson Hershbell, eds., *Iamblichus: On the Pythagorean Way of Life. Text, Translation, and Notes* (SBLTT 29, Graeco-Roman Religion Series 11; Atlanta: Scholars Press, 1991) 29, cf. 1–28, 155–235; Michael von Albrecht, "Das Menschenbild in Iamblichs Darstellung der pythagoreischen Lebensformen," *Antike und Abendland* 12 (1966) 51–63.

ing to the initial education and training of students in a philosophical school. The concentration on the virtues appears to represent a fairly effective procedure both for summarizing the school's doctrines and for demonstrating that they entail also a whole way of life that must be actualized in the pupils' thinking and conduct.

In light of the discussion so far, it comes as no surprise that the canon of virtues also worked its way into the corpus of Hellenistic Judaism, particularly in those texts that were most open to the influence of Greco-Roman philosophy and ethics. The author of the Wisdom of Solomon (first century B.C.), for instance, cites the Platonic tetrad in 8.7.[34] The canon enjoys a place of central importance for the author of 4 Maccabees (first century A.D.) as well, who refers to it in the prologue of his treatise as a means of establishing his philosophical presuppositions and of clarifying the ethical nature of his subject matter in cross-cultural terms.[35] The canon also appears to be functioning in the design of Ben Sira 36.23–38.23, where the author's gnomic instruction re-

---

[34] καὶ εἰ δικαιοσύνην ἀγαπᾷ τις, οἱ πόνοι ταύτης εἰσὶν ἀρεταί· σωφροσύνην γὰρ καὶ φρόνησιν ἐκδιδάσκει, δικαιοσύνην καὶ ἀνδρείαν, ὧν χρησιμώτερον οὐδέν ἐστιν ἐν βίῳ ἀνθρώποις. "And if one prizes justice, the fruits of Wisdom's labor are virtues; self-control and understanding are her teaching, justice and courage, and in the life of man nothing is more useful than these." See David Winston, *The Wisdom of Solomon* (AB 43; Garden City, New York: Doubleday, 1979) 191, 194; Larcher, *Le Livre de la Sagesse*, 2.527–530. Further, Martin Dibelius and Hans Conzelmann, *The Pastoral Epistles* (Hermeneia; Philadelphia: Fortress, 1972) 142–143; Mott, "Greek Ethics," 22–48.

[35] 4 Maccabees 1.1–4:
φιλοσοφώτατον λόγον ἐπιδείκνυσθαι μέλλων, εἰ αὐτοδέσποτός ἐστιν τῶν παθῶν ὁ εὐσεβὴς λογισμός, συμβουλεύσαιμ' ἂν ὑμῖν ὀρθῶς ὅπως προσέχητε προθύμως τῇ φιλοσοφίᾳ. καὶ γὰρ ἀναγκαῖος εἰς ἐπιστήμην παντὶ ὁ λόγος καὶ ἄλλως τῆς μεγίστης ἀρετῆς, λέγω δὴ φρονήσεως, περιέχει ἔπαινον. εἰ ἄρα τῶν σωφροσύνης κωλυτικῶν παθῶν ὁ λογισμὸς φαίνεται ἐπικρατεῖν, γαστριμαργίας τε καὶ ἐπιθυμίας, ἀλλὰ καὶ τῶν τῆς δικαιοσύνης ἐμποδιστικῶν παθῶν κυριεύειν ἀναφαίνεται, οἷον κακοηθείας, καὶ τῶν τῆς ἀνδρείας ἐμποδιστικῶν παθῶν, θυμοῦ τε καὶ φόβου καὶ πόνου.
"Highly philosophical is the subject I propose to discuss, namely whether devout reason is absolute master of the passions, and I would strictly counsel you to give earnest attention to my philosophical exposition. The subject is an indispensable branch of knowledge but it also includes a eulogy of the greatest of virtues, by which I mean of course prudence. If reason is shown to be master of the passions that hinder temperance, namely gluttony and lust, it is also demonstrated that it is lord of the passions that impede justice, such as malice, and over the passions that impede courage, such as rage and fear and pain."
Here φρόνησις, which appears to be roughly equivalent to ὁ εὐσεβὴς λογισμός, supersedes the other members of the tetrad. Because it controls the passions, a subject of primary concern for the author, he refers to it as the greatest virtue, and to a certain extent it encompasses or represents the other three. Translation: H. Anderson, trans., "4 Maccabees (First Century A.D.)," in Charlesworth, *Pseudepigrapha*, 2.544, cf. 531–564; cf. 4 Maccabees 1.5 ff., 18, 5.23–24; Moses Hadas, *The Third and Fourth Books of Maccabees* (New York: Harper, 1953) 144–149; Robert Renehan, "The Greek Philosophic Background of Fourth Maccabees," *RMP* 115 (1972) 223–238; Urs Breitenstein, *Beobachtungen zu Sprache, Stil*

lates first to the topic of justice (36.23–37.15), then to the topics of wisdom (37.16–26), moderation (37.27–31), and finally courage (38.1–23).[36]

Most germane to our study, however, is the use of the canon by Philo of Alexandria, a "contemporary, compatriot, and coreligionist" of Pseudo-Phocylides.[37] The impetus for Philo's employment of the canon originates in his attempt to relate the Mosaic law to the so-called ideal law in accordance with nature as described by numerous Greco-Roman philosophical schools.[38] In conjunction with this, Philo endeavors on a number of occasions to demonstrate how the commandments of the Jewish law in their entirety aim to regulate life in accordance with virtue, which constituted one of the ultimate objectives of the ideal philosophical law. On a more concrete level, Philo's writings also explain how individual laws were established with a view to inculcating specific virtues in those who obey the Torah. This pertains especially to the commandments of the second table of the Decalogue, and then to the particular laws subordinate to them. The injunctions regarding jurisprudence and commerce, for instance, were designed to promote the virtue of justice, whereas those concerning marriage and diet foster moderation.

Although Philo's corpus conveys no single scheme for classifying the commandments and the virtues,[39] the analysis of the Law beginning in *De Specialibus Legibus* and continuing in *De Virtutibus* is of special interest.[40] The former treatise consists largely of an examination of the specific laws, which Philo arranges under the main headings of the ten commandments as presented in *De Decalogo*. Beginning at 4.132, however, the presentation of the Torah moves in a different direction. After noting that he has adequately

---

und Gedankengut des vierten Makkabäerbuchs (2nd ed.; Basel and Stuttgart: Schwabe, 1978) 131 ff.

[36] Cf. Skehan and DiLella, *Ben Sira*, 424–444.

[37] Van der Horst, "Pseudo-Phocylides Revisited," 26.

[38] Here I am following Harry A. Wolfson, *Philo: Foundations of Religious Philosophy in Judaism, Christianity, and Islam* (2 vols.; Cambridge: Harvard University Press, 1947) 2.200–225; cf. North, *Sophrosyne*, 323–328; Samuel Sandmel, "Virtue and Reward in Philo," *Essays in Old Testament Ethics: J. Philip Hyatt, In Memoriam* (ed. James L. Crenshaw and John T. Willis; New York: KTAV, 1974) 215–223; Mott, "Greek Ethics," 25–26, 28–30; further see David Winston, "Philo's Ethical Theory," *ANRW* II.21.1 (1984) 372–416.

[39] For some other examples of Philo's use of the canon cf. *De Abrahamo* 219, *De Agricultura* 18, *De Cherubim* 5, *De Ebrietate* 23, *De Opificio Mundi* 73, *De Posteritate Caini* 128–129, *De Sacrificiis Abelis et Caini* 84, *De Specialibus Legibus* 2.62, *De Vita Mosis* 2.185, 216, *Legum Allegoriae* 1.63–65, *Quaestiones in Genesim* 1.12, *Quod Omnis Probus Liber Sit* 67, 70; cf. Daniel N. Jastram, "Philo's Concept of Generic Virtue," *SBLSP* 30 (ed. Eugene H. Lovering; Atlanta: Scholars Press, 1991) 323–347.

[40] For text and translation see Francis H. Colson, trans., *Philo*, Volume 8 (LCL; Cambridge: Harvard University Press; London: Heinemann, 1939); further see Richard D. Hecht, "Preliminary Issues in the Analysis of Philo's De Specialibus Legibus," *Studia Philonica* 5 (1978) 1–55.

treated the ten commandments and the injunctions dependent upon them, Philo states that they additionally correspond with "the virtues of universal value" (αἱ κοινωφελεῖς ἀρεταί), and that these virtues are exemplified in the various laws. Both individually and as a group the commandments exhort (προτρέπειν) the obedient to follow the company of virtues, which includes piety, wisdom, and temperance (which Philo claims to have already discussed sufficiently), as well as justice (discussed in *De Specialibus Legibus* 4.136–238), courage (discussed in *De Virtutibus* 1–50), and humanity (discussed in *De Virtutibus* 51–174).[41] These discussions of the individual virtues, in turn, indicate some of the specific ethical obligations and objectives that are associated with each of them, including in many instances illustrations from the Torah.

As Annewies van den Hoek has pointed out, Philo's analysis in *De Specialibus Legibus* and *De Virtutibus* taken as a whole represents "an attempt to pull the law of Moses out of its isolation and to give it a respected position within the thought of his time and environment."[42] Of course, the plan that he follows in explicating the teachings of the Law involves more on Philo's part than simply expressing Jewish ethical norms in the guise of Greek philosophy, though clearly one of the tasks before him is to make the Law more intelligible to a Hellenized audience. We must also take into account any factors that may have motivated Philo's composition of these treatises as evidenced in their argumentative features. Van den Hoek notes that, "Philo's point of departure seems to be an apologetic one; this intention generally emerges between the lines rather than overtly; but in *De Virtutibus* 141, he protests openly against slanderous ideas to the effect that Jewish laws were asocial and particularistic. His book is in large part occupied with giving examples to demonstrate the contrary. Bringing many, often unrelated laws under the common denominators of a few virtues must have been motivated by these outside attacks."[43] Thus in linking the Mosaic laws with the Greek virtues in a constructive man-

---

[41] Appended to the *De Virtutibus* are two comparatively short sermons on repentance (περὶ μετανοίας: 175–186) and on nobility (περὶ εὐγενείας: 187–227). It is not clear to what extent the topics of these sections should be understood as virtues in the same way as what precedes.

[42] Annewies van den Hoek, *Clement of Alexandria and his Use of Philo in the Stromateis: An Early Christian Reshaping of a Jewish Model* (VCSup 3; Leiden: E.J. Brill, 1988) 112; cf. S. Lilla, "Middle Platonism, Neoplatonism and Jewish-Alexandrine Philosophy in the Terminology of Clement of Alexandria's Ethics," *AISP* 3 (1962) 3–36; C.J. Classen, "Der platonisch-stoische Kanon der Kardinaltugenden bei Philon, Clemens Alexandrinus und Origenes," *Kerygma und Logos: Beiträge zu den geistesgeschichtlichen Beziehungen zwischen Antike und Christentum. Festschrift für Carl Andresen zum 70. Geburtstag* (ed. Adolf M. Ritter; Göttingen: Vandenhoeck & Ruprecht, 1979) 68–88.

[43] Van den Hoek, *Clement of Alexandria*, 111; cf. Gregory E. Sterling, "Philo and the Logic of Apologetics: An Analysis of the Hypothetica," *SBLSP* 29 (ed. David J. Lull; Atlanta: Scholars Press, 1990) 412–430.

ner, Philo underscores the universally valid qualities of the Torah and makes it feasible for the principles and ideals of the Law to be expressed and actualized in a more multicultural context. An important strategy that Philo employs both in devising his apologetic argument and in analyzing the Jewish law emerges in the form of what van den Hoek describes as his "doctrine of virtues". As van den Hoek observes, "Philo focuses on general virtues like justice, prudence, temperance, courage and self-restraint, to which he adds piety and humanity. Philo develops a kind of doctrine of virtues from apologetic motives on the basis of the law of Moses. The concept of doctrine must be understood in a restricted sense, however, since the above-mentioned virtues are an arbitrary series that can be extended or abbreviated at will." Van den Hoek goes on to observe that for Philo, "[t]he prescriptions of the law represent the virtues and not visa versa; the virtues are attributes of the law, labels that make the qualities of the law recognizable in broader terms. The law offers people a primary training that leads them on their way to God."[44] On one hand, according to Philo's reasoning, the Law constitutes an integral manifestation of virtue itself while, on the other, the prescriptions incorporated in the Law delineate the means by which individuals learn how to live virtuously. We should also note that the presentation of the teachings of the Law in this manner also entails a certain shift in the nature of its moral objectives and the type of hermeneutic that it recommends for itself. As van den Hoek notes, the virtues establish "labels that make the qualities of the law recognizable in broader terms"; we may qualify this observation by adding that these labels make certain *particular* qualities of the law more comprehensible. Above, we saw how the Stoics emphasized the rational and dispositional aspects of virtue, and in this regard their outlook may be considered fairly representative of the general understanding of virtue in the Hellenistic world.[45] In their view, an essential quality of virtuous activity is that it is guided both by the rational mind and by a consistent disposition of the human soul. In connecting the Jewish law with virtues as he has, Philo tends to bring its intellectual and character-developing features into sharper relief. His presentation of the Torah underscores the critical component of Jewish ethics while placing the center of attention more on the development of the moral character and moral disposition of the actor, rather than on the enumeration of moral obligations or actions in any systematic way. For this reason, Philo is able to express the essentials of the Jewish ethic as he understands it without mentioning every precept or obligation found in the Torah; it is sufficient for him to demonstrate how the Law is a means of training in the different virtues. As Samuel Sandmel writes, "Philo is not so much concerned with deeds as deeds, as he is with deeds as reflective of,

---

[44] Van den Hoek, *Clement of Alexandria*, 111.
[45] See above, p. 45.

or as embodying virtues; the deeds, indeed, only exemplify the perceptible virtues. The commandments in the Law are susceptible of being allegorized, and normally in Philo such allegorization turns a specific commandment (a deed to be done) into a facet of the specific virtues."[46] As we will see in Part Two of our study, a comparable integration of Jewish with Greco-Roman literary conventions, ethical concepts, and rhetorical tactics appears to be at work in Pseudo-Phocylides' *Sententiae* as well, though with significant differences in terms of the poem's mode of presentation, its level of explicit argumentation, and its moral content and objectives.

---

[46] Sandmel, "Virtue and Reward," 218–219; he refers to *De Specialibus Legibus* 4.132–135 as an example; cf., more generally, Robert E. Rodes, "On Law and Virtue," *Virtue: Public and Private* (ed. Richard J. Neuhaus; The Encounter Series 1; Grand Rapids: Eerdmans, 1986) 30–42.

Part Two

Analysis of the Poem

Chapter Three

Summary Rendition of the Decalogue (verses 3–8)

The surveys of the genres of gnomic wisdom prominent in antiquity (Chapter One) and of the use of the Canon of Cardinal Virtues by various ancient philosophers and moralists (Chapter Two) provide us with a framework for analyzing the genre and composition of Pseudo-Phocylides' *Sentences*, indicating, at least in a preliminary manner, some of the types of materials that may be profitably employed for comparative purposes. In Part One, I also discussed some of the more salient issues and problems associated with the literary, generic, and rhetorical investigation of such materials. At this point we can turn to the *Sententiae* itself, beginning with a conspectus of the analysis in outline form:

	I. [Title]
1–2	II. Prologue
3–227	III. Body of the poem
3–8	A. Summary rendition of the Decalogue
9–131	B. Exhortation structured according to the Canon of Cardinal Virtues
9–54	1. Exhortation on topics relating to justice
55–96	2. Exhortation on topics relating to moderation
97–121	3. Exhortation on topics relating to courage, specifically fortitude
122–131	4. Exhortation on the topic of wisdom and speech
132–227	C. Exhortation structured according to the different relationships in which one lives
132–152	1. Exhortation on dealing with social 'outsiders'
153–174	2. Exhortation concerning the nature and importance of work
175–227	3. Exhortation concerning personal responsibilities within the household
228–230	IV. Epilogue

Most modern critics agree that verses 3–227 comprise the main body of the poem; this section, in turn, consists of three closely related segments according to our interpretation: a summary rendition of the Decalogue (verses 3–8), exhortation structured according to the Canon of Cardinal Virtues (verses 9–131), and exhortation structured according to the different types of relationships in which one lives (verses 132–227). These passages will be discussed in Chapters Three, Four, and Five respectively. Because the formal elements that envelop this core – the title, the prologue (verses 1–2), and the epilogue (verses 228–230) – include many references that pertain to or describe the work in its entirety, our examination of these sections presupposes something of an understanding of the poem's overall message and argument, and so will follow afterwards in Chapter Six. It is also useful to examine the prologue and epilogue at the same time, since the author has quite deliberately, it seems, linked these elements together through the literary device of inclusio (see below). My plan for the analysis of the poem is to present an outline, text,[1] and translation[2] of each passage (or subsection) followed by some specific observations pertinent to its structure and message, particularly as they compare with relevant exhortatory and gnomic passages from other ancient sources.

As I will discuss in some detail in Chapter Six, our poem begins with the title and the prologue (verses 1–2), the latter constituting the text's poetic σφραγίς. This "seal" serves to identify the author and his work, emphasizing its divine source and suggesting its connection with Torah. These opening lines are formally and functionally coordinated with the epilogue of the poem, verses 228–230, by means of inclusio.

Immediately after this prologue, we find the opening section of the main body of the work, verses 3–8, where the author provides a versified summary of the Decalogue, especially (but not exclusively) the second table, which concentrates on ethical and social obligations.[3] Although it is selective, and Pseudo-Phocylides fails to maintain the original order of the commandments, the summary represents by implication the entire Decalogue, which, in turn, stands for the Jewish law.[4] It should be quickly added, though, that none of the injunctions employed in the rendition are exclusively Jewish in nature, and so no allusions to the ritual observances or cultic practices peculiar to Judaism are included. Instead, the author's principle of selection demonstrates a prefer-

---

[1] Unless otherwise noted, the text used throughout is Derron, *Sentences*, 2–18; cf. Young, *Theognis*, 95–112.

[2] The translation throughout is my own unless noted otherwise; cf. van der Horst, *Sentences*, 89–103; idem, "Pseudo-Phocylides," in Charlesworth, *Pseudepigrapha*, 574–582; Walter, *Poetische Schriften*, 197–216; Derron, *Sentences*, 2–18.

[3] Jacob Bernays, *Gesammelte Abhandlungen* (ed. Hermann Usener; 2 vols.; Berlin: Wilhelm Hertz, 1885) [originally, *Über das phokylideische Gedicht: Ein Beitrag zur hellenistischen Literatur* (Berlin: Wilhelm Hertz, 1856)] 227–228; Crouch, *Colossian Haustafel*, 88; van der Horst, *Sentences*, 110–117; Walter, *Poetische Schriften*, 197; Niebuhr, *Gesetz und Paränese*, 10–20, 25–26; Derron, *Sentences*, 19, n. 5; cf. Klaus Berger, *Die Gesetzesauslegung Jesu. Ihr historischer Hintergrund im Judentum und im Alten Testament I: Markus und Parallelen* (WMANT 40; Neukirchen-Vluyn: Neukirchener Verlag, 1972) 272–273; Eckart Reinmuth, *Geist und Gesetz: Studien zu Voraussetzungen und Inhalt der paulinischen Paränese* (ThA 44; Berlin: Evangelische Verlagsanstalt, 1985) 29–31; Thomas, *Der jüdische Phokylides*, 89–102, 404–413, 442.

[4] Though Pseudo-Phocylides' inversed order for the first two commandments of the second table (in vv. 3–4) does reflect their order as recorded in the LXX and elsewhere in Hellenistic Judaism and early Christianity; cf. Bo Reicke, *Die Zehn Worte in Geschichte und Gegenwart: Zählung und Bedeutung der Gebote in den verschiedenen Konfessionen* (BGBE 13; Tübingen: J.C.B. Mohr [Paul Siebeck], 1973) 21 ff.; Niebuhr, *Gesetz und Paränese*, 16; also cf. the citation of Philo, *De Decalogo* 50–51 below, n. 23.

ence for those moral ideas that would win the most universal acceptance, as evidenced by numerous parallels from Greco-Roman sources.[5] The following outline is proposed for the rendition:

3–7	I.	Primary responsibilities in 'horizontal' relations
3		A. Prohibitions concerning sexual relations
3a		1. Against adultery
3b		2. Against homosexual relations
4		B. Prohibitions concerning transgressions against others
4a		1. Against plotting treachery
4b		2. Against murder
5–6		C. Commands concerning material possessions
5		1. Observe justice in making a living
6		2. Against covetousness
7		D. On honesty
8	II.	Primary responsibilities in 'vertical' relations
8a		A. Honor God foremost
8b		B. Secondly honor parents

Text:

3   μήτε γαμοκλοπέειν μήτ' ἄρσενα κύπριν ὀρίνειν
4   μήτε δόλους ῥάπτειν μήθ' αἵματι χεῖρα μιαίνειν.
5   μὴ πλουτεῖν ἀδίκως, ἀλλ' ἐξ ὁσίων βιοτεύειν.
6   ἀρκεῖσθαι παρεοῦσι καὶ ἀλλοτρίων ἀπέχεσθαι.
7   ψεύδεα μὴ βάζειν, τὰ δ' ἐτήτυμα πάντ' ἀγορεύειν.
8   πρῶτα θεὸν τιμᾶν, μετέπειτα δὲ σεῖο γονῆας.

Translation:

3   Do not commit adultery nor rouse male passion.
4   Do not contrive deceptions nor defile your hands with blood.
5   Be not unjustly rich but live from lawful means.
6   Be satisfied with what is at hand[6] and refrain from what belongs to others.
7   Speak not falsehoods but always say things that are true.
8   First of all honor God and thereafter your parents.

Pseudo-Phocylides divides the material of the summary into two categories of ethical teaching depending on the nature of the referents involved.[7] In both sections the instruction is highly condensed and paradigmatic, illustrating a number of fundamental moral principles to be expanded upon by exhortation later in the poem. The first section, verses 3–7, which constitutes the bulk of

---

[5] Van der Horst, *Sentences*, 110–117; Niebuhr, *Gesetz und Paränese*, 16–17, 20; Derron, *Sentences*, 19–20, 38–39.

[6] Following the conjecture of Ernest Diehl, ed., *Anthologia Lyrica Graeca* (4 vols.; Leipzig: Teubner, 1936) 2.97: παρεοῦσι (in Σ) instead of παρ' ἑοῖσι in M, V, and P², printed by Young, *Theognis*, 96; van der Horst, *Sentences*, 113–114; Derron, *Sentences*, 2. Theodorus Bergk (*Poetae Lyrici Graeci II* [4th ed.; Leipzig: Teubner, 1882] 81) prints παρ' ἑοῖς. P and L have παρεοῖσι. B reads παρέουσι. Cf. Walter, *Poetische Schriften*, 197, who translates our reading: "Begnüge dich mit dem, was vorhanden ist, usw."

[7] To some extent this division mirrors the common practice in antiquity of grouping the commandments of the Decalogue into two tables (see below).

the summary, addresses some of the primary responsibilities that the recipients must observe in 'horizontal' or communal relationships. This includes precepts about sexual conduct, offenses against others, wealth and possessions, and honesty; these commands are mostly negative in their orientation.[8] The author begins with injunctions attacking certain types of unacceptable sexual conduct, specifically adultery (verse 3 a) and homosexuality (verse 3 b). Next come orders not to harm others either through treachery (verse 4 a) or violence (verse 4 b). Verses 5–6, both antithetically constructed, counsel the reader on proper attitudes concerning material wealth: the plea in verse 5 contrasts just and unjust means of living, while verse 6 argues for the audience to be content with what they have, and not to covet or steal. In verse 7, which is also antithetically constructed, Pseudo-Phocylides commands the reader always to tell the truth and not to lie. The second section, verse 8, prescribes in a very condensed form the readers' obligations in 'vertical' or transcendent relationships; these commands, in contrast to the first section, are positive in their orientation. The chief responsibilities stipulated are to honor God first of all, and then also one's parents.[9]

The creation of literary summaries, renditions, or representative selections based upon the Decalogue such as we find in these verses of the *Sententiae* represents a fairly common practice in Hellenistic-Jewish and early Christian moral writings.[10] For an example of the utilization of such a summary we may turn to Didache 2.2–3:[11]

οὐ φονεύσεις, οὐ μοιχεύσεις, οὐ παιδοφθορήσεις, οὐ πορνεύσεις, οὐ κλέψεις, οὐ μαγεύσεις, οὐ φαρμακεύσεις, οὐ φονεύσεις τέκνον ἐν φθορᾷ, οὐδὲ γεννηθὲν ἀποκτενεῖς, οὐκ ἐπιθυμήσεις τὰ τοῦ πλησίον, οὐκ ἐπιορκήσεις, οὐ ψευδομαρτυρήσεις, οὐ κακολογήσεις, οὐ μνησικακήσεις.

Do not murder; do not commit adultery; do not corrupt boys; do not fornicate; do not steal; do not practice magic; do not go in for sorcery; do not murder a child by abortion or kill a newborn infant. Do not covet your neighbor's property; do not commit perjury; do not bear false witness; do not slander; do not bear grudges.

---

[8] Also note how vv. 3–5 begin and end similarly: μή- ... -ειν.

[9] On the pairing of gods and parents in moral literature see Leopold Schmidt, *Die Ethik der alten Griechen* (2 vols.; Berlin: Wilhelm Hertz, 1882) [reprint, Stuttgart: Friedrich Frommann, 1964] 2.141–149; Berger, *Die Gesetzesauslegung Jesu*, 278–290; Niebuhr, *Gesetz und Paränese*, 18–19; Thom, *Golden Verses*, 97–98; Thomas, *Der jüdische Phokylides*, 99–101, 166, 308–309, 413–415; cf. Hock and O'Neil, *The Chreia*, # 41 (p. 324).

[10] On such summaries see F. E. Vokes, "The Ten Commandments in the New Testament and in First Century Judaism," *Studia Evangelica* 5 (ed. F. L. Cross; TU 103; Berlin: Akademie-Verlag, 1968) 146–154; Berger, *Die Gesetzesauslegung Jesu*, 258–277; Niebuhr, *Gesetz und Paränese*, 15–20; Reginald H. Fuller, "The Decalogue in the New Testament," *Int* 43 (1989) 243–255; cf. Str-B 1.810–814.

[11] Text: Niederwimmer, *Die Didache*, 117; translation: Cyril C. Richardson, trans., *Early Christian Fathers* (LCC 1; Philadelphia: Westminster, 1953) 172; cf. Niederwimmer, *Die Didache*, 116–120.

The structure of the exhortation here follows a loose interpretation of the second table of the Decalogue, exhibiting considerable freedom in selection, formulation, and arrangement. The tractate's editor also incorporates some prohibitions from outside the Decalogue, which, although they appear to be primarily Jewish in nature, could be expected to find a sympathetic hearing with a Hellenistic audience.[12] Consistent with this is the absence of any reference to particularly Jewish (or Jewish-Christian) practices or beliefs, or any explicit acknowledgment of the use of the Decalogue as a source. The specific injunctions found in this rendition exhibit numerous parallels with Pseudo-Phocylides, *Sentences* 3–7, including commands against murder, adultery, theft, covetousness, and speaking falsely. Also, in each passage the format of the exhortation is predominantly negative in its orientation, the commands appear to be arranged seriatim, and the gnomic style dominates both the context and the mode of communication. It may be significant, too, that in both cases the summary of the Decalogue occurs near the beginning of the text (see below).

Also formally comparable is Pseudo-Philemon, *Fragmenta* 1.8–16, a short excerpt taken from a fragmentary poetic and gnomic text composed by a Hellenistic-Jewish author who, like Pseudo-Phocylides, assumes the guise of a famous Greek poet:[13]

δεῖ γὰρ τὸν ἄνδρα χρήσιμον πεφυκέναι,
μὴ παρθένους φθείροντα καὶ μοιχώμενον,
κλέπτοντα καὶ σφάττοντα χρημάτων χάριν·
τἀλλότρια βλέποντα, κἀπιθυμοῦντα
ἤτοι γυναικὸς πολυτελοῦς ἢ δώματος
ἢ κτήσεως παιδός τε παιδίοκης θ' ἁπλῶς,
ἵππων, βοῶν τὸ σύνολον ἢ κτηνῶν. τί δή;
μηδὲ βελόνης ἔναμμα ἐπιθυμήσῃς, [Πάμ]φιλε·
ὁ γὰρ θεὸς βλέπει σε πλησίον παρών.

For man must honorable be
and must not seduce women, nor commit adultery
nor steal nor slay for sake of gain,
nor look to other's property, nor covet
either wealthy woman or house
or goods or even slave or servant lass
or horses, cattle or any beast at all. What then?
Covet not, O friend, even a needle's thread.
For God is nearby and is watching you.

---

[12] Some of these are paralleled elsewhere in Pseudo-Phocylides' *Sententiae*, for example, vv. 149, 184–185.

[13] The excerpt is from Pseudo-Justin, *De Monarchia* 4; several of these lines are preserved also in Clement of Alexandria, *Stromata* 5.14.119 and Eusebius, *Praeparatio Evangelica* 13.13.45–46, both of whom attribute the poem to Menander rather than Philemon. Text: Albert-Marie Denis, *Fragmenta Pseudepigraphorum Quae Supersunt Graeca* (PVTG 3; Leiden: E.J. Brill, 1970) 169–170; translation: Attridge, "Fragments of

In their renditions of the Decalogue both Jewish poets warn against adultery, murder, theft, and covetousness, while mentioning nothing that plainly betrays the Jewish origin of their exhortation. Pseudo-Philemon concludes this section in a manner somewhat reminiscent of the command in verse 8 a at the end of Pseudo-Phocylides' summary, supporting his recommendations by reminding the audience of God's omnipresence and omniscience.

In terms of both its content and its format, Pseudo-Phocylides' rendition of the Decalogue participates also in certain conventions governing the formulation and presentation of ethical duties familiar from different Greco-Roman sources. To begin with, modern critics have documented how most of the injunctions in verses 3–8 are analogous to the sorts of moral obligations enumerated in various popular ethical codes.[14] Some of these codes were known in antiquity as the "unwritten laws". The numerous extant summaries of these ἄγραφοι νόμοι manifest a host of special modifications as to the number, order, and types of duties listed, though prescriptions to revere the gods, to honor one's parents, to abhor murder, and to abstain from incest and other unacceptable sexual activities appear regularly.[15] A number of these summaries are also employed in gnomic contexts, for example, Pseudo-Isocrates, *Ad Demonicum* 16.[16] Other popular Greco-Roman codes comparable in form and substance to these collections of unwritten laws include the varying compilations of the so-

---

Pseudo-Greek Poets," 2.830. Cf. Walter, *Poetische Schriften*, 267–269; Reinmuth, *Geist und Gesetz*, 28–29; Niebuhr, *Gesetz und Paränese*, 229–231; also cf. above, p. 19, n. 12.

[14] In addition to the references given below see F. E. Adcock, "Literary Tradition and Early Greek Code Makers," *Cambridge Historical Journal* 2 (1927) 95–109.

[15] See Rudlof Hirzel, *ΑΓΡΑΦΟΣ ΝΟΜΟΣ* (ASGW.PH 20.1; Leipzig: Teubner, 1900); Isaak Heinemann, "Die Lehre vom ungeschriebenen Gesetz im jüdischen Schriftum," *HUCA* 4 (1927) 149–171; Crouch, *Colossian Haustafel*, 37–46; Küchler, *Weisheitstraditionen*, 227–235, 244–245; Niebuhr, *Gesetz und Paränese*, 53–57; Thom, *Golden Verses*, 82–104; Thomas, *Der jüdische Phokylides*, 468–469; also cf. the literature listed above, p. 7, n. 22. Some examples: Aeschylus, *Supplices* 701–709; Xenophon, *Memorabilia* 4.4.18–25; Plato, *Leges* 838A–839D; Philo, *Hypothetica* 8.7.6–8; Plutarch, *De Liberis Educandis* 7E.

[16] Also significant here is the fact the Pseudo-Isocrates links his presentation of some of the unwritten laws with a scheme of virtues, much in the same way that Pseudo-Phocylides does (see the discussion on vv. 9–131 below):

ἡγοῦ μάλιστα σεαυτῷ πρέπειν κόσμον, αἰσχύνην δικαιοσύνην σωφροσύνην· τούτοις γὰρ ἅπασι δοκεῖ κρατεῖσθαι τὸ τῶν νεωτέρων ἦθος. μηδέποτε μηδὲν αἰσχρὸν ποιήσας ἔλπιζε λήσειν· καὶ γὰρ ἂν τοὺς ἄλλους λάθῃς, σεαυτῷ συνειδήσεις. τοὺς μὲν θεοὺς φοβοῦ, τοὺς δὲ γονεῖς τίμα, τοὺς δὲ φίλους αἰσχύνου, τοῖς δὲ νόμοις πείθου.

"Consider that no adornment so becomes you as modesty, justice, and self-control; for these are the virtues by which, as all men are agreed, the character of the young is held in restraint. Never hope to conceal any shameful thing which you have done; for even if you do conceal it from others, your own heart will know. Fear the gods, honour your parents, respect your friends, obey the laws."

Text and translation: Norlin, *Isocrates*, 1.12–13; cf. Wefelmeier, *Die Sentenzensammlung*, 78 ff.

called laws of Buzyges[17] and the Praecepta Delphica.[18] Within the literature of Judaism we also encounter on a number of occasions the Noachian, or Noachite, commandments. These were presented as precepts fundamental for the moral conduct of the entire human race; consequently they were held to be equally valid for Gentiles as well as for Jews. Although the number of commandments varied considerably, the seven mentioned most frequently were prohibitions of idolatry, blasphemy, murder, adultery, robbery, and eating flesh torn from a living animal, and the command to establish systems of justice.[19] It should be emphasized that while a concentration of parallels with these different moral codes appears in verses 3–8 of the *Sentences*, similarities can be detected also at various and numerous points throughout the poem. This suggests that traditional collections of moral laws comparable to those described above may have constituted basic sources for the author in addition to his primary legal source, the Torah. By drawing upon these kinds of widely approved materials, Pseudo-Phocylides establishes the moral tone and argumentative stance of his instruction, indicating as well its popular, multicultural nature. Consistent with this is the fact that there is much here that would have appeared quite ancient and hence authoritative to the intended audience.[20]

---

[17] Schmidt, *Die Ethik der alten Griechen*, 1.88, 2.278–279; Jacob Bernays, "Philon's Hypothetika und die Verwünschungen des Buzyges in Athen," *Monatsbericht der Königlichen Akademie der Wissenschaften zu Berlin* (Oktober, 1876) 589–609 [reprint, idem, *Gesammelte Abhandlungen*, 262–282]; Hendrik Bolkestein, *Wohltätigkeit und Armenpflege im vorchristlichen Altertum: Ein Beitrag zum Problem "Moral und Gesellschaft"* (Utrecht: A. Oosthoeck, 1939) 69–71; Crouch, *Colossian Haustafel*, 87; Hans von Geisau, "Buzyges," *KP* 1 (1964) 977; Berger, *Gesetzesauslegung Jesu*, 380–381; Küchler, *Weisheitstraditionen*, 227–235, 245; Niebuhr, *Gesetz und Paränese*, 55–56.

[18] Derron (*Sentences*, 19–20, nn. 5, 7, 9–11) notes Delphic parallels for vv. 3–8, particularly with the collection attributed to Sosiades preserved in Stobaeus, *Anthologium* 3.1.173. Also similar are the so-called "Sayings of the Seven Sages", cf. Küchler, *Weisheitstraditionen*, 241–244.

[19] Samuel Krauss, "Les Préceptes des Noachides," *REJ* 47 (1903) 32–40; Michael Guttmann, *Das Judentum und seine Umwelt* (Berlin: Philo Verlag, 1927) 98 ff.; Ernst L. Dietrich, "Die 'Religion Noahs', ihre Herkunft und ihre Bedeutung," *ZRGG* 1 (1948) 301–315; Louis Ginzberg, *The Legends of the Jews* (7 vols.; Philadelphia: Jewish Publication Society, 1909–1938) 5.92–93, n. 55; Str-B 3.36–38; Crouch, *Colossian Haustafel*, 91–98; F. J. Foakes Jackson and Kirsopp Lake, *The Beginnings of Christianity: The Acts of the Apostles* (5 vols.; London: Macmillan, 1920–1933) [reprint, Grand Rapids: Baker Book House, 1979] 1.43–45, 4.117, 119, 5.81, 208; Steven S. Schwarzschild and Saul Berman, "Noachide Laws," *EncJud* 12 (1971) 1189–1191; Folker Siegert, "Gottesfürchtige und Sympathisanten," *JSJ* 4 (1973) 109–164, especially 125; van der Horst, *Sentences*, 73–75; Thomas, *Der jüdische Phokylides*, 228–235.

[20] Also in the background of this type of exhortation are prohibitions against the so-called three cardinal sins (adultery, murder, and idolatry), see, for example, Harald Sahlin, "Die drei Kardinalsünden und das Neue Testament," *ST* 24 (1970) 93–112; cf. Reinhard Staats, "Hauptsünden," *RAC* 13 (1985) 734–770.

Turning now to the structure of this summary, Pseudo-Phocylides appears to have borrowed from the common procedure in antiquity of categorizing moral responsibilities according to the so-called Canon of Two Virtues. The first of these virtues (usually referred to as either εὐσέβεια or ὁσιότης) pertains to the obligations that one owes to one's superiors, especially the gods, parents, and the dead. The second virtue (usually referred to as either δικαιοσύνη or φιλανθρωπία) refers to the obligations owed to one's peers, such as friends, neighbors, fellow citizens, and so forth.[21] The practice of applying such a scheme to an ethical analysis of the Decalogue is reflected also in Philo's writings, where he sometimes arranges the commandments into two sets (or tables) of five each; the first set deals with duties towards God whereas the second addresses duties towards humanity.[22] An illustration of this organizational scheme comes from *De Decalogo* 50–51, where Philo notes that the first set of commands begins with God and ends with parents, drawing together referents similar to those of verse 8 in the *Sentences*. He also observes that the second set contains all the prohibitions, listing adultery before murder, much in the same way Pseudo-Phocylides does in verses 3 ff.[23] In *De Decalogo* 50–51, as

---

[21] Albrecht Dihle, *Der Kanon der zwei Tugenden* (Arbeitsgemeinschaft für Forschung des Laudes Nordrhein-Westfalen, Reihe: Geisteswissenschaften, Heft 44; Cologne and Opladen: Westdeutscher Verlag, 1968); Hans Dieter Betz, "Christianity as Religion: Paul's Attempt at Definition in Romans," *JR* 71 (1991) 315–344, especially 339–343; Berger, *Die Gesetzesauslegung Jesu*, 142–168; Dorothy I. Sly, "Philo's Practical Application of Δικαιοσύνη," *SBLSP* 30 (ed. Eugene H. Lovering; Atlanta: Scholars Press, 1991) 303.

[22] *De Decalogo* 50–51 (cited in the next note), *Quis Rerum Divinarum Heres Sit* 167–173; cf. Berger, *Die Gesetzesauslegung Jesu*, 151–152, 156–160; Yehoshua Amir, "The Decalogue according to Philo," *The Ten Commandments in History and Tradition* (ed. Ben-Zion Segal and Gershon Levi; Jerusalem: Magnes, 1990) 121–160 [originally, *Die hellenistische Gestalt des Judentums bei Philo von Alexandria* (Forschungen zum jüdisch-christlichen Dialog 5; Neukirchen: Neukirchener Verlag, 1983) 131–163]; Jastram, "Generic Virtue," 332.

[23] δέκα τοίνυν ὄντα διένειμεν εἰς δύο πεντάδας, ἃς δυσὶ στήλαις ἐνεχάραξε, καὶ ἡ μὲν προτέρα πεντὰς τὰ πρωτεῖα ἔλαχεν, ἡ δ' ἑτέρα δευτερείων ἠξιοῦτο· καλαὶ δ' ἀμφότεραι καὶ βιωφελεῖς, εὐρείας ὁδοὺς καὶ λεωφόρους ἑνὶ τέλει περατουμένας ἀναστέλλουσαι πρὸς ἄπταιστον ψυχῆς ἐφιεμένης ἀεὶ τοῦ βελτίστου πορείαν. ἡ μὲν οὖν ἀμείνων πεντὰς τοιάδε ἦν· περὶ μοναρχίας, ᾗ μοναρχεῖται ὁ κόσμος· περὶ ξοάνων καὶ ἀγαλμάτων καὶ συνόλως ἀφιδρυμάτων χειροκμήτων· περὶ τοῦ μὴ λαμβάνειν ἐπὶ ματαίῳ θεοῦ πρόσρησιν· περὶ τοῦ τὴν ἱερὰν ἑβδόμην ἄγειν ἱεροπρεπῶς· περὶ γονέων τιμῆς καὶ ἰδίᾳ ἑκατέρου καὶ ἀμφοτέρων κοινῇ· ὡς εἶναι τῆς μιᾶς γραφῆς τὴν μὲν ἀρχὴν θεὸν καὶ πατέρα καὶ ποιητὴν τοῦ παντός, τὸ δὲ τέλος γονεῖς, οἳ μιμούμενοι τὴν ἐκείνου φύσιν γεννῶσι τοὺς ἐπὶ μέρους. ἡ δ' ἑτέρα πεντὰς τὰς πάσας ἀπαγορεύσεις περιέχει· μοιχείας, φόνου, κλοπῆς, ψευδομαρτυριῶν, ἐπιθυμιῶν.

"We find that God divided the ten into two sets of five which were engraved on two tables, and the first five obtained the first place, while the other was awarded the second. Both are excellent and profitable for life; both open out broad highroads leading at the end to a single goal, roads along which the soul which ever desires the best can travel without stumbling. The superior set of five treats the following matters: the monarchical principle by which the world is governed; idols of stone and wood and images in general made by hu-

elsewhere, Philo pairs together the two virtues as a means of depicting the full range of potential civic and religious responsibilities addressed by the Mosaic law, suggesting that there are two extensive though related areas of moral accountability for Jews.[24] By availing himself of this Canon of Virtues in conjunction with the "unwritten laws" for his rendition of the Decalogue in verses 3–8, Pseudo-Phocylides demonstrates from the outset how his poem will be significantly broad in the scope of its ethical content and application as well as multicultural in the literary and rhetorical nature of its appeal, while at the same time predicated upon the moral perspective and specific directives of the Torah.

Besides its role as a summary of the Decalogue, it is also possible to think of verses 3–8 as operating in the role of a summary or preview of the poem itself. As such, these lines serve a foundational role, constructing an ideational basis and point of reference for the text's instruction and indicating its fundamental ethical outlook, tone, and standards. In this regard the section corresponds functionally to what Greco-Roman rhetoricians called the πρόθεσις, or *propositio*, a concise statement placed near the beginning of an oration that sets forth the matters to be discussed in a clear and complete way.[25] In this capacity, the section in verses 3–8 enunciates but does not explicate certain principles and requirements that set the stage for the exhortation that follows, implying its moral stance and material presuppositions while anticipating many of its essential ethical themes.[26] If the analogy is carried one step further, then

---

man hands; the sin of taking the name of God in vain; the reverent observance of the sacred seventh day as befits its holiness; the duty of honouring parents, each separately and both in common. Thus one set of enactments begins with God the Father and Maker of all, and ends with parents who copy God's nature by begetting particular persons. The other set of five contains all the prohibitions, namely adultery, murder, theft, false witness, covetousness or lust."

Text and translation: Colson, *Philo*, 7.30–33.

[24] *De Abrahamo* 107–118, 208, *De Decalogo* 110–111, *De Iosepho* 240, *De Specialibus Legibus* 1.304, 2.62–64, 3.209, 4.170, *De Virtutibus* 51, 54, 76, 94–95, 175, *De Vita Mosis* 1.198, 2.108, 163, *Hypothetica* 6.8, *Legatio ad Gaium* 213; cf. *Quaestiones et Solutiones in Exodum* 1.12, *Quod Omnis Probus Liber Sit* 79, 81–85; Winston, "Philo's Ethical Theory," 394–396; Berger, *Die Gesetzesauslegung Jesu*, 151–165; further also Josephus, *Antiquitates Judaicae* 6.265, 8.121, 295, 314, 9.16, 10.50, 11.55, 14.283, 15.182, 375, *Contra Apionem* 2.213; *Epistula Aristeas* 24, 131.

[25] It was also known as the *partitio* or *divisio*; see Aristotle, *Rhetorica* 3.13; Cicero, *De Inventione* 1.22.31–1.23.33; Pseudo-Cicero, *Rhetorica ad Herennium* 1.10.17; Quintilian, *Institutio Oratoria* 4.4.1–4.5.28; cf. 3.9.2, 5; 3.11.27; Jean Cousin, *Etudes sur Quintilian* (2 vols.; Paris: Boivin, 1935–1936) [reprint, Amsterdam: Schippers, 1967] 247–252; Lausberg, *Handbuch*, § 346, cf. §§ 343–345, 347, 671; Josef Martin, *Antike Rhetorik: Technik und Methode* (HAW 2.3; München: Beck, 1974) 91–95. As Hans Dieter Betz observes (*Galatians: A Commentary on Paul's Letter to the Churches in Galatia* [Hermeneia; Philadelphia: Fortress, 1979] 114), the *propositio* may consist of short formulaic summaries of doctrines.

[26] Derron, *Sentences*, 19, n. 5.

we may describe the bulk of the text, verses 9–227, as the πίστις, or *probatio*. This is that part of the oration, usually the longest and most complex, that marshals various arguments or proofs in support of the *propositio*.[27] The designation of this part of the poem as the *probatio* is not intended to suggest that the summary of the Decalogue in verses 3–8 is in need of 'proof' in the sense that the author sought validation or confirmation for it. Rather, the heart of the poem strives to develop in the audience an improved understanding about the nature, the authority, and the value of the *propositio* as well as the conviction necessary to put its principles into action in their own ethical decision-making and conduct. The proof section thus expands upon and explains the proposition, indicating its implications and significance for the reader.

As the observations made so far have suggested, it appears that Pseudo-Phocylides' summary of the Decalogue in verses 3–8, together with the σφραγίς in verses 1–2 (see Chapter Six below), plays an important material and argumentative role as the text's introduction. In the same manner as many other poetic texts, the opening lines of our poem are especially crucial for seizing the audience's attention, for articulating the author's persona and objectives, and for indicating the basis and character of what will be said. As we have seen, in constructing this opening segment, the author not only draws from the Torah for his material, but also benefits from different popular sources and rhetorical strategies familiar from the moral discourse of the time. It comes as no surprise that we can observe some of these same strategies at work in the introductions designed for other ancient gnomic texts. The manner in which the formulation of verses 1–8 of the *Sentences* corresponds with these texts serves as an indication of the extent to which it participates in the contemporaneous literary and exhortatory conventions that governed the presentation of materials of this type, and provides clues as to both the author's designs in writing and the type of poem he intended to write.

The prologue to the *Theognidea*, to begin with, while not employing a summary of the Decalogue like Pseudo-Phocylides' *Sententiae*, exhibits similar features in the context of gnomic exhortation. After an invocation of the gods, indicating the author's divine inspiration (Apollo and Artemis in verses 1–14, the Muses and the Graces in verses 15–18), we have the σφραγίς proper (verses 19–26). A preview of the text's basic principles and objectives in outline form follows in verses 27–38: (1) Theognis intends to bequeath to the reader ("Kyrnos") ethical instruction that he acquired in his youth from the ἀγαθοί, (2) in conjunction with this, he orders Kyrnos to do nothing

---

[27] It was also known as the *confirmatio* or *argumentatio*; see Aristotle, *Rhetorica* 3.17; Cicero, *De Inventione* 1.24.34; Pseudo-Cicero, *Rhetorica ad Herennium* 1.10.18; Quintilian, *Institutio Oratoria* 5; Cousin, *Quintilian*, 253–307; Lausberg, *Handbuch*, §§ 348–430; Martin, *Antike Rhetorik*, 95–137; Betz, *Galatians*, 128–129.

dishonorable or unjust, and (3) he makes a moral appeal for the reader to consort with the ἀγαθοί while avoiding the κακοί.[28] Like Pseudo-Phocylides, Theognis demonstrates in his introduction some concern to suggest the divine origin as well as the traditional nature of the advice contained in his poetic verses. Both authors also tend to conceptualize their opening appeals antithetically, contrasting two opposing types of conduct. In this regard, their prologues are reminiscent of the "Two Ways" doctrine familiar from numerous ancient sources.[29]

The preamble for the *Carmen Aureum*, verses 1–8, also demonstrates some affinities with the introduction to our *Sentences*, chiefly in its division of primary moral duties according to first 'vertical' and then 'horizontal' relationships. This poet begins by exhorting the reader to honor (τιμᾶν; verses 2 and 4) first of all (πρῶτα; verse 1) the gods, and then (ἔπειθ'; verse 2) also the heroes, the spirits of the dead, and one's parents (compare Pseudo-Phocylides, *Sententiae* 8). Beginning at verse 5, the author's attention turns to the reader's peers, targeting the moral obligations owed to one's friends. The author expects his audience to select companions who excel in virtue (a central theme of the poem), espousing an attitude based on fairness and compassion (verses 5–8).[30]

With respect to its structure and function, the prologue to the sapiential text known as the *Sentences* of Syriac Menander offers perhaps the most instructive parallel to verses 1–8 of our poem. Like Pseudo-Phocylides' *Sentences*, this work represents a pseudonymous Hellenistic-Jewish document that is predominantly gnomic in character, and, in fact, the two compositions share a number of themes and features. The extant Syriac text of Menander is probably a translation from the Greek, originally composed perhaps during the late second or early third century A.D.[31] After a σφραγίς identifying the author (verse 1), which forms an inclusio with the poem's epilogue (verse 474), the section opens with a programmatic maxim: "Prior to the words of man are all his activities." This is followed by a number of commands in summary form (verses 3–19), all of which have analogues in verses 3–8 of Pseudo-Phocylides' *Sentences*; the readers are instructed to (1) beget children (verses 3–8, suggesting, at least indirectly, proper sexual conduct; compare Pseudo-Phocylides, *Sententiae* 3); (2) fear God (verse 9; compare Pseudo-Phocylides, *Sententiae* 8 a); (3) honor their parents (verses 10–14; compare Pseudo-

---

[28] Also compare Theognis' use of ταῦτα in vv. 31 and 37 with Pseudo-Phocylides, *Sententiae* 1.

[29] Cf. Hesiod, *Opera et Dies* 1–10; also below, p. 149, n. 12.

[30] Cf. Thom, *Golden Verses*, 82–104; also below, pp. 189–190.

[31] See T. Baarda, trans., "The Sentences of the Syriac Menander (Third Century A.D.)," in Charlesworth, *Pseudepigrapha*, 2.583–606; also Jean-Paul Audet, "La Sagesse de Ménandre l'Egyptien," *RB* 59 (1952) 55–81; Küchler, *Weisheitstraditionen*, 303–318; Schürer, *History*, 692–694; cf. van der Horst, *Sentences*, 64, n. 1, 76, n. 21.

Phocylides, *Sententiae* 8 b); and (4) refrain from murder (verses 15–19; compare Pseudo-Phocylides, *Sententiae* 4). Afterwards the author has assembled a lengthy collection of gnomic sayings and other ethical materials arranged by topic, for which verses 1–19 serve in part as a material and rhetorical foundation. As this brief description suggests, the prologue to Syriac Menander displays several features that are akin to those observed in Pseudo-Phocylides, *Sentences* 1–8 in terms of its content, structure, context, and function. Like Pseudo-Phocylides, the author of this prologue has utilized a σφραγίς followed by a summary of the Decalogue that incorporates some of the 'unwritten laws' as an introduction for his gnomic text.[32] The substance and ethical perspective of both texts appear to be primarily Jewish in nature, though both authors benefit significantly from the employment of non-Jewish materials and structures that are consistent with the more universalistic posture that they seek to establish. Precisely what these materials and structures are for Pseudo-Phocylides' gnomic appeal, and how they relate to the summary of the Decalogue that stands in vv. 3–8, will be explored in greater detail in the chapters that follow.

---

[32] Cf. the introduction to the *Epitome* of Syriac Menander, vv. 1–6.

Chapter Four

Exhortation Structured According to the Canon of Cardinal Virtues (verses 9–131)

The survey of the interpretation and application of the Canon of Cardinal Virtues in antiquity conducted in Chapter Two provides an interpretive framework for conducting our investigation of the literary composition of Pseudo-Phocylides' *Sentences*, verses 9–131 in particular. As we saw, while the tetrad appears in many contexts, it is employed especially in philosophical and exhortatory materials, including a fair number of Jewish as well as Greco-Roman sources. The analysis that follows will show that Pseudo-Phocylides also has recourse to the canon in these verses and that the nature of his application of the tetrad as a compositional device is consonant with its employment in other gnomic texts, such as Isocrates' *Ad Nicoclem* 10–39, Sextus, *Sententiae* 167–182, Ben Sira 36.23–38.23, and the Pythagorean *Carmen Aureum* 9–20, all inspected as part of the survey in Chapter Two. Because Pseudo-Phocylides applies the canon this way at an implicit level (rather than at an explicit level in a discussion of the definition and nature of virtue and the virtues) it would be incorrect for us to anticipate a tightly argued or systematic exposition of any of the virtues or a comprehensive series of injunctions intended to represent all of their facets. Instead, the author characterizes the individual virtues in effect by indicating through gnomic exhortation the sorts of moral activities and attitudes he associates with them. By including paraenesis that relates to all four of the cardinal virtues, he provides the audience with a number of essential insights as to his ethical program, its content, nature, and purpose, while leaving many of the details to them. The gnomic style is appropriate for this kind of message since it invites critical moral reflection while at the same time eliciting a proper and concrete response from the readers that has implications for the development of their ethical judgment.

The placement of this section on the principal virtues immediately after the summary of the Decalogue in verses 3–8 apparently proceeds according to an intentional design. The general objective evident in this literary scheme may be compared to certain inquiries relating to the meaning and function of the Jewish law conducted by Philo. As we saw above, he presents and interprets the Law in terms of the Greek virtues, asserting that the way of life mapped out by the commands of the Decalogue and the special laws associated with them serves to inculcate these virtues in those who obey the Torah. The same sort of argument appears to underlie the composition of this passage in the *Sentences*, where exhortation organized according to the tetrad immediately follows a rendition of the Decalogue. Consistent with this observation is the fact that much of the substance and tone of verses 9–131 (and indeed the entire poem) is familiar from the LXX as well as other Jewish moral writings, as a number of contemporary studies have documented. Here the author subsumes exhortation from disparate sources and traditions, including non-Jewish ones, and gives it new form under a scheme of the cardinal virtues, indicating that these materials have been critically appropriated, molded, and redirectioned according to a certain plan and objective. Thus the literary composition of the text evidences the author's specific views on the nature of virtue and of the particular virtues, their positive relationship with Torah, and the relationship between Jewish and Greek ethics more generally.

As befits the section's basic character, the author has arranged the maxims in verses 9–131 into four units, each pertaining to one of the cardinal virtues: Exhortation on Topics Relating to Justice (verses 9–54), Exhortation on Topics Relating to Moderation (verses 55–96), Exhortation on Topics Relating to Courage, Specifically Fortitude (verses 97–121), Exhortation on the Topic of Wisdom and Speech (verses 122–131). These units will be investigated individually below.

Exhortation on Topics Relating to Justice (verses 9–54)

Outline:

9–21	I.	A paragraph of maxims on the theme of justice, organized by ring-composition (see below for outline)
22–54	II.	Exhortation organized according to ethical topics associated with the theme of justice
22–41		A. Maxims on φιλανθρωπία, organized according to different referents
22–30		1. Those in need, especially the poor
22–26		a. Admonitions concerning different types of needy persons
22–23		i. The poor
24a		ii. The homeless
24b		iii. The blind
25		iv. The shipwrecked
26a		v. Those who have fallen
26b		vi. The helpless
27–30		b. Supporting argumentation and evidence
27a		i. On the universality of suffering
27b–c		ii. On the vicissitudes of life and prosperity
28		iii. That charity is contingent upon one's resources
29		iv. Possessions are from God
30		v. Unity of life should be the goal

32–34	2. Enemies
32–33	a. Instruction on the use of violent force
32	i. Rule: violence, if used, should be for self-defense, not murder
33	ii. Intensification: but avoiding violence altogether is most desirable
34	b. Reason: homicide defiles the aggressor
35–38	3. Neighbors
35	a. Do not trespass your neighbor's property
38	b. Do not harm the fruits of the land
39–41	4. Strangers
39	a. Command to respect strangers
40–41	b. Supporting observations
40	i. Universality of poverty and wandering
41	ii. The land is unpredictable
42–54	B. Exhortation about different personal sources of injustice
42–47	1. On greed
42	a. Thesis statement: greed is the source of all evil
43–47	b. Supporting material
43	i. Maxim on the constant allure of wealth
44–47	ii. An apostrophe to Gold
44a	α. Direct address
44b–d	β. Three negative epithets
45	γ. A wish that wealth was not such a fatal attraction
46–47	δ. Elaboration: greed is the source of violence and alienation
48–54	2. On hybris
48–50	a. Against hypocrisy
48–49	i. Negative commands
48	α. Against lying
49	β. Against opportunism
50	ii. Positive commands: be sincere
51–52	b. Against willful or presumptuous wrongdoing
51a	i. Rule: whoever does wrong ἑκών is evil
51b–52	ii. Qualification
51b–52a	α. No judgment is possible regarding someone who is coerced
52b	β. Reason: it is the intention that matters
53–54	c. Against arrogance
53	i. Warning against human pride
54	ii. Reason: only God has reason for pride

Text:

9	πάντα δίκαια νέμειν, μὴ δὲ κρίσιν ἐς χάριν ἕλκειν.
10	μὴ θλίψῃς πενίην ἀδίκως, μὴ κρῖνε πρόσωπον·
11	ἢν σὺ κακῶς δικάσῃς, σὲ θεὸς μετέπειτα δικάσσει.
12	μαρτυρίην ψευδῆ φεύγειν· τὰ δίκαια βραβεύειν.
13	παρθεσίην τηρεῖν, πίστιν δ᾽ ἐν πᾶσι φυλάσσειν.
14	μέτρα νέμειν τὰ δίκαια, καλὸν δ᾽ ἐπὶ μέτρον ἅπασι.
15	σταθμὸν μὴ κρούειν ἑτερόζυγον, ἀλλ᾽ ἴσον ἕλκειν.
16	μὴ δ᾽ ἐπιορκήσῃς μήτ᾽ ἀγνὼς μήτε ἑκοντί·
17	ψεύδορκον στυγέει θεὸς ἄμβροτος ὅστις ὀμόσσῃ.
18	σπέρματα μὴ κλέπτειν· ἐπαράσιμος ὅστις ἕληται.
19	μισθὸν μοχθήσαντι δίδου, μὴ θλῖβε πένητα.
20	γλώσσῃ νοῦν ἐχέμεν, κρυπτὸν λόγον ἐν φρεσὶν ἴσχειν.

21   μήτ' ἀδικεῖν ἐθέλῃς μήτ' οὖν ἀδικοῦντα ἐάσῃς.
22   πτωχῷ δ' εὐθὺ δίδου μὴ δ' αὔριον ἐλθέμεν εἴπῃς·
23   πληρώσεις ἔο χεῖρ'· ἔλεον χρήζοντι παράσχου.
24   ἄστεγον εἰς οἶκον δέξαι καὶ τυφλὸν ὁδήγει.
25   ναυηγοὺς οἴκτειρον, ἐπεὶ πλόος ἐστὶν ἄδηλος.
26   χεῖρα πεσόντι δίδου, σῶσον δ' ἀπερίστατον ἄνδρα.
27   κοινὰ πάθη πάντων· ὁ βίος τροχός· ἄστατος ὄλβος.
28   πλοῦτον ἔχων σὴν χεῖρα πενητεύουσιν ὄρεξον·
29   ὧν σοι ἔδωκε θεός, τούτων χρήζουσι παράσχου.
30   ἔστω κοινὸς ἅπας ὁ βίος καὶ ὁμόφρονα πάντα.
[31]
32   τὸ ξίφος ἀμφιβαλοῦ μὴ πρὸς φόνον, ἀλλ' ἐς ἄμυναν.
33   εἴθε δὲ μὴ χρήζοις μήτ' ἔκνομα μήτε δικαίως·
34   ἢν γὰρ ἀποκτείνῃς ἐχθρόν, σέο χεῖρα μιαίνεις.
35   ἀγροῦ γειτονέοντος ἀπόσχεο, μὴ δ' ἄρ' ὑπερβῇς.
[36]
[37]
38   μηδέ τιν' αὐξόμενον καρπὸν λωβήσῃ ἀρούρης.
39   ἔστωσαν δ' ὁμότιμοι ἐπήλυδες ἐν πολιήταις·
40   πάντες γὰρ πενίης πειρώμεθα τῆς πολυπλάγκτου,
41   χώρης δ' οὔ τι βέβαιον ἔχει πέδον ἀνθρώποισιν.
42   ἡ φιλοχρημοσύνη μήτηρ κακότητος ἁπάσης.
43   χρυσὸς ἀεὶ δόλος ἐστὶ καὶ ἄργυρος ἀνθρώποισιν.
44   χρυσέ, κακῶν ἀρχηγέ, βιοφθόρε, πάντα χαλέπτων,
45   εἴθε σε μὴ θνητοῖσι γενέσθαι πῆμα ποθεινόν·
46   σεῦ γὰρ ἕκητι μάχαι τε λεηλασίαι τε φόνοι τε,
47   ἐχθρὰ δὲ τέκνα γονεῦσιν ἀδελφειοί τε συναίμοις.
48   μὴ δ' ἕτερον κεύθῃς κραδίῃ νόον ἀλλ' ἀγόρευων,
49   μηδ' ὡς πετροφυὴς πολύπους κατὰ χῶρον ἀμείβου.
50   πᾶσιν δ' ἁπλόος ἴσθι, τὰ δ' ἐκ ψυχῆς ἀγόρευε.
51   ὅστις ἑκὼν ἀδικεῖ, κακὸς ἀνήρ· ἢν δ' ὑπ' ἀνάγκης,
52   οὐκ ἐρέω τὸ τέλος· βουλὴ δ' εὐθύνεθ' ἑκάστου.
53   μὴ γαυροῦ σοφίῃ μήτ' ἀλκῇ μήτ' ἐνὶ πλούτῳ·
54   εἷς θεός ἐστι σοφὸς δυνατός θ' ἅμα καὶ πολύολβος.

Translation:

9   Always dispense just things and prolong no decision to gain favor.[1]
10   Do not unjustly oppress[2] a poor man; judge not by his countenance.[3]
11   If you judge evilly, God will afterwards judge you.
12   Shun false testimony; decide what's right.
13   Safeguard a deposit, and protect your integrity in all circumstances.
14   Dispense just measures; it is good to have measure in all circumstances.[4]

---

[1] Cf. van der Horst, *Sentences*, 117–118: "... stretch not judgement for a favor." Walter, *Poetische Schriften*, 198: "... verdrehe nach Gunst nicht das Urteil." Derron, *Sentences*, 3: "... ne pas fausser un jugement pour une faveur."

[2] Following Bernays, *Gesammelte Abhandlungen*, 216, n. 1, who conjectures θλίψῃς instead of ῥίψῃς, which is in the mss. and printed by Young, *Theognis*, 96; Derron, *Sentences*, 3; cf. van der Horst, *Sentences*, 118.

[3] On v. 10b cf. Betz, *Galatians*, 94–95.

[4] Following West (*CR* 30 [1980] 137), who reads ἐπὶ μέτρον ἅπασι instead of ἐπίμετρον ἁπάντων in Young, *Theognis*, 96; van der Horst, *Sentences*, 121–122; Derron, *Sentences*, 3 (which appears to be supported only by B). Cf. Arthur Ludwich, "Über das Spruchbuch des

15 Tip not a scale to one side[5], but weigh (both sides) equally.
16 Do not commit perjury, either unknowingly or deliberately.
17 Immortal God detests anyone who swears falsely.[6]
18 Do not steal seeds; cursed is whoever takes them.[7]
19 Give to a worker his wage; oppress not a poor man.
20 Be mindful of your tongue; keep in your heart a word given in confidence.[8]
21 Be unwilling to do wrong, and therefore check a wrong-doer.[9]
22 To a beggar give immediately, and do not tell him to come tomorrow.[10]
23 You are to fill[11] your hand; give alms to one in need.
24 Receive a homeless person into your house, and guide a blind man.
25 Pity a shipwrecked person, since sailing is uncertain.
26 To one who falls give a hand, and save an unprotected man.
27 Common to all is suffering; life's a wheel; unstable is happiness.
28 Having wealth extend your hand to the poor.
29 From what God has given you provide for those in need.
30 Let all of life be in common and let all things have unity of purpose.[12]
[31][13]
32 Gird on your sword not for murder but for defense.
33 But may you not need it at all, unlawfully or justly.
34 For if you slay a foe, you stain your hand.
35 Keep away from a neighbor's field, and so do not trespass.
[36]
[37][14]
38 Harm not any crop growing in a field.
39 Let foreigners be held in equal honor among citizens.

---

falschen Phokylides," *Programm Königsberg* (Königsberg, 1904) 16: καλὸν δ' ἐπὶ μέτρον ἀπαντᾶν. Cf. *Carmen Aureum* 38b.

[5] Cf. Walter, *Poetische Schriften*, 198: "Drücke die Waage nicht nach einer Seite, usw."

[6] Following M. L. West's proposed translation as reported in van der Horst, "Pseudo-Phocylides Revisited," 17–18.

[7] Following the translation of van der Horst, *Sentences*, 124–125.

[8] Cf. Walter, *Poetische Schriften*, 199: "... ein Wort im Vertrauen behalte fest für dich."

[9] Following Edward O'Neil's proposed translation (personal communication, 5/15/92).

[10] For non-Jewish parallels to this sentiment see, for example, Publilius Syrus, *Sententiae* 164, 274.

[11] There are numerous textual problems and conjectures for this line, see van der Horst, *Sentences*, 128–130, and Derron, *Sentences*, 21, n. 2. Derron's (*Sentences*, 4) reading (printed above) seems as probable as any. Young (*Theognis*, 97) and van der Horst (*Sentences*, 128–130) print πληρώσει σέο χεῖρ'. ἔλεον χρήζοντι παράσχου. Diehl (*Anthologia*, 2.99) has πληρώσας σέο χεῖρ' ἐλέου χρήζοντι παράσχου (cf. Lᵞᵒ and P). Cf. Morton Smith's proposal reported in van der Horst, "Pseudo-Phocylides Revisited," 18: πληρώσει σέο χεῖρ' ἔλεον χρήζοντι παρασχεῖν. Also cf. Walter (*Poetische Schriften*, 199): πληρώσῃ (aor. mid. subj. 2nd sg.) σέο χεῖρ' ἔλεον χρήζοντι παράσχου.

[12] Edward O'Neil (personal communication, 5/15/92) suggests "Let every mode of life be common, and all things be united."

[13] V. 31 (αἷμα δὲ μὴ φαγέειν, εἰδωλοθύτων ἀπέχεσθαι. "Consume not blood; abstain from food offered to idols.") is spurious; see van der Horst, *Sentences*, 135–136.

[14] Vv. 36–37 (πάντων μέτρον ἄριστον, ὑπερβασίαι δ' ἀλεγειναί. κτῆσις ὀνήσιμός ἐσθ' ὁσίων, ἀδίκων δὲ πονηρά. "Best of all is moderation, but excesses are grievous. Possession of honest things is useful, of dishonest things, wicked.") are spurious; see van der Horst, *Sentences*, 137–138.

40 For we all experience the poverty that comes from roaming widely,[15]
41 and a tract of land has nothing certain for people.[16]
42 The love of money is the mother of every evil.
43 Gold and silver are always a delusion for people.
44 Gold, you cause of evils, destroyer of life, crushing everything,[17]
45 would that you were not such a longed-for calamity to mortals!
46 On your account there are fights and robberies and murders,
47 and children are enemies to their parents, and brothers to their kinfolk.
48 Hide not one intention in your heart while expressing another;
49 and do not vary with the situation like the rock-clinging polyp.
50 In all circumstances be sincere, and speak what comes from the heart.
51 Whoever on purpose acts unjustly is an evil man; but if he acts thus perforce
52 I will not predict the outcome; but it is the intention of each that is called to account.
53 Pride not yourself on wisdom, might, or wealth.
54 God alone is wise, mighty, and also very wealthy.

The ordering of the sections on the cardinal virtues in verses 9–131 shows signs of some planning, particularly the placement of the exhortation on justice, which comes first. In philosophical writings of the Greco-Roman period, justice was the virtue most closely associated with the law. Accompanying this, ethical thinkers generally considered it to be the most social or civic in orientation.[18] It follows that this virtue takes on special prominence in Jewish contexts, with Leviticus 19 frequently serving as a basic source of instruction, which is also the case with this section of our poem.[19] Furthermore, as commentators on the *Sentences* have pointed out, justice appears to operate as a key moral theme and standard for the text as a whole, as indicated, for instance, by verses 229–230. The importance allotted to this idea by Pseudo-

---

[15] Or perhaps, "For we all have experience of wide-ranging poverty, etc."

[16] Cf. the alternatives for translation proposed by van der Horst, *Sentences*, 140–142: "... and the land has nothing constant for men"; Walter, *Poetische Schriften*, 201: "... und nirgends gibt es einen sicheren Platz auf Erden für die Menschen"; and Derron, *Sentences*, 5: "... et la terre n'a point de lieu sûr pour les hommes."

[17] With regard to v. 44d, Edward O'Neil (personal communication, 5/15/92) suggests that πάντα could be taken as equivalent to ἀεί and that χαλέπτω is intransitive (as it sometimes is in the active), in which case the phrase πάντα χαλέπτων could mean "always vexatious" or "always vexing."

[18] The literature on this subject is vast, and only a few of the more important titles can be mentioned here: Erik Wolf, *Griechisches Rechtsdenken* (4 vols.; Frankfurt: Klostermann, 1950–1970); Albrecht Dihle, "Gerechtigkeit," *RAC* 10 (1978) 236–289; Bengt Hägglund, "Gerechtigkeit VII. Ethisch," *TRE* 12 (1984) 440–443; Bernhard Taureck, "Gerechtigkeit VIII. Philosophisch," *TRE* 12 (1984) 443–448; Wolfgang von Leyden, *Aristotle on Equality and Justice: His Political Argument* (New York: St. Martin's Press, 1985); Johannes Triantaphyllopoulos, *Das Rechtsdenken der Griechen* (MBPF 78; München: Beck, 1985).

[19] Gottlob Schrenk, "δικαιοσύνη," *TDNT* 2 (1964) 193–198; Martin Fiedler, "Δικαιοσύνη in der diaspora-jüdischen und intertestamentarischen Literatur," *JSJ* 1 (1970) 120–143; Dihle, "Gerechtigkeit," 289–306; Ceslaus Spicq, *Notes de Lexicographie Neó-testamentaire* (OBO 22; 3 vols.; Fribourg: Editions Universitaires; Göttingen: Vandenhoeck & Ruprecht, 1978–1982) 3.120–151; Josef Scharbert, "Gerechtigkeit I. Altes Testament," *TRE* 12 (1984) 404–411; Asher Finkel, "Gerechtigkeit II. Judentum," *TRE* 12 (1984) 411–414; cf. Niebuhr, *Gesetz und Paränese*, 20–26; Thomas, *Der jüdische Phokylides*, 161–170.

Phocylides in the unveiling of his ethical perspective and appeal is shared by other ancient authors – Cicero and Philo for instance – who ranked it as the foremost of the canon of virtues. Philo's treatment of δικαιοσύνη is particularly instructive inasmuch as it additionally reflects the general tendency in Second Temple Judaism to present justice as the recapitulation of the Torah and one of its central objectives for human life.[20] Judging at least from the extant fragments, the original Phocylides, Phocylides of Miletus, also valued justice above all other virtues;[21] this common standpoint may supply another reason why the author of our poem appropriated the pseudonym that he did.

Two distinct sections comprise Pseudo-Phocylides' teaching on justice in verses 9–54. The first, verses 9–21, arrays a series of maxims that address more or less directly the subject of justice whereas the second, verses 22–54, raises a number of different topics all of which are associated with the explication of justice though they do not speak to it directly. Another way of putting this is that the first section conveys exhortation on justice in a more narrow, technical sense, while the second conveys exhortation on its broader implications for moral thought and action. The logical progression of the exhortation is somewhat reminiscent of the Stoic subdivisions of the virtues in so far as the headings of the second section may be understood as being subordinate or auxiliary to the main topic. In this way the exhortation on justice in verses 9–21 appears to have generated or attracted additional thematic groups of sayings by way of clarification and elaboration. In verses 9–54, as throughout the poem, a number of formal devices are at work connecting individual verses in order to create unified clusters and paragraphs. Among the more important devices are ring composition, inclusio, catchword (including anaphoric and epistropic catchword), and linkword.

The maxims in the first section regarding justice, verses 9–21, have been organized according to ring composition, a literary pattern that occurs regularly in gnomic writings.[22] Here the author renders advice in the area of justice in its stricter, particularly legal, sense. Accordingly, the language of the courtroom echoes throughout the passage, and terms containing the δικ stem run throughout these lines as a thread,[23] though other catchwords are used here as well.[24] The contents of the paragraph may be outlined as follows:

---

[20] See below, pp. 171–172; see also van der Horst, *Sentences*, 75, n. 19.

[21] See below, pp. 153–154, 171.

[22] See Wilson, *Love Without Pretense*, s.v. ring composition.

[23] δίκαια (v. 9), ἀδίκως (v. 10), δικάσῃς, δικάσσει (v. 11), τὰ δίκαια (v. 12), τὰ δίκαια (v. 14), ἀδικεῖν, ἀδικοῦντα (v. 21); for similar applications of this stem cf. Hesiod, *Opera et Dies* 213–224, 274–285 (with West, *Works and Days*, 209–212, 226–229); Theognis 731–752; Sextus, *Sententiae* 63–66; *Comparatio Menandri et Philistionis* 4.39–52.

[24] κρίσιν (v. 9) and κρῖνε (v. 10); πᾶσι (v. 13) and ἄπασι (v. 14); ἐπιορκήσῃς (v. 16) and ψεύδορκον (v. 17); and ὅστις (vv. 17 and 18). Also note how vv. 12 and 13 begin and end similarly: μαρτυρίην ... βραβεύειν (v. 12) and παρθεσίην ... φυλάσσειν (v. 13).

9	A. On striving for justice
10	B. Against oppressing the poor
11	C. God's punishment of injustice
12	D. Against false witness
13	E. An example of fair dealing: guarding a deposit
14	F. General principle on just measures
15	E'. An example of fair dealing: honest balances
16	D'. Against perjury
17	C'. God's anger with perjurers
18–20	B'. Against oppressing others, among them the poor
21	A'. On striving for justice

It should be emphasized that the arrangement of verses in this ring composition, like most, does not rely on precise formal or ideational connections, and the different structural pairs (A and A', etc.) correspond in various ways.[25] Here, as elsewhere, the elements located at the extremities (A and A') and the center (F) take on special prominence. The maxims in verses 9 and 21 (A and A') contain broad topical statements, antithetically formulated, that establish the material focus and rhetorical stance of the section, forming an envelope around the more concrete injunctions and illustrations of justice and injustice in verses 10–20. The precept in verse 14, which constitutes the turning-point of the ring (F), conveys a similarly broad appeal that seems to be especially foundational for the section, particularly in its reference to τὸ μέτρον, "due measure".[26] In verses 10 and 18–20 (B and B') the author counsels against oppressing and taking advantage of others. This applies above all to the poor (verses 10 and 19b), though the advice pertains also to those whose seeds are vulnerable to theft (verse 18), to laborers (verse 19a), and to those who have taken the reader into their confidence (verse 20). The subject of both verses 11 and 17 (C and C') is God, who punishes individuals who act unjustly, specifically anyone who judges evilly (verse 11) or falsely swears (verse 17). Both verses 12 and 16 (D and D') advise against dishonest speech, with the injunction against perjury (whether it be done unknowingly or deliberately) in verse 16 perhaps entailing an intensification of the charge to flee false witness and choose just things in verse 12. In verses 13 and 15 (E and E') we meet with imperatives regarding relatively specific actions – safeguarding a deposit and weighing with an honest scale – each of which provides an illustration of fair dealing that involves the handling of goods or money.[27]

Following Derron, the maxims in the next paragraph, verses 22–41, may be grouped under the title περὶ φιλανθρωπίας. This term, to be sure, does not occur anywhere in the paragraph. It is clear, however, that all of its individual

---

[25] The repetition of specific terms strengthens the correspondence of structural pairs in certain cases: δίκαια (v. 9) and ἀδικεῖν, ἀδικοῦντα (v. 21); μὴ θλίψῃς (v. 10) and μὴ θλῖβε (v. 19); πενίην (v. 10) and πένητα (v. 19); θεός (vv. 11 and 17).

[26] Cf. Thomas, *Der jüdische Phokylides*, 141–159.

[27] Cf. Philo, *De Specialibus Legibus* 4.30 ff., 4.193–194.

precepts address in one way or another the humane treatment of different sorts of people. Additionally, these verses furnish as a whole a fairly effective picture of the ethical ideals and criteria for action generally associated in antiquity with φιλανθρωπία, such as mercy, fairness, and goodwill in one's conduct towards others.

As Derron also notes, the exhortation in this paragraph constitutes an extension of the preceding instruction on justice (verses 9–21), amplifying its humanitarian dimension. The way that the author carries forward the argument here is by-and-large consistent with the more widespread body of thought in ancient ethics that maintained that justice not only entails obedience to the law and the avoidance of harmful deeds but also ought to encourage positive actions motivated by a sense of fairness and compassion.[28] Moral philosophers frequently voiced the opinion that justice in its higher or more adequate sense makes ethical demands beyond mere compliance with the law or the equitable distribution of goods, and, in connection with this, that it is predicated upon moral standards of humanity (φιλανθρωπία) that are to some extent above and separate from the law.[29] Typical of Jewish attitudes is Wisdom of Solomon 12.19, which declares that the person who is righteous must also be humane and that God's actions in history are models of such humanity.[30] Another Jewish author, Philo, often introduces certain concepts and topics generally associated with φιλανθρωπία and ἔλεος ("mercy")[31] into his analysis of δικαιοσύνη

---

[28] The objectives of "equity" (ἐπιείκεια) and "equality" (ἰσότης) often figured prominently in ancient discussions of justice; see Spicq, *Notes*, 1.263–267, 3.351–360; Triantaphyllopoulos, *Das Rechtsdenken der Griechen*, 17–23, 142–179, and s.v. ἐπιείκεια.

[29] φιλανθρωπία is a prominent concept in ancient ethics and it has an important connection with justice; see Bolkestein, *Wohltätigkeit und Armenpflege*, 102–114, 133–149, and s.v. φιλανθρωπία; Glanville Downey, "Philanthropia in Religion and Statescraft in the Fourth Century After Christ," *Historia* 4 (1955) 199–208; Ferguson, *Moral Values*, 42–45, 102–117; Jürgen Kabiersch, *Untersuchungen zum Begriff der Philanthropia bei dem Kaiser Julian* (KPS 21; Wiesbaden: Otto Harrassowitz, 1960) 26–48, 64–72; Ulrich Luck, "φιλανθρωπία, φιλανθρώπως," *TDNT* 9 (1974) 107–112; Hans Dieter Betz, ed., *Plutarch's Ethical Writings and Early Christian Literature* (SCHNT 4; Leiden: E.J. Brill, 1978) s.v. φιλανθρωπία, φιλάνθρωπος, φιλανθρώπως; Dihle, "Gerechtigkeit," 272–274; Spicq, *Notes*, 2.922–927; Triantaphyllopoulos, *Das Rechtsdenken der Griechen*, 137–139; Eilert Herms, "Humanität," *TRE* 15 (1986) 661–682.

[30] Cf. Wisdom of Solomon 1.6, 7.23; cf. Winston, *The Wisdom of Solomon*, 243–244; Larcher, *Le Livre de la Sagesse*, 1.179, 3.731; A. Pelletier, "La Philanthropia de Tous les Jours chez les Ecrivains Juifs Hellénisés," *Paganisme, Judaïsme, Christianisme: Influences et Affrontements dans le Monde Antique. Mélanges Offerts à Marcel Simon* (Paris: Editions E. de Boccard, 1978) 35–44.

[31] Mercy is central to the ancient Jewish conception of justice; see Bolkestein, *Wohltätigkeit und Armenpflege*, 34–66, 401–417, 428–429; Wolfson, *Philo*, 445–455; Rudolf Bultmann, "ἔλεος, κτλ.," *TDNT* 2 (1964) 477–487; Horst D. Preuß, "Barmherzigkeit I. Altes Testament," *TRE* 5 (1980) 215–224; Michael A. Signer, "Barmherzigkeit III. Judentum," *TRE* 5 (1980) 228–232; Henning G. Reventlow, "Gnade I. Altes Testament," *TRE* 13 (1984) 459–464; Robert Goldenberg, "Gnade II. Judentum," *TRE* 13 (1984) 465–

in an effort to bring the humanitarian dimension of justice into sharper relief.[32] We can detect such a fusion at work in the treatment of justice located in *De Specialibus Legibus* 4.136–238, where he allies with the virtue a number of moral obligations that pertain to φιλανθρωπία, many of which are familiar also from the commands offered in Pseudo-Phocylides' *Sentences* 22–41. For example, rulers should strive to extend justice to the helpless, strangers, widows, and orphans (4.176–178, compare 4.183–187), no one should mistreat the deaf or the blind (4.197–202), restraint should be demonstrated when confronting enemies (4.219–225), and crops should be spared from needless destruction (4.226–229). Not surprisingly, comparable themes turn up when Philo investigates the concept of φιλανθρωπία itself, for example, in *De Virtutibus* 51–174. Among those who must be dealt with humanely, says Philo, are the poor (§§ 90–94, 97–98, 121–123), strangers (§§ 102–108), and enemies (§§ 109–120); similar concern should be shown to the crops of the land, since people depend upon them for their survival (§§ 148–159). In *De Officiis* 1.7.20 ff., Cicero orients his presentation of justice in a similar fashion, linking justice with the goals of *beneficentia*, *benignitas*, and *liberalitas*. He proceeds at some length to demonstrate why and in what manner acts of kindness and generosity ought to be considered part of the virtue of justice, which should be extended not only to fellow citizens, family, and friends (1.17.53–59), but even to enemies (1.11.34–1.13.40), slaves (1.13.41), and strangers (1.16.51–52).[33]

Pseudo-Phocylides' paraenesis relating to φιλανθρωπία in *Sententiae* 22–41 contains four clusters of sayings, each based upon a different sort of named or implied referent: people who are destitute or in need (verses 22–30), enemies (verses 32–34), neighbors (verses 35, 38), and strangers (verses 39–41). These clusters appear to be arranged in no particular order, except perhaps for the priority attached to the advice concerning the needy in verses 22–30, which enjoys both the first position and the fullest treatment. This initial segment, which encourages the reader to be merciful to various types of individuals who are impoverished or otherwise in want, has been subdivided into two parts, distinguished by their function. The first part, verses 22–26, consists solely of

---

467; Hans-Helmut Esser, "Mercy," *NIDNTT* 2 (1986) 593–601; Ferdinand Staudinger, "ἔλεος," *EDNT* 1 (1990) 429–431. Also cf. the Testament of Zebulon, especially 5.1–4, 7.1–4, 8.1–6 on ἔλεος and εὐσπλαγχνία, with Hollander and de Jonge, *Testaments*, 253–275.

[32] For example, *De Decalogo* 164, *De Mutatione Nominum* 225, *De Specialibus Legibus* 2.63, 72, 96, *De Vita Mosis* 2.9. Philo also links the virtue of φιλανθρωπία with concepts such as κοινωνία ("fellowship"), ὁμόνοια ("concord"), ἰσότης ("equality"), and χάρις ("grace"); cf. *De Specialibus Legibus* 1.295, *De Virtutibus* 51; further cf. Wolfson, *Philo*, 2.218–221; Berger, *Die Gesetzesauslegung Jesu*, 156–160; M. D. van Veldhuizen, "Moses: A Model of Hellenistic Philanthropia," *Reformed Review* 38 (1985) 215–224.

[33] Cf. Ibscher, *Der Begriff des Sittlichen*, 19–54; Cicero, *De Officiis* 2.15.54 ff., 2.18.61–64; Plutarch, *De Stoicorum Repugnantiis* 1040 A–1042 A.

direct commands; these commands instruct the audience to render assistance of various kinds to different types of unfortunate people, many of whom belong to well-known categories in moral literature.[34] The sequence of referents – πτωχός ("a beggar"), χρήζων ("one in need"), ἄστεγος ("a homeless person"), τυφλός ("a blind man"), ναυηγός ("a shipwrecked sailor"), πεσών ("someone who has fallen"), ἀπερίστατον ἀνήρ ("an unprotected man") – creates thematic catchwords that link the verses together, while the use of the imperative δίδου at either end of the sequence (in both verses 22 and 26) creates an inclusio setting the segment apart from its immediate context. Verses 27–30 then support and expand upon the commands of verses 22–26 by providing some motivations and explanations germane to a consideration of mercy, supplying reasons why it is important and suggestions on how such acts should be fulfilled. This includes observations on the ubiquitous and indiscriminate nature of suffering and the instability of prosperity (verse 27), followed by an implicit acknowledgment that one must possess the necessary resources before it is possible to aid others (verse 28), and finally reminders about the origin of all sustenance in God and the unity of human existence (verses 29–30). The repetition of the key terms κοινός and ὁ βίος in verses 27 and 30 forms a frame around the subsection.[35]

The remainder of the paragraph illustrates φιλανθρωπία in three other types of social circumstances. Pseudo-Phocylides exhorts the recipients to refrain from unnecessary force against enemies (verses 32–34), not to trespass the property of others or destroy their crops (verses 35, 38), and to treat strangers with respect (verses 39–41). In verses 32–34, we find an appeal to refrain from unprovoked violence, particularly against an adversary. This cluster begins with a rule stating that when it is necessary to resort to violent force, one should use it only for self-protection and not for murder (verse 32). The next verse intensifies (and to some degree corrects) this rule by observing that ideally the reader ought to avoid violence altogether, even when some justification can be provided for such conduct. Verse 34 bolsters this line of reasoning by pointing out some of the negative implications of such acts, asserting that homicide defiles the aggressor. In verses 35 and 38, the author has placed two

---

[34] Cf. Bolkestein, *Wohltätigkeit und Armenpflege*, 34–66, 401–417; Hendrik Bolkestein and W. Schwer, "Almosen," *RAC* 1 (1950) 301–307; Hendrik Bolkestein and A. Kalsbach, "Armut I," *RAC* 1 (1950) 698–705; Franz Rosenthal, "Sedaka, Charity," *HUCA* 23 (1950–51) 411–430; Friedrich Hauck, "πένης, πενιχρός," *TDNT* 6 (1968) 37–40; Friedrich Hauck and Ernst Bammel, "πτωχός, κτλ.," *TDNT* 6 (1968) 885–915; W. den Boer, *Private Morality in Greece and Rome: Some Historical Aspects* (Mnemosyne Sup. 57; Leiden: E.J. Brill, 1979) 162–178; Diethelm Michel, "Armut II. Altes Testament," *TRE* 4 (1979) 72–76; Johann Maier, "Armut IV. Judentum," *TRE* 4 (1979) 80–85; Helmut Merklein, "πτωχός, κτλ.," *EWNT* 3 (1983) 466–472.

[35] Note also the repetition of χείρ in vv. 23, 26, and 28, and the similar endings of vv. 23 (χρήζοντι παράσχου) and 29 (χρήζουσι παράσχου).

prohibitions pertaining to the treatment of neighbors, the first a command not to trespass the property of one's neighbor, the second a warning against damaging the fruits of the land.[36] The final cluster of the paragraph contains advice for the audience to respect foreigners (verse 39), buttressed by the observations that both poverty and one of its primary causes, itinerancy, represent universal dilemmas (verse 40). Pseudo-Phocylides argues furthermore that at the root of such problems often lies the unpredictability of living off the land (verse 41).[37] These statements serve to remind the readers indirectly of how they themselves are susceptible to the same sorts of dangers that have forced other people to abandon their homes and wander in strange places.

Individually, each of the specific topics Pseudo-Phocylides raises in verses 22–41 – mercy for the poor and downtrodden, advice against unprovoked violence, and so forth – constitutes a fairly prominent heading in ancient gnomic sources, as recent studies have documented.[38] Also noteworthy are gnomic paragraphs that unite these or similar subjects in order to create unified appeals comparable to this passage with reference to their literary and argumentative character. *Papyrus Insinger* 15.21–16.19 is of special interest since it links its advice on φιλανθρωπία with injunctions against greed (15.8–20) in a manner akin to Pseudo-Phocylides' *Sentences* (see verses 42–47). Other parallels include Proverbs 3.27–35[39] and Ben Sira 3.17–4.10[40] and 29.1–20.[41]

At first glance the maxims of the next section of our poem, verses 42–54, seem unrelated to the central theme of justice. However, if it is recognized that each of the topical clusters here addresses different sources of injustice, particularly as they relate to individual ethical conduct, then the section plays an effective role in the overall presentation in so far as it stands as a negative

---

[36] Note how these verses end similarly: ἄρ' ὑπερβῇς (v. 35) and ἀρούρης (v. 38).

[37] Vv. 35, 38, and vv. 39–41 may be connected by thematic linkword: ἀγρός (v. 35), ἄρουρα (v. 38), χώρης ... πέδον (v. 41). Also, the reference to "poverty" (πενίη) in v. 40 recalls the "poor man" (πτωχός) of v. 20, forming an inclusio of sorts for the section.

[38] Van der Horst, *Sentences*, 128–142; Derron, *Sentences*, lii–lv, 4–5, 21–22. Pseudo-Aristotle, *De Virtutibus et Vitiis* 5.4–5 associates φιλανθρωπία and φιλοξενία with the virtue of ἐλευθεριότης; cf. Aristotle, *Ethica Nicomachea* 4.1.1–45.

[39] This passage opens with an exhortatory section stipulating the readers' obligations to render assistance to those in need (vv. 27–28) and to refrain from doing evil and violence (vv. 29–31), buttressed by an extended motivation in the form of antithetical wisdom sentences (vv. 32–35) that raise some prominent sapiential contrasts: transgressors vs. the righteous, cursing vs. blessing, the proud vs. the humble, and the wise vs. the unfaithful. Cf. McKane, *Proverbs*, 299–302; Wilson, *Love Without Pretense*, 96–105.

[40] Here the author joins together paraenesis on humility (3.17–29), almsgiving (3.30–4.6), and humanitarian conduct (4.7–10). Cf. Skehan and DiLella, *Ben Sira*, 158–168.

[41] The theme of Ben Sira 29.1–20 is the importance of generosity to people in need of assistance, with the subheadings of lending to others (vv. 1–7), giving alms to the poor (vv. 8–13), and going surety for a neighbor (vv. 14–20). Cf. Skehan and DiLella, *Ben Sira*, 368–372. Further cf. Isocrates, *Ad Nicoclem* 15–28, especially 15, 19–26.

counterpart to verses 22–41, which explored some of the positive aspects of the virtue for moral behavior. Comparison with the analysis of ἀδιϰία (the opposite of διϰαιοσύνη) in Pseudo-Aristotle's *De Virtutibus et Vitiis* 7.1–6 (1251A–B) sheds some light on the principle at work in the addition of verses 42–54 and on the logic of the section's internal construction. 'Aristotle' observes that there are three kinds (εἴδη) of unrighteousness – ἀσέβεια, πλεονεξία, and ὕβϱις – and then proceeds to define each of these vices.[42] Given the generally multicultural slant and ethical focus of Pseudo-Phocylides, as well as his tendency to omit references to anything specifically Jewish in nature, it comes as no surprise that he includes in his discussion of justice no detailed treatment of the first of these topics (though see verse 54). However, he does seem to raise the last two topics in this passage on justice. Verses 42–47 contain an invective against a particular type of greed, ἡ φιλοχϱημοσύνη, while the maxims in verses 48–54 attack particular types of wrongful behavior (hypocrisy, presumptuous intentions, and arrogance) all of which contribute in one fashion or another to the broader theme of hybris.[43]

For the most part, ancient moral thinkers concur that the various personal motives associated with greed are among the foremost sources of unjust actions, and that such motives characterize the vice of injustice. In the *Ethica Nicomachea*, for instance, Aristotle generally associates πλεονεξία with ἀδιϰία.[44] As he argues, if justice entails the fair distribution of goods, honor, and so forth according to what each person is legally entitled, the πλεονέϰτης brings about the unjust disruption of this balance by wanting more than he legally deserves or by wanting what rightfully belongs to someone else.[45] It follows that Jewish authors of the Hellenistic era also frequently attacked greed and related vices as being unjust and contrary to the divine order.[46]

---

[42] The author goes on to relate unrighteousness to such things as the transgression of agreements, lying, imposture, pretentiousness, and unscrupulousness.

[43] Cf. Thom, *Golden Verses*, 119.

[44] Cf. Bernard Williams, "Justice as a Virtue," *Essays on Aristotle's Ethics* (ed. Amélie O. Rorty; Major Thinkers Series 2; Berkeley, Los Angeles, London: University of California Press, 1980) 189–199; Troels Engberg-Pedersen, *Aristotle's Theory of Moral Insight* (Oxford: Clarendon, 1983) 39–40, 53–62. Cf. Theognis 465–466.

[45] On greed as a topic in ancient ethical thought see Gerhard Delling, "πλεονέϰτης, πλεονεϰτέω, πλεονεξία," *TDNT* 6 (1968) 266–274; Dihle, "Gerechtigkeit," 262, 269–271; Spicq, *Notes*, 2.704–706, 928–929; Karl Suso Frank, "Habsucht (Geiz)," *RAC* 13 (1986) 227–238; Kenneth J. Dover, *Greek Popular Morality in the Time of Plato and Aristotle* (Berkeley: University of California Press, 1974) 170–175, 180–184, 193. For illustrations of such critiques cast in the form of gnomic utterances see Stobaeus, *Anthologium* 3.10.

[46] Delling, "πλεονέϰτης," 269–270; van der Horst, *Sentences*, 142–146; Frank, "Habsucht," 235–238. Some examples: Ben Sira 8.2, 26.29–27.3, 31.6, 13; 4 Maccabees 1.26–30; Didache 3.5; this vice is regularly condemned in the Testaments of the Twelve Patriarchs also, for instance, Levi 14.6, Judah 17.1, 18.2, 19.1–2, 21.8, Dan 5.7, Naphtali 3.1, Gad 2.4, Benjamin 5.1; also in Philo's corpus, for instance, *De Confusione Linguarum*

In verses 42–47 of the *Sentences*, Pseudo-Phocylides critiques what was perhaps the most notorious species of greed, the love of money.[47] The initial gnome (verse 42), which has the appearance of a reformulated proverb, stands as a general heading and 'text', with verses 43–47 serving as a more specific commentary or elucidation.[48] Thus the opening verse operates as a condensation-point for additional, subordinate maxims and other materials (including an extended apostrophe to Gold in verses 44–47), creating a cluster of related sayings.[49] In keeping with the general tenor of the section on justice, the author highlights the social aspects of this vice, especially in verses 46–47, where he laments the fact that greed incites heinous crimes and breaks families apart. Comparably formulated paragraphs on this theme are located elsewhere in gnomic literature, for example, Ben Sira 26.29–27.3[50] and *Papyrus Insinger* 15.12–19.[51]

In verses 48–54, the author has placed different maxims that fall under the heading of hybris, a popular though complex and multi-faceted concept in Hellenistic philosophy and literature. It represented an especially prominent topic in gnomic sources, and beginning at least with Hesiod and Theognis gnomic authors tended to view hybris as the moral antithesis of justice.[52] Generally, they employed the term hybris to characterize both the insolent or arrogant attitude of an individual and the destructive actions that could stem from such a disposition. This arrogance could be interpreted as a form of self-deception or self-deceit that has negative ramifications for one's relationships

---

46–48, *De Specialibus Legibus* 1.281, *De Vita Mosis* 2.186, *Legum Allegoriae* 1.75–76, *Quod Omnis Probus Liber Sit* 21.

[47] This section elaborates on a theme touched upon earlier in the poem, cf. vv. 5–6, 13–15, 18–19, 28–30.

[48] Cf. Wilson, *Love Without Pretense*, 48–49; Thomas, *Der jüdische Phokylides*, 170, 429–430.

[49] Cf. Skehan and DiLella, *Ben Sira*, 24–25.

[50] Cf. Skehan and DiLella, *Ben Sira*, 353–356; also cf. Ben Sira 31.12–21 and the Testament of Judah (regarding φιλαργυρία) especially 17.1–19.4, with Harm W. Hollander and Marinus de Jonge, *The Testaments of the Twelve Patriarchs: A Commentary* (SVTP 8; Leiden: E.J. Brill, 1985) 184–232.

[51] Cf. Lichtheim, *Late Egyptian Wisdom*, 212; van der Horst, "Pseudo-Phocylides Revisited," 19; also cf. Pseudo-Isocrates, *Ad Demonicum* 36–39; Isocrates, *Nicocles* 29–35, 48 ff.

[52] On ὕβρις as the antithesis of justice see Hesiod, *Opera et Dies* 213–285, with West, *Works and Days*, 209–229; Theognis 40, 151, 153, 291, 307, 379, 541, 603, 732, 835, 1103, 1174, and Figueira and Nagy, *Theognis of Megara*, s.v. hybris; von Arnim, *Stoicorum Veterum Fragmenta*, 3.152.28–36; Schmidt, *Die Ethik der alten Griechen*, s.v. ὕβρις; also the sources listed below in n. 53. Hybris was also understood as the opposite of *sophrosyne*, and, in so far as the admonitions in vv. 48–54 also relate to the explication of this virtue, these verses operate as a transition to the following section (vv. 55–96) as well as the conclusion of vv. 9–54. See Plato, *Leges* 906 A–B, *Philebus* 45 D–E; Aristotle, *Politica* 7.13.18; Isocrates, *De Pace* 119; Iamblichus, *De Vita Pythagorica* 30.174–175; North, *Sophrosyne*, 58–61; Wilson, *Love Without Pretense*, s.v. σωφροσύνη.

with others, particularly with the deity or deities.[53] To be sure, the word ὕβϱις itself does not occur in these lines of our poem and the author makes no attempt to equip his audience with anything like a thorough treatment of its moral characteristics or negative implications. Rather, the exhortation in each of the three thematic sub-divisions in verses 48–54 introduces one specific type of hybristic conduct that is in some manner illustrative of the vice itself. The first cluster of sayings, verses 48–50, conveys an appeal for the reader to refrain from hypocrisy and opportunism and to be sincere in all circumstances.[54] The argument proceeds in verses 51–52 with the assertion that although it is impossible for the author to ascertain what consequences await those who act unjustly under compulsion, those who act unjustly freely or willfully (ἑκών ἀδικεῖ) he judges to be plainly κακοί. Thus the paraenesis here involves an attack on unjust intentions and on plotting to do wrong.[55] The final lines of the section, verses 53–54, counsel the recipients against arrogance by reminding them that the only true wisdom, power, and wealth belong to God.[56] This advice most clearly relates to the critique of hybris, and may serve as a

---

[53] See Jozua J. Fraenkel, *Hybris* (Utrecht: P. den Boer, 1941); North, *Sophrosyne*, s.v. hybris; Hans von Gersau, "Hybris," *KP* 2 (1967) 1257–1258; Georg Betram, "ὕβϱις, κτλ.," *TDNT* 8 (1972) 295–307; Douglas M. MacDowell, "Hybris in Athens," *Greece and Rome* 23 (1976) 14–31; N. R. E. Fisher, "Hybris and Dishonour," *Greece and Rome* 23 (1976) 177–193; idem, *Hybris: Study in Values* (Warminster: Aris & Phillips, n.d.); Wilson, *Love Without Pretense*, 179–186.

[54] On the critique of hypocrisy in antiquity see BAGD s.v. ὑποκϱίνομαι, ὑπόκϱισις, ὑποκϱιτής; Günther Bornkamm, "Heuchelei," *RGG³* 3 (1959) 305–306; Ulrich Wilckens, "ὑποκϱίνομαι, κτλ.," *TDNT* 8 (1972) 559–571; idem, with Alois Kehl and Karl Hoheisel, "Heuchelei," *RAC* 14 (1988) 1205–1231, especially 1206–1215; Heinz Giesen, "ὑπόκϱισις, ὑποκϱιτής," *EWNT* 3 (1983) 963–966; Spicq, *Notes*, 3.650–657; Wilson, *Love Without Pretense*, 152–155, 180–186; cf. Harald Patzer's review of Bruno Zucchelli, *ΥΠΟΚΡΙΤΗΣ: Origine e Storia del Termine* (Brescia: Paideia, 1963) in *Gnomon* 42 (1970) 641–652 [reprint, idem, *Gesammelte Schriften* (Stuttgart: Steiner, 1985) 261–272]. On vv. 48–50 cf. Joseph Amstutz, *ΑΠΛΟΤΗΣ: Eine begriffsgeschichtliche Studie zum jüdisch-christlichen Griechisch* (Theophaneia, Beiträge zur Religions- und Kirchengeschichte des Altertums 19; Bonn: Peter Hanstein, 1968) 42. Note also how vv. 48 and 50 end similarly: ἀγοϱεύων (v. 48) and ἀγόϱευε (v. 50). Also, to a certain extent the thoughts here have been anticipated by previous maxims, especially vv. 7 and 20.

[55] In the background of vv. 51–52 is the distinction drawn in LXX Numbers 15.29–30 between sinning inadvertently and sinning presumptuously: τῷ ἐγχωϱίῳ ἐν υἱοῖς Ἰσϱαὴλ καὶ τῷ πϱοσηλύτῳ τῷ πϱοσκειμένῳ ἐν αὐτοῖς νόμος εἷς ἔσται αὐτοῖς, ὃς ἂν ποιήσῃ ἀκουσίως. καὶ ψυχή, ἥτις ποιήσει ἐν χειϱὶ ὑπεϱηφανίας ἀπὸ τῶν αὐτοχθόνων ἢ ἀπὸ τῶν πϱοσηλύτων, τὸν θεὸν οὗτος παϱοξυνεῖ· κτλ.; see van der Horst, *Sentences*, 123, who also refers to 1QS 8.17–24; Str-B 2.264; Friedrich Hauck, "ἑκών, κτλ.," *TDNT* 2 (1964) 469–470; Ceslaus Spicq, *Les Epitres Pastorales* (4th ed.; EBib; 2 vols.; Paris: J. Gabalda, 1969) 1.342; also cf. LSJ s.v. ὑπεϱηφανία.

[56] Note the catchword, σοφίη (v. 53) and σοφός (v. 54), as well as several thematic linkwords. Cf. Thomas, *Der jüdische Phokylides*, 193–194. Also, the phrase εἷς θεός κτλ. at the beginning of v. 54 recalls the earlier references to God, particularly πϱῶτα θεόν κτλ. in v. 8 (cf. vv. 1, 11, 17, 29), and these phrases bracket the section on justice in vv. 9–54.

concluding summary of the preceding exhortation in verses 42 ff. In this respect these maxims function similarly to what teachers of Greco-Roman oratory sometimes termed the ἐπιφώνημα or *clausula* (compare also verses 69 B and 131).[57]

A number of Cicero's remarks in *De Officiis* attest to how the sorts of considerations Pseudo-Phocylides raises in verses 42–54 can be integrated into an explication of the virtue of justice. Cicero notes, for example, that greed and ambition often cause individuals to lose sight of the responsibilities dictated by justice, adding that in measuring the culpability of an unjust act one must take into account whether the offender committed it willfully and with premeditation or not (1.8.25–27). Elsewhere he arrives at a similar conclusion regarding those people who are absorbed with their own self-interest (1.9.29–30), and he demonstrates how such misdeeds as chicanery, fraud, and false posturing can foment injustice (1.10.33). Analogous combinations of themes occur in Hellenistic gnomic exhortation as well, for example, Ben Sira 5.1–6.4, which links prescriptions against arrogance (especially verses 1–2) and sinning (verses 4–6) with a condemnation of deceitful wealth (verse 8) and hypocrisy (verses 9 ff.).[58]

We can draw the analysis of this section to a close by noting how literary patterns comparable to those at work in Pseudo-Phocylides' discussion of justice in verses 9–54 as a unit are visible in other gnomic documents as well, for example, the 21st instruction of *Papyrus Insinger* (25.14–27.21), entitled "The teaching not to slight lest you be slighted."[59] Although in organizing the aphorisms of this text the author follows logical and literary principles that are clearly looser in nature than those of the *Sententiae*, he has assembled similar types of gnomic materials, all of which relate to the overriding theme of justice. Accordingly, within the instruction we come across a paragraph of injunctions repudiating unjust conduct, particularly in monetary and legal matters (26.18–27.1),[60] among clusters of sayings on ethical issues analogous to those set forth in verses 22–54 of the *Sentences*, including greed (25.15–19), lying (25.21–23), violence (27.4–9), and arrogance (27.16–21). The unit also embraces a sequence of maxims that advise on correct behavior vis-à-vis different sorts of individuals, among them the needy, enemies, and neighbors (26.1–6). Given the prominent place they occupy in works like the *Sentences* and *Papyrus Insinger*, it should occasion no surprise that justice and the vari-

---

[57] Pseudo-Aristotle, *Rhetorica ad Alexandrum* 39; Demetrius, *De Elocutione* 2.106–110; Quintilian, *Institutio Oratoria* 8.5.10–14; Lausberg, *Handbuch*, §§ 875, 879; Martin, *Rhetorik*, 257; Wilson, *Love Without Pretense*, 49–50, 197–198.

[58] Cf. Skehan and DiLella, *Ben Sira*, 179–185. Also cf. Syriac Menander, *Sentences* 176–180.

[59] Cf. Lichtheim, *Late Egyptian Wisdom*, 223–225.

[60] See above, pp. 81–82; cf. *Papyrus Insinger* 27.11–15.

ous moral topics associated with it represented subjects of keen interest for gnomic writers, as texts such as Ben Sira 7.1–14,[61] Ankhsheshonqy 14.18–15.25,[62] Pseudo-Isocrates' *Ad Demonicum* 36–39,[63] and Isocrates' *Ad Nico-clem* 15–29[64] also attest.

Exhortation on Topics Relating to Moderation (verses 55–96)

The second major division of the exhortation structured according to the Canon of Cardinal Virtues is verses 55–96; it contains paragraphs of moral sayings that contribute to the theme of σωφϱοσύνη. The positioning of this unit and the relatively large number of lines it occupies appear to represent a meaningful decision. As noted above, moral philosophers sometimes ranked justice and self-restraint together as the most significant or the most beneficial of the four, and the configuration of the paraenesis structured according to the virtues in the *Sententiae* suggests that its author shared in this view.[65] In addition, these two virtues share something on the ideational level. As Thom observes, Greek thinkers beginning at least with Democritus depicted σωφϱοσύνη as the internalization by the individual of those principles dictated by δικαιοσύνη, principles that primarily concern the regulation of social life. Thus moderation and justice are moral counterparts, so to speak, the former being "the internal principle of moral control, with justice as its external social

---

[61] The group of injunctions in Ben Sira 7.1 ff. commences with topic sentences attacking evil and injustice: "Do no evil, neither let evil overtake you; avoid wickedness, and it will turn aside from you. Sow not in the furrows of injustice, lest you harvest it sevenfold." The author proceeds with counsel against arrogance and abuses of justice, particularly in a court of law (vv. 4–8), coupled with advice to render honest and humble service to God (vv. 9 and 14), not to scorn an unfortunate person (v. 11), to contrive no mischief against others (v. 12), and to tell no lies (v. 13). Cf. Skehan and DiLella, *Ben Sira*, 197–202.

[62] The text here includes recommendations not to trespass on a neighbor's land (14.21), to do good to others without expectation of acknowledgment (15.5–6), and to avoid deceit (15.9, 18–19), greed (15.10, 14), and evil (15.17, 19); it includes also a version of the golden rule in 15.23. Cf. Lichtheim, *Late Egyptian Wisdom*, 43–45.

[63] In this unit, 'Isocrates' asserts the noble and enduring character of δικαιοσύνη, encouraging the reader to strive for justice from a sense of ἐπιείκεια, not from a position of weakness or for the sake of gain. As a means of achieving this goal the reader should imitate the character and conduct of those in positions of authority, obeying the laws, selecting trustworthy people for important positions, and supporting only just causes. Cf. Norlin, *Isocrates*, 48–57.

[64] See above, pp. 49–51. Further cf. *Gnomologium Democrateum* 43–50.

[65] For example Plato, *Phaedo* 82A–B, *Protagoras* 323A; Isocrates, *Nicocles* 29–30; Philo, *De Abrahamo* 103, *De Opificio Mundi* 81, *De Praemiis et Poenis* 15, *Quod Deterius Potiori Insidiari Soleat* 143; cf. Christopher J. Rowe, "Justice and Temperance in Republic IV," *Arktouros: Hellenic Studies Presented to Bernard M. W. Knox* (ed. Glen W. Bowersock, Walter Burkert, Michael C. J. Putnam; Berlin and New York: de Gruyter, 1979) 336–344.

manifestation."[66] Thus Pseudo-Phocylides raises the logical complement to the preceding exhortation pertaining to justice in this section on moderation, which I have outlined as follows:

55–69 B	I.	Maxims on exercising self-control, especially regarding the emotions
55–59		A. Introduction
55–58		1. Complementary injunctions on a specific level
55–56		a. On self-control with respect to personal actions
55		i. Command: don't be emotionally overwhelmed by evils already committed
56		ii. Reason: events of the past cannot be altered
57–58		b. On self-control with respect to social actions
57		i. Commands
57 a		a. Avoid rash violence
57 b		b. Control anger
58		ii. Reason: uncontrolled violence can lead to unintended murder
59		2. A general rule on moderation: let your emotions be moderate
60–68		B. Sequence of indicative statements against excessiveness
60–64		1. First list, mostly in the form of cause-and-effect statements
60		a. General statement: anything gained that is not good is superfluous
61–64		b. More specific ancillary statements
61		i. Great luxuriousness leads to ignoble desires
62		ii. Great wealth leads to hybris
63		iii. Overwhelming anger leads to fury
64		iv. Excessive wrath leads to madness
65–68		2. Second list, mostly in the form of contrastive statements
65		a. General statement: emulation of good things vs. emulation of bad things
66–68		b. More specific ancillary statements
66		i. Daring in evil deeds vs. daring in good deeds
67		ii. Love of virtue vs. love of passion
68		iii. The one who tries to please everyone is a fool (contrast of intention and result)
69–69 B		C. Conclusion
69		1. Complementary injunctions on a specific level
69 a		a. On self-control with respect to personal actions: eat and drink in moderation
69 b		b. On self-control with respect to social actions: talk in moderation
69 B		2. A general rule on moderation: moderation is best of all, but excesses are grievous
70–96	II.	Exhortation on avoiding envy through moderation
70		A. Thesis statement: admonition against envy
71–75		B. Descriptive section: the example of the cosmos
71		1. An assertion regarding the lack of envy among the "heavenly ones"
72–74 a		2. Three specific illustrations of this assertion
72		a. The moon does not envy the sun
73		b. The earth does not envy the heavens
74 a		c. The rivers do not envy the seas

---

[66] Thom, *Golden Verses*, 113, cf. 111–112; he cites also Dihle, "Gerechtigkeit," 250–252; North, *Sophrosyne*, 9, 87, 189; Acts 24.25; *Corpus Hermeticum* 13.18.

Text:

55 μὴ δὲ παροιχομένοισι κακοῖς τρύχου τεὸν ἧπαρ·
56 οὐκέτι γὰρ δύναται τὸ τετυγμένον εἶναι ἄτυκτον.
57 μὴ προπετὴς ἐς χεῖρα, χαλίνου δ᾽ ἄγριον ὀργήν·
58 πολλάκι γὰρ πλήξας ἀέκων φόνον ἐξετέλεσσεν.
59 ἔστω κοινὰ πάθη· μηδὲν μέγα μηδ᾽ ὑπέροπλον.
60 οὐκ ἀγαθὸν πλεονάζον ἔφυ θνητοῖσιν ὄνειαρ·
61 ἡ πολλὴ δὲ τρυφὴ πρὸς ἀσέμνους ἕλκετ᾽ ἔρωτας·
62 ὑψαυχεῖ δ᾽ ὁ πολὺς πλοῦτος καὶ ἐς ὕβριν ἀέξει.
63 θυμὸς ὑπερχόμενος μανίην ὀλοόφρονα τεύχει.
64 ὀργὴ δ᾽ ἐστὶν ὄρεξις, ὑπερβαίνουσα δὲ μῆνις.
65 ζῆλος τῶν ἀγαθῶν ἐσθλός, φαύλων δ᾽ ὑπέρογκος.
66 τόλμα κακῶν ὀλοή, μέγ᾽ ὀφέλλει δ᾽ ἐσθλὰ πονεῦντα.
67 σεμνὸς ἔρως ἀρετῆς, ὁ δὲ κύπριδος αἶσχος ὀφέλλει.
68 ἡδὺς ἄγαν ἄφρων κικλήσκεται ἐν πολιήταις.
69 μέτρῳ ἔδειν, μέτρῳ δὲ πιεῖν καὶ μυθολογεύειν.
69B πάντων μέτρον ἄριστον, ὑπερβασίαι δ᾽ ἀλεγειναί.
70 μὴ φθονέοις ἀγαθῶν ἑτάροις, μὴ μῶμον ἀνάψῃς.
71 ἄφθονοι οὐρανίδαι καὶ ἐν ἀλλήλοις τελέθουσιν.
72 οὐ φθονέει μήνη πολὺ κρείσσοσιν ἡλίου αὐγαῖς,
73 οὐ χθὼν οὐρανίοισ᾽ ὑψώμασι νέρθεν ἐοῦσα,
74 οὐ ποταμοὶ πελάγεσσιν· ἀεὶ δ᾽ ὁμόνοιαν ἔχουσιν·
75 εἰ γὰρ ἔρις μακάρεσσιν ἔην, οὐκ ἂν πόλος ἔστη.
76 σωφροσύνην ἀσκεῖν, αἰσχρῶν δ᾽ ἔργων ἀπέχεσθαι.
77 μὴ μιμοῦ κακότητα, δίκῃ δ᾽ ἀπόλειψον ἄμυναν.
78 πειθὼ μὲν γὰρ ὄνειαρ, ἔρις δ᾽ ἔριν ἀντιφυτεύει.
79 μὴ πίστευε τάχιστα, πρὶν ἀτρεκέως πέρας ὄψει.
80 νικᾶν εὖ ἔρδοντας ἐπὶ πλεόνεσσι καθήκει.
81 καλὸν ξεινίζειν ταχέως λιταῖσι τραπέζαις
82 ἢ πλείσταις θαλίαισι βραδυνούσαις παρὰ καιρόν.
83 μηδέποτε χρήστης πικρὸς γένῃ ἀνδρὶ πένητι.
84 μηδέ τις ὄρνιθας καλιῆς ἅμα πάντας ἑλέσθω,
85 μητέρα δ᾽ ἐκπρολίποις, ἵν᾽ ἔχῃς πάλι τῆσδε νεοσσούς.
86 μηδέποτε κρίνειν ἀδαήμονας ἄνδρας ἐάσῃς.
[87]
88 τὴν σοφίην σοφὸς εὐθύνει, τέχνας δ᾽ ὁμότεχνος.
89 οὐ χωρεῖ μεγάλην διδαχὴν ἀδίδακτος ἀκουή·
90 οὐ γὰρ δὴ νοέουσ᾽ οἱ μηδέποτ᾽ ἐσθλὰ μαθόντες.
91 μὴ δὲ τραπεζοκόρους κόλακας ποιεῖσθαι ἑταίρους·
92 πολλοὶ γὰρ πόσιος καὶ βρώσιός εἰσιν ἑταῖροι
93 καιρὸν θωπεύοντες, ἐπὴν κορέσασθαι ἔχωσιν,

94 ἀχθόμενοι δ᾽ ὀλίγοις καὶ πολλοῖς πάντες ἄπληστοι.
95 λαῷ μὴ πίστευε, πολύτροπός ἐστιν ὅμιλος·
96 λαὸς ⟨γὰρ⟩ καὶ ὕδωρ καὶ πῦρ ἀκατάσχετα πάντα.

Translation:

55 Exhaust not your liver over bygone ills;
56 for what's been done can be undone no more.
57 Be not prone to acts of violence; bridle your wild anger;
58 for often with a blow one unintentionally commits murder.
59 Let emotions be moderate; let nothing be grandiose or insolent.[67]
60 A gain that is not good is superfluous for mortals.[68]
61 Great luxuriousness leads to ignoble[69] desires.
62 Great wealth is boastful and fosters hybris.
63 Anger that steals over one brings on baneful fury.
64 Wrath is a desire, but when it goes too far it is madness.
65 Emulation of good things is noble, but of bad things, monstrous.[70]
66 Boldness is destructive in evil deeds, but greatly profits one laboring for good ones.
67 Love of virtue is noble, but love of passion earns shame.
68 One who is too pleasant[71] is among the citizens called senseless.
69 Eat in moderation, drink in moderation, and converse (in moderation).
69B Of all things moderation is best, but excesses are grievous.
70 Envy not the goods of friends; do not place blame on them.
71 The heavenly ones are quite without even envy among themselves:
72 the moon does not envy the sun's much stronger rays,
73 nor the earth the heavenly heights though it is below,[72]
74 nor the rivers the seas. Rather they always have concord.
75 For if strife were among the blessed ones, the firmament would not stand firm.
76 Practice moderation, and refrain from shameful deeds.
77 Do not imitate evil, but leave vengeance to justice.[73]
78 For while persuasion is an advantage, strife sows strife in turn.

---

[67] Following the proposed translation of Edward O'Neil (personal communication, 5/15/92); cf. Derron, *Sentences*, 7: "Il faut des sentiments normaux: point d'excès ni d'orgueil."

[68] Cf. van der Horst, *Sentences*, 153: "Excess, even of good, is never a boon to mortals"; Walter, *Poetische Schriften*, 203: "Denn (selbst) Gutes bringt, (wenn es) im Übermaß (kommt), den Sterblichen kein Heil"; and Derron, *Sentences*, 7: "Surabondance de bien ne profite pas aux mortels."

[69] Reading ἀσέμνους with P, L, V, and printed by Bergk (*Poetae Lyrici Graeci*, 90) and Bernays (*Gesammelte Abhandlungen*, 256), against ἀμέτρους ("boundless") in M, B, Vᵞᵖ, Σ, which is printed by Diehl (*Anthologia*, 2.102), Young (*Theognis*, 101), and Derron (*Sentences*, 7), followed by van der Horst (*Sentences*, 154) and Walter (*Poetische Schriften*, 203).

[70] Only one ms., M, reads ὑπέρογκος. B, P, L²ᵞᵖ, V have ὑποεργός. Vᵞᵖ has ἄδηλος (printed by Bergk [*Poetae Lyrici Graeci*, 90] and Bernays [*Gesammelte Abhandlungen*, 256]; cf. v. 194). For discussion see van der Horst, *Sentences*, 157–158. On the translation cf. Walter, *Poetische Schriften*, 204: "Eifer um Gutes ist edel, um Schlimmes ist er unerträglich"; Derron, *Sentences*, 7: "L'émulation pour le bien est noble; pour de vils objets, elle est exagérée."

[71] Cf. van der Horst, *Sentences*, 159–160: "A man who is too simple, etc." Walter, *Poetische Schriften*, 204: "(Wer sich jedermann) allzu angenehm (macht), usw." Derron, *Sentences*, 7: "L'homme trop conciliant, etc." Cf. van der Horst, "Pseudo-Phocylides Revisited," 20–21.

[72] Following the translation for v. 73 of van der Horst, *Sentences*, 164–165.

[73] Following the translation of van der Horst, *Sentences*, 166–167.

79   Trust not quickly before you truly see the end.
80   To outdo one's benefactors with further benefactions is fitting.
81   It is better to entertain guests promptly with simple meals
82   than with many festivities[74] extending beyond due time.
83   Never become a harsh creditor to a poor man.
84   Let no one take all the birds from a nest at the same time,
85   but leave behind the mother so that you may again have her young.
86   Never allow untrained men to judge.
[87][75]
88   A wise man manages wisdom, a fellow-craftsman, crafts.
89   An untaught ear does not grasp a great teaching;
90   for surely those who never learned good things do not comprehend.
91   Make not table-clearing flatterers your companions.
92   For many are companions of drinking and eating,[76]
93   beguiling time whenever they can satisfy themselves,
94   all being annoyed with little and insatiable with much.[77]
95   Trust not the people: the mob is shifty.
96   ‹For› people and water and fire are ever uncontrollable.

Helen North has admirably chronicled the fairly long and complex history of *sophrosyne* in Greek, Roman, Jewish, and Christian thought.[78] As a general observation, it appears that, especially in the philosophical literature, this virtue encompasses both the intellectual and spiritual objective of proper self-understanding (often being linked with the interpretation of the Delphic maxim γνῶθι σαυτόν) and the goal of obtaining self-mastery and observing moderation in one's moral decision-making and conduct. It comes as no surprise that the latter interpretation is more prominent in paraenetic materials, and there survives an extensive and varied body of advice exhorting readers to master their irrational impulses and to control their passions as they pertain both to matters of personal welfare and to matters of a more inter-personal nature. As a practical matter, then, in the moral literature σωφροσύνη often overlaps in meaning with the prevalent Greek virtue of ἐγκράτεια, "self-control".[79] In

---

[74] Following Richard F. Ph. Brunck, *Gnomici Poetae Graeci* (2nd ed.; Leipzig: G. Fleischeri, 1817) 159, and van der Horst, *Sentences*, 93, n. 1, 170 who read θαλίαισι instead of δολίαισι, which is printed in Young, *Theognis*, 102, and Derron, *Sentences*, 8 (with the mss.). With the latter reading we might translate, "... than with many contrived (meals) that are long in coming," or "... than with many diversions that drag on too long."

[75] V. 87 (μηδὲ δίκην δικάσῃς, πρὶν ‹ἂν› ἄμφω μῦθον ἀκούσῃς. "Pass not judgment before you hear the word of both sides.") is spurious; see van der Horst, *Sentences*, 173–174.

[76] Edward O'Neil (personal communication, 5/15/92) suggests "... at drinking and eating," or "... over food and drink."

[77] For vv. 91–94, Edward O'Neil (personal communication, 5/15/92) refers to Plautus' description of the parasite Peniculus in the *Menaechmi* 77–119 and passim.

[78] Helen North, *Sophrosyne: Self-Knowledge and Self-Restraint in Greek Literature* (CSCP 35; Ithaca: Cornell University Press, 1966).

[79] On ἐγκράτεια see, for example, Plato, *Respublica* 430 D–431 D, *Definitiones* 412 A–B; Xenophon, *Memorabilia* 2.1.1–7, 4.5.1–11; Aristotle, *Ethica Nicomachea* 3.10.1–3.12.10, 7.1.1–7.9.7, with H. H. Joachim, *Aristotle: The Nicomachean Ethics* (Oxford: Clarendon,

turn, ancient ethicists associated both of these concepts with other social and ethical ideals, especially those relating to order (ὁμόνοια, κοσμιότης, εὐταξία, etc.) and to propriety (πρέπον).[80] These ideals are among the chief themes of gnomic wisdom as well, particularly in connection with the interpretation of the Delphic maxims μηδὲν ἄγαν and μέτρον ἄριστον. The traditions associated with these sayings, like a great deal of Greek ethical thought, urged individuals both to eschew excess and to aim for the ethical mean, what is generally considered measured or balanced.[81]

1951) 122–123, 219–233; Pseudo-Aristotle, *Magna Moralia* 2.4.1–2.6.44; von Arnim, *Stoicorum Veterum Fragmenta*, 3.64.23, 34, 3.65.12, 3.66.40, 3.67.20; Stobaeus, *Anthologium* 3.17; Philo, *De Iosepho* 153, *De Somniis* 1.124, *De Vita Contemplativa* 34; *Epistula Aristeas* 278; Aristobulus, *Fragmenta* 13.12.8; cf. North, *Sophrosyne*, s.v. enkrateia; Ferguson, *Moral Values*, 35; Dover, *Popular Morality*, 124–126; Walter Grundmann, "ἐγκράτεια, κτλ.," *TDNT* 2 (1964) 339–342; Henry Chadwick, "Enkrateia," *RAC* 5 (1965) 343–365; Betz, *Plutarch's Ethical Writings*, s.v. ἐγκράτεια; van der Horst, *Sentences*, 210; Spicq, *Notes*, 1.61–63; Thom, *Golden Verses*, 108–110; also cf. Galatians 5.23, with Betz, *Galatians*, 288–289. Further cf. David Wiggens, "Weakness of Will, Commensurability, and the Objects of Deliberation and Desire," in Rorty, *Essays*, 241–265; Amélie O. Rorty, "Akrasia and Pleasure: Nicomachean Ethics Book 7," in Rorty, *Essays*, 267–284. Also worth consulting are the series of articles assembled in Ugo Bianchi, ed., *La Tradizione dell'Enkrateia: Motivazioni Ontologiche e Protologiche* (Rome: Edizioni dell'Ateneo, 1985).

[80] For example, Plato, *Respublica* 430D–431D, 431E–432A; Pseudo-Aristotle, *De Virtutibus et Vitiis* 4.5; von Arnim, *Stoicorum Veterum Fragmenta*, 3.27.7, 3.64.22, 3.72.9, 3.73.6, 3.264; Cicero, *De Officiis* 1.27.93–1.42.151, with Lotte Labowsky, *Die Ethik des Panaitios: Untersuchungen zur Geschichte des Decorum bei Cicero und Horaz* (Leipzig: F. Meiner, 1934) 1–73; cf. Max Pohlenz, "Τὸ πρέπον: Ein Beitrag zur Geschichte des griechischen Geistes," *Nachrichten von der Gesellschaft der Wissenschaften zu Göttingen: Philologisch-historische Klasse* (Berlin: Weidmannsche Buchhandlung, 1933) 53–92; North, *Sophrosyne*, s.v. homonoia, kosmiotês, prepon; Ferguson, *Moral Values*, 118–132; Hans Armin Gärtner, *Cicero und Panaitios: Beobachtungen zu Ciceros De Officiis* (SHAW.PH; Heidelberg: Carl Winter, 1974) 26 ff., 54–56.

[81] North, *Sophrosyne*, s.v. mêden agan; Ulrich Luck, "σώφρων, κτλ.," *TDNT* 7 (1971) 1097–1104; van der Horst, *Sentences*, 137–138; Spicq, *Notes*, 2.867–874; Engberg-Pedersen, *Aristotle's Theory of Moral Insight*, 68–70; Thom, *Golden Verses*, 108–109. Most important for the history of *sophrosyne* is the discussion of the term in the Platonic dialogues, especially the *Charmides*, see North, *Sophrosyne*, 150–196; also Charles L. Griswold, *Self-Knowledge in Plato's Phaedrus* (New York and London: Yale University Press, 1986); cf. Irwin, *Plato's Moral Theory*, s.v. temperance; Walter T. Schmid, "Socratic Moderation and Self-Knowledge," *JHP* 21 (1983) 349–358. Also cf. Vincent L. Wimbush, "Sophrosyne: Greco-Roman Origins of a Type of Ascetic Behavior," *Gnosticism and the Early Christian World: In Honor of James M. Robinson* (ed. James E. Goehring, Charles W. Hedrick, Jack T. Sanders, with Hans Dieter Betz; FF 2; Sonoma, CA: Polebridge, 1990) 89–102; Dieter Zeller, "σωφροσύνη, κτλ.," *EWNT* 3 (1983) 790–792. For some examples of gnomic instruction on *sophrosyne* see Stobaeus, *Anthologium* 3.5, 21. Also cf. Aristotle, *Ethica Nicomachea* 3.10.1–3.12.10, with Joachim, *Nicomachean Ethics*, 122–123; Iamblichus, *De Vita Pythagorica* 31.187–213; Cicero, *De Officiis* 1.93–143, with Ibscher, *Der Begriff des Sittlichen*, 90–105.

Given that *sophrosyne* constituted a major, characteristic theme of the gnomic style, it makes sense that a fairly large number of gnomic exhortations from antiquity resemble Pseudo-Phocylides' *Sententiae* 55–96 formally and materially. We may compare, for example, Pseudo-Isocrates' *Ad Demonicum* 21–32. Although from a literary standpoint this block of sayings betrays fewer signs of internal coherency than our poem, the topical clusters seemingly arranged only seriatim, the author does raise several comparable themes.[82] For instance, 'Isocrates' advises his readers to show discretion in choosing friends (§§ 24–25; compare Pseudo-Phocylides, *Sentences* 79, 95–96), to surpass their friends in doing kindness (§§ 25–26; compare Pseudo-Phocylides, *Sentences* 80), and to avoid envious friends (§ 26; compare Pseudo-Phocylides, *Sentences* 70–75). There is also exhortation to be tasteful in one's dress (§§ 27–28; compare Pseudo-Phocylides, *Sentences* 61), to be moderate in acquiring wealth (§ 28; compare Pseudo-Phocylides, *Sentences* 62), not to taunt others in their misfortune (§ 29; compare Pseudo-Phocylides, *Sentences* 83–85), to abhor flatterers (§ 30; compare Pseudo-Phocylides, *Sentences* 91–94), never to be quarrelsome or angry (§ 31; compare Pseudo-Phocylides, *Sentences* 75–78), and to avoid drinking parties (§ 32; compare Pseudo-Phocylides, *Sentences* 69, 81–82, 92–94). Other gnomic texts that could be included in a comparative discussion are Isocrates' *Ad Nicoclem* 29–35[83] and *Nicocles* 36–42,[84] the seventh instruction of *Papyrus Insinger* (2.21–5.11),[85] Ben Sira 18.30–19.3,[86] Syriac Menander's *Sentences* 45–75,[87] and Sextus' *Sententiae* 67–102, 132–142, 200–209, 265–282.[88]

The maxims on *sophrosyne* in the *Sententiae* of Pseudo-Phocylides are organized in two major sub-sections, verses 55–69 B, which admonish the readers to exercise self-control over their emotions, and verses 70–96, moral guidance on how to avoid envy by practicing self-restraint. As with the treatment

---

[82] It does appear to have a coordinated introduction (21) and conclusion (32 c), however.

[83] See above, pp. 49–51.

[84] This unit, subtitled περὶ σωφροσύνης, focuses on self-mastery in matters of sex and passion, particularly as they impact one's married and family life. Isocrates calls upon Nicocles to observe moderation in order to preserve the ὁμόνοια of his household and thereby set a positive example for the citizens. Text and translation: Norlin, *Isocrates*, 96–101.

[85] This section is entitled "The teaching to be measured in everything, so as to do nothing but what is fitting"; cf. the eighth instruction (5.12–7.19), especially 6.15–24; see Lichtheim, *Late Egyptian Wisdom*, 198–203; also cf. van der Horst, "Pseudo-Phocylides Revisited," 20, who cites 4.16–21.

[86] Most Greek and Latin mss. have this section entitled ἐγκράτεια ψυχῆς ("[On] self-control of the soul"); cf. Skehan and DiLella, *Ben Sira*, 292.

[87] The block consists of material regarding moderation in sex (vv. 45–51) and drinking (vv. 52–66), and exhortation against laziness (vv. 67–75).

[88] The themes of moderation and self-control are central to this gnomologium; see Chadwick, *The Sentences of Sextus*, 97–106. Further cf. *Gnomologium Democrateum* 69–78.

of justice in verses 9–41, the author appears to move from a thematic section whose topic is on the whole more general in its depiction of the virtue in question to a section whose topics explore some of more specific aspects or auxiliary components of that virtue.

Formally, the main body of the first paragraph is comprised entirely of a series of indicative statements (verses 60–68) that counsel against excessiveness, especially as it influences the emotions. This sequence is flanked by an introduction (verses 55–59) and conclusion (verses 69–69 B) that parallel each other logically and structurally. Each of these framing elements begins with two complementary commands to observe moderation in certain matters, the first pertaining to more-or-less personal activities (vexing one's liver in verses 55–56 and eating and drinking in verse 69 a), and the second to activities that may more often affect others (violent anger in verses 57–58 and speaking in verse 69 b). The implicit contrasts drawn here between the personal and social aspects of self-restraint typify the way moral thinkers generally understood this virtue to encompass the mastery both of personal appetites (especially eating, drinking, and sleeping) and of desires that affect other people more directly (especially talking, sex, and anger).[89] These specific injunctions in verses 55–58 and 69, which appear to be offered by way of example, are then joined to maxims that elicit from them general rules, conveying the main theme of the paragraph, moderation: "Let emotions be moderate; let nothing be grandiose or insolent" (verse 59) and, "Of all things moderation is best, but excesses are grievous" (verse 69 B).

The body of the paragraph, verses 60–68, presents a series of indicative statements alerting the reader to the destructive nature of excessive emotions and irrational impulses. The roster may be separated into two lists, judging by their forms. To begin with, verses 60–64 largely contain maxims that appear to be in the form of cause-and-effect statements. Thus Pseudo-Phocylides declares that wrongful gain or advantage becomes superfluous for human beings (verse 60), that great luxury breeds dishonorable desires (verse 61), that great wealth, which is boastful, fosters hybris (verse 62), that anger, when it overcomes someone, incites baneful fury (verse 63), and that wrath, if it goes too far, degenerates into madness (verse 64). By comparison, the next roster, verses 65–68, communicates ideas mostly in the form of contrastive statements. Here Pseudo-Phocylides contrasts the noble character of emulating good things with the monstrous results of emulating bad things (verse 65), the destructive nature of boldness in evil deeds with the profitable outcome of boldness in good deeds (verse 66), and the noble love of virtue with the

---

[89] Cf. *Carmen Aureum* 9b–11 a, with Thom, *Golden Verses*, 107–110; Pseudo-Isocrates, *Ad Demonicum* 21; Philo, *De Specialibus Legibus* 2.193–199. The topic of moderation in sexual affairs appears to be postponed by Pseudo-Phocylides until vv. 175 ff.

shameful love of passion (verse 67). The antithesis in verse 68 is not as obvious as in the previous lines, though at least implicitly the author contrasts the intention of the person who is ἡδὺς ἄγαν with the ironic and unintended consequences of his actions. As for the internal structure of these sub-lists, it appears that within each roster the first gnome (verses 60 and 65) gives expression to the broadest subject matter and so functions as a sort of topic sentence, introducing what follows. In addition to these formal considerations, the lists are bound together by various catchwords and linkwords.[90]

Exhortation on avoiding envy through moderation constitutes the theme of the second major sub-section, verses 70–96. As 'Aristotle' notes in the *De Virtutibus et Vitiis*, the avoidance of envy represents an essential part of training in moderation.[91] The poet who composed the *Carmen Aureum* apparently shares this opinion, incorporating a warning against envy in his teaching on moderation and self-control in verses 32–38.[92] The nature of the recommendations that Pseudo-Phocylides includes in this section suggests that he has in mind not only the avoidance of envy on the readers' part but also their refraining from the sorts of things that arouse envy in others. As a saying attributed to Cato the Elder observes, since people generally do not envy other people themselves but rather their circumstances, the ability to refrain from excess and ostentation reduces the risk of inciting this vice. Thus "those who use their good fortune reasonably and moderately are least envied," (ἥκιστα δὲ φθονεῖσθαι τοὺς τῇ τύχῃ χρωμένους ἐπιεικῶς καὶ μετρίως.").[93] Both envy and

---

[90] Some of the catchwords are based on phonetic similarities: πολλή (v. 61) and πολύς (v. 62); ὑψαυχεῖ (v. 62) and ὑπερχόμενος (v. 63); μανίην (v. 63) and μῆνις (v. 64); ἐσθλός (v. 65) and ἐσθλά (v. 66); ὀφέλλει (v. 66) and ὀφέλλει (v. 67); μέτρῳ (v. 69 bis) and μέτρον (v. 69B); also note that five of the poem's six words containing ὑπερ- occur here (vv. 59, 63, 64, 65, 69B, cf. 35, [36]); also note the similar endings for vv. 62 and 63: -ξει (v. 62) and -χει (v. 63). Cf. Thomas, *Der jüdische Phokylides*, 289–290.

[91] Pseudo-Aristotle, *De Virtutibus et Vitiis* 4.5.

[92] οὐ δ' ὑγιείας τῆς περὶ σῶμ' ἀμέλειαν ἔχειν χρή,
ἀλλὰ ποτοῦ τε μέτρον καὶ σίτου γυμνασίων τε
ποιεῖσθαι. μέτρον δὲ λέγω τόδ' ὃ μή σ' ἀνιήσει.
εἰθίζου δὲ δίαιταν ἔχειν καθάρειον ἄθρυπτον
καὶ πεφύλαξο τοιαῦτα ποιεῖν ὁπόσα φθόνον ἴσχει.
μὴ δαπανᾶν παρὰ καιρὸν ὁποῖα καλῶν ἀδαήμων
μηδ' ἀνελεύθερος ἴσθι. μέτρον δ' ἐπὶ πᾶσιν ἄριστον.
"You should not be careless about your physical health,
but you should practice due measure in drinking, eating, and physical
exercises. By due measure I mean that which will not distress you.
Become accustomed to have a pure way of life, not an enervated one,
and guard against doing the kind of thing that incurs envy.
Do not spend money at the wrong time like someone ignorant of good manners,
nor be tight-fisted. Due measure is in everything the best."
Text and translation: Thom, *Golden Verses*, 73, 78, cf. 138–145.

[93] Plutarch, *Regum et Imperatorum Apophthegmata* 119A; cited by Thom, *Golden Verses*, 142.

the incitement of envy entail actions and attitudes in which individuals exceed the acceptable limits of common sense and due measure in moral matters.

In these lines of the poem, Pseudo-Phocylides has accommodated his message to a three-part literary scheme that has structural and functional analogues elsewhere in Hellenistic-Jewish and early Christian sapiential literature: verse 70 fills the role of a thesis statement, verses 71–75 is a descriptive section on the example of the cosmos, while verses 76–96 serves as a prescriptive section that contains various instructions on the theme of σωφροσύνη, particularly as it relates to controlling envy.[94]

The thesis statement, verse 70, consists of a pair of parallel wisdom admonitions against φθόνος ("envy") in social relations: "Envy not the goods of friends; do not place blame on them."[95] The admonitions here establish the theme and guide the purpose of the sub-section; in the ensuing lines the author endeavors to equip the audience with reasons, motivations, and specific recommendations on how they may evade jealousy and the personal moral conflicts that it breeds.

The ethical model of the cosmos, a common theme in ancient paraenesis and the subject of the descriptive section (verses 71–75), supplies the basis of the injunction against envy in the thesis statement of verse 70.[96] Because the "heavenly ones" always exhibit ὁμόνοια ("harmony") and are without φθόνος and ἔρις ("strife"), the audience must imitate their example and pursue these same qualities. The passage starts with a general assertion about the "heavenly ones" (verse 71) linked to the thesis statement logically with καί. The author demonstrates this assertion by offering three specific illustrations of harmony in the universe: the moon does not envy the sun, nor the earth the heaven, nor the rivers the seas (verses 72–74 a). This is flanked by another ethical assertion regarding the members of the cosmos, this time formulated positively: since no jealousy or resentment disrupts their relationships, they constantly enjoy

---

[94] The analysis of this section is based upon my previous work in *Love Without Pretense*, 112–119.

[95] On this topic in ancient ethics see the extensive survey by Ernst Milobenski, *Der Neid in der griechischen Philosophie* (KPS 29; Wiesbaden: Otto Harrassowitz, 1964), particularly 116–134 on 'Die Kynisch-Stoische Popular-Philosophie'; also Schmidt, *Die Ethik der alten Griechen*, 1.78–84, 256–260; van der Horst, *Sentences*, 161–162; Spicq, *Notes*, 2.919–921; Peter Walcot, *Envy and the Greeks: A Study of Human Behavior* (Warminster: Aris & Phillips, 1978); Luke T. Johnson, "James 3.13–4.10 and the Topos ΠΕΡΙ ΦΘΟΝΟΥ," *NovT* 25 (1983) 327–347. Cf. also the *Testament of Simeon* (subtitled περὶ φθόνου) especially 3.1–5.3, with Hollander and de Jonge, *Testaments*, 109–128; Dio Chrysostom, *Orationes* 77, 78; Plutarch, *De Invidia et Odio* 536E–538E; Stobaeus, *Anthologium* 3.38; Str-B 1.833 ff.; Galatians 5.26, with Betz, *Galatians*, 294–295.

[96] For more on this theme see van der Horst, *Sentences*, 163–165; Thomas, *Der jüdische Phokylides*, 204–205. The descriptive section here is linked with the thesis statement in v. 70 by means of catchword: φθονέοις (v. 70), ἄφθονοι (v. 71), and φθονέει (v. 72).

harmony and concord. In verse 75 Pseudo-Phocylides draws a conclusion from the preceding discussion in the form of a gnomic utterance, maintaining that if there was rivalry or contention among the "heavenly ones" the universe itself could not endure.

The central message of the prescriptive section (verses 76–96) is that the means by which a reader can avoid envy and strife, and so imitate the οὐρανίδαι, is to σωφροσύνην ἀσκεῖν ("practice moderation"), an injunction that sets the tone for the section and names its governing virtue (verse 76a). In the ensuing lines, the author composes direct and extended exhortation, indicating the nature of the audience's personal obligations in definite terms. In this way he indicates some of the distinct ethical actions and attitudes that derive from the broader goals articulated in the thesis statement, the descriptive section, and the opening injunction in verse 76a. Formally, the section exhibits a variety of paraenetic materials, consisting of a number of admonitions (verses 76, 77, 79, 83, 86, 87, 91, 95) accompanied by wisdom sentences (verses 78, 80, 81–82, 88, 89, 90, 96), examples and illustrations (verses 84–85, 92–94). Pseudo-Phocylides has divided the instruction here into two subsections, distinguished by their function and means of organization. The first unit concisely introduces the section's essential ethical principles in the form of three antithetical maxims that articulate the basis for conducting one's life free of envy (verses 76–78).[97] Above all, it is σωφροσύνη, which appears as the first word of the leading maxim (as well as of the entire paragraph), that functions as the theme for the prescriptive section and for the advice that it contains. The contrasts made in these first three lines are fundamental to the ethos that the passage extols; together they develop an image of σωφροσύνη in broad terms and so are of use in establishing the readers' moral perspective on this topic. The audience is charged to practice σωφροσύνη and to refrain from shameful acts (verse 76); they are to renounce vengeance and retaliation and to allow justice to take its course (verse 77); and they are to value the advantages of πειθώ ("persuasiveness"), shunning ἔρις, which produces only further conflict (verse 78, compare verse 75).

The second unit, verses 79–96, relates a series of subordinate sayings that explicate the basic principles of verses 76–78 with a number of commands and sage observations, all of which connect directly or indirectly with the topic of moderation. By providing some concrete, paradigmatic injunctions and illustrations, the author suggests how exactly the reader is to practice σωφροσύνη and in this way he clarifies and applies the moral premises of the first unit. With regard to subject matter, the advice rendered in verses 79–96 pertains to a wide range of referents: benefactors (verse 80), guests (verses 81–82), the poor (verses 83–85), untrained people (verse 86), the wise (verse 88), the un-

---

[97] Note the use of α- alliteration to help bind these three verses together.

educated (verses 89–90), flatterers (verses 91–94), and the mob (verses 95–96). Although the themes of self-restraint and moderation run as a thread through these lines, no apparent attempt has been made to create sub-categories depending on specific topics and the progression of thought from the subject of any one maxim or illustration to that of the next is often loose or unclear. So the author has not provided a tight linear argument or a systematic treatment of σωφροσύνη. All the same, the maxims in verses 79–86 have been organized according to a literary pattern common in gnomic materials, namely, ring composition.[98] The main exhortatory themes of the advice here can be arranged in the following manner:

79–80	A. Don't trust too quickly (but it is fitting to be generous with those who have demonstrated trust in you)
81–82	B. Provide guests with a simple meal, not lengthy festivities
83–85	C. Show restraint in collecting debts and in using nature's resources
86	D. Don't allow the untrained (or uninformed) to be judges
88	E. On the discipline of the wise sage
89–90	D'. The uneducated do not comprehend
91	C'. Don't take on parasitic flatterers as companions
92–94	B'. Against over-indulgence in eating and drinking
95–96	A'. Don't trust the mob

As with most gnomic ring compositions, the correlation of structural pairs here relies upon varying material and literary aspects of the particular lines and the relationships are not precise in every case. The injunctions to show restraint in trusting others found in verses 79–80 (A) and 95–96 (A') take on special prominence as a result of their respective positions, and together they set the tone and direction of the entire sub-section: as a rule, the readers should exercise care and restraint in dealing with others (with verse 80 attached to verse 79 in A stipulating one type of allowable exception). The inclusio created by μὴ πίστευε in these parts of the segment (verses 79 and 95) helps to reinforce the boundaries of the ring composition.[99] Both B (verses 81–82) and B' (verses 92–94) somehow praise moderation in matters of eating and drinking: in B Pseudo-Phocylides recommends quick, simple meals for guests rather than many elaborate festivities that drag on too long, and in B' he complains about those annoying types of guests who are insatiable (and sometimes rude) when it comes to dining. The point common to both C (verses 83–85) and C' (verse 91) concerns the necessity of exercising restraint when taking something from others: in verses 83–85 the author encourages the audience to show mercy when collecting debts from the poor (verse 83) and when removing birds from a nest (verses 84–85);[100] in verse 91 they are advised not to ac-

---

[98] Note also the use of catchword: ἑταίρους (v. 91) and ἑταῖροι (v. 92) [epistophic]; λαῷ (v. 95) and λαός (v. 96) [anaphoric].

[99] Note also the use of καιρόν in vv. 82 (B) and 93 (B').

[100] Perhaps vv. 84–85 is intended to serve as a supporting illustration for v. 83.

cept as associates individuals whom the poet labels "table-clearing flatterers", that is, sycophants who exercise no self-restraint when consuming the sustenance of their companions. D (verse 86) and D' (verses 89–90) share similar referents: untrained individuals in D, who should never be allowed to judge, and the uneducated and those who have never learned good things in D', who cannot grasp "a great teaching" (μεγάλη διδαχή). At the center of the ring composition stands a wisdom sentence on the discipline of the σοφός (verse 88), whose wisdom he compares (or contrasts) with the skillful work of a craftsman.[101] Given the sapiential qualities of the *Sentences* as a whole, the references to wisdom and the wise sage at this pivotal point in the sub-section are both appropriate and effective. The σοφός serves as a paradigm of the ethos that the passage strives to develop, and the wisdom that he manages ensures that his moral conduct and outlook are proper and disciplined, in keeping with σωφροσύνη.

Exhortation on Topics Relating to Courage, Specifically Fortitude (verses 97–121)

Outline:

---

[101] On the different possibilities of interpretation for this line see van der Horst, *Sentences*, 174–175.

Text:

97   μὴ δὲ μάτην ἐπὶ πῦρ καθίσας μινύθῃς φίλον ἦτορ·
98   μέτρα δὲ τεῦχε γόοισι· τὸ γὰρ μέτρον ἐστὶν ἄριστον.
99   γαῖαν ἐπιμοιρᾶσθαι ἀταρχύτοις νεκύεσσιν.
100   μὴ τύμβον φθιμένων ἀνορύξῃς μηδ' ἀθέατα
101   δείξῃς ἠελίῳ καὶ δαιμόνιον χόλον ὄρσῃς.
102   οὐ καλὸν ἁρμονίην ἀναλυέμεν ἀνθρώποιο·
103   καὶ τάχα δ' ἐκ γαίης ἐλπίζομεν ἐς φάος ἐλθεῖν
104   λείψαν' ἀποιχομένων· ὀπίσω δὲ θεοὶ τελέθονται·
105   ψυχαὶ γὰρ μίμνουσιν ἀκήριοι ἐν φθιμένοισιν·
106   πνεῦμα γάρ ἐστι θεοῦ χρῆσις θνητοῖσι καὶ εἰκών·
107   σῶμα γὰρ ἐκ γαίης ἔχομεν κἄπειτα πρὸς αὖ γῆν
108   λυόμενοι κόνις ἐσμέν· ἀὴρ δ' ἀνὰ πνεῦμα δέδεκται.
109   πλουτῶν μὴ φείδου· μέμνησ' ὅτι θνητὸς ὑπάρχεις·
110   οὐκ ἔνι εἰς Ἅιδην ὄλβον καὶ χρήματ' ἄγεσθαι.
111   πάντες ἴσον νέκυες, ψυχῶν δὲ θεὸς βασιλεύει.
112   κοινὰ μέλαθρα δόμων αἰώνια καὶ πατρὶς Ἅιδης,
113   ξυνὸς χῶρος ἅπασι, πένησί τε καὶ βασιλεῦσιν.
114   οὐ πολὺν ἄνθρωποι ζῶμεν χρόνον, ἀλλ' ἐπίκαιρον·
115   ψυχὴ δ' ἀθάνατος καὶ ἀγήρως ζῇ διὰ παντός.
[116]
[117]
118   μήτε κακοῖσ' ἄχθου μήτ' οὖν ἐπαγάλλεο χάρμῃ·
119   πολλάκις ἐν βιότῳ καὶ θαρσαλέοισιν ἄπιστον
120   πῆμα καὶ ἀχθομένοισι κακοῦ λύσις ἤλυθεν ἄφνω.
121   καιρῷ λατρεύειν, μὴ δ' ἀντιπνέειν ἀνέμοισιν.

Translation:

97 Weaken not your heart sitting in vain by the fire.
98 Make moderate your lamentations,[102] for moderation is best.
99 Reserve a share of earth for the unburied dead.
100 Do not dig up the grave of the deceased, nor reveal
101 what may not be seen to the sun and incite divine wrath.
102 It is not good to destroy a human frame.
103 And we hope, too, that quickly will the remains of the departed come
104 from the earth to the light. And then they become gods.[103]
105 For souls remain deathless[104] in the deceased.
106 For the spirit is a loan from God to mortals, and is God's image.[105]
107 For we possess a body out of earth; and then when we are resolved
108 into earth again we are dust; but the air has received our spirit.
109 When you are wealthy do not be sparing; remember that you are a mortal.
110 It is impossible to carry wealth and goods with you into Hades.
111 All the dead are alike, and God rules over (their) souls.
112 Our shared, eternal dwelling-place and fatherland is Hades,
113 a common place for all, both poor and kings.[106]
114 We humans live no long time, but only briefly.
115 But the soul lives immortal and ageless through all time.
[116]
[117][107]
118 Neither be grieved by evils nor overjoyed with delight.[108]
119 Often in life unbelievable suffering comes to the confident
120 and to the distressed a sudden release from evil.
121 Go with the times:[109] blow not against the winds.

In its plainest sense ἀνδρεία refers to physical bravery, especially valor on the battlefield. For the most part, ethical philosophers found this meaning too restricted and they often extended the term's meaning to include courage in fac-

---

[102] Following Bernays (*Gesammelte Abhandlungen*, 200–202), Diehl (*Anthologia*, 2.105) and van der Horst (*Sentences*, 95, n. 2, 180) who read γόοισι instead of θεοῖσι in the mss. Derron (*Sentences*, 9, 25–26) opts for the latter, translating: "mais honore modérément les dieux ...". Young (*Theognis*, 103) conjectures τεῦχ' ἔθ' ἑοῖσι, which he translates: "modum impone etiam tuis" (cf. Walter, *Poetische Schriften*, 206: "‹rate auch den Deinen zur Mäßigung›"), but cf. West (*CR* 30 [1980] 137) and Derron (*Sentences*, 25–26). Also cf. H. J. de Jonge in *Nederlands Theologisch Tijdschrift* 33 (1979) 246: τεῦχ' ἐθέεσσι.

[103] Following the proposed translation for vv. 103–104 of Edward O'Neil (personal communication, 5/15/92).

[104] Or perhaps "unharmed"; cf. van der Horst, *Sentences*, 188.

[105] Following the translation of van der Horst, *Sentences*, 189–190.

[106] Following the translation for v. 113 of van der Horst, *Sentences*, 194.

[107] Vv. 116–117 (οὐδεὶς γινώσκει, τί μετ' αὔριον ἢ τί μεθ' ὥραν. ἄσκοπός ἐστι βροτῶν θάνατος, τὸ δὲ μέλλον ἄδηλον. "No one knows what is to be after tomorrow or after an hour. Obscure is the death of mortals; the future is unclear.") are spurious; see van der Horst, *Sentences*, 195–196.

[108] Edward O'Neil (personal communication, 5/15/92) suggests a translation that treats χάρμῃ as an adverb: "Neither be grieved by evils nor joyfully exult in them."

[109] Cf. the translation of van der Horst, *Sentences*, 197–198: "Accommodate yourself to the circumstances, etc."

ing dangers and difficulties of all sorts, and so the virtue took on new moral, personal, and social connotations.[110] Most influential in this regard was the evaluation of courage in the Platonic dialogues, particularly the *Laches*.[111] Two aspects about this type of philosophical analysis of courage bear upon the present analysis. First, moral thinkers often depicted courage as the capacity to face death and the possible consequences of the hereafter without anxiety or fear. Indeed, questions raised concerning the nature of death and of life after death constituted quite prominent topics of discussion and debate for both Greco-Roman[112] and Jewish[113] writers of antiquity. This aspect of courage appears to be Pseudo-Phocylides' focus in part II of the outline above, verses 99–113. According to the philosophical literature, the ability to remain undismayed by the fear of death stems generally from a correct understanding about

---

[110] In ancient discussions the moral ideal of courage takes on many different forms and applications, see René-Antonin Gauthier, *Magnanimité: L'Idéal de la Grandeur dans la Philosophie Païenne et dans la Théologie Chrétienne* (Bibliothèque Thomiste 28; Paris: J. Vrin, 1951) 144–164; Ferguson, *Moral Values*, 28–30, 40–42, 46–50, 159–178; Dover, *Popular Morality*, 167–169; Betz, *Plutarch's Ethical Writings*, s.v. ἀνδρεία; Thom, *Golden Verses*, 121–127; Engberg-Pedersen, *Aristotle's Theory of Moral Insight*, 48–49, 65–68, 83–84; Stephen A. White, *Sovereign Virtue: Aristotle on the Relation Between Happiness and Prosperity* (Stanford Series in Philosophy; Stanford: Stanford University Press, 1992) 226–228, 272–276; cf. J. F. Procope, "Quiet Christian Courage: A Topic in Clemens Alexandrinus and its Philosophical Background," *Studia Patristica* 15 (1984) 489–494; Aristotle, *Ethica Nicomachea* 3.6.1–3.9.7; Pseudo-Aristotle, *Magna Moralia* 1.20.1–12; Pseudo-Aristotle, *De Virtutibus et Vitiis* 4.4; Cicero, *De Officiis* 1.18.61–1.26.92, with Ibscher, *Der Begriff des Sittlichen*, 55–89; Iamblichus, *De Vita Pythagorica* 32.214–221; Stobaeus, *Anthologium* 3.7.

[111] Walter T. Schmid, *On Manly Courage: A Study of Plato's Laches* (Philosophical Explorations; Carbondale, IL: Southern Illinois University Press, 1992); cf. Gerasimos Santas, "Socrates at Work on Virtue and Knowledge in Plato's Laches," *Review of Metaphysics* 22 (1969) 433–460; Stewart Umphrey, "Plato's Laches on Courage," *Apeiron* 10 (1976) 14–22; Daniel Devereux, "Courage and Wisdom in Plato's Laches," *JHP* 15 (1977) 129–141; Irwin, *Plato's Moral Theory*, 198–199; cf. further Plato, *Leges* 633C-D, *Politica* 306A–311C, *Republica* 429A–430C, etc.

[112] Ernst Benz, *Das Todesproblem in der stoischen Philosophie* (TBAW 7; Stuttgart: W. Kohlhammer, 1929) 48–109; Ramsay MacMullen, *Paganism in the Roman Empire* (New Haven and London: Yale University Press, 1981) 53–57; Robert Garland, *The Greek Way of Death* (Ithaca: Cornell University Press, 1985) 13–20; Matthias Baltes, "Die Todesproblematik in der griechischen Philosophie," *Gymnasium* 95 (1988) 97–128; Thom, *Golden Verses*, 117–121, 210–215. The third book of Lucretius' *De Rerum Natura* is of special interest in this regard, see Barbara P. Wallach, *Lucretius and the Diatribe Against the Fear of Death: De Rerum Natura 3, 830–1094* (Mnemosyne Sup. 40; Leiden: E.J. Brill, 1976); Martha C. Nussbaum, "Mortal Immortals: Lucretius on Death and the Voice of Nature," *PPR* 50 (1989) 303–351; Charles Segal, *Lucretius on Death and Anxiety: Poetry and Philosophy in De Rerum Natura* (Princeton: Princeton University Press, 1990).

[113] For Jewish materials see Paul Volz, *Jüdische Eschatologie von Daniel bis Akiba* (Tübingen and Leipzig: J.C.B. Mohr [Paul Siebeck], 1903) 126–161; Albrecht Oepke, "Auferstehung II (des Menschen)," *RAC* 1 (1950) 930–938; Rudolf Bultmann, "θάνατος, κτλ.," *TDNT* 3 (1965) 7–25; George W. E. Nickelsburg, *Resurrection, Immortality and*

the nature of life, death, and the afterlife, and what should and should not be feared. Hence the common notion that "courage is knowledge".[114] This may account for the relatively large number of declarative sentences in this section of the poem, as the author makes certain assertions apropos of a moral discussion of the nature of death and the afterlife.

A second moral quality often embraced by ἀνδρεία was the individual's ability to bear well both good and bad fortune, a trait sometimes referred to as μακροθυμία or μεγαλοψυχία, which could be treated as virtues in their own right.[115] As Cicero observes, those counted among the courageous are very often not warriors, but those who exhibit a spirit superior to the vicissitudes of earthly life and an attitude marked by perseverance and indifference to external circumstances or worldly standards. This entails not only the fortitude to be resolute in times of difficulty but also the strength to be humble in times of success or prosperity. One place where he raises such issues is *De Officiis* 1.26.90, comments made within the context of a Stoic analysis of courage as a virtue:[116]

> Atque etiam in rebus prosperis et ad voluntatem nostram fluentibus superbiam magnopere, fastidium arrogantiamque fugiamus. Nam ut adversas res, sic secundas immoderate ferre levitatis est, praeclaraque est aequabilitas in omni vita et idem semper vultus eademque frons ...

> Again, when fortune smiles and the stream of life flows according to our wishes, let us diligently avoid all arrogance, haughtiness, and pride. For it is as much a sign of weakness to give way to one's feelings in success as it is in adversity. But it is a fine thing to keep an unruffled temper, an unchanging mien, and the same cast of countenance in every condition of life ...

Such an ability to persevere can be realized above all by developing one's intellectual capacity to anticipate the future and respond accordingly.[117] This seems to be the focus of part III in the outline above, verses 114–121.

As these remarks suggest, it appears that in this part of the poem Pseudo-Phocylides does not so much address the theme of courage per se as he does some of its more specific motivations and manifestations in the realm of eth-

---

Eternal Life in Intertestamental Judaism (HTS 26; Cambridge: Harvard University Press, 1972); also the references below in n. 120.

[114] For example, Plato, *Gorgias* 495C ff., *Laches* 190B–201C, *Protagoras* 360C–D; Xenophon, *Memorabilia* 4.6.11; Aristotle, *Ethica Nicomachea* 3.6.1–12; Cicero, *De Officiis* 1.23.81; Philo, *De Specialibus Legibus* 4.145, *De Virtutibus* 1–2.

[115] Aristotle, *Ethica Nicomachea* 4.3.1–34; Pseudo-Aristotle, *De Virtutibus et Vitiis* 5.6–7 (cf. φιλοπονία in 4.4); Schmidt, *Die Ethik der alten Griechen*, 2.450–453; Gauthier, *Magnanimité*, 144–164, 199–208, 212–222; Ferguson, *Moral Values*, s.v. megalopsuchia; Johannes Horst, "μακροθυμία, κτλ.," *TDNT* 4 (1967) 374–387; Betz, *Plutarch's Ethical Writings*, s.v. μακροθυμία, μεγαλόψυχος; Colin Brown, Ulrich Falkenroth, and Wilhelm Mundle, "Patience," *NIDNTT* 2 (1986) 764–776; Harm W. Hollander, "μακροθυμία, κτλ.," *EDNT* 2 (1991) 380–381.

[116] Text and translation: Miller, *Cicero*, 90–93.

[117] For example, Cicero, *De Officiis* 1.23.81.

ics, which he no doubt viewed as more compatible with the general objectives of the work. In this sense, then, we may say that the exhortation here concentrates on the topic of moral fortitude, καρτερία or ὑπομονή, which ancient philosophers often linked with the virtue of courage or categorized as one of its species.[118]

The teaching on fortitude in verses 97–121 consists of three formal segments. The first two lines operate as a thesis statement, introducing the main body of the section and establishing the central theme: the reader should not give in to excessive mourning, worry, or grief (verses 97–98). Presumably foremost in the author's mind are the moral dangers involved in becoming overwhelmed by grief over *death*, though it should be noted that distress of this sort is not explicitly mentioned, and so the warnings extend at least potentially to grief as it pertains to other matters, such as those set forth in verses 114 ff.[119] Two blocks of material based on this theme constitute the main body of the section on courage: verses 99–113 address proper attitudes and behavior in comprehending and confronting death, while verses 114–121 advise on enduring the vicissitudes of earthly existence.[120]

The first block, verses 99–113, contains two paragraphs, each beginning with specific directives backed by more general reasons and explanations submitted as supporting evidence. In the first paragraph, verses 99–108, the au-

---

[118] On καρτερία, ὑπομονή, and their relationship with courage see Plato, *Laches* 192 B–194 A, *Alcibiades* 122 C, *Definitiones* 412 C; Aristotle, *Ethica Nicomachea* 3.6.1–3.9.7, 7.1.1–7.9.7, with Joachim, *Nicomachean Ethics*, 116–122, 219–233; Aristotle, *Politica* 7.13.18; von Arnim, *Stoicorum Veterum Fragmenta*, 1.49.33, 1.129.1, 3.64.6, 18, 23, 3.65.13, 3.66.13, 29, 3.67.24, 40, 3.70.19, 22, 3.73.3, 3.264.23–24, 35–40; Pseudo-Aristotle, *De Virtutibus et Vitiis* 4.4; Philo, *De Cherubim* 78, *De Mutatione Nominum* 153, *Legum Allegoriae* 1.65, *Quod Deterius Potiori Insidiari Soleat* 17–18, 51, *Quod Deus Sit Immutabilis* 13. Further, A. M. Festugière, "ΥΠΟΜΟΝΗ dans la Tradition Grecque," *RSR* 30 (1931) 477–486; Gauthier, *Magnanimité*, 148–150, 199–202; Walter Grundmann, "καρτερέω, κτλ.," *TDNT* 3 (1965) 617–620; Friedrich Hauck, "ὑπομένω, ὑπομονή," *TDNT* 4 (1967) 581–588; Michael Spanneut, "Geduld," *RAC* 9 (1976) 245–260; Spicq, *Notes*, 1.61–63, 3.658–665; Walter Radl, "ὑπομονή," *EWNT* 3 (1983) 969–971; Heinz-Horst Schrey, "Geduld," *TRE* 12 (1984) 139–144; Brown, Falkenroth, and Mundle, "Patience," 767–768, 772–776; Thom, *Golden Verses*, 121–127.

[119] As van der Horst observes (*Sentences*, 179), the central thought here seems to be exhortation towards μετριοπάθεια; see LSJ s.v.; cf. Thomas, *Der jüdische Phokylides*, 209–210.

[120] On vv. 97 ff., in addition to the commentaries, see Hans C. C. Cavallin, *Life After Death: Paul's Argument for the Resurrection of the Dead in 1 Corinthians 15*, Part 1: *An Enquiry into the Jewish Background* (ConBNT 7.1; Lund: Gleerup, 1974) 151–155; idem, "Leben nach dem Tode im Spätjudentum und im frühen Christentum: I. Spätjudentum," *ANRW* II.19.1 (1979) 295–296, cf. 240–345; Felix Christ, "Das Leben nach dem Tode bei Pseudo-Phokylides," *TZ* 31 (1975) 140–149; Ulrich Fischer, *Eschatologie und Jenseitserwartung im hellenistischen Diasporajudentum* (BZNW 44; Berlin: de Gruyter, 1978) 125–143; Thomas, *Der jüdische Phokylides*, 205–212, 325–326.

thor offers some directives relating to the treatment of corpses that are supplemented by a number of observations on the nature of death and the afterlife.[121] He opens with two contrastive injunctions: a positive command to guarantee the dead a proper burial (verse 99) coupled with a negative prohibition against opening up graves (verses 100–101a). These commands are buttressed by certain statements in verses 101b–108, which, like verses 99–101a, have been divided into contrastive positive and negative components, though here the order is reversed. The inclusio created by ἀναλυέμεν in verse 102 and λυόμενοι in verse 108 helps to demarcate the boundaries of this supporting segment. In verses 101b–102 we find two negatively formulated reasons for the initial directives: tomb-violation will incur divine wrath (verse 101b) and the dissection (or dismemberment)[122] of corpses is simply οὐ καλόν (verse 102). A lengthier section positive in orientation counters these threats by delving into certain beliefs concerning the afterlife that the author and the audience share (verses 103–108).[123] This section, in turn, alternates between particular religious claims and their ancillary explanations. The first set of claims, verses 103–104, advocates a belief in bodily resurrection (verses 103–104a) and the hope of eventual (quasi-)deification (verse 104b).[124] The subsequent reasons in verses 105–106, which appear to apply especially to the second claim, maintain that the soul[125] of a person survives in the corpse (verse 105) and that this soul is divine both in origin and in nature (verse 106).[126] The last set of claims, verses 107–108, which attest to religious sentiments that are to a certain degree contradictory to those mentioned in verses 103–104, raises the subject of spiritual resurrection.[127] As the poet contends, even though human

---

[121] Note also the application of inclusio: γαῖαν (v. 99) and γαίης, γῆν (v. 107).

[122] On the different possible interpretations for this verse see van der Horst, *Sentences*, 183–184. Adela Yarbro Collins (*The Beginning of the Gospel: Probings of Mark in Context* [Minneapolis: Fortress, 1992] 143, cf. 138–142) suggests that the rejected practice may be secondary burial, referring to Jack Finegan, *The Archaeology of the New Testament* (Princeton: Princeton University Press, 1969) 216–218.

[123] As van der Horst's parallels show (*Sentences*, 185–192), there is little here that is exclusively Jewish in nature; cf. Derron, *Sentences*, 25–26; Thomas, *Der jüdische Phokylides*, 211–212, 352.

[124] Most likely this refers primarily to the immortal character of the resurrected; see van der Horst, *Sentences*, 186–188.

[125] On the interchangability of ψυχή and πνεῦμα in this context see van der Horst, *Sentences*, 189; van der Horst also notes the logical connection of v. 105 to v. 104.

[126] Note the interesting anaphoric thematic progression in vv. 105–107: ψυχαὶ γάρ (v. 105), πνεῦμα γάρ (v. 106), and σῶμα γάρ (v. 107); also linkword: ψυχαί (v. 105), ψυχῶν (v. 111), and ψυχή (v. 115).

[127] As van der Horst (*Sentences*, 188–189) writes, "... belief in the immortality of the soul as an inherent quality, distinguishing it from the body that will be dissolved without any resurrection, seems to be maintained in vv. 106–108; this apparently contradicts vv. 103–104." But he also observes (citing Arthur Darby Nock, *Essays on Religion and the Ancient World* [ed. Zeph Stewart; 2 vols.; Cambridge: Harvard University Press, 1972] 1.507,

corpses revert to the earth out of which they were originally created, the air receives their spirits.[128]

It should be emphasized that the basic observations set forth in verses 101b–108 not only reinforce the concrete injunctions of verses 99–101a but pertain also to the main thought articulated in the thesis statement, verses 97–98. By amplifying some of the positive aspects of what the readers (apparently) already believe about the nature of the afterlife, Pseudo-Phocylides prevails upon them to exhibit fortitude in dealing with death and their apprehensions about it.[129] The arguments marshaled by the poet in this section parallel to a certain extent some of the topics familiar from that branch of paraenetic literature known as consolation, a fairly prevalent mode of exhortation in the ancient world. In attempting to console readers overwrought with grief after the death of a loved one, authors of this genre would sometimes employ motifs and strategies similar to those applied in verses 97–108 (as well as verses 109–121) of the *Sententiae*. For example, a consolatory author might urge his audience to observe moderation in grieving, since overreacting to the death of another person is not only unnecessary and accomplishes nothing for the deceased but may also have ill effects for the mourner. The consolatory writer might also remind his readers that death is the final and inescapable destiny of all mortals, rich and poor alike (see also below). He might argue, too, that death has released the departed from the difficulties and the evils of human life, or, in the same vein, he might point out that death can lead to some better state of existence for the deceased in the hereafter.[130] As Hubert Martin

---

n. 19), "the widespread tendency of language about the afterlife to admit inconsistencies." Cf. Cavallin, *Life After Death*, 212: "In the same writings, and even in the same passages, concepts and symbols from widely differing anthropologies are used in order to express the hope of personal survival of death: immortality of the soul or resurrection of the body. The writers intend to state that the *personality* survives." Cf. Fischer, *Eschatologie und Jenseitserwartung*, 257–258; Thom, *Golden Verses*, 210–215.

[128] On this motif see J. H. Waszink, "Aether," *RAC* 1 (1950) 150–158; Erwin Rohde, *Psyche: The Cult of Souls and Belief in Immortality Among the Greeks* (trans. W. B. Hillis; New York: Arno, 1972) s.v. aether; van der Horst, *Sentences*, 191–192; Thom, *Golden Verses*, 211–212.

[129] In comparison with most of the rest of the poem this section is very factual and informative in nature, using a large number of indicative sentences; for an overview see Küchler, *Weisheitstraditionen*, 266–274.

[130] On consolation literature see Rudolf Kassel, *Untersuchungen zur griechischen und römischen Konsolationsliteratur* (Zetemata 18; München: C.H. Beck, 1958); Otto Schmitz and Gustav Stählin, "παρακαλέω, παράκλησις," *TDNT* 5 (1967) 773–799; Traudel Stork, *Nil Igitur Mors est ad Nos: Der Schlussteil des dritten Lukrezbuchs und sein Verhältnis zur Konsolationsliteratur* (Habelts Dissertationsdrucke, Reihe klassische Philologie 9; Bonn: Rudolf Habelt, 1970) 9–22; Robert C. Gregg, *Consolation Philosophy: Greek and Christian Paideia in Basil and the Two Gregories* (Patristic Monograph Series 3; Cambridge, MA: Philadelphia Patristic Foundation, 1975) 1–123; Johannes Thomas, "παρακαλέω, παράκλησις," *EWNT* 3 (1983) 54–64; Stanley K. Stowers, *Letter Writing in Greco-Roman*

and Jane E. Phillips have observed in their study of Plutarch's *Consolatio ad Uxorem*, gnomic wisdom ordinarily formed part of a consolatory author's repertoire: "Contributions to [the] miscellany of consolatory themes came from several sources. The most obvious is the common cultural heritage, the accumulated folk wisdom that spoke to generation after generation through the old poets and tragedians on the one hand and through proverbs and wise sayings on the other."[131]

In the second paragraph of part II, verses 109–113, Pseudo-Phocylides shares his thoughts on the meaninglessness of riches in the face of death. Since all people, rich and poor alike, must die, and money is of no value after death, the readers should make sensible use of their wealth and share it with others while they are still alive. Similar in design to the first paragraph, this segment begins with a concrete directive for the recipients not to concern themselves unduly with saving money (verse 109a) backed by more general reasons and explanations in verses 109b–111. First, the poet laments the ephemeral quality of the present mode of life, reminding the audience of their mortality (verse 109b). Three assertions follow, each depicting some aspect of the condition of life after death (verses 110–111): money and possessions are worthless in Hades (verse 110), everyone is alike in the afterlife (verse 111a), and God rules over all souls after they die (verse 111b). Verses 112–113 function as a summarizing statement, expressing the common belief that Hades is the shared and eternal resting place for all people, regardless of their previous stations in life.[132]

The topics of the third and final segment of the section on courage (verses 114–121) also relate to the virtue of fortitude, though here we discover not exhortation concerning death and the afterlife, but prescriptions on dealing with the hardships of earthly existence with dignity and endurance.[133] The paragraph opens with the universal complaint that life is short, but quickly adds by way of encouragement that the soul, by contrast, is immortal (verses 114–115). In verses 118–120, the readers are exhorted not to be discouraged by misfortune nor over-confident in prosperity, but rather to accept whatever comes with resilience, since life is so unpredictable and sudden twists of fate

---

Antiquity (LEC 5; Philadelphia: Westminster, 1986) 142–152; Menander of Laodicea, ΠΕΡΙ ΕΠΙΔΕΙΚΤΙΚΩΝ 413.5–414.30.

[131] Hubert Martin and Jane E. Phillips, "Consolatio ad Uxorem (Moralia 608A–612B)," in Betz, *Plutarch's Ethical Writings*, 403, cf. 394–441.

[132] Note the use of linkword: βασιλεύει (v. 111) and βασιλεῦσιν (v. 113); ῞Αιδην (v. 110) and ῞Αιδης (v. 112); also a thematic catchword: ἴσον (v. 111), κοινά (v. 112), and ξυνός (v. 113).

[133] Cf. Thom, *Golden Verses*, 121–127; as he notes on p. 122, "Bearing up under misfortune falls under the heading of fortitude (καρτερία) which is a species of moral courage (ἀνδρεία)." See also Musonius Rufus, *Fragmenta* 7 (ΟΤΙ ΠΟΝΟΥ ΚΑΤΑΦΡΟΝΗΤΕΟΝ, "That One Should Disdain Hardships"), with Lutz, *Musonius Rufus*, 56–59.

can affect both the fortunate and the unfortunate. The author offers a concluding recommendation in verse 121 that the best course in light of these facts is
accommodation to circumstances rather than vain resistance: "Go with the
times: blow not against the winds." Taken as a whole, Pseudo-Phocylides' re-
flections in this paragraph on the apparent caprice of human fortune echo elements from a wide variety of discussions in antiquity on the subject of fate (ἡ
τύχη, ἡ εἱμαρμένη, ἡ μοῖρα, etc.), a theme that occupied a central place in the
history of Greek and Latin thought.[134] Formally, the section is demarcated by
inclusio (ἐπίκαιρον in verse 114 and καιρῷ in verse 121) and unified by a
number of catchwords.[135]

As already indicated, the fundamental issues and general format of Pseudo-
Phocylides' exhortation on fortitude possess a number of analogues in the
comparative paraenetic, particularly gnomic, literature. The author of *Papyrus
Insinger*, for example, sub-divides 20.7–13 into three similarly designed formal segments. The paragraph starts in 20.7 with an introductory injunction
that announces the theme ("Do not worry your heart with the bitterness of one
who is dying"), bolstered by indicative statements about the nature of death
and the afterlife (20.8–11) and continuing with instruction not to be vexed by
the hardships of daily life (20.12–13).[136] In Ben Sira 38.16–23, the author explicitly connects exhortation to observe proper burial rites while avoiding excessive grief with the virtue of courage (compare 30.21–24).[137] The *Sentences*
of Syriac Menander 385–401 also counsels against the anxieties caused by the

---

[134] Derron, *Sentences*, 10, n. 3; further see Wilhelm Gundel, "Heimarmene," *PW* 7.2
(1912) 2622–2645; Samson Eitrem, "Moira," *PW* 15.2 (1932) 2449–2497; William C.
Greene, *Moira: Fate, Good, and Evil in Greek Thought* (Cambridge: Harvard University
Press, 1948) 277–398; Konrat Ziegler, "Tyche," *PW* 7A.2 (1948) 1643–1696; Bernard C.
Dietrich, *Death, Fate and the Gods: The Development of a Religious Idea in Greek Popular
Belief and in Homer* (University of London Classical Studies 3; rev. ed.; London: Athlone,
1967); Heinrich O. Schröder, "Fatum (Heimarmene)," *RAC* 7 (1969) 525–579; David
Amand, *Fatalisme et Liberté dans l'Antiquité Grecque* (Recueil de Travaux d'Histoire et de
Philologie 3.19; Amsterdam: Adolf M. Hakkert, 1973) 1–188; Jutta Krause, *ΑΛΛΟΤΕ
ΑΛΛΟΣ: Untersuchungen zum Motiv des Schicksalswechsels in der griechischen Dichtung
bis Euripides* (Tuduv Studies, Reihe Kulturwissenschaften 4; München: Tuduv-Verlags-
gesellschaft, 1976) especially 67–74 (on Hesiod) and 81–90 (on Phocylides and Theognis);
Valerio Neri, "Dei, Fato e Divinazione nella Letteratura Latina del I sec. d.C.," *ANRW*
II.16.3 (1986) 1974–2051; Thom, *Golden Verses*, 121–127. Of special interest are philo-
sophical treatises on fate such as those written by Cicero and Alexander of Aphrodisias, see
H. Rackham, trans., *Cicero* (LCL; London: Heinemann; Cambridge: Harvard University
Press, 1942) 4.187–249; R. W. Sharples, *Alexander of Aphrodisias, On Fate: Text, Transla-
tion, and Commentary* (Duckworth Classical Editions; London: Duckworth, 1983).

[135] ζῶμεν (v. 114) and ζῇ (v. 115); ἄχθου (v. 118) and ἀχθομένοισι (v. 120); κακοῖσ' (v.
118) and κακοῦ (v. 120).

[136] Cf. 2.9–13, 7.13–19, 17.5–10, 18.5–14, 20.14 ff.

[137] Cf. Skehan and DiLella, *Ben Sira*, 439, 443–444. Also cf. Ben Sira 14.11–19, 40.1 ff.,
41.1–4; Thomas, *Der jüdische Phokylides*, 210.

fear of death and the shortness of life. In verses 444–473, the author contends that people should not despair because of the vicissitudes of human existence (verses 444–457), nor mourn excessively over the deceased (verses 458–462), but give the dead a proper burial (verses 463–467), remembering that someday they too will die (verses 468–469) and descend to Sheol (verses 470–473).[138] Pseudo-Isocrates' *Ad Demonicum* 42–43 integrates recommendations to grieve and rejoice in moderation with advice to face death nobly, despite the sobering fact that eventually all mortals must die. Finally, Isocrates' *Ad Nicoclem* 35–39 connects injunctions to perish with honor rather than to live in shame with appeals to bear bravely the good and evil chances of human existence.[139]

Exhortation on the Topic of Wisdom and Speech (verses 122–131)

As most modern critics observe, the final paragraph of the section on the cardinal virtues, verses 122–131, constitutes a unified block of sayings on the topic of σοφία,[140] which is mentioned explicitly in verse 131.[141] Within this discussion, the center of attention is λόγος. We may think of the term as it is employed here as representing one special aspect or category of wisdom, encompassing excellence in both the faculties of speech and of reason.[142] As the

---

[138] Cf. 126–132, 314–321, 368–376.

[139] See the analysis above, pp. 49–51; further cf. Qohelet 6.3–6; Theognis 133–142, 557–560, 585–594, 657–660, 1162 A–F; *Carmen Aureum* 15–20, with Thom, *Golden Verses*, 116–127; *Comparatio Menandri et Philistionis* 1.65–76, 254–255, 2.166–181; Thomas, *Der jüdische Phokylides*, 309–312.

[140] On σοφία and its role in virtue see Joachim, *Nicomachean Ethics*, s.v. σοφία; Hartmut Gese, "Weisheit," *RGG³* 6 (1962) 1574–1577; Ulrich Wilckens and Georg Fohrer, "σοφία, σοφός, σοφίζω," *TDNT* 7 (1971) 465–509, cf. 510–528; P. W. Gooch, "The Relation Between Wisdom and Virtue in Phaedo 69 A–C3," *JHP* 12 (1974) 153–159; Olof Gigon, "Phronesis und Sophia in der Nikomachischen Ethik des Aristotles," *Kephalaion: Studies in Greek Philosophy and its Continuation Offered to Professor Cornelia J. de Vogel* (ed. Jaap Mansfeld and Lambertus M. de Rijk; Assen: van Gorcum, 1975) 91–104; Engberg-Pedersen, *Aristotle's Theory of Moral Insight*, 96–101, 223 ff., 240 ff.; Irwin, *Plato's Moral Theory*, 200–208; van der Horst, *Sentences*, 174–175, 202–203; Richard Sorabji, "Aristotle on the Role of Intellect in Virtue," in Rorty, *Essays*, 201–219; Aristotle, *Ethica Nicomachea* 6.1.1–6.13.8; Pseudo-Aristotle, *De Virtutibus et Vitiis* 4.1–2; Pseudo-Aristotle, *Magna Moralia* 1.34.1–32; Iamblichus, *De Vita Pythagorica* 29.157–166; Cicero, *De Officiis* 1.6.18–19.

[141] Van der Horst entitles the section "Speech and Wisdom, Man's Distinction" (*Sentences*, 97, 198); cf. Walter, *Poetische Schriften*, 208–209 ("Über rechte Rede und rechte Weisheit"); Derron, *Sentences*, xxvii, 11 ("περὶ λόγου καὶ σοφίας" or "Parole et sagesse"); Thomas, *Der jüdische Phokylides*, 191–193 ("Logos und Sophia").

[142] As van der Horst observes (*Sentences*, 201) the close connection between these two concepts is exhibited especially in the use of λόγος (vv. 124, 128), which conveys the mean-

author of the *De Virtutibus et Vitiis* observes, one of the important components of wisdom (in this case φρόνησις) is τὸ ἀγχίνως χρήσασθαι καὶ λόγῳ καὶ ἔργῳ, "to employ both *logos* and action shrewdly".[143] In the opinion of antiquity, speech frequently represented one of the plainest ways in which one's wisdom could be tested for its true value in practical social circumstances. Hence speaking both well and correctly were among the main attributes of the wise sage,[144] and eloquence itself – when informed by reason – could be elevated to a place among the primary virtues.[145] The following outline is proposed for the section:

122–123	I.	Introduction, antithetically formulated
122		A. A command against arrogant boastfulness, which leads to madness
123		B. A command to "practice speaking well", which benefits others
124–128	II.	Descriptive section on the λόγος of humankind
124		A. Thesis statement: λόγος is humankind's most effective weapon
125–128		B. Comparison of humankind's λόγος with the natural attributes of various animals (a priamel)
125a		1. Introduction: God has allotted every animal a "weapon"
125b–128		2. List of animals and their respective "weapons"
125b–126a		a. Birds: flight
126b		b. Horses: speed
126c		c. Lions: strength
127a		d. Bulls: horns
127b–128a		e. Bees: stingers
128b		f. Human beings: λόγος
130–131	III.	Conclusion, antithetical in nature
130		A. Claim: a wise man is better than a strong one
131		B. Reason: σοφία guides human civilization

Text:

122　μὴ μεγαληγορίη φυσῶν φρένα λυσσωθείης.
123　εὐεπίην ἀσκεῖν, ἥτις μάλα πάντας ὀνήσει.
124　ὅπλον τοι λόγος ἀνδρὶ τομώτερόν ἐστι σιδήρου·
125　ὅπλον ἑκάστῳ νεῖμε θεός, φύσιν ἠερόφοιτον

---

ing of "speech" as well as of "reason". Cf. Derron, *Sentences*, 27, n. 4; Emile Bréhier, *Les Idées Philosophiques et Religieuses de Philon d'Alexandrie* (Etudes de Philosophie Médiévale 8; 2nd ed.; Paris: J. Vrin, 1925) 83–111; Burton L. Mack, *Logos und Sophia: Untersuchungen zur Weisheitstheologie im hellenistischen Judentum* (SUNT 10; Göttingen: Vandenhoeck & Ruprecht, 1973) 97–102, 135–138, 141–154. Also cf. Aristotle's use of the term ὀρθὸς λόγος in *Ethica Nicomachea* VI, with Joachim, *Nicomachean Ethics*, 163 ff., and s.v. λόγος.

[143] Pseudo-Aristotle, *De Virtutibus et Vitiis* 4.1; text: Rackham, *Aristotle*, 492; my translation.

[144] See, for example, William McKane, "Functions of Language and Objectives of Discourse According to Proverbs 10–30," *La Sagesse de l'Ancien Testament* (ed. Maurice Gilbert; BETL 51; 2nd ed.; Leuven: Leuven University Press, 1990) 166–185.

[145] For example, Euripides, *Fragmenta* 282.23–28 (and Adkins, *Merit and Responsibility*, 191–192); "Anonymus Iamblichi," in Diels and Kranz, *Die Fragmente der Vorsokratiker*, 2.400.1–3, 2.401.16–19; Aeschines, *In Ctesiphontem* 168.

126 ὄρνισιν, πώλοις ταχυτῆτ', ἀλκήν τε λέουσιν,
127 ταύροις δ' αὐτοφύτως κέρα ἐστίν, κέντρα μελίσσαις
128 ἔμφυτον ἄλκαρ ἔδωκε, λόγον δ' ἔρυμ' ἀνθρώποισιν.
[129]
130 βέλτερος ἀλκήεντος ἔφυ σεσοφισμένος ἀνήρ·
131 ἀγροὺς καὶ πόλιας σοφίη καὶ νῆα κυβερνᾷ.

Translation:

122 Do not puff up[146] your mind with boastfulness and grow mad.
123 Practice speaking well, which will greatly profit everyone.
124 Surely the word is for a man a sharper weapon than iron.
125 To each God has allotted a weapon: power to roam the air
126 to birds, to horses swiftness, strength to lions;
127 he has clothed bulls with self-growing[147] horns; stingers he's given
128 to bees as an inborn defense, but reason to humans for protection.
[129][148]
130 Better than a strong man is one who's by nature wise.[149]
131 Wisdom steers the course of lands and states and ships.

In this paragraph, as elsewhere in the poem, the treatment of the virtue in question accentuates its practical and social aspects; Pseudo-Phocylides identifies λόγος as a ὅπλον ("weapon") given to human beings for their protection (verses 124, 128) that they should employ for the benefit of others (verse 123). In verse 131, the author describes σοφίη itself as directing the course of lands, states, and ships. Implicit in these statements is the opinion that wisdom must be pragmatic and beneficial to the community; therefore it should not be reduced to merely theoretical or esoteric applications. By indicating his position on this matter, Pseudo-Phocylides participates in an ongoing critique of wisdom as a virtue in ancient moral literature. Cicero, for example, contends that although the search for wisdom and truth possesses certain noble aspects, such pursuits should not detract from the active life or the fulfillment of one's moral duties to others. He complains that, "some people devote too much industry

---

[146] Reading, with Diehl (*Anthologia*, 2.107), φυσῶν (cf. V), against τρυφῶν, which is printed by Young, *Theognis*, 105; van der Horst, *Sentences*, 198; Derron, *Sentences*, 11. West (*CR* 30 [1980] 137) argues that τρυφῶν is in fact a corruption of τυφῶν. For the translation cf. van der Horst, *Sentences*, 198: "Become not mad in your mind by revelling in boastfulness"; Derron, *Sentences*, 11: "Par les délices de propos arrogants ne sois pas en ton coeur emporté"; Walter, *Poetische Schriften*, 208: "Berausche dich nicht selbst in deinem Sinn, indem du in Großsprecherei schwelgst."

[147] Reading, with Bernays (*Gesammelte Abhandlungen*, 217, n. 2) and van der Horst (*Sentences*, 97, n. 3, 200), αὐτοφύτως. Young (*Theognis*, 105) reads ταύρους δ' αὐτοχύτως κέρα ἔσσεν κτλ.; Derron (*Sentences*, 11, 27, n. 3) has ταύροις δ' αὐτοχύτως κέρα ἐστίν κτλ., which she translates, "chez les taureaux, les cornes viennent d'elles mêmes, etc."

[148] V. 129 (τῆς δὲ θεοπνεύστου σοφίης λόγος ἐστὶν ἄριστος. "Speech of divinely inspired wisdom is best.") is spurious; see van der Horst, *Sentences*, 201–202.

[149] Following the proposed translation of Edward O'Neil (personal communication, 5/15/92).

and too deep study to matters that are obscure and difficult and useless as well."[150]

Formally, a coordinated introduction (verses 122–123) and conclusion (verses 130–131) frame the body of the passage; each of these elements is constructed antithetically, contrasting real as opposed to apparent excellence in the area of speech and wisdom. The introduction contains two commands, the first warning against vain boastfulness, since it results in madness,[151] the second urging the reader instead to practice εὐεπία ("speaking well," or perhaps "eloquence") on account of the benefits it confers on all those associated with it. The conclusion, on the other hand, contrasts the wise sage, exercising his dynamic and useful wisdom, with the man whose strength is merely physical in nature; the former is better since the wisdom of which he partakes guides the course of vital human endeavors and institutions (verse 131). These elements flank the main body of the paragraph, a descriptive section that evaluates the λόγος of humankind by comparing it with the gifts allotted by God to other creatures (verses 124–128).[152] This comparative segment opens with a thesis statement (verse 124) connected to the main description in verses 125–128 by catchword and inclusio.[153] Pseudo-Phocylides asserts that λόγος equips the human race with a "sharper weapon than iron", that is, a tool indispensable for human survival and advancement.[154] He expands upon this idea in verses 125–128, where we learn that God has apportioned to each species of creature its own unique and characteristic "weapon". A list of vivid examples from the animal world illustrates this observation: birds have flight, horses speed, lions strength, bulls horns, bees stingers, but most important, of course, is the λόγος given human beings. The nature of the descriptive section's design and argument is reminiscent of the priamel, a popular device in Greco-Roman litera-

---

[150] ... quod quidam nimis magnum studium multamque operam in res obscuras atque difficiles conferunt easdemque non necessarias. *De Officiis* 1.6.19; text and translation: Miller, *Cicero*, 20–21; cf. Ibscher, *Der Begriff des Sittlichen*, 106–112.

[151] As van der Horst observes (*Sentences*, 198), v. 122 constitutes a warning against ὑπερηφανία, a common theme in Greek, Jewish, and Christian literature; cf. Georg Betram, "ὑπερήφανος, ὑπερηφανία," *TDNT* 8 (1972) 525–529; Spicq, *Notes*, 3.644–649; cf. above, n. 55.

[152] This was a common theme in ancient philosophical literature; for references see van der Horst, *Sentences*, 200–201; for comparable gnomic paragraphs cf. *Gnomologium Democrateum* 51–56; Ankhsheshonqy 8.17–23.

[153] ὅπλον in vv. 124 and 125; λόγος (v. 124) and λόγον (v. 128); ἀνδρί (v. 124) and ἀνθρώποισιν (v. 128). On the use of chiasm in these lines see van der Horst, *Sentences*, 200. The descriptive section is linked to the conclusion by catchword as well: ἄλκαρ (v. 128) and ἀλκήεντος (v. 130); ἀνθρώποισιν (v. 128) and ἀνήρ (v. 130). The two lines of the conclusion also exhibit catchword: σεσοφισμένος (v. 130) and σοφίη (v. 131).

[154] On λόγος as humankind's most important possession cf. Hock and O'Neil, *The Chreia*, # 2 (p. 301).

ture, particularly poetry.[155] Often, as here in verses 125–128, a priamel will open with a general introductory statement that provides the theme, while the final item in the comparative catalogue is allotted special significance in one way or another. Such constructions were also employed on a regular basis in conjunction with gnomic forms, as Ovid, *Amores* 3.4.17–26 illustrates:[156]

> nitimur in vetitum semper eupimusque negata;
>   sic interdictis imminet aeger aquis.
> centum fronte oculos, centum cervice gerebat
>   Argus – et hos unus saepe fefellit Amor;
> in thalamum Danae ferro saxoque perennem
>   quae fuerat virgo tradita, mater erat;
> Penelope mansit, quamvis custode carebat,
>   inter tot iuvenes intemerata procos.
> Quidquid servatur eupimus magis, ipsaque furem
>   eura vocat; pauci, quod sinit alter, amant.

> We ever strive for what is forbid, and ever covet what is denied;
>   so the sick man longingly hangs over forbidden water.
> A hundred eyes before, a hundred behind, had
>   Argus – and these Love alone did oft deceive;
> the chamber of Danae was eternally strong with iron and rock,
>   yet she who had been given a maid to its keeping became a mother.
> Penelope, although without a guard,
>   remained inviolate among so many youthful wooers.
> Whatever is guarded we desire the more, and care itself
>   invites the thief; few love what another concedes.

In this paragraph the maxims occupying lines 17 and 25–26 flank the priamel itself in lines 18–24, which consists of a roster of four well-known examples illustrating the human propensity to desire most things that are forbidden or closely guarded by others (lines 18, 19–20, 21–22, 23–24). In addition to their

---

[155] Walter Kröhling (*Die Priamel [Beispielreihung] als Stilmittel in der griechisch-römischen Dichtung, nebst einen Nachwort: Die altorientalische Priamel, von Franz Dornseiff* [GBLS 10; Greifswald: Hans Dallmeyer, 1935] 63) identifies vv. 125–128 of the *Sentences* as a priamel. See further W. A. A. van Otterlo, "Beitrage zur Kenntnis der griechischen Priamel," *Mnemosyne* 8 (1940) 145–176; Ulrich Schmid, *Die Priamel der Werte im Griechischen von Homer bis Paulus* (Wiesbaden: Otto Harrassowitz, 1964); Tilman Krischer, "Die logischen Formen der Priamel," *Grazer Beiträge* 2 (1974) 79–91; William H. Race, *The Classical Priamel from Homer to Boethius* (Mnemosyne Sup. 74; Leiden: E. J. Brill, 1982).

[156] Text and translation: Grant Showerman, trans., *Ovid: Heroides and Amores* (LCL; 2nd ed.; Cambridge: Harvard University Press; London: Heinemann, 1977) 460–461. For other examples of priamels utilized within a gnomic context see Ovid, *Amores* 1.2.10–18, 2.17.14–24, 3.8.45–50, *Tristia* 1.2.4–12, 2.266–276, *Ex Ponto* 1.5.35–42, 4.3.35–48; Propertius, *Elegies* 2.1.57–64; Theognis 699–718 (with Schmid, *Die Priamel*, 22–26); Plato, *Leges* 660 E–661 C (with Schmid, *Die Priamel*, 27–33); cf. Kröhling, *Die Priamel*, 59–63; Race, *The Classical Priamel*, 29–30; also Archer Taylor, *The Proverb and an Index to the Proverb* (2nd ed.; Hatboro, PA: Folklore Associates; Copenhagen: Rosenkilde and Bagger, 1962) 179–180.

structural role, the gnomic utterances that introduce and conclude the segment provide a means for the poet to elicit from the specific examples some general rules or observations on human behavior and decision-making in a form that is striking and memorable.

The theme and perspective of Pseudo-Phocylides' paragraph on speech and wisdom would be at home also in the moral literature of the time; among gnomic sources we may compare especially various topical clusters in the *Sententiae* of Sextus, where the author consistently identifies observing truthfulness, moderation, and reason in speech as attributes of the wise sage (see, for example, lines 151–168, 350–368, and 426–432).[157] Also analogous is Ben Sira 37.16–26, where the author depicts speech, understood as the origin of all of one's actions, both good and bad, as the means by which the sage may be wise not only to his own advantage, but for the benefit of his people as well.[158]

This concludes our analysis of verses 9–131 of the *Sententiae*. As we have seen, in this, the longest sub-section of the poem, Pseudo-Phocylides has subsumed exhortatory material based upon the Torah and various non-biblical sources under the headings of each of the four virtues of the Platonic-Stoic canon. In doing so, we see him implicitly endorsing, while at the same time utilizing for his own purposes and in his own manner, the most common form of the canon in antiquity. By deploying it in this manner, the poet highlights both the philosophical and the multi-cultural, Hellenistic nature of his instruction, demonstrating the positive and practical connection between Jewish and Greco-Roman morality. The canon also benefits our author in so far as it indicates the range and the scope of moral responsibilities that he has in mind, suggesting the balance of both personal and social concerns necessary in developing an agenda for ethical action in a cosmopolitan milieu. Although verses 122–131 brings to a conclusion a major subsection of the *Sentences*, rounding off the author's exhortation structured according to the Canon of Cardinal Virtues, the poem's gnomic appeal does not end here. As we will see in the next chapter, Pseudo-Phocylides extends his teaching in verses 3–131 by linking with it exhortation structured according to a distinct, though related, literary and rhetorical pattern that complements and develops the moral principles and arguments articulated thus far.

---

[157] Cf. Chadwick, *The Sentences of Sextus*, 105–106, 169–170, 178, 180–181.

[158] Cf. Skehan and DiLella, *Ben Sira*, 434–437; further Ben Sira 8.8–9, 21.13–17, 27.4–7, 28.12–26, 38.31–39.11; also cf. Ahiqar, *Sayings* 92–109; *Comparatio Menandri et Philistionis* 2.35–48, 182–194.

Chapter Five

Exhortation Structured According to the Relationships in Which One Lives (verses 132–227)

The third and last major formal section of the body of Pseudo-Phocylides' *Sentences* is verses 132–227. The organizing principle at work in this block of material is no longer the Canon of Cardinal Virtues, as it was in verses 9–131, but rather the sub-sections here have been arranged according to different areas or spheres of social life, with the topic of each sub-section addressing a more specific and more familiar domain of ethical responsibility. From a material standpoint, the section may be viewed as a series of three concentric rings, each somewhat more restricted or focused in its point of reference than the last. Thus the first paragraph of sayings (verses 132–152) discusses what we might call social 'outsiders', that is, assorted referents on the periphery of moral life and conduct, with an emphasis on how one ought to deal with evil persons. The second paragraph (verses 153–174) concentrates on how the reader ought to earn a living, treating a more specific topic as well as a more pertinent and common area of life than the preceding paragraph, though the activities described here take place mostly outside the household (see especially verses 160–161, 164 a). The third and final sub-section offers advice on the most familiar referents and the most customary aspects of social life, namely, ethical obligations within the household and among members of the family (verses 175–227).

It should be underscored that although the means for organizing the maxims into topical units changes beginning at verse 132, many of the basic ethical subjects and presuppositions of the individual sayings are compatible with those found earlier in the poem. So, for example, the advice of a number of precepts in verses 132 ff. relates to the general themes of justice and moderation, even while the topics of the paragraphs in which these precepts are situated address different concerns. Similarly, there is no discernible shift in the maxims' level of specificity or argumentative stance. We should also note that there is nothing fundamentally new here in the author's attempt to enumerate moral duties as they relate to different types of referents (compare, for example, the exhortation on *philanthropia* in verses 22–41). It seems safe to conclude, then, that no change takes place in the ethical character or tone of the poem, just in its mode of literary composition. Moreover, the organization of

ethical material according to the various relationships in which a person lives
not only represents a fairly common practice in ancient paraenesis, but, judging at least from some sources (see below), it would have also constituted a
natural and expected corollary to instruction constructed around the canon of
primary virtues.

One place where exhortation structured according to the different relationships in which one lives occurs is the Stoic lists of καθήκοντα, mentioned
above with reference to recent scholarship on verses 175–227. The *Epitome* of
Hierocles (second century A.D.), for instance, preserved in the *Anthologia* of
Stobaeus, summarizes Stoic ethical teaching in a format based upon the traditional lists of duties. While reconstruction of the text remains tentative, the
Epitome appears to have been divided into a number of 'chapters' based on
different referents which may have been organized as follows:[1]

1   Τίνα τρόπον θεοῖς χρηστέον
2   Πῶς πατρίδι χρηστέον
3   Πῶς χρηστέον τοῖς γονεῦσιν
4   Περὶ φιλαδελφίας
5   Πῶς συγγενέσι χρηστέον
6   Οἰκονομικός
7   Περὶ γάμου (καὶ παιδοποιίας)

Although the *Sentences* contains no paragraphs with topics comparable to
those of the first three chapters in Hierocles' *Epitome*, both the themes and ordering of chapters 4–7 show some basic similarities with those of verses 132–
227. Thus chapters 4 and 5 discuss respectively how to treat all people with
consideration and regard (including certain 'outsiders') and how to conduct
oneself towards relatives outside the immediate family. Chapter 6 then summarizes the types of labor that are appropriate for different members of the
household. Finally, chapter 7 instructs the reader on the importance of marriage and on the responsibilities that parents have towards their children. The
same general arrangement of topics is discernible in verses 132–227 of the
Sententiae: first a broadly defined group of 'outsiders', then labor, marriage,
and finally children. Thus the καθήκοντα-scheme that modern critics have
seen at work only in verses 175–227 may be extended in its application to include the instruction in verses 132–174 as well. A literary format of this type
would be comparable to treatments of moral duties found in other Hellenistic-
Jewish gnomic sources, for example, Ben Sira 7.1–28. This unit opens with
miscellaneous precepts against evil, injustice, and sinning (verses 1–14), fol-

---

[1] Karl Praechter, *Hierokles der Stoiker* (Leipzig: Dieterich'sche Verlags-Buchhandlung,
1901) 14–90; Hans F. A. von Arnim, *Hierokles ethische Elementarlehre (Papyrus 9780)*
(Berliner Klassikertexte 4; Berlin: Weidmannsche Buchhandlung, 1906); Powell and Barber, *New Chapters*, 36–40; Crouch, *Colossian Haustafel*, 67–70; Malherbe, *Moral Exhortation*, 85–104.

lowed by directives for the readers not to feel that they are above manual labor (verses 15–17), and finally advice that touches upon the moral obligations owed to different members of the household, including wives, slaves, children, and parents (verses 18–28).[2]

Also of special interest are texts that in some manner connect exhortation organized according to the different relationships in which one lives with exhortation organized according to the Canon of Cardinal Virtues. Indeed, it appears that the application of these two literary schemes in conjunction with one another represents something of an argumentative convention among both Greco-Roman and Jewish authors for articulating a program relating to matters of ethical action and decision-making within a philosophical context. This can be discerned most clearly, perhaps, in the *De Officiis*, where, as we observed in Chapter One, Cicero organizes the first major section of the discussion of moral duties (καθήκοντα) according to the Stoic Canon of Cardinal Virtues.[3] Additionally, in the course of analyzing each of the virtues, Cicero is able to list some of the duties dictated by that particular virtue as it pertains to various referents, for example, in 1.17.53–58 and 1.34.122–125.[4] Cicero's association of the canon with his exploration of moral duties apparently evokes a fairly standard procedure in Stoic philosophy, as evidenced by some of the more substantial extant 'summaries' of its moral system located in Diogenes Laertius, *Vitae Philosophorum* 7.84–131, Cicero, *De Finibus* 3.4.15–3.22.76, and the *Epitome* of Arius Didymus, preserved in Book 2 of Stobaeus' *Eclogae*.[5] Each of these authors employs both the canon of virtues and an evaluation of καθήκοντα (in collaboration with other literary schemes) as they summarize Stoic ethics.[6]

---

[2] Cf. Skehan and DiLella, *Ben Sira*, 197–206; also cf. above, p. 7, n. 21. Also cf. Syriac Menander, *Sentences* 126–228, which is divided into three major units: (1) counsel regarding different 'outsiders' and unjust behavior (enemies [vv. 126–132], public arguments [vv. 133–144], theft [vv. 145–147], bad men [vv. 148–153], bad servants [vv. 154–169], lascivious old men [vv. 170–172], and a transitional summary [vv. 173–180]); (2) advice on dining at banquets and loaning money (vv. 181–188); (3) exhortation about the household (brothers and friends [vv. 189–193], sons and brothers [vv. 194–210], fathers [vv. 211–212], friends [vv. 213–226], and slaves [vv. 227–228]). For translation see Baarda, "Syriac Menander," 595–598; also cf. vv. 328 ff.

[3] See above, pp. 46–47.

[4] Cf. Seneca, *Epistulae Morales* 95.47–55.

[5] On Arius Didymus see Michelangelo Giusta, *I Dossografi di Etica* (2 vols.; Turin: Giappichelli, 1964, 1967) [and the reviews by G. B. Kerford in *CR* 81 (1967) 156–158 and *CR* 85 (1971) 371–373]; Charles H. Kahn, "Arius as Doxographer," *On Stoic and Peripatetic Ethics: The Work of Arius Didymus* (ed. William W. Fortenbaugh; Rutgers University Studies in Classical Humanities 1; New Brunswick, NJ and London: Transaction Books, 1983) 3–13; Anthony A. Long, "Arius Didymus and the Exposition of Stoic Ethics," in Fortenbaugh, *Ethics*, 41–65.

[6] Praechter (*Hierokles*, 7–14) also raises the possibility that the Epitome of Hierocles opened with a (now lost) analysis of the virtues, continuing with the exhortation on duties

The literary procedures to which these Stoic summaries bear witness correspond with more widespread conceptions regarding the logical connection between the cultivation of virtue and the recognition of moral responsibilities in different spheres of life. One place where such ideas are expressed in a rather succinct form is the introduction to the Pythagorean tractate περὶ γυναικὸς ἁρμονίας of Pseudo-Periktione:[7]

> τὴν ἁρμονίην γυναῖκα νώσασθαι δεῖ φρονήσιός τε καὶ σωφροσύνης πλείην· κάρτα γὰρ ψυχὴν πεπνῦσθαι δεῖ εἰς ἀρετήν, ὥστ' ἔσται καὶ δικαίη καὶ ἀνδρηίη καὶ φρονέουσα καὶ αὐταρκείῃ καλλυνομένη καὶ κενὴν δόξην μισέουσα. ἐκ τούτων γὰρ ἔργματα καλὰ γίνεται γυναικὶ ἐς αὑτήν τε καὶ ἄνδρα καὶ τέκεα καὶ οἶκον· πολλάκις δὲ καὶ πόλει, εἴ γε πόλιας ἢ ἔθνεα ἡ τοίη γε κρατύνοι, ὡς ἐπὶ βασιληίης ὀρέομεν.

> A woman must deem harmony to be the greater part of both prudence and moderation. For her soul must be truly wise in virtue, so that she shall be just, courageous, and prudent, priding herself in her independence and despising vain judgment. For from these (virtues), she does noble deeds towards herself, her husband, her children, and her household. And often towards cities as well, if such a woman in fact governs cities or nations, as we (may) see in a kingdom.

The possession of the virtues in the woman's soul generates the noble deeds (ἔργματα καλά) that she may carry out towards a whole spectrum of referents, ranging from herself and her husband to the οἶκος (including responsibilities towards kindred and slaves, as the treatise goes on to show) and even (potentially) to entire cities, which presumably involves moral obligations towards all sorts of people. On one hand, as the author maintains, in order to become fully realized virtue must be manifested through the recognition and performance of moral duties, whereas, on the other, in order for these concrete actions to be fully praiseworthy and fully integrated into a noble life they must be motivated by the cultivation of virtue. These two approaches to moral growth, then, complement, correct, and interpret one another.

Moral rudiments informed by this type of reasoning left their mark on Jewish thinkers of the Second Temple period as well. Philo's allegorical exegesis of the trees and the rivers in the Garden of Eden located in *Legum Allegoriae* 1.56–64 provides an example. Here the author develops a hierarchical framework that relates virtue as an absolute with both the canon of virtues and the καθήκοντα. Philo situates at the top of this hierarchy "generic virtue" (ἡ γενικωτάτη ἀρετή), which, he argues, is the ontological source for the virtues of the Platonic tetrad, each of which, in turn, is manifested through various ac-

---

that we have. There may have been, in fact, within Stoicism a school of thought that utilized the canon of cardinal virtues as a framework for the analysis of duty.

[7] Text: Holger Thesleff, ed., *The Pythagorean Texts of the Hellenistic Period* (Acta Academiae Aboensis A.30.1; Åbo: Åbo Akademi, 1965) 142–143; my translation. Cf. Kurt von Fritz, "Periktione," *PW* 19.1 (1937) 794–795; also, more generally, Kathleen O. Wicker, "Mulierum Virtutes (Moralia 242E–263C)," in Betz, *Plutarch's Ethical Writings*, 106–134.

tivities, identified as either moral accomplishments (κατορθώματα) or moral duties (καθήκοντα). Finally, at the bottom of the hierarchy, he identifies noble deeds (καλαὶ πράξεις) as the specific acts that constitute these moral accomplishments or moral duties.[8] In this manner, Philo demonstrates how one's moral obligations to different types of people, and the concrete actions associated with these obligations, develop from and correspond to the primary virtues as well as to virtue in its perfect, divine sense. This sort of hierarchy appears to drive the formation of other Philonic texts, such as *De Virtutibus* 102 ff., where he illustrates how the virtue of φιλανθρωπία applies to different categories of people and things. Thus one ought to demonstrate humanity in dealing with strangers (§§ 102–108), enemies (§§ 109–120), slaves (§§ 121–124), animals (§§ 125–147), and plants (§§ 148–160).[9] Such organizational schemes resemble those employed by Isocrates in the *Ad Nicoclem* 20–29, where, as we saw above, the paraenesis on justice contains advice on how to manage with fairness situations that pertain to an array of different moral referents.

Mention should be made lastly of Josephus, *Contra Apionem* 2.190–219, a summary of the Torah that exhibits numerous parallels with Pseudo-Phocylides' *Sententiae*.[10] Of particular interest for the analysis of verses 132–227 is the literary format at work in 2.199–213. The summary in its entirety can be outlined as follows:

190–198	I.	On εὐσέβεια
190–192a		A. On the nature of God
192b–198		B. On the worship of God: the temple and its operation
192b		1. Introduction: the practice of virtue is the best form of worship
193a		2. The temple
193b–194		3. The priests
195		4. The sacrifices
196–197		5. Prayer
198		6. Purifications

---

[8] Jastram, "Generic Virtue," 327–330.

[9] Cf. Crouch, *Colossian Haustafel*, 48, 55–56, 60–61, 81.

[10] On this summary see Klein, *Der älteste christliche Katechismus*, 143–153; Crouch, *Colossian Haustafel*, 74–101; Ehrhard Kamlah, "Frömmigkeit und Tugend: Die Gesetzesapologie des Josephus in c Ap 2, 145–195," *Josephus-Studien. Untersuchungen zu Josephus, dem antiken Judentum und dem Neuen Testament: Otto Michel zum 70. Geburtstag gewidmet* (ed. Otto Betz, Klaus Haacker, and Martin Hengel; Göttingen: Vandenhoeck & Ruprecht, 1974) 220–232; Küchler, *Frühjüdische Weisheitstraditionen*, 210–222; David L. Balch, "Two Apologetic Encomia: Dionysius on Rome and Josephus on the Jews," *JSJ* 13 (1982) 102–122; Geza Vermes, "A Summary of the Law by Flavius Josephus," *NovT* 24 (1982) 289–303; Niebuhr, *Gesetz und Paränese*, 39–41 and passim; Carras, "Philo's Hypothetica," 431–450.

The first two sections, which comprise 2.190–213, recount the various obligations imposed by the Torah on the Jewish people, whereas the concluding segment, 2.214–219, stipulates the rewards bestowed on those who obey (§§ 217b–219)[11] and the punishment that awaits those who fail to do so (§§ 214–217a). The first section on obligations (§§ 190–198) addresses some of the significant aspects of the Jewish conception of God (§§ 190–192a) and then the proper manner of worshipping God (§§ 192b–198), subjects that relate to the topic of the virtue εὐσέβεια. The second section, 2.199–213, which constitutes the heart of the summary, proceeds to enumerate Jewish obligations and concerns in the domain of human relations. As Geza Vermes has observed, the main thrust of the text at this point is the idea that such relations ought to be governed by the virtue of φιλανθρωπία, explicitly mentioned in 2.213.[12] Thus it appears that Josephus has applied a schema familiar from the Canon of Two Virtues[13] as an organizational device in his presentation of the Torah's moral requirements. Furthermore, he classifies the directives that are placed under the heading of φιλανθρωπία (section II) in a manner comparable to the approach detected in verses 132–227 of our poem, though the order of analogous topical units is reversed.

To begin with, Josephus mentions rules of the Mosaic law that pertain to personal obligations within the household (§§ 199–206). This section incorporates counsel on responsibilities to one's spouse, especially in matters of sexual behavior (§§ 199–203; compare *Sententiae* 175 ff., 195 ff.), duties that pertain to the upbringing of children (§ 204; compare *Sententiae* 207–217), and obligations to parents and elders (§ 206; compare *Sententiae* 220–222)

---

[11] Cf. Pseudo-Phocylides, *Sentences* 229–230.

[12] Vermes, "A Summary of the Law," 299.

[13] Cf. above, pp. 70–71.

much in the same way as Pseudo-Phocylides' teaching on household duties in verses 175–227. The middle paragraph of Josephus' treatment of φιλανθρωπία (§§ 207–208) contains a miscellany of precepts that advise the reader on duties to different members of the community who are neither part of the household nor reckoned as 'outsiders' (compare §§ 209–213); with regard to the nature of its referents, then, the advice here occupies a sort of middle ground between the teaching in sections II.A and II.C. While a number of themes emerge in this section, some of its directives touch upon economic and monetary matters, which are also part of Pseudo-Phocylides' middle section in verses 153–174, exhortation concerning the nature and importance of work. In drawing section II to a close, Josephus discusses the Jewish treatment of different social 'outsiders' (§§ 209–213), a theme that is also central to verses 132–152 in the *Sentences*. It follows that a number of the referents mentioned in 2.209–213 match those in this part of our poem, particularly enemies and evildoers (§§ 211–212; compare *Sententiae* 132–136, 141–143, 151–152) and animals (§ 213; compare *Sententiae* 139–140, 147–148). Most important to Josephus' presentation at this juncture is the obligation to show mercy, ἐπιείκεια (§ 214), a concern that resonates throughout verses 132–152 of the *Sentences*, too.[14]

So in the matter of the nature of its overall literary composition, the section on φιλανθρωπία in Book II of Josephus' *Contra Apionem* manifests the same sort of three-part concentric ring structure observed in verses 132–227 of our poem. We should bear in mind additionally that both authors in some manner link their καθήκοντα-schemes with literary configurations informed by a canon of virtues. There are, of course, some important differences to be noted between the two texts as well. An obvious one is that Josephus begins his discussion at the center of the ring structure and works outwards whereas Pseudo-Phocylides moves in the opposite direction, starting at the periphery and moving inwards. Also, Josephus bases his summary of Torah obligations on the Canon of Two Virtues and allows exhortation organized according to the virtues and exhortation organized according to duties to overlap (like Cicero in the *De Officiis*) whereas Pseudo-Phocylides avails himself of the Platonic-Stoic tetrad, separating the teaching structured around the cardinal virtues from that on duties in different areas of life. These variations evidence the authors' differing ethical presuppositions and objectives as well as their the different literary characteristics and modes of communication of their respective texts.

---

[14] Cf. Triantaphyllopoulos, *Das Rechtsdenken der Griechen*, 23–24, 178–190.

Exhortation Concerning Social 'Outsiders' (verses 132–152)

The sequence of sayings in verses 132–153 is in many respects the most miscellaneous and incoherent of the poem, and its analysis presents special problems both with regard to its internal design and its relationship with the rest of
the text. It appears to contain a number of thematic clusters that have been organized by ring composition, though the structure here is rougher and more
uneven than those detected in verses 9–21 and 79–96. As mentioned above,
these clusters are affiliated materially in so far as they offer recommendations
concerning referents who are social 'outsiders'.[15] The rendering of advice on
how to evaluate and handle such types is characteristic of the gnomic style, as
passages such as Ankhsheshonqy 19.3–25,[16] *Papyrus Insinger* 11.22–15.6,[17]
and Ben Sira 8.1–19,[18] 11.29–12.18[19] attest. Although the range of referents
that these texts exhibit is often considerable (enemies, fools, and evildoers being the most popular), emphasis is placed throughout upon the importance of
exercising extreme caution and discrimination when interacting with such
people, while at the same time displaying as humane an outlook as possible.[20]

Although the paragraph on 'outsiders' makes significant use of catchwords
as a unifying device,[21] its central organizing strategy is to be found in the use
of ring composition:

---

[15] On outsiders as a reference group for moral exhortation cf. Wayne A. Meeks, "The
Circle of Reference in Pauline Morality," *Greeks, Romans, and Christians: Essays in
Honor of Abraham J. Malherbe* (ed. David L. Balch, Everett Ferguson, and Wayne A.
Meeks; Minneapolis: Fortress, 1990) 305–317. On the biblical background of vv. 132–152
see Thomas, *Der jüdische Phokylides*, 171–179, 326.

[16] Cf. Lichtheim, *Late Egyptian Wisdom*, 84–85.

[17] This passage embraces the twelfth (entitled, "Do not trust one whom you do not know
in your heart, lest he cheat you with cunning"), the thirteenth (entitled, "Do not trust a thief,
lest you come to grief"), and the fourteenth (entitled, "Do not let the inferior man rule, lest
he make your name that of a fool") instructions; cf. Lichtheim, *Late Egyptian Wisdom*, 208–
212.

[18] These verses contain advice on dealing prudently with a whole array of different types
of people, including many 'outsiders': fools, sinners, evildoers, strangers, and so forth; cf.
Skehan and DiLella, *Ben Sira*, 209–214.

[19] Here the author recommends discretion and caution in selecting associates and in how
one does good to others, with many observations pertinent to dealing with 'outsiders', for
example, slanderers, evildoers, the wicked, sinners, enemies, and the proud; cf. Skehan and
DiLella, *Ben Sira*, 242–248.

[20] Also cf. *Gnomologium Democrateum* 87–97; Ahiqar, *Sayings* 162–172; Didache 3.1–
6, with Niederwimmer, *Die Didache*, 123–130; H. van de Sandt, "Didache 3.1–6: A Transformation of an Existing Jewish Hortatory Pattern," *JSJ* 23 (1992) 21–41.

[21] κακοεργόν (v. 133) and κακοῖσ' (v. 134); δέξῃ (v. 135) and δεξάμενος (v. 136);
κλοπίμην (v. 135) and κλῶπες, κλέψας (v. 136); πᾶσιν (v. 137) and πάντων (v. 138); μὴ
τέρμ' (v. 138) and μέτρον (v. 139); κτήνους (v. 139) and κτῆνος (v. 140); ὁδόν (v. 140) and
ἀλίτροπον (v. 141); ἐχθροῖο (v. 140) and ἐχθροῦ (v. 142); θηρόβορον (v. 147) and θηρῶν,
θῆρες (v. 148). Note also the α- alliteration in vv. 132–133.

132–136   A. Exhortation not to associate with evildoers
137   B. A rule on the fair treatment of children
138   C. A general rule on moderation: be sparing
139–140   D. Maxims concerning the treatment of animals
141–143   E. On overcoming evil with kindness
147–148   D'. Further advice concerning animals
149   C'. Specific command on moderation: use no magic
150   B'. A command not to hurt children
151–152   A'. Exhortation to avoid strife and evildoers

Text:

132   οὐχ ὅσιον κρύπτειν τὸν ἀτάσθαλον ἄνδρ' ἀνέλεγκτον,
133   ἀλλὰ χρὴ κακοεργὸν ἀποτρωπᾶσθαι ἀνάγκῃ·
134   πολλάκι συνθνῄσκουσι κακοῖσ' οἱ συμπαρεόντες.
135   φωρῶν μὴ δέξῃ κλοπίμην ἄδικον παραθήκην·
136   ἀμφότεροι κλῶπες, καὶ ὁ δεξάμενος καὶ ὁ κλέψας.
137   μοίρας παισὶ νέμειν, ἰσότης δ' ἐν πᾶσιν ἄριστον.
138   ἀρχόμενος φείδου πάντων, μὴ τέρμ' ἐπιδεύσῃ.
139   μὴ κτήνους θνητοῖο βορὴν κατὰ μέτρον ἕληαι.
140   κτῆνος κἢν ἐχθροῖο πέσῃ καθ' ὁδόν, συνέγειρε.
141   πλαζόμενον δὲ βροτὸν καὶ ἀλίτροπον μήποτ' ἐλέγξῃς.
142   βέλτερον ἀντ' ἐχθροῦ τεύχειν φίλον εὐμενέοντα.
143   ἀρχόμενον τὸ κακὸν κόπτειν ἕλκος τ' ἀκέσασθαι.
[144]
[145]
[146]
147   μὴ δέ τι θηρόβορον δαίσῃ κρέας, ἀργίποσιν δέ
148   λείψανα λεῖπε κυσίν· θηρῶν ἄπο θῆρες ἔδονται.
149   φάρμακα μὴ τεύχειν, μαγικῶν βίβλων ἀπέχεσθαι.
150   νηπιάχοις ἁπαλοῖς μὴ μάρψῃ χεῖρα βιαίως.
151   φεῦγε διχοστασίην καὶ ἔριν πολέμου προσιόντος.
152   μὴ κακὸν εὖ ἔρξῃς· σπείρειν ἴσον ἔστ' ἐνὶ πόντῳ.

Translation:

132   It is unholy to conceal unconvicted the guilty man;
133   but it is necessary to deter an evildoer with force.
134   Often those who go with the wicked perish with them.
135   Take not into illegal deposit the thievery of criminals:[22]
136   both are thieves, the one who accepts and the one who's stolen.
137   Pay due respect to children;[23] equality is best in everything.
138   When you begin, use all things sparingly lest you end up in want.[24]

---

[22] Cf. van der Horst, *Sentences*, 204: "Accept not from thieves a stolen, unlawful deposit."

[23] Reading παισί with M (cf. B), Brunck (*Gnomici Poetae Graeci*, 164), and Bergk (*Poetae Lyrici Graeci*, 99) against πᾶσι in P, L, V, Young (*Theognis*, 106), van der Horst (*Sentences*, 205), and Derron (*Sentences*, 12). See Walter (*Poetische Schriften*, 209) who translates: "Teile den Kindern ihre (Erb-)Anteile (gleichmäßig) zu – Gleichheit unter allen ist am besten." Cf. Ben Sira 42.3; van der Horst, "Pseudo-Phocylides Revisited," 24; Juvenal, *Saturae* 14.38–58.

[24] Following Edward O'Neil's (personal communication, 5/15/92) suggested emendation ἐπιδεύσῃ. Cf. Bergk's (*Poetae Lyrici Graeci*, 100) and Bernay's (*Gesammelte Abhand-*

139 Take not for yourself the daily food of a man's animal.[25]
140 And if[26] an enemy's animal falls along the way, help to lift it up.
141 Never blame an errant man or a transgressor.[27]
142 It is better to make a gracious friend in place of an enemy.
143 Nip evil in the bud and so heal the wound.[28]
[144]
[145]
[146][29]
147 Eat no meat torn by wild beasts, but to swift-footed dogs
148 leave the remains: beasts feed on beasts.
149 Concoct no potions; from books of magic keep away.
150 On tender children lay not a hand in violence.[30]
151 Flee dissension and strife when war approaches.
152 Do no good to an evil man: it's like sowing in the sea.

The teaching of this passage concentrates primarily on different strategies for how the reader ought to respond to evil and evildoers. This is clear not only from the number of lines devoted to this topic (ten of the section's eighteen – eleven if we include verse 140), but also from the prominent position assigned to the clusters that occupy these lines, that is, at the beginning, the middle, and the end of the passage.

---

lungen, 258) conjecture ἐπιδεύῃ, against ἐπιδεύῃς, printed by Diehl (*Anthologia*, 2.108), Young (*Theognis*, 106), van der Horst (*Sentences*, 205), and Derron (*Sentences*, 12).

[25] On the difficulties of interpreting this verse see van der Horst, *Sentences*, 206; idem, "Pseudo-Phocylides Revisited," 24–25.

[26] Reading κἤν with P, L, V, Bernays (*Gesammelte Abhandlungen*, 258), Bergk (*Poetae Lyrici Graeci*, 100), Diehl (*Anthologia*, 2.108), and Walter (*Poetische Schriften*, 210). M, B, Young (*Theognis*, 106), van der Horst (*Sentences*, 207), and Derron (*Sentences*, 12) have δ' ἤν instead.

[27] There are many textual problems in this line; see van der Horst, *Sentences*, 207–208, and Derron, *Sentences*, 12, 28, n. 5. The text printed above (μήποτ' ἐλέγξῃς) is from Bergk (*Poetae Lyrici Graeci*, 100) and Diehl (*Anthologia*, 2.108), following P and L (cf. Walter, *Poetische Schriften*, 210). Young (*Theognis*, 106), van der Horst (*Sentences*, 207–208), and Derron (*Sentences*, 12) read οὔποτ' ἐλέγξεις with Pa^vo and Rb. On the translation cf. van der Horst, *Sentences*, 207–208: "Never expose a wandering man and a sinner"; Walter, *Poetische Schriften*, 210: "Einem verirrten und umhergetriebenen Menschen mache niemals Vorhaltungen"; Derron, *Sentences*, 12: "Tu ne repousseras jamais un homme errant et égaré."

[28] Following van der Horst's (*Sentences*, 208–209) translation for vv. 142–143; cf. Walter, *Poetische Schriften*, 210: "(Man soll) das Übel schon zu Beginn ersticken, eine Wunde (schon beim Entstehen) heilen."

[29] Vv. 144–146 (ἐξ ὀλίγου σπινθῆρος ἀθέσφατος αἴθεται ὕλη. ἐγκρατὲς ἦτορ ἔχειν, καὶ λωβητῶν δ' ἀπέχεσθαι. φεῦγε κακὴν φήμην, φεῦγ' ἀνθρώπους ἀθεμίστους. "From a tiny spark a mighty woods burns. Have a steadfast heart and refrain from baneful thoughts as well. Avoid evil gossip; avoid lawless people.") are spurious; see van der Horst, *Sentences*, 209–211.

[30] Reading ἁπαλοῖς μὴ μάρψῃ with Diehl (*Anthologia*, 2.109), which is supported by M² and V. Cf. Bergk (*Poetae Lyrici Graeci*, 102) and Bernays (*Gesammelte Abhandlungen*, 259): ἀταλοὺς μὴ μάρψῃς. Also cf. Young (*Theognis*, 107), van der Horst (*Sentences*, 213–214), and Derron (*Sentences*, 12): ἀταλοῖς μὴ ἄψῃ. The translation follows the suggestion of Edward O'Neil (personal communication, 5/15/92).

At the extremities of the ring composition, A (verses 132–136) and A' (verses 151–152), we find exhortation pertaining to evil and evildoers that is largely negative in its orientation: the reader is to avoid evildoers and not to become involved in their schemes. The poet contends that to hide or to protect someone guilty of a crime so that he remains unconvicted is unholy (verse 132); rather, those who transgress the law must be deterred from doing wrong (verse 133). The next verse offers one possible rationale for following these directives, namely, that those who accompany evildoers and abet their cause will also share their fate, which frequently can be death. Cluster A also includes the author's caution not to accept any deposit that is the result of thievery, since this is illegal and entails complicity in the transgression (verses 135–136). At the opposite end of the ring composition, A', Pseudo-Phocylides charges his readers to avoid dissension and strife when war is in the offing (verse 151) and to recognize the futility that is frequently involved when one does good to those who are evil: kind deeds of this sort, he says, are "like sowing in the sea" (verse 152). At the center or turning-point of the ring, E (verses 141–143), the same types of referents occur, though here the advice is noticeably more positive in its tone and objectives: the reader should treat sinners humanely by not blaming them (verse 141), try to make friends instead of enemies (verse 142), and heal the wounds that evil inflicts by acting promptly against it (verse 143).[31]

The remaining clusters of the paragraph either introduce different types of referents that can be included in one fashion or another under the broad category of 'outsiders' or are somehow related materially to the main topics named in A, E, and A'. The clusters D (verses 139–140) and D' (verses 147–148) are connected in so far as both make mention of animals. Verses 139–140 urge their decent treatment: the readers must not disturb an animal's daily rations (verse 139), and they should help raise a fallen beast, even when it might be the property of an enemy (verse 140).[32] This is countered in D', where the author reasons that since only beasts should feed on beasts (verse 148 b) it is unacceptable for humans to consume any meat torn by wild animals; rather, such remains should be left for swift-footed dogs to eat (verses 147–148 a). The most problematic pairing of the ring is C (verse 138) and C' (verse 149), with the latter element, a warning against potions and books of magic, perhaps offering a specific instance of the universal rule on moderation and planning ahead expressed in the former. It may be that Pseudo-Phocylides included these clusters in the paragraph because he associated the types of practices that

---

[31] Note also the repetition of the κακ- stem in parts A, E, and A', vv. 133, 134, 143, and 152.

[32] The reference to an enemy in v. 140 indicates the topical link made between D and A, E, and A'.

they depict with the sordid characters of verses 132–136, 141–143, and 151–152. B (verse 137) and B' (verse 150) represent the final pair, with both elements rendering advice on the treatment of children. This sort of referent seems to be out of place in a context of this nature, though the author's consideration of the illegal and violent acts of criminals and so forth in the bulk of the paragraph may have brought to mind the mistreatment of those who are unable to deter the wicked or even defend themselves against misdeeds, such as children. In verse 137, Pseudo-Phocylides recommends that children receive their fair share, since equality is best in everything, while verse 150 appeals for their fair treatment, without recourse to violence.

Exhortation Concerning the Nature and Importance of Work
(verses 153–174)

As van der Horst observes, verses 153–174 represent a coherent block of exhortatory material on the importance and the nature of labor.[33] Beginning at least with Hesiod[34] and Phocylides of Miletus[35] these constituted prominent themes in Greek and Roman gnomic wisdom, and they occur in Jewish sapiential sources as well (see especially LXX Proverbs 6.6–8). In terms of the overall design of verses 132–227, this paragraph occupies a sort of middle ground between the advice concerning evildoers et alii in verses 132–152 and the material on members of the family and household in verses 175–227. In so far as this paragraph addresses a narrower sphere of social life and is more concrete in its relevance and application to the everyday ethical duties of the individual, it lies 'closer to home', as it were, though its subject matter is presented for the most part as distinct from and occurring outside the οἰκία. The following outline is proposed for the paragraph:

153–163	I. Prescriptive section
153–157	A. On hard work and self-sufficiency
153–154	1. Work vs. idleness
153a	a. Command: work hard
153b–154	b. Contrasting reasons
153b	i. Positive reason: so that you can be self-sufficient
154	ii. Negative reason: idleness leads to crime
156–157	2. Contrastive commands on obtaining sustenance
156	a. Don't depend on others' refuse
157	b. Live from your own means without shame

---

[33] On this entire section, in addition to the commentaries, see Küchler, *Weisheitstraditionen*, 292–298; Thomas, *Der jüdische Phokylides*, 292–294, 326.

[34] See especially *Opera et Dies* 286–319, with West, *Works and Days*, 229–237.

[35] See Derron, *Sentences*, lvi, cf. 29, n. 3, 49–50.

153   ἐργάζευ μοχθῶν, ὡς ἐξ ἰδίων βιοτεύσῃς·
154   πᾶς γὰρ ἀεργὸς ἀνὴρ ζώει κλοπίμων ἀπὸ χειρῶν.
[155]
156   μὴ δ' ἄλλου παρὰ δαιτὸς ἔδοις σκυβάλισμα τραπέζης,
157   ἀλλ' ἀπὸ τῶν ἰδίων βίοτον διάγοις ἀνύβριστος.
158   εἰ δέ τις οὐ δεδάηκε τέχνην, σκάπτοιτο δικέλλῃ.
159   ἔστι βίῳ πᾶν ἔργον, ἐπὴν μοχθεῖν ἐθέλησθα.
160   ναυτίλος εἰ πλώειν ἐθέλεις, εὐρεῖα θάλασσα·
161   εἰ δὲ γεηπονίην μεθέπεις, μακραί τοι ἄρουραι.
162   οὐδὲν ἄνευ καμάτου πέλει ἀνδράσιν εὐπετὲς ἔργον
163   οὐδ' αὐτοῖς μακάρεσσι· πόνος δ' ἀρετὴν μέγ' ὀφέλλει.
164   μύρμηκες γαίης μυχάτους προλελοιπότες οἴκους
165   ἔρχονται βιότου κεχρημένοι, ὁππότ' ἄρουραι
166   λήϊα κειράμεναι καρπῶν πλήθωσιν ἀλωάς.
167   οἱ δ' αὐτοὶ πυροῖο νεοτριβὲς ἄχθος ἔχουσιν
168   ἢ κριθῶν, αἰεὶ δὲ φέρων φορέοντα διώκει,
169   ἐκ θέρεος ποτὶ χεῖμα βορὴν σφετέρην συνάγοντες
170   ἄτρυτοι· φῦλον δ' ὀλίγον τελέθει πολύμοχθον.
171   κάμνει δ' ἠεροφοῖτις ἀριστοπόνος τε μέλισσα
172   ἠὲ πέτρης κοίλης κατὰ χηραμὸν ἢ δονάκεσσιν
173   ἢ δρυὸς ὠγυγίης κατὰ κοιλάδος ἔνδοθι σίμβλων
174   σμήνεσι μυριότρητα κατ' ἄγγεα κηροδομοῦσα.

Translation:

153   Work with every effort so that you may survive by your own means;
154   for every man who's idle lives off thieving hands.
[155]³⁶

---

³⁶ V. 155 (τέχνη ‹γὰρ› τρέφει ἄνδρα, ἀεργὸν δ' ἵψατο λιμός. "‹For› a craft sustains a man, but hunger oppresses an idler.") is spurious; see van der Horst, *Sentences*, 217.

156   You should not eat from the refuse from the meal of another's table,[37]
157   but you should live life from your own means without shame.[38]
158   And if someone does not know a craft,[39] he should dig with a mattock.
159   There is in life all sorts of work, if you are willing to toil.
160   If as a mariner you want to sail, vast is the sea;[40]
161   but if you want to attend to farming, quite large are the fields.
162   No work is wont to be light (or) without trouble for men,
163   not even for the blessed ones themselves; but toil greatly strengthens virtue.
164   Ants, once they have left homes very deep underground,
165   come in need of food, whenever fields,
166   sheared of their crops, fill threshing floors with grain.
167   And they themselves have a newly threshed load of wheat
168   or barley – and bearer ever follows bearer –
169   from summer to winter gathering[41] their food
170   untiringly. The tiny folk is quite hard-working.
171   And the air-roving and industrious bee labors,
172   in the crevice of a hollow rock or in reeds,
173   or in the hollow of a primal oak, inside beehives,
174   in swarms building with wax at thousand-celled honeycombs.

The block of exhortation in verses 153–174 consists of two segments, distinguished by their function and argumentative stance. The first, prescriptive, segment, offers advice on the necessity and value of hard work and the importance of learning some sort of craft (verses 153–163). The author has coordinated these instructions with two supporting illustrations in the second, descriptive, segment (verses 164–174). Thematic inclusio helps to demarcate each of these segments formally: μοχθῶν (verse 153) and πόνος (verse 163) occur at either end of Section I, while οἴκους (verse 164) and κηροδομοῦσα (verse 174) mark the boundaries of Section II.

The exhortatory segment (verses 153–163) is comprised of two thematically distinct clusters of sayings, verses 153–157 and 158–161, rounded off with a summarizing statement in verses 162–163. Beginning with the first cluster, the author calls upon the readers not to be idle, but to labor diligently. This way they can survive from their own means without shame (verses 153, 157) and not be compelled by circumstances to resort to either theft (verse 154) or sur-

---

[37] On the subject of this line cf. Ramsay MacMullen, *Roman Social Relations, 50 B.C. to A.D. 284* (New Haven and London: Yale University Press, 1974) 14, with n. 50.

[38] Reading βίοτον διάγοις ἀνύβριστος with Diehl (*Anthologia*, 2.109); cf. Bernays (*Gesammelte Abhandlungen*, 259) and Bergk (*Poetae Lyrici Graeci*, 102). Derron, *Sentences*, 13: βιότων φαγέοις. Young (*Theognis*, 107) and van der Horst (*Sentences*, 218) print μισθῶν φαγέοις.

[39] Reading τέχνην with Bergk (*Poetae Lyrici Graeci*, 102), Diehl (*Anthologia*, 2.109), P, and L. Young (*Theognis*, 107), van der Horst (*Sentences*, 218), and Derron (*Sentences*, 13) have τέχνης in M and B.

[40] Cf. Derron, *Sentences*, 13: "Marin, si tu veux naviguer, la mer est vaste."

[41] Reading συνάγοντες with P, V, Bergk (*Poetae Lyrici Graeci*, 103), Bernays (*Gesammelte Abhandlungen*, 259), and Diehl (*Anthologia*, 2.110) against ἐπάγοντες printed by M, L, Young (*Theognis*, 108), van der Horst (*Sentences*, 222), and Derron (*Sentences*, 14).

viving off the refuse of others (verse 156).[42] The second cluster, in conjunction with the first, argues that all sorts of work are possible, even if one has not learned a τέχνη, although toil will be involved (verses 158–159). A pair of representative examples is offered by way of support: working on the sea as a mariner (verse 160) and working on the land as a farmer (verse 161).[43] Taken together, these examples cover a full range of the types of locales that people can possibly work and earn a living. The summarizing statement in verses 162–163 elicits from the preceding discussion some more universal observations about work: although it is seldom easy, it is of great use in so far as it strengthens virtue, even for the blessed ones.

The second segment (verses 164–174) portrays two highly descriptive illustrations with animals as their subjects,[44] the first about ants (verses 164–170), the second about bees (verses 171–174).[45] Here we discern one of the few places in the poem where some narrative element drives the ordering of the verses. To begin with, we learn how ants, a traditional symbol in antiquity for industry and methodicalness, diligently set out from their subterranean dwellings to gather food for themselves. In the second description, Pseudo-Phocylides enumerates some of the various locations where bees may labor: in the crevice of a rock, in reeds, in the hollow of a primal oak, and within their beehives.

Together these sketches provide supporting examples or moral paradigms for the more direct paraenesis in verses 153–163. Additionally, it should be observed that each illustration relates on a more specific level to one of the two exhortatory clusters detected in verses 153–161. Thus the depiction of the ants in verses 164–170 (II.A) highlights their untiring hard work and self-sufficiency, which was the main theme of the commands in verses 153–157 (I.A). Similarly, the pertinent aspect of the illustration of the bees' toil in verses 171–174 (II.B) seems to be that they busy themselves in all sorts of different settings; this aspect of human labor appears as a prominent theme in the argument of verses 158–161 (I.B), where Pseudo-Phocylides points to the land and the sea as possible locales for plying one's trade. Such interlocking structures that alternate precepts with the descriptive examples corroborating them are

---

[42] Cf. Hesiod, *Opera et Dies* 397–400; *Papyrus Insinger* 27.2–3.

[43] Note the use of catchwords in this cluster: εἰ (vv. 158, 160, and 161); ἐθέλησθα (v. 159) and ἐθέλεις (v. 160). Also, Kröhling (*Die Priamel*, 63, cf. 59–63) identifies vv. 159–161 as a priamel; see the discussion of vv. 125–128 above, pp. 116–118.

[44] Pseudo-Phocylides frequently makes use of animal imagery for his moral examples or illustrations, for example, vv. 49, 84–85, 125–128, 164–174, 191, 201–202; cf. vv. 139–140, 147–148, 185, 188.

[45] In addition to their common themes, style, and function, the two illustrations are linked by thematic catchword: πολύμοχθον (v. 170) and ἀριστοπόνος (v. 171). Note also other catchwords: κατά (vv. 172, 173, and 174); κοίλης (v. 172) and κοιλάδος (v. 173).

not uncommon in gnomic literature. Compare, for example, the *Sentences* of
Syriac Menander 99–112, exhortation on how one ought to treat those who are
less well-off, which can be outlined as follows:

99–101	I. Prescriptive section
99–100	A. Do not scorn the elderly
101	B. Do not despise the poor
102–112	II. Descriptive section
102–104	A. On old age
105–112	B. On poverty and reversal of fortune

Here the description of old age in II.A (verses 102–104) supplements the prohibitions not to scorn the elderly in I.A (verses 99–100), whereas the description of poverty and the reversal of fortune in II.B (verses 105–112) augments
the appeal not to despise the poor in I.B (verse 101).[46] Structures of this type
enable moral writers to integrate instruction on two (or sometimes more) distinct items; in this manner they discover new types of logical or argumentative
cohesion between the different topics involved while simultaneously synthesizing these topics into an intelligible unit containing both prescriptive and
descriptive elements.

Exhortation Concerning Personal Relationships
Within the Household (verses 175–227)

The final major section of the poem, verses 175–227, has attracted a fair
amount of scholarly attention because of the parallels it exhibits with the so-
called *Haustafeln* literature, found particularly in Stoic, Jewish, and Christian
sources. Although it seems clear that the author of our *Sentences* employs the
Haustafel-scheme in a general way as a framework for this material, dealing
successively with obligations concerning marriage, children, and slaves, in
certain regards his composition is unique.[47] For instance, the first paragraph of
the section, verses 175–206, consists largely of warnings against immoral
sexual activities, having little to say about mutual duties, while in between the
paragraphs on children (verses 207–21) and slaves (verses 223–227) he inserts

---

[46] Cf. *Papyrus Insinger* 4.17–5.1, which can be outlined as follows:

4.17–18	I. Descriptive section
4.17	A. Thoth set a balance to measure the earth
4.18	B. He also placed a heart in man to measure its owner
4.19–5.1	II. Prescriptive section
4.19–21	A. On being balanced
4.22–5.1	B. On knowing one's heart

In contrast with the paragraphs discussed above, here the descriptive section is placed
first, though the interlocking structure is still evident. Cf. *Papyrus Insinger* 13.14–18.

[47] Cf. Thomas, *Der jüdische Phokylides*, 57–59, 326–327, 378–391.

precepts urging respect to kinfolk (verse 219) and the elderly (verse 220–222). We should bear in mind, too, that the section in its entirety is part of a larger literary context (verses 132–227; see above), and should be interpreted within this structural and conceptual framework.[48] Comparison with similar schemes in Hellenistic-Jewish literature, particularly Josephus, *Contra Apionem* 2.199–206 (see above) and Philo, *Hypothetica* 7.1–9, reveals numerous other differences with respect to content and mode of organization. The following outline is proposed for the block in verses 175–227 of the *Sentences*:

175–194	I.	Prohibitions concerning various sexual relations and sexual acts
175–186		A. Exhortation organized according to referent
175–178		1. Wife
175		a. On marriage
175a		i. Command to marry
175b		ii. Reason: to avoid dying without an heir
176		b. Command to beget children
177–178		c. On prostitution
177a		i. Warning against inducing one's wife to prostitution
177b–178		ii. Reason: this practice stigmatizes the children
179–181		2. Father's companions
179–180		a. On sexual relations with one's step-mother
179–180a		i. Commands
179		α. Negative: Have no sexual relations with your step-mother
180a		β. Positive: Honor her
180b		ii. Reason: she holds the position once held by your mother
181		b. Command to have no sexual relations with the concubines of one's father
182–183		3. Sisters and sisters-in-law
182		a. Command to have no sexual relations with one's sister
183		b. Command to have no sexual relations with one's sister-in-law
184–186		4. Infants and the unborn
184		a. A command against abortion
185		b. A command against exposure
186		c. Another command against abortion (?)
187–193		B. Injunctions against miscellaneous sexual practices
187		1. Against castration
188		2. Against bestiality
189		3. Against 'shameful intercourse'
190–191		4. Against homosexual relations
190		a. Command not to transgress the natural limits of sexuality
191		b. Reason: even animals are not pleased by such acts
192		5. Against lesbian sexual relations
193		6. Against unrestrained lust for women
194		C. Summarizing sentence on the true nature of Eros

---

[48] Also note that a number of the commands in the section are not necessarily restricted to members of the household, for example, vv. 188, 190–191, 220–222, 226.

195–227 II. Exhortation pertaining to various members of the household
195–206   A. Wife
195–197   1. On proper love between man and wife
195a   a. Command to love one's wife
195b–197   b. Reason: nothing is better than a good marriage
198–206   2. On obtaining a spouse
198   a. A rule on sex and wooing
199–204   b. On the proper criteria for choosing a spouse
199   i.   Command not to marry a bad and wealthy women
200   ii. Reason: you will become a slave of your wife
201–204   iii. Descriptive section contrasting the selection processes for
                             animals and spouses
201–202   α. Positive observation on how people select horses, bulls,
                                and dogs
203–204   β. Contrasting negative observations on how people select
                                spouses
203   1. Men do not marry good wives
204   2. Women do not reject bad men when they are wealthy
205   c. Command against digamy / polygamy
206   d. Command against strife over inheritances
207–217   B. Children
207–209   1. General advice on the correction of children
207   a. Command on the treatment of children
207a   i.   Negative: don't be harsh
207b   ii. Positive: be gentle
208–209   b. Recommendations on who should carry out the correction of
                        children
208   i.   The mother
209a   ii. The elders of the family
209b   iii. The chiefs of the people
210–212   2. Concerning boys' personal appearance
210–211   a. Prohibitions
210   i.   Don't let a boy's hair grow long
211   ii. Don't fix a boy's hair elaborately
212   b. Reason: These practices are appropriate only for women
213–217   3. Concerning the protection of children
213–214   a. On protecting boys from pederasty
213   i.   Command to guard an attractive boy
214   ii. Reason: many people will desire immoral sexual relations
                             with him
215–216   b. Commands to guard an unmarried girl
215   i.   Keep a virgin safe inside
216   ii. Don't let her be seen outside before she is married
217   c. General observation on the difficulties of protecting children
219   C. Kinfolk: observe φιλότης and ὁμόνοια
220–222 D. The elderly
220a   1. Revere the elderly
220b–221a   2. Yield your seat to the elderly
221b–222   3. Give honor to a man who is like your father in age and descent
223–227 E. Slaves
223   1. See to it that they are fed
224   2. On the duties assigned to slaves
224a   a. Command: apportion tasks fairly
224b   b. Reason: this will foster a good relationship

225   3. Don't brand a slave
226   4. Don't slander a slave to his master
227   5. Accept advice from a prudent slave

Text:

175   μὴ μείνῃς ἄγαμος, μή πως νώνυμνος ὄληαι·
176   δός τι φύσει καὐτός, τέκε δ' ἔμπαλιν, ὡς ἐλοχεύθης.
177   μὴ προαγωγεύσῃς ἄλοχον σέο τέκνα μιαίνων·
178   οὐ γὰρ τίκτει παῖδας ὁμοίους μοιχικὰ λέκτρα.
179   μητρυιῆς μὴ ψαῦ', ἅτε δεύτερα λέκτρα γονῆος·
180   μητέρα δ' ὡς τίμα τὴν μητέρος ἴχνια βᾶσαν.
181   μηδέ τι παλλακίσιν πατρὸς λεχέεσσι μιγείης.
182   μηδὲ κασιγνήτης ἐς ἀπότροπον ἐλθέμεν εὐνήν.
183   μηδὲ κασιγνήτων ἀλόχων ἐπὶ δέμνια βαίνειν.
184   μηδὲ γυνὴ φθείρῃ βρέφος ἔμβρυον ἔνδοθι γαστρός,
185   μηδὲ τεκοῦσα κυσὶν ῥίψῃ καὶ γυψὶν ἕλωρα.
186   μηδ' ἐπὶ σῇ ἀλόχῳ ἐγκύμονι χεῖρα βάλῃαι.
187   μηδ' αὖ παιδογόνον τέμνειν φύσιν ἄρσενα κούρου.
188   μηδ' ἀλόγοις ζῴοισι βατήριον ἐς λέχος ἐλθεῖν.
189   μηδ' ὕβριζε γυναῖκα ἐπ' αἰσχυντοῖς λεχέεσσιν.
190   μὴ παραβῇς εὐνὰς φύσεως ἐς κύπριν ἄθεσμον·
191   οὐδ' αὐτοῖς θήρεσσι συνεύαδον ἄρσενες εὐναί.
192   μηδέ τι θηλύτεραι λέχος ἀνδρῶν μιμήσαιντο.
193   μηδ' ἐς ἔρωτα γυναικὸς ἅπας ῥεύσῃς ἀκάθεκτον·
194   οὐ γὰρ ἔρως θεός ἐστι, πάθος δ' ἀίδηλον ἁπάντων.
195   στέργε τεὴν ἄλοχον· τί γὰρ ἡδύτερον καὶ ἄρειον,
196   ἢ ὅταν ἀνδρὶ γυνὴ φρονέῃ φίλα γήραος ἄχρις
197   καὶ πόσις ᾗ ἀλόχῳ, μηδ' ἐμπέσῃ ἄνδιχα νεῖκος;
198   μὴ δέ τις ἀμνήστευτα βίῃ κούρῃσι μιγείη.
199   μὴ δὲ γυναῖκα κακὴν πολυχρήματον οἴκαδ' ἄγεσθαι·
200   λατρεύσεις ἀλόχῳ λυγρῆς χάριν εἵνεκα φερνῆς.
201   ἵππους εὐγενέας διζήμεθα γειαρότας τε
202   ταύρους ὑψιτένοντας, ἀτὰρ σκυλάκας πανάριστον·
203   γῆμαι δ' οὐκ ἀγαθὴν ἐριδαίνομεν ἀφρονέοντες·
204   οὐδὲ γυνὴ κακὸν ἄνδρ' ἀπαναίνεται ἀφνεὸν ὄντα.
205   μηδὲ γάμῳ γάμον ἄλλον ἄγοις ἔπι, πήματι πῆμα.
206   μηδ' ἀμφὶ κτεάνων συνομαίμοσιν εἰς ἔριν ἔλθῃς.
207   παισὶν μὴ χαλέπαινε τεοῖσ', ἀλλ' ἤπιος εἴης.
208   ἢν δέ τι παῖς ἀλίτῃ σε, κολουέτω υἱέα μήτηρ
209   ἢ καὶ πρεσβύτατοι γενεῆς ἢ δημογέροντες.
210   μὴ μὲν ἐπ' ἄρσενι παιδὶ τρέφειν πλοκάμους ἐπὶ χαίτης·
211   μὴ κορυφὴν πλέξῃς μήθ' ἄμματα λοξὰ κορύμβων·
212   ἄρσεσιν οὐκ ἐπέοικε κομᾶν, χλιδαναῖς δὲ γυναιξίν.
213   παιδὸς δ' εὐμόρφου φρουρεῖν νεοτήσιον ὥρην·
214   πολλοὶ γὰρ λυσσῶσι πρὸς ἄρσενα μεῖξιν ἔρωτος.
215   παρθενικὴν δὲ φύλασσε πολυκλείστοις θαλάμοισιν,
216   μὴ δέ μιν ἄχρι γάμων πρὸ δόμων ὀφθῆμεν ἐάσῃς.
217   κάλλος δυστήρητον ἔφυ παίδων τοκέεσσιν.
[218]
219   συγγενέσιν φιλότητα νέμοις ὁσίην θ' ὁμόνοιαν.
220   αἰδεῖσθαι πολιοκροτάφους, εἴκειν δὲ γέρουσιν
221   ἕδρης καὶ γεράων πάντων· γενεῇ δ' ἀτάλαντον
222   πρέσβυν ὁμήλικα πατρὸς ἴσαις τιμαῖσι γέραιρε.

223   γαστρὸς ὀφειλόμενον δασμὸν παρέχειν θεράποντι.
224   δούλῳ τακτὰ νέμοις, ἵνα τοι καταθύμιος εἴη.
225   στίγματα μὴ γράψῃς ἐπονειδίζων θεράποντα.
226   δοῦλον μὴ βλάψῃς τι κακηγορέων παρ' ἄνακτι.
227   λάμβανε καὶ βουλὴν παρὰ οἰκέτου εὖ φρονέοντος.

Translation:

175   Remain not unmarried, lest you perish nameless.[49]
176   And give something to nature yourself:[50] beget in turn as you were begotten.
177   Do not prostitute your wife, defiling your children;
178   for an adulterous bed does not produce similar offspring.
179   Touch not your step-mother, since[51] she is your father's second wife;
180   but honor as mother the one who follows the footsteps of a mother.[52]
181   In no way consort with your father's mistresses.
182   Approach not your sister's bed, which should be avoided.
183   Go not to the bed of your brothers' wives.
184   A woman should not destroy an unborn babe in the womb,
185   nor after bearing it should she cast it out as prey for dogs and vultures.
186   Lay not a hand on your wife while she is pregnant.
187   Do not cut the male procreative nature of a youth.
188   Do not engage in sexual relations with irrational animals.
189   Do not outrage a woman with shameful acts of sex.
190   Do not violate the natural limits of sex for illicit passion;
191   male-with-male relations are not pleasing even to beasts.[53]
192   Let not women mimic the sexual role of men at all.
193   Be not inclined to utterly unrestrained lust for a woman.
194   For Eros is not a god, but a destructive passion of all humanity.
195   Love your wife: for what is sweeter and more splendid
196   than when a wife is lovingly disposed to her husband into old age
197   and husband to his wife, and strife does not split them asunder?
198   Let no one have sexual relations with maidens forcibly (or)[54] without
          honorable wooing.
199   Bring not into your house an evil, wealthy wife;
200   you will be a hireling to your wife all for a wretched dowry.[55]
201   We seek well-bred horses and ploughers of earth –
202   strong-necked bulls – and of dogs the best of all.
203   But foolishly we do not contend to marry a good woman;

---

[49] Following the translation of van der Horst, *Sentences*, 225–227.

[50] Cf. van der Horst, *Sentences*: "Give nature her due"; Walter, *Poetische Schriften*, 213: "Gib auch du der Natur das Deine."

[51] Following Bergk's (*Poetae Lyrici Graeci*, 104) conjecture μὴ ψαῦ', ἅτε κτλ. Young (*Theognis*, 109) and Derron (*Sentences*, 14, 29, n. 4) print μὴ ψαῦε τὰ κτλ. Or we could adopt Young's and Derron's version and place a raised stop after ψαῦε, as van der Horst (*Sentences*, 229–230) suggests.

[52] Following the proposed translation of Edward O'Neil (personal communication, 5/15/92).

[53] Cf. Edward O'Neil's (personal communication, 5/15/92) proposed translation: "Nor is male-with-male sex in accord with even wild beasts."

[54] Cf. van der Horst, *Sentences*, 242–243: "Let no one violently have intercourse with maidens without honorable wooing."

[55] Following Edward O'Neil's (personal communication, 5/15/92) proposed translation.

204 nor[56] does a woman reject a wicked man if he's wealthy.
205 You should not add marriage to marriage, misery to misery.
206 Engage not in a dispute over possessions with your kinfolk.
207 Be not severe with your children, but be gentle.
208 If a child sins against you, let the mother judge[57] her son,
209 or else the elders of the family or the chiefs of the people.[58]
210 Do not grow locks in the hair of a male child.
211 Braid not his crown or the cross-knots of the top of his head.[59]
212 For men to wear long hair is not seemly, just for delicate women.
213 Protect the youthful beauty of a comely boy;[60]
214 for many rage with lust for sex with a male.
215 Guard a virgin in closely shut chambers,
216 and let her not be seen before the house until her nuptials.
217 The beauty of children is hard for parents to defend.
[218][61]
219 Bestow on your kinfolk love and genuine harmony.
220 Respect those with gray hair on the temples, and yield to the aged
221 a seat and all privileges. To an elder equal in descent
222 and of like age with your father show the same honors.
223 Furnish a servant with the portion he needs for his stomach.[62]
224 Apportion to a slave what is prescribed so that he will be to your liking.
225 Mark not a servant with brands, disgracing him.
226 Harm not a slave by speaking ill of him to his master.
227 Even accept counsel from a (household) slave who's prudent.

Formally, the section on personal moral obligations within the household has been divided into two large paragraphs. The first paragraph, verses 175–194, concerns sexual behavior in assorted types of relationships, the majority of which relate to members of the household.[63] As Johannes Thomas observes,

---

[56] Reading οὐδέ following van der Horst's (*Sentences*, 245) suggestion.

[57] Reading κρινάτω with V and Diehl, *Anthologia*, 2.113. Cf. Bergk's (*Poetae Lyrici Graeci*, 107) conjecture κολουέτω, followed by Young (*Theognis*, 111), van der Horst (*Sentences*, 248–249), and Derron (*Sentences*, 16) but in no mss.

[58] Following van der Horst's (*Sentences*, 248) translation for v. 209.

[59] On the translation of this line cf. van der Horst, *Sentences*, 249–250: "Braid not his crown nor make cross-knots at the top of his head"; Walter, *Poetische Schriften*, 215: "nicht sollst du das Scheitel(haar) flechten oder Zöpfe zu Haarknoten (winden)."

[60] Following van der Horst's (*Sentences*, 250–251) translation for v. 213.

[61] V. 218 (στέργε φίλους ἄχρις θανάτου· πίστις γὰρ ἀμείνων. "Love your friends till death, for faithfulness is better.") is spurious; see van der Horst, *Sentences*, 252–253.

[62] Cf. van der Horst, *Sentences*, 255: "Provide your slave with the tribute he owes his stomach"; Walter, *Poetische Schriften*, 215: "Gib deinem Diener, was er zu seiner Sättigung braucht"; and Derron, *Sentences*, 17: "Pour satisfaire son estomac, donner sa part au serviteur".

[63] It comes as no surprise that the themes of marriage and sexual conduct were popular in the moral literature of the time; for discussion see Praechter, *Hierokles*, 121–150; Albrecht Oepke, "Ehe," *RAC* 4 (1959) 650–666; Gerhard Delling, "Ehebruch, Ehegesetze, Ehehindernisse, Eheleben, Ehescheidung, Eheschliessung," *RAC* 4 (1959) 666–730; Claude Vatin, *Recherches sur le Mariage et la Condition de la Femme Mariée à l'Epoque Hellénistique* (BEFAR 216; Paris: E. de Boccard, 1970) especially 1–40, 115–206; Ze'ev W. Falk, *Introduction to Jewish Law of the Second Commonwealth* (AGJU 11; 2 vols.; Leiden: E.J. Brill,

this portion of the poem, with its list of forbidden sexual relations with relatives, is based largely upon the directives of Leviticus 18.[64] The exhortation in the *Sentences* consists largely of negative prohibitions, with every line beginning with μη- except verses 176, 178, 191, and 194. The paragraph is also unified by the repeated use of words that contain the λοχ or λεχ (λεκ) stem[65] as well as by the application of a number of catchwords.[66] The author has organized the first part of the paragraph, verses 175–186, into clusters of sayings depending on different referents, while the second part, verses 187–193, conveys a number of more miscellaneous warnings about sexual conduct that do not fall clearly into any of the categories delineated in the first part. The second paragraph, verses 195–227, then deals in orderly fashion with some broader moral responsibilities to be observed towards different members of the household – spouses, children, kinfolk, the elderly, and slaves – some of which are the same as those identified in the first paragraph.

The clusters in verses 175–186 (I.A.) appear to be arranged according to the importance of the referents involved: the wife, the father's companions, sisters and sisters-in-laws, and infants and the unborn. The author mentions marital relations first (verses 175–178); here emphasis lies on the responsibilities of marrying and of reproducing within the legitimate confines of the marriage.[67] The poet reminds the reader that marriage and procreation are in accord with φύσις, "nature" (verses 175–176), a belief popular in antiquity especially in Stoic and Jewish circles.[68] The poet couples this advice with a caution against prostituting one's own wife, since this form of adultery defiles the children, producing offspring who are not ὅμοιοι, that is, they are not similar to their legitimate sire (verses 177–178).[69] Afterwards there are injunctions to refrain

---

1972, 1978) 2.276–331; Carl H. Ratschow, et al., "Ehe, Eherecht, Ehescheidung," *TRE* 9 (1982) 308–362. For some examples of gnomic exhortation on this theme see Stobaeus, *Anthologium* 4.22, 24; cf. Musonius Rufus, *Fragmenta* 12–15, with Lutz, *Musonius Rufus*, 84–101.

[64] Thomas, *Der jüdische Phokylides*, 57–89, 425–428; cf. Niebuhr, *Gesetz und Paränese*, 26–31; for comparable gnomic paragraphs see *Papyrus Insinger* 7.20–8.20, *Derek Eretz Rabbah* 1.1–12.

[65] Vv. 176, 177, 178, 179, 181, 183, 186, 188, 189, and 192; cf. 195, 197, 200.

[66] τέκε (v. 176), τέκνα (v. 177), and τίκτει (v. 178); λέκτρα (v. 178) and λέκτρα (v. 179); κασιγνήτης (v. 182) and κασιγνήτων (v. 183); εὐνάς (v. 190) and εὐναί (v. 191); θήρεσσι (v. 191) and θηλύτεραι (v. 192); ἔρωτα (v. 193) and ἔρως (v. 194); ἅπας (v. 193) and ἁπάντων (v. 194).

[67] Cf. David M. Feldman, *Birth Control in Jewish Law: Marital Relations, Contraception and Abortion as Set Forth in the Classic Texts of Jewish Law* (2nd ed.; New York: Schocken, 1974) 46–80; Rachel Biale, *Women and Jewish Law: An Exploration of Women's Issues in Halakhic Sources* (New York: Schocken, 1984) 198–203.

[68] Van der Horst, *Sentences*, 225–227; Derron, *Sentences*, 14, n. 2.

[69] On the problems in interpreting these verses see van der Horst, *Sentences*, 227–229; Thomas, *Der jüdische Phokylides*, 68–70; cf. Biale, *Women and Jewish Law*, 183–192, and s.v. Bastard (mamzer).

from sexual relations with the companions of one's father, both his second wife (the reader's step-mother), since she follows the footsteps of the reader's mother (verses 179–180), and his mistresses or concubines (verse 181).[70] The next cluster, verses 182–183, conveys warnings against incestuous relations with one's sister or with one's sister-in-law.[71] Lastly, turning to the treatment of infants and the unborn, the author implores the audience not to resort to abortion or exposure as means of dealing with unwanted pregnancies (verses 184–185).[72]

In the second and final part of this paragraph, verses 187–193 (I.B.), Pseudo-Phocylides rejects an array of miscellaneous sexual practices as unacceptable: castration (verse 187), bestiality (verse 188), 'shameful acts of sex' with a woman (verse 189; referring perhaps to intercourse during menstruation or intercourse not intended for procreation, compare verses 175–176),[73] homosexual relations (verses 190–191),[74] lesbian sexual relations (verse 192),[75] and unrestrained lust for women (verse 193). The prohibitions appear to cover certain aspects of sexual behavior that are not associated with specific familial referents (as in verses 175–186) and are arranged seriatim. Some of the topics raised here, castration and bestiality for instance, represent forms of sexual debauchery abhorred generally in antiquity, whereas others, such as homosexuality, appear to have been strongly or consistently condemned for the most part only in Jewish circles. Thus the author develops a moral perspective on sexual conduct that tends to mesh Greek with Jewish sensibilities, while keeping the overall sense of moral accountability high. A summarizing

---

[70] Van der Horst (*Sentences*, 229–231) notes the traditional nature of the pairing of stepmother and concubine of the father; cf. Thomas, *Der jüdische Phokylides*, 65–66.

[71] On the placement of v. 183 see van der Horst, *Sentences*, 232; Derron, *Sentences*, 15; cf. Biale, *Women in Jewish Law*, 179–183.

[72] The meaning of the last verse of I.A. is unclear; it appears to be intended as a command against abortion (like v. 184), though it may instead forbid having sexual relations with a woman while she is with child; see van der Horst, *Sentences*, 234–235; Thomas, *Der jüdische Phokylides*, 71–73; cf. Josephus, *Contra Apionem* 2.202. On abortion in antiquity see Franz J. Dölger, "Das Lebensrecht des ungeborenen Kindes und die Fruchtabtreibung in der Bewertung der heidnischen und christlichen Antike," *Antike und Christentum: Kultur- und religionsgeschichtliche Studien*, Volume 4 (Münster: Aschendorff, 1934) [reprint, 1975] 1–61; J. H. Waszink, "Abtreibung," *RAC* 1 (1950) 55–60; Feldman, *Birth Control in Jewish Law*, 251–294; den Boer, *Private Morality*, 272–288; Biale, *Women and Jewish Law*, 219–238.

[73] For discussion of this line see van der Horst, *Sentences*, 237; Walter, *Poetische Schriften*, 213; Derron, *Sentences*, 30, n. 4; Thomas, *Der jüdische Phokylides*, 66–67.

[74] The directive not to violate "the natural limits of sex" in v. 190 probably refers to homosexual relations, and so fits with the thought of v. 191; see van der Horst, *Sentences*, 237–239; Derron, *Sentences*, 30, n. 5, who refers to Gerhard, *Phoinix*, 141–146; Felix Buffière, *Eros Adolescent: La Pédérastie dans la Grèce Antique* (Paris: Société d'Edition 'Les Belles Lettres', 1980) 485–490.

[75] Cf. van der Horst, *Sentences*, 239–240; Biale, *Women and Jewish Law*, 192–197.

maxim in verse 194 introduced by γάǫ concludes the paragraph by formulating a rule in support of the preceding warnings: ἔǫως – erotic love – is not a
divine or heavenly being to be pursued or venerated but a passion found in all
human beings that leads to destructive behavior and hence must be vigilantly
controlled.[76]

The second paragraph, verses 195–227, offers advice on the moral responsibilities that the reader should recognize with respect to various members of the
household; it has been arranged by referent throughout, again (like verses
175–186) apparently in order of the importance of the referents. The application of φǫονέω in both verses 196 and 227 as a framing device helps to demarcate the literary unit.[77] The discussion here, like that of the preceding paragraph, opens with paraenesis on marital relations. The presentation at first is
positive in its orientation, consisting of an injunction for the reader to love his
wife (verse 195a), buttressed by a supporting argument in the form of a rhetorical question that is fairly descriptive in nature (verses 195b–197). Seeking
his inspiration from Homer's *Odyssey* 6.182–184, the author reasons that
nothing is better for a man than to live as part of a married couple that is lovingly disposed towards one another throughout life, without contentiousness
interfering to disrupt the marriage.[78] Even though it is done rather indirectly,
the image of a kind and harmonious union established at this point effectively
contrasts with the general exhortatory pattern conveyed by the various negative injunctions in verses 175 ff. and 198 ff., which are for the most part pessi-
mistic in their moral view of human sexuality. In this way the author holds
forth a positive model of sexual relations and sexual roles for the audience to
emulate while at the same time itemizing the different sorts of sexual activities
that they must avoid.

The theme of marital relations continues in verses 198–206, a section that
counsels the readers about the moral criteria they should apply when selecting
a spouse; here the author returns to the prohibitory style that characterized
verses 175 ff. A rule on sex and courtship stands at the beginning of the section in verse 198: no one should have sexual relations with a woman forcibly

---

[76] The gnome also constitutes a warning against deceptive love; further see Carl
Schneider, "Eros," *RAC* 6 (1966) 306–311; Wilson, *Love Without Pretense*, 150–155; cf.
Stobaeus, *Anthologium* 4.20; *Comparatio Menandri et Philistionis* 1.272–273.

[77] The use of catchword and linkword also helps to unify the paragraph: anaphoric μὴ δέ
in vv. 198 and 199; ἀφǫονέοντες (v. 203) and ἀφνεὸν ὄντα (v. 204) [epistrophic]; anaphoric
μηδέ in vv. 205 and 206; παισίν (v. 207), παῖς (v. 208), παιδί (v. 210), παιδός (v. 213), and
παίδως (v. 217); ἄǫσενι (v. 210), ἄǫσεσιν (v. 212), and ἄǫσενα (v. 214); also note the alternation of anaphoric and epistrophic linkword in vv. 223–226: θεǫάποντι (v. 223) and
θεǫάποντα (v. 225); δούλῳ (v. 224) and δοῦλον (v. 226).

[78] Van der Horst, *Sentences*, 241–242; cf. Ahrens, *Gnomen in griechischer Dichtung*, 66,
79–80.

or without honorable wooing. A more developed argument that marriages should not be arranged for the sake of financial reward ensues; there is an injunction not to seek for a wife an evil and wealthy woman (verse 199). This is bolstered by the remark that the large dowry involved in marrying such a woman will ultimately reduce the reader to becoming her "hireling" (verse 200).[79] This leads to an amplifying descriptive section that unfavorably compares the foolish and lamentable way that people choose spouses with the more exacting processes ordinarily employed in selecting certain animals such as horses, bulls, and dogs (verses 201–204).[80] The author rounds off the section on marital relations in verses 205–206 with warnings against the misery of digamy (or polygamy)[81] and against quarreling over inheritances, presumably those resulting from a marriage. There appears to be a temporal principle at work in the author's thematic ordering of these lines, as the topics of the exhortation proceed from courtship (verse 198), to bringing a wife home (verse 199), to a discussion of the institution of marriage per se (verses 200–204), and finally remarriage and inheritances (verses 205–206).[82] Thus in a basic way the narrative progression of topics in the poem mirrors the typical steps of the marital process itself.

In the next group of sayings, verses 207–217 (II.B.), Pseudo-Phocylides focuses on the care of children by their parents.[83] He opens with exhortation pertaining to the proper correction of offspring (verses 207–209), then the personal appearance of boys (verses 210–212), and lastly the protection of children from harmful pre-marital sexual relations (verses 213–217). At the head of the cluster stands a rudimentary principle on the benevolent treatment

---

[79] "In this particular case, φερνή is the marriage-portion brought in by the wife, which had to be paid back by the husband in case of divorce. When the dowry was high, that made divorce more difficult ..."; van der Horst, *Sentences*, 244; he also cites Rafael Taubenschlag, *The Law of Greco-Roman Egypt in the Light of the Papyri* (2nd ed.; New York: Herald Square, 1955) 123–124. The use of λατρεύειν in this instance, as opposed to δουλεύειν, is appropriate in light of the hoped-for "wages" implied by the φερνή.

[80] As van der Horst observes (*Sentences*, 243, 245), vv. 199–204 form a topical unit and are based upon Theognis 183–190; inclusio helps bind the section together: γυναῖκα κακήν (v. 199) and γυνὴ κακόν (v. 204).

[81] On v. 205 see van der Horst, *Sentences*, 245–247; Derron, *Sentences*, 30, n. 3; and, more generally, Bernhard Kötting, "Digamus," *RAC* 3 (1957) 1016–1024.

[82] Note the α- alliteration in vv. 203–205; van der Horst (*Sentences*, 245) also notes the paronomasia of v. 205.

[83] On the responsibilities of parents as a topic in moral exhortation see Stobaeus, *Anthologium* 4.26; Albrecht Oepke, "παῖς, παιδίον, κτλ.," *TDNT* 5 (1967) 636–654; van der Horst, *Sentences*, 247–252; Georg Braumann and Colin Brown, "Child," *NIDNTT* 1 (1986) 280–291; cf. Rainer Lachmann, "Kind," *RAC* 18 (1989) 156–176. For examples from Jewish literature see especially Ben Sira 7.24–25, 30.1–13 (entitled in some manuscripts περὶ τέκνων), 42.9–14, with Skehan and DiLella, *Ben Sira*, 203, 206, 373–377, 477–478, 482–483, and s.v. Children.

of offspring that is antithetically formulated: "Be not severe with your children, but be gentle" (verse 207). This is supplemented by more specific recommendations on who ought to execute the correction of children when punishment becomes necessary: either the mother, the elders of the family, or the chiefs of the people, but not – by implication – the father (verses 208–209). Next the author observes that long or elaborately styled hair is effeminate and therefore not appropriate for boys (verses 210–212). The last unit contains complementary injunctions urging parents to guard their sons from pederasty, since many rage lustfully for sex with a male (verses 213–214), and to shelter their daughters from public life before they are given away in marriage (verses 215–216). A general remark on the difficulty that parents face in safeguarding their offspring from sexual immorality concludes the section in verse 217.[84]

The remaining clusters based upon referent (II.C, D, and E) are, by comparison, short and basic. It appears that they are organized in order according to the significance of the referents, with the most important coming first. There is, to begin with, a single exhortation on demonstrating φιλότης and ὁμόνοια among one's kinfolk (verse 219). A cluster on showing respect to the elderly – both inside and outside the family – follows in verses 220–222.[85] Thus the reader should revere those with gray hair on the temples (verse 220 a), yielding to the aged a seat and similar privileges (verses 220 b–221 a). In the same vein, due respect should be shown to an elder equal in descent and of comparable age with one's father (verses 221 b–222). Finally, we have a sequence of admonitions on the just treatment of slaves: they should be properly fed (verse 223), the duties assigned to them should not be unreasonable, so that the slaves will be to their owner's liking (verse 224), they ought not to be branded, since this brings disgrace (verse 225), nor slandered to their master, since this may cause them harm (verse 226).[86] Pseudo-Phocylides brings the paragraph to a close with the suggestion that an owner should be willing to accept counsel from a house-slave, provided that he is sensible (verse 227). In keeping with the generally humanitarian character of the text, the teaching in these lines stresses the responsibilities that masters must observe in handling their slaves.[87]

---

[84] Note the variation of terms in vv. 213–217 meaning "guard, protect, defend": φρουρέω in v. 213, φυλάσσω in v. 215, and δυστήρητος in v. 217.

[85] Note the use of catchword here: γέρουσιν (v. 220), γεράων (v. 221), and γέραιρε (v. 222).

[86] Note the different terms employed for "slave, servant" in these lines: θεράπων in vv. 223, 225; δοῦλος in vv. 224, 226; and οἰκέτης in v. 227. Cf. Thomas, *Der jüdische Phokylides*, 137–138.

[87] On slavery as a topic in moral literature see van der Horst, *Sentences*, 255–257, with references; also Falk, *Jewish Law*, 2.263–269; den Boer, *Private Morality*, 205–241; Spicq, *Notes*, 1.211–227; cf. Stobaeus, *Anthologium* 4.19.

This concludes our compositional analysis of the body of the *Sentences*, vv. 3–227. Before summarizing our findings and considering some possibilities for the genre of the poem, though, we have yet to investigate the literary elements that frame this body; in these segments the author reveals in a more explicit and self-conscious manner than elsewhere some key insights as to his literary persona, the nature of his work, its ideational and literary background, its intended function, and its potential value for the reader.

Chapter Six

Title, Prologue (verses 1–2), and
Epilogue (verses 228–230)

Three formal elements frame the main body of the *Sentences* of Pseudo-Phocylides, verses 3–227: the poem's title (assuming that it had one), the prologue (verses 1–2), which functions as the work's σφϱαγίς, and a coordinated epilogue (verses 228–230). As with many literary texts, the introductory and concluding segments of the poem are of special value for the interpretation of its general character and overall purpose. For this reason, their analysis in our study has been postponed until this point, after discussion of the message and composition of the main body of the *Sentences*. It is also appropriate to investigate these elements at the same time, since the poet has quite deliberately, it seems, linked them together through inclusio (see below). I have outlined these sections as follows:

	I. Title: "A Beneficial Poem of Phocylides the Philosopher"
1–2	II. Prologue: the poetic sphragis
1	A. Identification of the contents of the text: θεοῦ βουλεύματα ("resolutions of God") (compare δίκηϚ' ὁσίῃσι)
1	B. Identification of the means of communication: the author "reveals" (φαίνει) the contents of the text
2 a	C. Identification of the author: Φωκυλίδης ἀνδϱῶν ὁ σοφώτατος (compare Φωκυλίδου φιλοσόφου in the Title)
2 b	D. A promise of benefits: identification of the text as ὄλβια δῶϱα ("blessed gifts") (compare ὠφέλιμος in the Title)
....	
228–230	III. Epilogue (inclusio with the Prologue)
228	A. A rule on acts of ritual purification: spiritual and moral purity should accompany somatic purity
229 a	B. Identification of the contents of the text: δικαιοσύνης μυστήϱια ("the mysteries of righteousness") (compare θεοῦ βουλεύματα in verse 1)
229 b	C. Function of the poem: it outlines a "way of living" (τοῖα βιεῦντες κτλ.)
230	D. Promise of benefits: the reader will achieve "a good life" (ζωὴ ἀγαθή) (compare ὄλβια δῶϱα in verse 2)

Text:

Φωκυλίδου φιλοσόφου ποίησις ὠφέλιμος

1 ταῦτα δίκηϚ' ὁσίῃσι θεοῦ βουλεύματα φαίνει
2 Φωκυλίδης ἀνδϱῶν ὁ σοφώτατος ὄλβια δῶϱα.
....
228 ἅγν' εἴη ψυχῆς οὗ σώματός εἰσι καθαϱμοί.

229 ταῦτα δικαιοσύνης μυστήρια, τοῖα βιεῦντες
230 ζωὴν ἐκτελέοιτ᾽ ἀγαθὴν μέχρι γήραος οὐδοῦ.

Translation:

A Beneficial Poem of Phocylides the Philosopher

1 These resolutions of God through judgments divine
2 Phocylides, wisest of men, reveals as blessed gifts.
....
228 Let there be purity of the soul where there are (ritual) purifications of the body.[1]
229 These are the mysteries of righteousness; living by them
230 you may achieve a good life until the threshold of old age.

As a result of the considerable disagreement in the manuscript tradition regarding the title of the poem, it is impossible to say with certainty what its original title was, or even if it had one at all. Following manuscripts P and L, most editors print for the incipit Φωκυλίδου γνῶμαι, "Maxims of Phocylides", a title that corroborates the prevailing interpretation of our text as an anthology of individual sayings. However, two equally important (and older) manuscripts, M and B, have Φωκυλίδου φιλοσόφου ποίησις ὠφέλιμος, "A Beneficial Poem of Phocylides the Philosopher", a title that tends to underscore the work's unity and utility, as well as its philosophical nature. So although it appears that no firm decision can be reached on this matter, there are some significant indications that early copyists, and perhaps even the original author himself, presented the work in the title as a unified, philosophical ποίησις rather than as an anthology of γνῶμαι.[2] The evidence provided by the compositional analysis of the *Sentences* conducted in the preceding chapters would support this conclusion.

The description of the poem as ὠφέλιμος in the titles of manuscripts M and B could also carry some significance, especially in light of the author's self-designation as a philosopher[3] and as the wisest of men. Beginning at least in the fifth century B.C., an ongoing debate raged between philosophers and poets over the social and moral value of poetry, chiefly as to whether poetry can have any positive role to play in the cultivation of virtue, conveying the knowledge or moral models necessary for virtuous conduct in life. Perhaps the most famous instance of this debate takes place in the *Republic*, where Plato banishes the poets from his ideal *polis*, arguing that the powerful emotional

---

[1] Following West's conjecture in *CR* 30 (1980) 137. Cf. Young, *Theognis*, 112: ἁγνείη ψυχῆς, οὐ σώματός εἰσι καθαρμοί (followed by Derron, *Sentences*, 18) and Ludwich, "Spruchbuch," 23: ἁγνείη ψυχῆς, οὐ σώματός εἰσι καθαρμοί (followed by van der Horst, *Sentences*, 103, n. 4, 258).

[2] Cf. Küchler, *Weisheitstraditionen*, 262; Walter, *Poetische Schriften*, 197; Derron, *Sentences*, 2.

[3] The Suda identifies Phocylides of Miletus as a φιλόσοφος. Cf. van der Horst, *Sentences*, 61.

impact of verse weakens the control of reason in the soul of the listener.[4] In this excerpt from Book X, Plato explains under what conditions he might actually lift this banishment:[5]

ὅμως δὲ εἰρήσθω, ὅτι ἡμεῖς γε, εἴ τινα ἔχοι λόγον εἰπεῖν ἡ πρὸς ἡδονὴν ποιητικὴ καὶ ἡ μίμησις, ὡς χρὴ αὐτὴν εἶναι ἐν πόλει εὐνομουμένῃ, ἄσμενοι ἂν καταδεχοίμεθα· ὡς ξύνισμέν γε ἡμῖν αὐτοῖς κηλουμένοις ὑπ' αὐτῆς· ἀλλὰ γὰρ τὸ δοκοῦν ἀληθὲς οὐχ ὅσιον προδιδόναι. ἦ γάρ, ὦ φίλε, οὐ κηλεῖ ὑπ' αὐτῆς καὶ σύ, καὶ μάλιστα ὅταν δι' Ὁμήρου θεωρῇς αὐτήν;
Πολύ γε.
Οὐκοῦν δικαία ἐστὶν οὕτω κατιέναι, ἀπολογησαμένη ἐν μέλει ἤ τινι ἄλλῳ μέτρῳ;
Πάνυ μὲν οὖν.
Δοῖμεν δέ γέ που ἂν καὶ τοῖς προστάταις αὐτῆς, ὅσοι μὴ ποιητικοί, φιλοποιηταὶ δέ, ἄνευ μέτρου λόγον ὑπὲρ αὐτῆς εἰπεῖν, ὡς οὐ μόνον ἡδεῖα ἀλλὰ καὶ ὠφελίμη πρὸς τὰς πολιτείας καὶ τὸν βίον τὸν ἀνθρώπινόν ἐστι· καὶ εὐμενῶς ἀκουσόμεθα. κερδανοῦμεν γάρ που, ἐὰν μὴ μόνον ἡδεῖα φανῇ ἀλλὰ καὶ ὠφελίμη.

"But nevertheless let it be declared that, if the mimetic and dulcet poetry can show any reason for her existence in a well-governed state, we would gladly admit her, since we ourselves are very conscious of her spell. But all the same it would be impious to betray what we believe to be the truth. Is that not so, friend? Do not you yourself feel her magic and especially when Homer is her interpreter?"
"Greatly."
"Then may she not justly return from this exile after she has pleaded her defence, whether in lyric or other measure?"
"By all means."
"And we would allow her advocates who are not poets but lovers of poetry to plead her cause in prose without meter, and show that she is not only delightful but beneficial to orderly government and all the life of man. And we shall listen benevolently, for it will be clear gain for us if it can be shown that she bestows not only pleasure but benefit."

Plato concedes that poetry is delightful and bestows pleasure on those who hear it, possessing even a certain enchanting effect, especially when Homeric verses are considered. But in order for poetry to be found acceptable from a moral or philosophical standpoint, so the argument goes, it must first be proven to be "beneficial", ὠφελίμη, for the βίος of human beings and human society.[6] By claiming this very quality as a characterization of his own poetic

---

[4] Plato's evaluation of poetry in the *Republic* contains some rather complex arguments, involving also a critique of poetry as μίμησις ("imitation," "representation"); see Gerald F. Else, *The Structure and Date of Book Ten of Plato's Republic* (AHAW.PH 3; Heidelberg: Carl Winter, 1972); idem, *Plato and Aristotle on Poetry* (Chapel Hill: University of North Carolina Press, 1986) 17–46. Further see Mario Puelma, "Der Dichter und die Wahrheit in der griechischen Poetik von Homer bis Aristoteles," *Museum Helveticum* 46 (1989) 65–100, with bibliography on pp. 98–100.

[5] Plato, *Republic* 607D–E; text and translation: Paul Shorey, trans., *Plato: The Republic* (LCL; 2 vols.; Cambridge: Harvard University Press; London: Heinemann, 1930, 1935) 2.466–467.

[6] Cf. also Plutarch's treatise *Quomodo Adolescens Poetas Audire Debeat* (*Moralia* 14D–37B), which, as he relates in 30D, is written for those who are concerned that poetry be "beneficial" (ὠφελίμος) for the development of "moral character" (ἦθος); cf. 32F, 35F–37B.

composition in the title, Pseudo-Phocylides implicitly demonstrates an awareness of such philosophical criteria, arguing against potential critics that poetry is not a suitable medium for a message that bestows moral benefits on those who listen.[7] Apparently, he intends for the poem to stand in the tradition of poetic compositions that were either (a) deemed useful by general standards for philosophical purposes or inquiry (the works of Homer and Hesiod, for instance) or (b) were composed by the philosophers themselves, such as Aristotle's *Hymn to Virtue* or Cleanthes' *Hymn to Zeus*.[8] In this regard it should be noted that in the opinion of antiquity the verses of Phocylides of Miletus were thought to be beneficial for human life.[9] Precisely how and why the *Sentences* will be beneficial for the reader becomes more explicit in verses 1–2 and 229–230 with the language employed there to depict the poem and its author.

After the title, we have the prologue, verses 1–2, which operates as the poem's σφραγίς, a common device in classical literature. Ordinarily, such "seals" afforded authors an opportunity to identify themselves by name and to claim a composition as their own property, though they may reveal key facts about the nature and substance of a work as well.[10] The seal employed by Phocylides of Miletus, for example, consisted simply of καὶ τόδε Φωκυλίδεω.[11] The σφραγίς of Theognis, by contrast, exhibits more complex features, including, among other things, arguments for the poem's divine inspiration and authority as well as some indications of its moral and rhetorical objectives.[12]

---

[7] Cf. the Prologue to the *Comparatio Menandri et Philistionis II*, cited above, pp. 24–25.

[8] Poems of this sort were frequently gnomic in character; see Wilson, *Love Without Pretense*, 61–68. On the *Hymn to Virtue* see Cecil M. Bowra, "Aristotle's Hymn to Virtue," *CQ* 32 (1938) 182–189; John M. Crossett, "Aristotle as a Poet: The Hymn to Hermeias," *Philological Quarterly* 46 (1967) 145–155. On the *Hymn to Zeus* see Ernst Neustadt, "Der Zeushymnos des Kleanthes," *Hermes* 66 (1931) 387–401; Max Pohlenz, "Kleanthes' Zeushymnus," *Hermes* 75 (1940) 117–123; Günther Zuntz, "Zum Kleanthes-Hymnus," *HSCP* 63 (1958) 289–308; Lattke, *Hymnus*, 33; cf. above, p. 23, n. 31.

[9] In a discussion of the poetry of Phocylides of Miletus, Dio Chrysostom, *Orationes* 36.13 praises its beneficial quality, cf. 36.9–15; van der Horst, *Sentences*, 60.

[10] Walther Kranz, "Sphragis: Ichform und Namensiegel als Eingangs- und Schluszmotiv antiker Dichtung," *RMP* 104 (1961) 3–46, 97–124 [reprint, idem, *Studien zur Antiken Literatur und ihrem Nachwirken: Kleine Schriften* (ed. Ernst Vogt; Bibliothek der klassischen Altertumswissenschaften 1.3; Heidelberg: Carl Winter, 1967) 27–78]. It should be emphasized that the classical σφραγίς does not lay claim to originality or to authorship in the modern sense. The skill of the poet is evident rather in the artful and authoritative manner of expression; cf. Isocrates, *Ad Nicoclem* 40–41.

[11] See *Fragmenta* 1, [2], 3–6.

[12] Lines 1–38; see the analysis above, pp. 72–73. Further: L. Woodbury, "The Seal of Theognis," *Studies in Honor of Gilbert Norwood* (ed. Mary E. White; Phoenix Sup. 1; Toronto: University of Toronto Press, 1952) 20–41; Andrew L. Ford, "The Seal of Theognis: The Politics of Authorship in Archaic Greece," in Figueira and Nagy, *Theognis of Megara*, 82–95.

The first two lines of Pseudo-Phocylides' *Sentences* are comparable in form and function to such seals. Here, as throughout the poem, the author carefully integrates Greek and Jewish elements, avoiding reference to anything particularly Jewish. Thus he identifies himself as the famous Greek poet Φωκυλίδης while concurrently assuming a traditional epithet of the Jewish king Solomon, ἀνδρῶν ὁ σοφώτατος ("the wisest of men"; verse 2 a).[13] Along with the self-designation, the author provides two terms that are of interest for identifying the contents and message of the poem: he refers to the work as θεοῦ βουλεύματα ("resolutions of God"; verse 1) and as ὄλβια δῶρα ("blessed gifts"; verse 2b).[14] As van der Horst and other critics have noted, it seems clear that the author intends these formulae primarily (but not exclusively) as indirect references to the teachings of the Torah.[15] The same may also be said of δίκησ' ὁσίησι in verse 1, which may be translated "divine judgments" or "sacred statutes". As such, these designations clarify the poem's divine origin and suggest its revelatory character, underscoring the moral authority of the poet and his instruction. Appropriately, they indicate also the potential benefits that such teachings hold out for the recipients. We should note, additionally, that these terms both anticipate and summarize the ensuing material, providing initial clues as to the substance and function of the text, specifically, that it relates to the teaching of the Torah, its proper meaning for the audience, and that its presentation will be conducted within a moral context and mode of discourse that is cross-cultural in character.

The seal, as modern critics frequently observe, also plays a role in the literary structure of the *Sententiae*. In a manner similar to that of other classical and Hellenistic texts, Pseudo-Phocylides' sphragis corresponds logically and linguistically with the concluding lines of the poem, the epilogue in verses 228–230. The most striking indication of this correspondence comes from the verbal affinity of ταῦτα δίκησ' κτλ. at the beginning of the poem's first sen-

---

[13] It should be noted, however, that this predicate could be applied to others as well; van der Horst, *Sentences*, 108–109; idem, "Pseudo-Phocylides Revisited," 16–17. On the place of Pseudo-Phocylides in pseudepigraphical literature see Wolfgang Speyer, *Die literarische Fälschung im heidnischen und christlichen Altertum: Ein Versuch ihrer Deutung* (HAW 1.2; München: C.H. Beck, 1971) 167, cf. 150–168; Martin Hengel, "Anonymität, Pseudepigraphie und 'literarische Fälschung' in der jüdisch-hellenistischen Literatur," *Fondation Hardt pour l'Etude de l'Antiquité Classique, Entretiens* 18 (1972) 296–298, cf. 231–329; Derron, *Sentences*, xxxii–li; Thomas, *Der jüdische Phokylides*, 187–190, 322–323.

[14] It is interesting to note that Isocrates also refers to his advice in *Ad Nicoclem* as a δωρεά, and that these references also create an inclusio for the work (§§ 1–2, 54). Perhaps such identifications were a conventional device in gnomic or ethical writings of this type. On the epistle as a gift see Demetrius, *De Elocutione* 4.224; Klaus Thraede, *Grundzüge griechisch-römischer Brieftopik* (Zetemata 48; München: C. H. Beck, 1970) 17, 30.

[15] Van der Horst, *Sentences*, 107–109; he notes that the verb βουλεύομαι is frequently used of God in the LXX; cf. BAGD s.v. βούλημα; Berger, *Gesetzesauslegung Jesu*, 47; Niebuhr, *Gesetz und Paränese*, 71.

tence (verses 1–2) with ταῦτα δικαιοσύνης κτλ. at the beginning of the poem's final sentence (verses 229–230). This structural feature suggests also a material correlation of the designation θεοῦ βουλεύματα in verse 1 with the designation δικαιοσύνης μυστήρια in verse 229; the terms appear to be roughly synonymous, interpreting and clarifying each other. Additionally, both the prologue and the epilogue contend that the author's precepts bestow (at least potentially) some kind of blessing upon the reader: in verse 2 the author refers to the contents of his poem as "blessed gifts", whereas in verses 229 b–230 he promises that abiding by his precepts ensures one of a "good life" (ζωὴ ἀγαθή). These formal and rhetorical tactics create a frame, or inclusio, that delineates the boundaries of the work, contributing to its unity and cohesiveness while underscoring the significance of certain concepts, among them justice (compare above on verses 9 ff.).[16] The use of inclusio also indicates that the author intends the prologue and epilogue to complement one another materially and functionally, and so they should be interpreted not only as independent units but also in light of one another. It is for this reason that they are being studied together here in Chapter Six.

The nature of the identifications made in the prologue and the epilogue corresponds with what can be observed about the content of the verses of the poem itself, which betray a very large number of parallels with the moral directives of the Jewish Law. By the same token, these identifications are also consistent with the fact that the *Sententiae* makes significant use of non-Jewish sources and has selected those commands of the Torah that would be most likely to win acceptance in a Hellenistic environment. The terms employed in the prologue and epilogue to identify the poem and the poet are not culturally determined, and so are broad enough in scope to incorporate the full integration of disparate kinds of ethical material that the text represents. "God's resolutions", while related to the moral ethos and purpose of the Torah, are given a more universal formulation and application in the poem and thus can include directives of originally non-Jewish provenance presented without any distinction from their Jewish counterparts. It might be fair to say that, for the author, God's resolutions for the life of human kind find their perfect or most beneficial expression in the Torah, though they find expression pertinent for a Hellenized Jewish audience also in other sources, such as those that have played a role in the composition of the poem (for example, the *Haustafeln* or the "unwritten laws"). At the same time, he wants to underscore the significant

---

[16] Kranz, "Sphragis," 100; van der Horst, *Sentences*, 59, 260. On the authenticity (that is, their belonging to the original version of the poem) of vv. 1–2 see van der Horst, *Sentences*, 59; Derron, *Sentences*, xlv–xlvii. West (*CR* 30 [1980] 137) suggests also that vv. 1–2 correspond to "I am the Lord thy God" before the decalogue (cf. vv. 3–8), another argument for their authenticity.

degree to which Jewish and non-Jewish moral perspectives can agree. For this reason, he is able to provide a cross-cultural application of the divine resolutions by means of a gnomic poem in a classically Greek mode and style and in the guise of a famous Greek poet noted for his wisdom. The use of the pseudonym underscores the universal and timeless validity of those moral rules incorporated into the poem. According to the literary fiction, even a great teacher and poet of the Greeks recognizes and promotes the moral concepts of Judaism alongside (and practically indistinguishable from) their non-Jewish counterparts.

The meaning of the terminology in verses 1–2 and 229–230 ought to be interpreted as far as possible against what can be surmised generally about the poem's purpose and intended audience. In an important article written in Hebrew by G. Alon (and summarized by van der Horst in his commentary), it is argued quite correctly that the choice of a Greek pseudonym does not necessarily imply that the text was directed at a Greek audience. Rather, it seems most likely that the poem was written by a Jewish author for a Jewish audience: "The poem is a presentation of the principles of Jewish life as compared to the heathen way of life."[17] Our author, speaking in the guise of the famous Phocylides of Miletus, "seeks to demonstrate to the Jews who are engrossed in Hellenistic culture and imitate its manner and deeds, that even an ancient Greek writer of great acclaim recognizes Jewish moral requisites."[18] By means of the poem, 'Phocylides' presents to Hellenized Jews "a more or less current presentation of the (ethical) principles of the Torah in order to check further decline into a non-Jewish way of life."[19] The underlying argument seems to be that one can remain a Jew and live a morally upright life as such without abandoning Greek culture; the poem provides authoritative evidence that the two moral traditions can be reconciled in some manner. Alon goes on to situate the *Sentences* "within a current in ancient Judaism which tended to reduce the Torah to a limited set of ethical principles, which were meant for the Jews."[20] That comparable summaries of the Law, also incorporating Greco-Roman elements, such as those located in Philo's *Hypothetica* or Josephus' *Contra Apionem* 2.190–219, may have been employed for purposes of apologetics, proselytizing, or propaganda in no way compels us to assume similar functions for the *Sentences*. As van der Horst observes, in this regard the difference between our poem and these other summaries is substantial. In the *Sentences*, "there is not the slightest hint of apologetics or propaganda for the Jewish law *as Jewish law*, let alone a missionary aim."[21] This explanation is of use in un-

---

[17] Van der Horst, *Sentences*, 45.
[18] Van der Horst, *Sentences*, 45.
[19] Van der Horst, *Sentences*, 71.
[20] Van der Horst, *Sentences*, 46.
[21] Van der Horst, *Sentences*, 74; his italics.

derstanding not only the assumption of a Greek pseudonym but also the virtually complete absence in the work (including especially the prologue and the epilogue, where it would be most expected) of reference to any religious practice, event, author, writing, or concept that could be deemed particularly Jewish as well as the lack of any condemnation of idolatry, a regular feature of Jewish apologetics. The *Sentences* promotes basic Jewish ethical principles by capitalizing on the readers' fascination with Greek culture, underscoring the moral common ground of the two traditions of thought. In this manner Pseudo-Phocylides strikes a balance between their commitment to living as Jews and the necessity of participating in a pluralistic, fully Hellenized (and probably urban) society.[22] It should be noted that this phenomenon of a Jewish author addressing fellow Jews in the guise of a Greek, which is evident here in the *Sentences*, is paralleled by other works of the Second Temple period, including the *Sentences* of Syriac Menander, the *Epistula Aristeas*, the Pseudo-Orphica, the Sibylline Oracles, and the Hellenistic-Jewish philosophical and poetic fragments.

The reasoning behind our author's choice of the particular pseudonym Φωκυλίδης over against some other possible name remains a matter for conjecture. This is an area of particular difficulty especially since so little is known of the original Phocylides and only a few fragments of his poetry survive for comparison. It should be emphasized that, in contrast to modern times, among citizens of the Hellenistic era the name Phocylides commanded considerable respect and his poems won widespread approval. As van der Horst puts it, "[f]rom the first half of the fourth century B.C. till well into the Middle Ages the name Phocylides is regarded as a guarantee for wise and useful counsel for daily life."[23] We should note, too, that, inasmuch as Phocylides, like other poets such as Hesiod, Theognis, and Chares, was famous in ancient times for his gnomic verses, the choice of pseudonym is consistent with and emphasizes the relationship of the text with the Greek gnomic genres such as gnomic poetry. The fact that Phocylides was a revered figure of the distant past would also contribute something to our poet's apparent efforts to achieve a sense of ancient, traditional authority, adding also something of an oracular aura. Van der Horst notes additionally that Phocylides' mention of Ninevah in *Fragmenta* 4 may have been misconstrued in antiquity as a biblical allusion, another factor possibly influencing our author's choice of pseudonym.[24] Perhaps more pertinent is *Fragmenta* 17, where Phocylides voices the opinion that justice is the

---

[22] Further see van der Horst, *Sentences*, 45–46, 71–72; idem, "Pseudo-Phocylides Revisited," 15–16; Walter, *Poetische Schriften*, 191–193; Niebuhr, *Gesetz und Paränese*, 57–72; Derron, *Sentences*, xxxii–li; Thomas, *Der jüdische Phokylides*, 352–361.

[23] Van der Horst, *Sentences*, 62, cf. 59–63.

[24] Van der Horst, *Sentences*, 63.

greatest of all virtues, a thought that would have been most amenable to the author of our *Sentences* in light of the analysis of the poem conducted above.[25] A final consideration has to do with the possibility that the poems of the original Phocylides were perceived by some ancient readers as functioning in one manner or another as summaries of important ethical points under 'headings' or 'principal points' (κεφάλαια). It is interesting for comparative reasons that modern interpreters of the *Sentences* of Pseudo-Phocylides have made note of its function as a summary of the important ethical teachings of the Torah. Perhaps, along with other factors, our author believed that the choice of the pseudonym 'Phocylides' was appropriate to his task of summarizing ethical materials in the form of a gnomic poem.[26]

The significance for the exegetical task of the unmistakable care exhibited by the author in formulating the coordinated prologue and epilogue should not be overlooked. Indeed, it appears that these formal elements include a number of carefully selected terms and motifs that are paramount for deciphering the poem's general character and purpose, including clues as to its sources, religious assumptions, argumentative stance, and intended hermeneutic. In so far as the prologue and epilogue furnish us with relatively self-conscious, programmatic designations of the poem as a complete literary product, their contents are key indications of how the poem may have been interpreted and utilized against the broader literary and moral backdrop of its original, Hellenistic-Jewish environment. Most important is the identification of the work in verse 229 as δικαιοσύνης μυστήρια, "the mysteries of righteousness", a term that perhaps best expresses the body of ideas from which the author draws here. As van der Horst observes, these words indicate "the way of life" as depicted by the entire poem and summarize its contents.[27]

To be sure, Pseudo-Phocylides' identification of his poem as "mysteries" is highly condensed and formulaic. Yet at the presuppositional level the ideas evident here correlate with some profound and rather complex traditions involving the widespread utilization of mystery language, motifs, and concepts in philosophical and religious literature during the Greco-Roman era. In order to describe more precisely how Jewish authors of the Second Temple period like Pseudo-Phocylides participated in the development and application of such mystery concepts, it is necessary to begin by examining in general terms some significant historical trends of the Hellenistic era that pertain to the understanding of Torah, its patterns of presentation and interpretation, and to religious epistemology more broadly.

---

[25] See below, p. 171.
[26] See below, p. 190.
[27] Van der Horst, *Sentences*, 260.

John J. Collins and others have described a strand within Jewish thought that, while maintaining in some manner its Torah-centeredness, appeals to a higher revelation for religious insight and guidance.[28] One reason for this kind of appeal is the search for a deeper foundation for the expression of an ethic that the Jewish law shares with the surrounding culture. After surveying a wide range of texts that exhibit this sort of appeal, Collins observes that for their authors, "[t]he saving acts of God no longer provide an adequate basis for religion. True understanding depends on some supernatural knowledge which is not accessible to all."[29] In the great majority of such texts, "the emphasis on true understanding shifts the focus away from the specific demands of the law. In virtually all cases the distinctive Jewish requirements such as circumcision and the dietary laws are ignored. Further, the significance of membership in the actual Jewish community becomes ambiguous. The main requirement for salvation is the right understanding of wisdom ..."[30] Thus, potentially, this wisdom can be appropriated and expressed by non-Jews: "[t]he Jewish authors may generally have assumed that true wisdom was found primarily within the Jewish community ... Yet, in principle, the wise and righteous do not necessarily correspond exactly to those who are circumcised."[31] Thus the traditional basis of communal identity for Judaism presupposed by these writers has to some degree shifted, becoming more elusive and more complex to define. At the same time, the significance of the Torah extends beyond its application to the life of the Jewish community and takes on features of natural or universal law: "[b]y emphasizing those aspects of Jewish law which could command respect in a gentile context, the Hellenistic Jewish writers were able to project Judaism as a universal religion which was in accordance with the laws of nature."[32] The presence of these features at work in a text like the *Sentences* of Pseudo-Phocylides would be consistent with the attempt to play down the most distinctive elements of Jewish practice and belief; it would also be consistent with the choice of a Greek pseudonym and a Greek literary genre and style.

Alongside efforts on the part of Jewish writers to appeal to a higher revelation and to express an ethic more universal in scope, in most of these texts the

---

[28] John J. Collins, *Between Athens and Jerusalem: Jewish Identity in the Hellenistic Diaspora* (New York: Crossroad, 1983) 195–243.

[29] Collins, *Between Athens and Jerusalem*, 236.

[30] Collins, *Between Athens and Jerusalem*, 236.

[31] Collins, *Between Athens and Jerusalem*, 236.

[32] Collins, *Between Athens and Jerusalem*, 143; he refers to Dieter Georgi, *Die Gegner des Paulus in 2.Korintherbrief* (WMANT 11; Neukirchen-Vluyn: Neukirchener Verlag, 1964) 182–187; also cf. Wolfson, *Philo*, 2.165–200; Naomi G. Cohen, "The Jewish Dimension of Philo's Judaism: An Elucidation of de Spec. Leg. IV 132–150," *JJS* 38 (1987) 165–186, especially 169–170; further also Gerard Watson, "The Natural Law and Stoicism," *Problems in Stoicism* (ed. A. A. Long; London: Athlone, 1971) 216–238.

Torah continues to operate as a primary 'source', though the manner in which it does so takes on many new and different shapes. During the Hellenistic period there is sufficient evidence of the widespread belief among Jews in the Torah as the central means of divine revelation and as the decisive place where Israel is to learn how to carry out the Lord's will. Because of its divine origin, the true and complete meaning of the divine will as expressed in the Law remains essentially inaccessible to human knowledge and effort. Rather, God may disclose the secrets resident in the Torah through a process of inspired and dynamic interpretation that may be thought of as a form of 'hermeneutical' revelation, though extreme care should be observed in applying terms such as 'hermeneutical' or 'exegetical' to describe what is going on in such texts. Often in these cases Jewish authors do not refer to Torah per se or to any part of it; nor do they actually claim to be interpreting it, self-consciously explaining particular biblical passages according to certain set interpretive methods. Instead many texts present messages that are only informed by or based upon the Mosaic Law, or allude to portions of Scripture, or refer to it indirectly. Thus we frequently witness the reapplication and reformulation of the principles of the Torah in a multicultural context, with a view to their actualization within the Jewish community. The new revelations that constitute these reformulations may in some manner uncover the 'mysteries', 'secrets', or the 'hidden things' of the Torah and so explicate its implications for those who are morally, intellectually, and/or ritually qualified to become 'initiates' of these mysteries. In the depiction of such revelations, authors frequently underscore the advantages and blessings that will accrue to the initiates as a result of the new life that these insights foster. As we will see, a wide variety of Jewish texts testify to the use of revelatory formulae informed by such mystery concepts, though the precise schemes that they employ may vary considerably. Also variable is what the 'mysteries' themselves may consist of: the Torah itself, the secrets of its interpretation or application for a particular situation, or, more broadly, what the Torah expresses, namely, the will of God for humanity and the way to blessing and immortality.[33]

---

[33] For general discussions see, for example, Karl Prümm, "Mystères," *DBSup* 6 (1960) 1–225; John R. Bartlett, "Revelation and the Old Testament," *Witness to the Spirit: Essays on Revelation, Spirit, Redemption* (ed. Wilfrid Harrington; Proceedings of the Irish Biblical Association 3; Dublin: Irish Biblical Association; Manchester: Koinonia, 1979) 11–31; Devon H. Wiens, "Mystery Concepts in Primitive Christianity and its Environment," *ANRW* II.23.2 (1980) 1248–1284; Michael Fishbane, "Revelation and Tradition: Aspects of Inner-Biblical Exegesis," *JBL* 99 (1980) 343–361; idem, *Biblical Interpretation in Ancient Israel* (Oxford: Clarendon, 1985) especially 96–97, 258–261, 337–341, 435–440, 528–533; idem, "Inner Biblical Exegesis: Types and Strategies in Ancient Israel," *Midrash and Literature* (ed. Geoffrey H. Hartman and Sanford Budick; New Haven and London: Yale University Press, 1986) 19–37; Herbert Haag, "Révélation I. Ancien Testament," *DBSup* 56 (1982) 586–600.

Our first illustration comes from 1 Enoch 103, part of a speech where 'Enoch' reveals to the "righteous ones" a "mystery" concerning "the holy writings" (verses 1–4):[34]

> I now swear to you, righteous ones, by the glory of the Great One and by the glory of his kingdom; and I swear to you (even) by the Great One. For I know this mystery; I have read the tablets of heaven and have seen the holy writings, and I have understood the writing in them; and they are inscribed concerning you. For all good things, and joy and honor are prepared for and written down for the souls of those who died in righteousness. Many and good things shall be given you – the offshoot of your labors. Your lot exceeds even that of the living ones. The spirits of those who died in righteousness shall live and rejoice; their spirits shall not perish, nor their memorial from before the face of the Great One unto all the generations of the world.

The author professes to have special access and understanding that pertains to "the tablets of heaven" (an expression that brings to mind the Torah but is not necessarily coterminous with it) and their meaning for the righteous, who shall be rewarded by God with life after death as a result of their "labors". Here, as elsewhere in apocalyptic discourse, the substance of the revelation of this "mystery" derives primarily from scriptural sources and precedents, involving a phenomenon akin to what John J. Collins has referred to as "prophecy by interpretation".[35]

Comparable formulations may be found in the Qumran materials as well, for example, CD 3.12–16:[36]

> But with the remnant which held fast to the commandments of God He made His Covenant with Israel for ever, revealing to them the hidden things in which all Israel had gone astray. He unfolded before them His holy Sabbaths and his glorious feasts, the testimonies of His righteousness and the ways of His truth, and the desires of His will which a man must do in order to live.

Here, as elsewhere in the Damascus Rule, it is clear that the object of God's disclosure is the Torah itself. The revelation of its "hidden things" to the righteous remnant pertains not only to cultic matters such as "His holy Sabbaths and his glorious feasts" but also to "the testimonies of His righteousness" and

---

[34] Translation: E. Isaac, trans., "1 (Ethiopic Apocalypse of) Enoch (Second Century B.C. – First Century A.D.)," in Charlesworth, *Pseudepigrapha*, 1.83–84. Cf. 1 Enoch 104.12–13; also cf. Campbell Bonner, *The Last Chapters of Enoch in Greek* (SD 8; London and Toronto: Christophers, 1937) 62–65; Matthew Black, *The Book of Enoch, or 1 Enoch* (SVTP 7; Leiden: E.J. Brill, 1985) 96–97, 313–314.

[35] John J. Collins, "Jewish Apocalyptic Against its Hellenistic Near Eastern Environment," *BASOR* 220 (1975) 27–36; cf. Devorah Dimant, "Use and Interpretation of Mikra in the Apocrypha and Pseudepigrapha," *Mikra: Text, Translation, Reading and Interpretation of the Hebrew Bible in Ancient Judaism and Early Christianity* (ed. Martin Jan Mulder; CRINT 2.1; Assen and Maastricht: van Gorcum; Philadelphia: Fortress, 1988) 379–419.

[36] Translation: Geza Vermes, *The Dead Sea Scrolls in English* (3rd ed.; London: Penguin, 1987) 85; cf. Markus N. A. Bockmuehl, *Revelation and Mystery in Ancient Judaism and Pauline Christianity* (WUNT 2.36; Tübingen: J.C.B. Mohr [Paul Siebeck], 1990) 43–44.

"the desires of His will which a man must do" (compare Pseudo-Phocylides, *Sentences* 229–230). Thus the interpretation of the Law as it has been divulged to the sectarians exhibits an ethical intention and has ethical implications in so far as it enables them to know and obey God's will and thus "live". The Qumran documents insist that these matters of scriptural exposition are by no means self-evident. Rather, the community asserts its own special insight and privileges over against outsiders and opponents of the sect ("all Israel" above). Besides their stringent ethical and ritual standards, one of the keys to such exclusivist claims lies in the community's conviction that it – and the Teacher of Righteousness in particular[37] – enjoys special and unmatched access to divine revelation, which occurs in the intense study and inspired interpretation of the Law.[38]

It comes as no surprise that sapiential writings also attest to the application of such concepts. The sages' concentration during this period on the Law as the perfect expression of God's wisdom precipitated a growing trend that linked wisdom and Torah.[39] Thus the revelation of divine secrets can take place in the scribe's careful and inspired scrutiny of Torah mediated by wisdom and perceived as a divine gift. In conjunction with this, God's dispensation of wisdom was generally understood as elusive, not only in that it is to some degree ethnically or culturally restricted inasmuch as it is embodied in the Torah, but also because it relies on the privileged gift of divine disclosure.

---

[37] On the Teacher of Righteousness as a mediator of revelation see Bockmuehl, *Revelation and Mystery*, 49, who refers especially to the Qumran hymns, for example, 1QH 1.21, 4.23 ff., 8.16 ff., 12.12–13, 33–34; cf. Béda Rigaux, "Révélation des Mystères et Perfection à Qumran et dans le Nouveau Testament," *NTS* 4 (1958) 243–247, cf. 237–262; Otto Betz, *Offenbarung und Schriftforschung in der Qumransekte* (WUNT 6; Tübingen: J.C.B. Mohr [Paul Siebeck], 1960) 55–57.

[38] Cf. 1QS 1.9, 4.22, 5.9, 11–12, 8.1, 11–12, 15–16, 9.13, 19; CD 6.7, 7.18. Further see Betz, *Offenbarung*, especially 6–72; Hervé Gabrion, "L'Interprétation de l'Ecriture dans la Littérature de Qumrân," *ANRW* II.19.1 (1979) 779–848; Michael Fishbane, "Use, Authority and Interpretation of Mikra at Qumran," in Mulder, *Mikra*, 339–377; Bockmuehl, *Revelation and Mystery*, 42–56; also Martin Winter, *Pneumatiker und Psychiker in Korinth: Zum religionsgeschichtlichen Hintergrund von 1. Kor. 2,6–3,4* (Marburger Theologische Studien 12; Marburg: Elwert, 1975) 96–157; Anthony E. Harvey, "The Use of Mystery Language in the Bible," *JTS* 31 (1980) 323–324, cf. 320–336.

[39] Johann Marböck, *Weisheit im Wandel: Untersuchungen zur Weisheitstheologie bei Ben Sira* (BBB 37; Bonn: Hanstein, 1971) 77–96, 136–138; idem, "Gesetz und Weisheit: Zum Verstandnis des Gesetzes bei Jesus Sira," *BZ* 20 (1976) 1–21; Küchler, *Weisheitstraditionen*, 33–61, 547–548; Skehan and DiLella, *Ben Sira*, 75–80; Eckhard J. Schnabel, *Law and Wisdom from Ben Sira to Paul: A Tradition Historical Enquiry into the Relation of Law, Wisdom, and Ethics* (WUNT 2.16; Tübingen: J.C.B. Mohr [Paul Siebeck], 1985) s.v. Law – correlation with wisdom; David G. Meade, *Pseudonymity and Canon: An Investigation into the Relationship of Authorship and Authority in Jewish and Earliest Christian Tradition* (WUNT 39; Tübingen: J.C.B. Mohr [Paul Siebeck], 1986) 44–72; Bockmuehl, *Revelation and Mystery*, 57–68.

Many of the sages localized their encounter with wisdom and God's unfolding of 'secrets' and 'mysteries' in their reading of the Law, although the level of explicitness in utilizing and interpreting the scriptures among these writers varies considerably, as they strive to formulate an ethic in a multicultural environment.[40] We may thus speak of a process of sapiential inspiration which by nature is to some extent Torah-centered, a process that could be represented as a channel of revelation analogous to prophecy, suggesting the proximity of sapiential and prophetic vocations in certain regards.[41] While the disclosure associated with this practice may pertain to a number of different theological categories – eschatology, cosmology, redemption, and so forth – its primary point of reference lies in the realm of halakhah, and we notice in most sapiential writings a somewhat greater emphasis than elsewhere on the ethical aspects and implications of participation in the divine 'mysteries'.

The hymn in praise of wisdom preserved in Baruch 3.9–4.4 (perhaps first century B.C.) eloquently demonstrates the use of a number of these concepts, incorporating in a rather sophisticated fashion various motifs reminiscent not only of sapiential sources, but of prophetic and legal ones as well. For the hymnist, God's wisdom is incarnate in the Law, a divine gift and privilege ac-

---

[40] The connection with Torah is evident especially in sapiential texts such as Ben Sira and rabbinic tractates like *Pirke 'Avot*, and to a somewhat lesser degree in works like Wisdom of Solomon; cf. Marböck, *Weisheit im Wandel*, 171 ff.; Schnabel, *Law and Wisdom*, 69–92, 132–134; Bockmuehl, *Revelation and Mystery*, 63–68; for more on the rabbinic materials see Gershom G. Scholem, "Revelation and Tradition as Religious Categories in Judaism," *The Messianic Idea in Judaism and Other Essays on Jewish Spirituality* (New York: Schocken, 1971) 282–303; Jakob J. Petuchowski, "Zur rabbinischen Interpretation des Offenbarungsglaubens," *Offenbarung im jüdischen und christlichen Glaubenverständnis* (ed. idem and Walter Strolz; QD 92; Freiburg: Herder, 1981) 72–86; Ira Chernus, *Mysticism in Rabbinic Judaism: Studies in the History of Midrash* (SJ 11; Berlin and New York: de Gruyter, 1982) 1–16, 51–57; Rimon Kasher, "The Interpretation of Scripture in Rabbinic Literature," in Mulder, *Mikra*, 547–594; Bockmuehl, *Revelation and Mystery*, 104–123.

[41] See, for instance, Wisdom of Solomon 7.27:
καὶ κατὰ γενεὰς εἰς ψυχὰς ὁσίας μεταβαίνουσα
φίλους θεοῦ καὶ προφήτας κατασκευάζει·
οὐθὲν γὰρ ἀγαπᾷ ὁ θεὸς εἰ μὴ τὸν σοφίᾳ συνοικοῦντα.
"... and generation by generation she (wisdom) passes into holy souls
and renders them prophets and friends of God,
for God loves nothing except the one who lives with wisdom."
Text: Joseph Ziegler, ed., *Sapientia Salomonis* (Septuaginta: Vetus Testamentum Graecum Auctoritate Societatis Litterarum Gottingensis editum 12.1; Göttingen: Vandenhoeck & Ruprecht, 1962); my translation; cf. Winston, *Wisdom of Solomon*, 184, 188–189; Larcher, *Le Livre de la Sagesse*, 2.506–507. Further cf. Ben Sira 1.1–10, 24.33, 39.6–8; Martin Hengel, *Judaism and Hellenism: Studies in their Encounter in Palestine during the Early Hellenistic Period* (trans. John Bowden; 2 vols.; Philadelphia: Fortress, 1974) 153–175; Joseph Blenkinsopp, *Prophecy and Canon: A Contribution to the Study of Jewish Origins* (University of Notre Dame Center for the Study of Judaism and Christianity in Antiquity 3; Notre Dame and London: University of Notre Dame Press, 1977) 128–132.

cessible to the Jews but not enjoyed by any other nations, despite the impressiveness of their efforts, wealth, or power. Knowing the way to wisdom, then, is effectively equivalent to observing the Torah, through which "the things that please God" are revealed to Israel. Those who heed the Law share in wisdom's glory and "live" while those who abandon its teachings perish.[42]

An illustration from the wisdom literature particularly apt for our discussion of Pseudo-Phocylides' *Sententiae* comes from Wisdom of Solomon 8.4–7:[43]

μύστις γάρ ἐστιν τῆς τοῦ θεοῦ ἐπιστήμης
καὶ αἱρετὶς τῶν ἔργων αὐτοῦ.
εἰ δὲ πλοῦτός ἐστιν ἐπιθυμητὸν κτῆμα ἐν βίῳ,
τί σοφίας πλουσιώτερον τῆς τὰ πάντα ἐργαζομένης;
εἰ δὲ φρόνησις ἐργάζεται,
τίς αὐτῆς τῶν ὄντων μᾶλλόν ἐστιν τεχνῖτις;
καὶ εἰ δικαιοσύνην ἀγαπᾷ τις,
οἱ πόνοι ταύτης εἰσὶν ἀρεταί·
σωφροσύνην γὰρ καὶ φρόνησιν ἐκδιδάσκει,
δικαιοσύνην καὶ ἀνδρείαν,
ὧν χρησιμώτερον οὐδέν ἐστιν ἐν βίῳ ἀνθρώποις.

For she (that is, Wisdom) is initiate in the knowledge of God,
and chooser of (God's) works.
If riches be a possession to be desired in life,
what is richer than Wisdom, maker of all things?
If understanding is productive,
who more than she is the artificer of all that is?
And if one prizes justice,
the fruits of Wisdom's labor are virtues;
self-control and understanding are her teaching,
justice and courage,
and in the life of man nothing is more useful than these.

Here 'Solomon' depicts *sophia* as both initiate and mystagogue into the knowledge of God without assuming the association of wisdom with Torah made often by writers like Ben Sira or the author of the hymn in Baruch 3.9–

---

[42] This fascinating hymn, extant in Greek, may have been translated from a Hebrew original of Palestinian provenance; it has not been much studied in modern times; see Carey A. Moore, *Daniel, Esther, and Jeremiah: The Additions. A New Translation with Introduction and Commentary* (AB 44; Garden City, New York: Doubleday, 1977) 295–304; cf. Joseph J. Battistone, *An Examination of the Literary and Theological Background of the Wisdom Passage of the Book of Baruch* (Ph.D. Dissertation, Duke University, 1968); Gerald T. Sheppard, *Wisdom as a Hermeneutical Construct: A Study in the Sapientializing of the Old Testament* (BZAW 151; Berlin and New York: de Gruyter, 1980) 84–99; David G. Burke, *The Poetry of Baruch: A Reconstruction and Analysis of the Original Hebrew Text of Baruch 3.9–5.9* (SBLSCS 10; Chico, CA: Scholars Press, 1982); Mack and Murphy, "Wisdom Literature," 377–378; more generally, Charlesworth, "Jewish Hymns, Odes, and Prayers," 411–436. Also similar is the hymn in Ben Sira 24.1–33; see below, n. 73.

[43] Text: Ziegler, *Sapientia Salomonis*, 120; translation: Winston, *Wisdom of Solomon*, 191, cf. 194; Larcher, *Le Livre de la Sagesse*, 2.523–530.

4.4, discussed above.[44] Instead, he describes the divine gifts in characteristically Greek terms, with the effect that the presentation, although conducted in a Jewish context, takes on a more universalistic posture. For those who participate in the revelation of this knowledge through wisdom she functions, among other things, as the source of the four cardinal virtues, the most salutary assets for human life. The author describes these virtues as the "fruits" of those who treasure δικαιοσύνη (which in verse 7a appears to represent or embody the other virtues) and work at appropriating the teachings of wisdom.[45] Also of special interest is the author's employment in this passage, as well as elsewhere in the work, of revelatory terminology and ideas familiar from the pagan mystery cults. In this respect, the Wisdom of Solomon is indicative of a movement within Second Temple Judaism that borrowed from this body of prevalent terms and concepts.[46] Even so, in spite of the significant number and nature of such parallels, it would be incorrect to conclude from the evidence that Jewish communities conducted actual mystery rites in the same sense that we know them from non-Jewish sources. Rather, it appears that Jewish authors, primarily Greek-speaking ones, secondarily appropriated the vernacular of the mysteries, finding its religious ideas and patterns of thought an effective way of articulating their own theological traditions and understandings in connection with divine revelation and the moral transformation that took place in those who participated in this revelation. No doubt such adaptations partly entailed a response of Jews to their pluralistic environment as they sought for standards of communication that would help to bridge the cultural and religious gap between themselves and the gentile world.

Perhaps our most important witness to the employment of mystery terminology and concepts in Hellenistic Judaism is Philo, and his writings have

---

[44] On the relationship between wisdom and Torah in the Wisdom of Solomon, Winston's (*The Wisdom of Solomon*, 43) comments are illuminating: "Very likely he believed with Philo that the teachings of the Torah were tokens of the Divine Wisdom, and that they were in harmony with the laws of the universe and as such implant all the virtues in man (cf. Jos. *Ant.* 1. Proem 4.24; Ps-Aristeas 161; IV Macc 1.16–17, 5.25; Philo, *Op.* 3, *Mos.* 2.52), but when he concentrates his attention on Wisdom, it is philosophy, science, and the arts that are uppermost in his mind. Wisdom is conceived by him as a direct bearer of revelation, functioning through the workings of the human mind, and supreme arbiter of all values. She is clearly the Archetypal Torah, of which the Mosaic Law is but an image."

[45] Cf. Wisdom of Solomon 2.21–24, and Bockmuehl, *Revelation and Mystery*, 65, who notes that the 'mysteries' in this passage denote eternal life as the reward of the righteous. Further cf. David Winston, "The Sage as Mystic in the Wisdom of Solomon," *The Sage in Israel and the Ancient Near East* (ed. John G. Gammie and Leo G. Perdue; Winona Lake: Eisenbrauns, 1990) 383–397.

[46] In addition to the texts discussed here see also *Joseph and Asenenth*, especially chapters 8 and 16; further Dieter Sänger, *Antikes Judentum und die Mysterien: Religionsgeschichtliche Untersuchungen zu Joseph und Aseneth* (WUNT 2.5; Tübingen: J.C.B. Mohr [Paul Siebeck], 1980) especially 148 ff.

been the subject of intense scholarship in this area.[47] While it is clearly incorrect to search the Philonic corpus for evidence of Jewish mystery rites of the sort envisioned by E. R. Goodenough,[48] it behooves us all the same to take seriously the mystical, religious, and moral implications of Philo's appropriation of mystery conceptualities, and, as part of this task, to try to make sense of how his thoughts on these matters would have been interpreted within his religious and philosophical milieu. For Philo, it was in fact possible to characterize entry into the Jewish covenant as an initiation into God's most holy "mysteries" (μυστήρια or τελεταί). Moses, who is portrayed as both μύστης and ἱεροφάντης of these mysteries, teaches the divine rites to those whose ears "have been purified" (κεκαθαρμένοι).[49] Above all, these mysteries comprise the disclosure of God's will, which lies hidden in the Law and must be extracted through a mode of inspired interpretation that has been likened to "hermeneutical prophecy".[50] As with the pagan mysteries, exacting intellec-

---

[47] In addition to the titles cited below see Lucien Cerfaux, "Influence des Mystères sur le Judaïsme Alexandrin avant Philon," *Recueil Lucien Cerfaux: Etudes d'Exégèse et d'Histoire Religieuse de Monseigneur Cerfaux à l'Occasion de son Soixante-Dixième Anniversaire* (BETL 6–7; 2 vols.; Gembloux: Duculot, 1954) 1.65–112; Ulrich Wilckens, *Weisheit und Torheit: Eine exegetisch-religionsgeschichtliche Untersuchung zu 1 Kor. 1 und 2* (BHT 26; Tübingen: J.C.B. Mohr [Paul Siebeck], 1959) 139–159; Harald Hegermann, *Die Vorstellung vom Schöpfungsmittler im hellenistischen Judentum und Urchristentum* (TU 82; Berlin: Akademie-Verlag, 1961) 6–87; Winter, *Pneumatiker und Psychiker*, 96–157; Christoph Elsas, "Das Judentum als philosophische Religion bei Philo von Alexandrien," *Altes Testament – Frühjudentum – Gnosis: Neue Studien zu 'Gnosis und Bibel'* (ed. Karl-Wolfgang Tröger; Gutersloh: Gerd Mohn, 1980) 195–220; Helmut Burkhardt, *Die Inspiration heiliger Schriften bei Philo von Alexandrien* (Giessen: Brunnen, 1988); Bockmuehl, *Revelation and Mystery*, 69–81.

[48] E. R. Goodenough, *By Light, Light: The Mystic Gospel of Hellenistic Judaism* (New Haven: Yale University Press, 1935); idem, "Literal Mystery in Hellenistic Judaism," *Quantulacumque: Studies Presented to Kirsopp Lake* (ed. Robert P. Casey, Silva Lake, and Agnes K. Lake; London: Christophers, 1937) 227–241; cf. the review of Goodenough's book by Arthur Darby Nock, "The Question of Jewish Mysteries," in idem, *Essays*, 1.459–468 [originally in *Gnomon* 13 (1937) 156–165]; also Jakob J. Petuchowski, "Judaism as 'Mystery' – The Hidden Agenda?" *HUCA* 52 (1981) 141–152; Gary Lease, "Jewish Mystery Cults since Goodenough," *ANRW* II.20.2 (1987) 858–880.

[49] See, for example, *De Cherubim* 42, 48–49, *De Fuga et Inventione* 85, *De Gigantibus* 54, *De Sacrificiis Abelis et Caini* 60, *Legum Allegoriae* 3.71, *Quaestiones in Genesim* 4.8. At the same time, of course, Philo could condemn the actual practices of the pagan mystery cults themselves; see, for example, *De Specialibus Legibus* 1.319–323.

[50] David Winston, "Was Philo a Mystic?" *Studies in Jewish Mysticism: Proceedings of Regional Conferences Held at the University of California, Los Angeles and McGill University in April, 1978* (ed. Joseph Dan and Frank Talmage; Cambridge, MA: Association for Jewish Studies, 1982) 15–39; cf. J.-B. Frey, "La Révélation d'après les Conceptions Juives au Temps de Jésus-Christ," *RB* 13 (1916) 472–510; Richard D. Hecht, "Scripture and Commentary in Philo," *SBLSP* 20 (ed. Kent H. Richards; Chico: Scholars Press, 1981) 129–164.

tual and moral standards are established for initiates, and nothing must be divulged to the unqualified or untrained.[51]

Of special interest for our investigation of Pseudo-Phocylides' *Sententiae* is the manner in which Philo integrates the topic of the human cultivation of virtue into his discussion of the divine revelation of mysteries in the Mosaic law. In order to grasp – at least in a preliminary way – some of the complexities of this relationship between virtue and mystery in Philo's thought, it is worthwhile to examine the different procedural phases of the revelatory process that he distinguishes. Philo believed that the Jewish mysteries, like their Eleusinian counterparts, could be divided into lesser and greater (or perfect) mysteries, with membership in the former constituting a prerequisite for initiation into the latter.[52] Participation in each of these levels of mysteries encompasses, among other things, both the exegesis of the inner meaning of scripture and the imparting of the moral guidance towards virtue that derives from this type of revelation. As Harry Wolfson observes, initiation into the lesser mysteries entails indirect knowledge of God, the literal reading of scripture,[53] and marks "the passage from the life of the passions to the practice of virtue,"[54] by which Philo means above all obedience to the Mosaic law. Initiation into the greater mysteries, in turn, refers to the spiritualizing allegorical interpretation of the Torah, which facilitates for the initiate a more complete knowledge of virtue.[55] In this case, God, understood as the ultimate source of virtue, directly implants in the soul of the initiate "the natural growth of unpolluted virtues."[56] Thus Philo contends that the potentiality of human virtue, which guides one to mor-

---

[51] Cf. above, n. 33.

[52] See, for example, *De Abrahamo* 122, *De Cherubim* 49, *De Sacrificiis Abelis et Caini* 60, 62; cf. Christoph Riedweg, *Mysterienterminologie bei Platon, Philon und Klemens von Alexandrien* (UaLG 26; Berlin and New York: de Gruyter, 1987) 87–115.

[53] Cf. Montgomery J. Shroyer, "Alexandrian Jewish Literalists," *JBL* 55 (1936) 261–284; Wolfson, *Philo*, 1.115–138; Irmgard Christiansen, *Die Technik der allegorischen Auslegungswissenschaft bei Philo von Alexandrien* (BGBH 7; Tübingen: J.C.B. Mohr [Paul Siebeck], 1969) 134 ff.

[54] Wolfson, *Philo*, 1.47, cf. 1.36–55.

[55] The allegorical method itself could be regarded as a sort of mystery, for example, *De Fuga et Inventione* 32, 179. On Philo's interpretation of scripture, and his allegorical method in particular, see, for example, Wolfson, *Philo*, 1.87–163; Jean Pépin, "Remarques sur la Théorie de l'Exégèse Allégorique chez Philon," *Philon d'Alexandrie: Lyon 11–15 Septembre 1966* (Colloques Nationaux du Centre National de la Recherche Scientifique; Paris: Editions du Centre National de la Recherche Scientifique, 1967) 131–167; idem, *Myth et Allégorie: Les Origines Grecques et les Contestations Judéo-Chrétiennes* (2nd ed.; Paris: Etudes Augustiniennes, 1976) especially 231–242; Amir, *Die hellenistische Gestalt des Judentums*, 77–106; idem, "Authority and Interpretation of Scripture in the Writings of Philo," in Mulder, *Mikra*, 421–453; Burton L. Mack, "Philo Judaeus and Exegetical Traditions in Alexandria," *ANRW* II.21.1 (1984) 227–271.

[56] *De Cherubim* 50. Most important is Philo's discussion in *De Cherubim* 40–50; cf. Wolfson, *Philo*, 1.36–55; Riedweg, *Mysterienterminologie*, 71–96.

ally correct conduct, comes directly from God as a gracious revelation of the divine will that is embodied in the Law and accessible through inspired (allegorical) interpretation. The moral life, then, cannot just be had: it requires 'initiation' into the study of the inner meanings of scripture.[57]

It is important to recognize that the *Sitz im Leben* of Philo's mystery language, like that of other Hellenistic Jews, is to be located in the contemporaneous literary, religious, and philosophical idiom of the Greco-Roman world.[58] We can compare, for example, Philo's allegorical exegesis of scripture with the interpretation of the 'mysteries' of the Homeric epics in various philosophical schools, such as Stoicism and Neo-Platonism.[59] Practices of this sort evidence the fairly widespread utilization of mystery terminology by Hellenistic philosophers, who employed such concepts metaphorically to clarify the nature of their philosophical inquiries and insights. A key element underlying such discussions is the notion that one must become somehow 'initiated' into certain philosophical secrets or divine mysteries in order to learn virtue and to live virtuously. We may thus speak of a 'mysteriosophy' accompanying the epistemological and moral program of certain philosophical texts.[60]

---

[57] Cf. *De Cherubim* 42, *Legum Allegoriae* 3.3. Also comparable is Philo's discussion of the Therapeutae in *De Vita Contemplativa* 25; his description of their "mysteries of holy life" is a means of comparing their exemplary religious conduct with the ethical stringency generally associated with initiation and participation in the pagan mysteries; see Bockmuehl, *Revelation and Mystery*, 78, n. 62; cf. Harvey, "Mystery Language," 320–336. In *Quis Rerum Divinarum Heres Sit* 259–260, Philo argues that a man must be ἀστεῖος, σοφός, and δίκαιος to receive prophetic revelation, employing a sort of canon of cardinal virtues. Cf. Wolfson, *Philo*, 2.22–54; Winter, *Pneumatiker und Psychiker*, 96–157; Harvey, "Mystery Language," 323–324; Bockmuehl, *Revelation and Mystery*, 73.

[58] The bibliography on the Greco-Roman mysteries is vast, see Bruce M. Metzger, "A Classified Bibliography of the Graeco-Roman Mystery Religions 1924–1973 with a Supplement 1974–1977," *ANRW* II.17.3 (1984) 1259–1423; also Walter Burkert, *Greek Religion* (trans. John Raffan; Cambridge: Harvard University Press, 1985) 276–304; Marvin W. Meyer, ed., *The Ancient Mysteries: A Sourcebook* (San Francisco: Harper & Row, 1987); A. J. M. Wedderburn, *Baptism and Resurrection: Studies in Pauline Theology against its Graeco-Roman Background* (WUNT 44; Tübingen: J.C.B. Mohr [Paul Siebeck], 1987) 90–163; Kurt Rudolph, "Mystery Religions," *The Encyclopedia of Religion,* Volume 10 (ed. Mircea Eliade; New York and London: Macmillan, 1987) 230–239; cf. Pépin, *Myth et Allégorie*, 85–214, 231–242.

[59] See, for example, Christiansen, *Technik*, 29–46, 134–171; Amir, *Gestalt*, 119–128; Riedweg, *Mysterienterminologie*, 85–115; Bockmuehl, *Revelation and Mystery*, 78–81.

[60] This term is from Ugo Bianchi, *The Greek Mysteries* (Iconography of Religions 17.3; Leiden: E.J. Brill, 1976); cf. Günther Bornkamm, "μυστήριον, μυέω," *TDNT* 4 (1967) 809, cf. 802–828; Rudolph, "Mystery Religions," 230–239. Plutarch's *De Iside et Osiride* and Iamblichus's *De Mysteriis* are important examples of this sort of literature; see J. Gwyn Griffiths, *Plutarch: De Iside et Osiride* (Cambridge: University of Wales Press, 1970); Hans Dieter Betz and Edgar W. Smith, "De Iside et Osiride (Moralia 351 C–484 C)," *Plutarch's Theological Writings and Early Christian Literature* (SCHNT 3; Leiden: E.J. Brill, 1975) 36–84; Edouard des Places, ed., *Iamblichus: Les Mystères d'Egypte* (Budé; Paris: Société d'Edition 'Les Belles Lettres', 1966); Pierre Thillet, "Jamblique et les

In the Proem (*Fragmenta* 1) of Parmenides of Elea, for example, the poet-philosopher narrates his journey on a chariot guided by the daughters of Helios, who convey him far from the world of ordinary perception to "the gates of the pathways of Night and Day." But before the poet can be received by the nameless goddess, who will instruct him about the Way of Truth (ἀλήθεια) and the Way of Seeming (δόξα), the maidens must first persuade Justice (δίκη), who holds the keys to the portal, to grant them entrance. Once this is accomplished, the goddess can address the poet:[61]

χαῖρ᾽, ἐπεὶ οὔτι σε μοῖρα κακὴ προὔπεμπε νέεσθαι
τήνδ᾽ ὁδόν (ἦ γὰρ ἀπ᾽ ἀνθρώπων ἐκτὸς πάτου ἐστίν),
ἀλλὰ θέμις τε δίκη τε. χρεὼ δέ σε πάντα πυθέσθαι
ἠμὲν ἀληθείης εὐπειθέος ἀτρεμὲς ἦτορ
ἠδὲ βροτῶν δόξας, ταῖς οὐκ ἔνι πίστις ἀληθής.

Welcome; for it is no evil Moira that sent you to come
by this road (for indeed it lies far from the beaten track of mortals)
but Themis and Dike. And it is right that you should study everything:
not only the unshaken heart of persuasive[62] Truth
but also mortals' opinions, in which there is no true reliance.

Taken as a whole, the proem affords the philosopher an opportunity to depict his route of reflective inquiry and philosophical perception in terms of a supernatural experience and a special gift of divine revelation. As Werner Jaeger observes, Parmenides' account amounts to more than mere metaphor: "What Parmenides has done is to take over the religious form of expression and transpose it to the sphere of philosophy, so that in truth a whole new intellectual world takes shape." Jaeger argues that this "is a kind of experience that has no place in the religion of the official cults. Its prototype is rather to be sought in the devotions we find in the mysteries and initiation ceremonies; and as these were flourishing with some vigour in southern Italy in Parmenides' time, he presumably had become acquainted with them there."[63] 'Justice' plays a cru-

---

Mystères d'Egypte," *REG* 81 (1968) 172–195; Friedrich W. Cremer, *Die Chaldäischen Orakel und Jamblich De Mysteriis* (Beiträge zur klassischen Philologie 26; Meisenheim: A. Hein, 1969) especially 102–144.

[61] Parmenides, *Fragmenta* 1.26–30; text: David Gallop, *Parmenides of Elea: Fragments* (Phoenix Sup. 18; Toronto: University of Toronto Press, 1984) 52; my translation.

[62] Some witnesses print here either εὐκυκλέος ("well-rounded") or εὐφεγγέος ("bright"); see Gallop, *Parmenides*, 36, n. 55, 52.

[63] Werner Jaeger, *The Theology of the Early Greek Philosophers* (Oxford: Clarendon, 1947) [reprint, Westport, CN: Greenwood, 1980] 96, 97, cf. 90–108: "Parmenides' Mystery of Being". It should be emphasized that a number of different interpretations have been proposed concerning the religious presuppositions and characteristics of Parmenides' proem; see, for example, C.M. Bowra, "The Proem of Parmenides," *CP* 32 (1937) 97–112; Hermann Fränkel, "Studies in Parmenides," *Studies in Presocratic Philosophy* (ed. R. E. Allen and David J. Furley; International Library of Philosophy and Scientific Method; 2 vols.; New York: Humanities Press, 1970, 1975) 2.1–47; Leonardo Tarán, *Parmenides: A Text with Translation, Commentary, and Critical Essays* (Princeton: Princeton University

cial role in Parmenides' story in so far as this divine entity directs the inquiring philosopher to the 'right' means for appropriating the truth and even guides the process of philosophical insight itself, guaranteeing the legitimacy of the instruction of the unnamed goddess.

Another illustration comes from Book V of the *Bibliotheca Historica* of Diodorus Siculus, where he relates a myth of how the sacred rites of the Great Mother of the Gods (τὰ τῆς μεγάλης μητρὸς τῶν θεῶν ἱερά) were transferred to Asia.[64] As for the rituals themselves, he writes:[65]

καὶ τὰ μὲν κατὰ μέρος τῆς τελετῆς ἐν ἀπορρήτοις τηρούμενα μόνοις παραδίδοται τοῖς μυηθεῖσι· διαβεβόηται δ' ἡ τούτων τῶν θεῶν ἐπιφάνεια καὶ παράδοξος ἐν τοῖς κινδύνοις βοήθεια τοῖς ἐπικαλεσαμένοις τῶν μυηθέντων. γίνεσθαι δέ φασι καὶ εὐσεβεστέρους καὶ δικαιοτέρους καὶ κατὰ πᾶν βελτίονας ἑαυτῶν τοὺς τῶν μυστηρίων κοινωνήσαντας.

Now the details of the initiatory rite are guarded among the matters not to be divulged and are communicated to the initiates alone; but the fame has travelled wide of how these gods[66] appear to mankind and bring unexpected aid to those initiates of theirs who call upon them in the midst of perils. The claim is also made that men who have taken part in the mysteries become both more pious and more just and better in every respect than they were before.

Diodorus' report of the claim that the mysteries render the initiate both more pious and more just alludes to the so-called Canon of Two Virtues, one pertaining to 'vertical' relationships (εὐσέβεια or ὁσιότης), the other to 'horizontal' relationships (δικαιοσύνη or φιλανθρωπία).[67] An important presupposition here concerns the belief that these virtues are in some sense divine and really only accessible to mortals through participation in divine secrets. The mysteries edify the μύστης in so far as they enhance the knowledge of virtue and facilitate the ability to live virtuously, drawing one closer to the gods while improving one's sense of moral and religious responsibility.

That initiation somehow marks the beginning of a new mode of existence and a new direction in life for the *mystes* is in truth a feature of most all pagan mysteries, though it is perhaps most pronounced in the Orphic rites. The *bios* of initiates into this mystery religion was generally characterized by various

---

Press, 1965) 7–31; Alexander P. D. Mourelatos, *The Route of Parmenides: A Study of Word, Image, and Argument in the Fragments* (New Haven and London: Yale University Press, 1970) 146–163; idem, "Some Alternatives in Interpreting Parmenides," *The Monist* 62 (1979) 3–14; Jonathan Barnes, *The Presocratic Philosophers* (2 vols.; London: Routledge and Kegan Paul, 1979) 1.155–230.

[64] Cf. Maarten J. Vermaseren, *Cybele and Attis: The Myth and the Cult* (New York and London: Thames and Hudson, 1977).

[65] Diodorus Siculus, *Bibliotheca Historica* 5.49.5–6; text and translation: C. H. Oldfather, et al., trans., *Diodorus of Sicily* (LCL; 12 vols.; Cambridge: Harvard University Press; London: Heinemann, 1933–1967) 3.234–235; also cf. *Bibliotheca Historica* 3.64.3–7 (on the Dionysiac mysteries).

[66] I.e. the Cabeiri; cf. 4.43.1–2.

[67] See above, pp. 70–71 and pp. 123–125.

purifications and abstinences that were intended to cleanse the soul and to prepare one for life in the hereafter. In this manner, participation in the mysteries involved a self-chosen and self-confirming life of special purity that in effect corresponded to the rites of purification that preceded the initiation ceremony itself. This way of life represented a mechanism for marking the identity and mission of the religious-philosophical community, distinguishing it from other groups and from society at-large.[68]

Turning now to the prologue and epilogue of Pseudo-Phocylides' *Sentences*, we can observe how many of these types of ideas and objectives inform the author's language.[69] He summarizes the contents of the poem as "resolutions of God", "blessed gifts", and "the mysteries of righteousness", which he, as a "philosopher" and "the wisest of men", "reveals" through "divine judgments". Such designations presuppose an appeal to divine revelation for the source of the author's ethical teaching in a manner similar to that described by Collins with respect to other 'universalizing' Hellenistic-Jewish texts. The commands included in the *Sentences* are not predicated simply upon human insight or talent but it is asserted that the author has privileged access to divine disclosure as to God's will for human life and conduct. This reflects the opinion in antiquity that determining the criteria by which one lives a virtuous life in accord with the divine will requires some sort of 'initiation' into the revelation of divine secrets. That the substance of the revelation in our poem relates in some manner to Torah is made plain not only by the identification of the text as θεοῦ βουλεύματα, which appears to be an indirect reference to the Mosaic Law, but also by the contents of the work itself, which depends extensively on its moral directives, beginning with the summary rendition of the Decalogue in the sec-

---

[68] Burkert, *Greek Religion*, 301–304, cf. 290–300; further, Rohde, *Psyche*, 335–361; Larry J. Alderink, *Creation and Salvation in Ancient Orphism* (American Classical Studies 8; Chico, CA: APA, 1981) 55–96; Walter Burkert, "Craft Versus Sect: The Problem of Orphics and Pythagoreans," *Jewish and Christian Self-Definition*, Volume 3: *Self-Definition in the Greco-Roman World* (ed. Ben F. Meyer and E. P. Sanders; Philadelphia: Fortress, 1982) 1–22; Robert Parker, *Miasma: Pollution and Purification in Early Greek Religion* (Oxford: Clarendon, 1983) 289–307; M. L. West, *The Orphic Poems* (Oxford: Clarendon, 1983). Comparable motives are discernable in the Mithraic mysteries; see Robert Turcan, *Mithras Platonicus: Recherches sur l'Hellénisation Philosophique de Mithra* (EPRO 47; Leiden: E.J. Brill, 1975), with the review by John Dillon, "The Platonizing of Mithra," *Journal of Mithraic Studies* 2 (1977) 79–85; Ugo Bianchi, "The Religio-Historical Question of the Mysteries of Mithra," *Mysteria Mithrae* (EPRO 80; Leiden: E.J. Brill, 1979) 3–60; Gary Lease, "Mithraism and Christianity: Borrowings and Transformations," *ANRW* II.23.2 (1980) 1306–1332; Reinhold Merkelbach, *Mithras* (Königstein/Ts.: Anton Hain, 1984) 188–193.

[69] Concerning μυστήρια, van der Horst (*Sentences*, 261) observes that, "in spite of the currency of a metaphorical use of μυστήριον, the word retains something of the sense of secrecy"; the author "sets forth these secrets for those who would read his poem. He seems to say: the secret of life is to live δικαίως, as it is described in my poem." But it is not clear what van der Horst means by "metaphorical" or by "the secret of life".

tion that immediately follows the prologue and introduces the main body of the text, verses 3–8. It should be emphasized, though, that at no point does Pseudo-Phocylides explicitly relate his revelation of divine mysteries to the Torah as such; nor does he claim to be interpreting the divine revelation embodied within it. The author's appeal, rather, appears to be to a higher source of revelation that is more universal in scope, allowing for the inclusion of many non-biblical and non-Jewish sources. This type of presentation is in keeping also with the author's choice of a Greek pseudonym and his apparent efforts to exclude anything that might be construed as peculiarly Jewish, concentrating on instruction that would gain approval among a thoroughly Hellenized readership. Such an approach would be consistent, too, with what we have seen regarding both the use the Torah and the understanding of the relationship between Torah and wisdom in other Jewish sapiential texts. What we see here, as often in Hellenistic-Jewish wisdom literature, is the reapplication and reformulation of the basic principles of the Law in a multicultural context, with a view to their actualization in the realm of ethical judgment and conduct. Because God's wisdom includes Torah but is not restricted to it, membership in the Jewish community is not a prerequisite for gaining access to the divine revelation that guides this reformulation. Rather, wisdom and righteousness seem to be the main characteristics of the one who may reveal God's will, characteristics that 'Phocylides' apparently claims for himself.

Most important with regard to the modality of this revelation in the *Sentences* is the author's choice of the verb φαίνειν in verse 1. Jewish writers commonly employ this term and its various cognates in revelatory contexts, including passages where the Torah or God's wisdom (or both) constitutes the subject of revelation.[70] In Ben Sira 24, for instance, the author prefaces the second major division of his book (chapters 24–50) with a hymn in praise of wisdom. In verses 3–22, *sophia*, speaking in the first person, proclaims her own glory, enumerating her many attributes and the many blessings she bestows on Israel. Starting at verse 23, the author himself takes over, equating these benefits of wisdom with the Torah:[71]

---

[70] In addition to the discussion that follows cf. Philo, *De Specialibus Legibus* 3.6: ἰδού γέ τοι τολμῶ μὴ μόνον τοῖς ἱεροῖς Μωυσέως ἑρμηνεύμασιν ἐντυγχάνειν, ἀλλὰ καὶ φιλεπιστημόνως διακύπτειν εἰς ἕκαστον καὶ ὅσα μὴ γνώριμα τοῖς πολλοῖς διαπτύττειν καὶ ἀναφαίνειν. ("So behold me daring, not only to read the sacred messages of Moses, but also in my love of knowledge to peer into each of them and unfold and reveal what is not known to the multitude.") Text and translation: Colson, *Philo*, 7.476–479. Also *De Cherubim* 28–29, *De Confusione Linguarum* 169, *De Ebrietate* 88, *De Specialibus Legibus* 1.155, 2.257–258, *Legum Allegoriae* 3.169–170, *Quis Rerum Divinarum Heres Sit* 96, *Quod Deterius Potiori* 159; Ben Sira 1.6–7, 39.6–8; Romans 16.25–26; Colossians 1.26; also cf. the use of ἐπιφάνεια in the quotation from Diodorus Siculus, *Bibliotheca Historica* 5.49.5–6 above, p. 166. Cf. Wolfson, *Philo*, 1.186–187, 2.36–43.

[71] My translation.

ταῦτα πάντα βίβλος διαθήκης θεοῦ ὑψίστου,
νόμον ὃν ἐνετείλατο Μωυσῆς, κληρονομίαν συναγωγαῖς Ἰακώβ.
ὁ πιμπλῶν ὡς Φισὼν σοφίαν,
καὶ ὡς Τίγρις ἐν ἡμέραις νέων·
ὁ ἀναπληρῶν ὡς Εὐφράτης σύνεσιν,
καὶ ὡς Ἰορδάνης ἐν ἡμέραις θερισμοῦ·
ὁ ἐκφαίνων ὡς φῶς παιδείαν,
ὡς Γηὼν ἐν ἡμέραις τρυγητοῦ.

All these things are the book of the covenant of the most high God,
the law which Moses established as a heritage for the congregations of Jacob.
It fills all things with wisdom,
like the Phison and the Tigris in the days of new fruits.
It makes understanding abound like the Euphrates,
and like the Jordan in the days of harvest.
It reveals instruction like the light,
and as the Geon in the days of vintage.

Thus "the book of the covenant", that is, the Mosaic law, fills the world with wisdom and understanding as it "reveals" (ἐκφαίνειν) divine paideia like the light that shines on the earth or like great rivers water the crops. Afterwards, the author appropriates the same motifs in order to describe his own mission in life:[72]

οὐ συνετέλεσεν ὁ πρῶτος γνῶναι αὐτήν,
καὶ οὕτως ὁ ἔσχατος οὐκ ἐξιχνίασεν αὐτήν.
ἀπὸ γὰρ θαλάσσης ἐπληθύνθη διανόημα αὐτῆς,
καὶ ἡ βουλὴ αὐτῆς ἀπὸ ἀβύσσου μεγάλης.
κἀγὼ ὡς διῶρυξ ἀπὸ ποταμοῦ,
καὶ ὡς ὑδραγωγὸς ἐξῆλθον εἰς παράδεισον.
εἶπα, ποτιῶ μου τὸν κῆπον,
καὶ μεθύσω μου τὴν πρασιάν·
καὶ ἰδοὺ ἐγένετό μοι ἡ διῶρυξ εἰς ποταμόν,
καὶ ὁ ποταμός μου ἐγένετο εἰς θάλασσαν.
ἔτι παιδείαν ὡς ὄρθρον φωτιῶ,
καὶ ἐκφανῶ αὐτὰ ἕως εἰς μακράν.
ἔτι διδασκαλίαν ὡς προφητείαν ἐκχεῶ,
καὶ καταλείψω αὐτὴν εἰς γενεὰς αἰώνων.
ἴδετε ὅτι ἐμοὶ μόνῳ ἐκοπίασα,
ἀλλὰ πᾶσι τοῖς ἐκζητοῦσιν αὐτήν.

The first person did not have perfect knowledge of her,
and likewise the last person will not find her out.
For her thoughts are more than the sea,
and her counsel more profound than the great deep.
I, too, came out like a brook from a river,
and like a conduit into a garden.
I said, "I will water my best garden,
and will water abundantly my garden bed."
And behold, my brook became a river,
and my river became a sea.

---

[72] My translation.

> Still I will make instruction shine like the morning,
> and I will reveal her light afar off.
> Still I will pour out teaching like prophecy,
> and leave it to all generations forever.
> Behold that I have not labored only for myself,
> but for all those that seek her.

Here the sage depicts his task as a teacher of the Law in relation to prophetic inspiration, as he "reveals" (ἐκφαίνειν) the paideia of wisdom incorporated in the Torah as he understands it to those that seek *sophia*.[73] Ben Sira's comments here presuppose a two-fold revelatory process: God reveals Torah to the Jews, while Ben Sira himself (and presumably others like him) reveals instruction to his students based on his ever-increasing insights on Torah; divine *sophia* mediates both of these processes.

The connection between revelation and wisdom evident in Ben Sira, as well as many other Hellenistic-Jewish texts, appears to be at work in the *Sentences*, too. This is evident chiefly in Pseudo-Phocylides' self-designation as a φιλοσόφος in the title, where he assumes a typically Greek title as a lover of wisdom, and as "the wisest of men" in verse 2, where he assumes a traditional epithet of King Solomon, to whom God gave wisdom surpassing that of all others.[74] The choice of these epithets suggests that σοφία, understood as a divine gift, mediates the author's revelation of mysteries in the poem. As the person who partakes of *sophia* more than any other mortal, 'Phocylides' would be the most appropriate and warranted person to "reveal" in quasi-prophetic fashion the true meaning of God's wisdom for the life of the audience. Such linkage is appropriate within the context of our poem, which is so manifestly sapiential in its orientation and structure.

The framing sections also provide some vital clues as to the exact content and objectives of Pseudo-Phocylides' revelation, particularly the epilogue. At first sight, the specification of the poem's mysteries in verse 229 as pertaining to δικαιοσύνη may seem somewhat restrictive, but this term is probably intended to operate on several different levels of meaning. First, in the sense that it was discussed in Chapters Two and Four, righteousness appears to constitute for Pseudo-Phocylides the foremost virtue, and it is no coincidence that the topic of justice occupies the first major section of the poem (verses 9–54;

---

[73] Further see Skehan and DiLella, *Ben Sira*, 327–338; cf. Marböck, *Weisheit im Wandel*, 34–96; O. Rickenbacher, *Weisheitsperikopen bei Ben Sira* (OBO 1; Freiburg [Schweiz]: Universitätsverlag; Göttingen: Vandenhoeck & Ruprecht, 1973) 111–172; Maurice Gilbert, "L'Eloge de la Sagesse (Siracide 24)," *RTL* 5 (1974) 326–348; Gerald T. Sheppard, "Wisdom and Torah: The Interpretation of Deuteronomy Underlying Sirach 24.23," *Biblical and Near Eastern Studies: Essays in Honor of William S. LaSor* (Gary A. Tuttle, ed.; Grand Rapids: Eerdmans, 1978) 166–176.

[74] Cf. Josephus, *Antiquitates Judaicae* 8.24; van der Horst, *Sentences*, 108–109; Derron, *Sentences*, 19, n. 4.

see Chapter Four). As we saw in several of the examples above, authors sometimes confined participation in the mysteries to those who seek after righteousness, ordering that the contents of the mysteries never be divulged to the unrighteous. Initiation into the mysteries could also be understood as a prerequisite for grasping the essence of this virtue and for living a just life. Above, I noted how a number of ancient moralists ranked justice above the other cardinal virtues; this seems to have been true especially of Jewish authors, for example, Philo, who nicely encapsulates his views on the issue in *De Congressu Quaerendae Eruditionis Gratia* 90: "τὸ δίκαιον in the soul is perfect and the true end of our life's actions."[75] In this sense of the term, Pseudo-Phocylides identifies that virtue which more than any other informs his moral outlook and best recapitulates the moral objective of his instruction. Thus, to begin with, the revelation of his poem may be related to this topic.

In connection with this, ancient writers could also interpret justice as a virtue in a more extended way, namely, as a sort of 'umbrella' virtue within the canon, encompassing all others. This appears to be the case, for instance, in the Wisdom of Solomon 8.7a, cited above, where the author assigns to justice a primary role in the attainment of the virtues of the Platonic tetrad through participation in the mysteries of wisdom.[76] Also, at certain junctures in Philo's corpus, it appears that doing justice is synonymous with being virtuous; thus righteousness is to a greater extent than other virtues an abstract principle that is valid for representing moral excellence in all aspects of human existence.[77] That our author shares in this perspective on righteousness may help account for his appropriation of the 'Phocylides' pseudonym, since, at least judging from *Fragmenta* 17, Phocylides of Miletus affirmed its role as the all-encompassing virtue: ἐν δὲ δικαιοσύνῃ συλλήβδην πᾶσ' ἀρετή 'στιν ("In righteousness is the sum of all virtue").[78] In this sense of the term, the poem's mysteries relate to cultivation of all the primary virtues and to generic virtue as well.[79]

We should note, finally, that it was also possible for Hellenistic-Jewish authors to equate the virtue of righteousness with doing the Torah itself. In *De Somniis* 2.224, for example, Philo speaks of the two as a pair: "justice and God's covenant are identical."[80] In *De Specialibus Legibus* 4.143, he identifies

---

[75] Cf. Sly, "Δικαιοσύνη," 298–308.

[76] Judging from the introduction (1.1–15), righteousness is a key theme for the work as a whole; see Winston, *Wisdom of Solomon*, 99–110.

[77] For example, *De Decalogo* 108–110; cf. Fiedler, "Δικαιοσύνη," 124; Sly, "Δικαιοσύνη," 302.

[78] Cf. Theognis 147; Aristotle, *Ethica Nicomachea* 5.1.15.

[79] Cf. the discussion of Philo's allegorical exegesis of the trees and the rivers in the Garden of Eden in *Legum Allegoriae* 1.56–64 above, pp. 122–123.

[80] τὸ δίκαιον ἀδιαφορεῖ διαθήκης θεοῦ. Text and translation: Colson, *Philo*, 5.542–543. Cf. *De Opificio Mundi* 46, *De Agricultura* 51, *De Sobrietate* 6; cf. the phrase "the covenant of justice" in 1QS 8.9.

the purpose of the Law as the cultivation of justice: "The wise legislator has omitted nothing which can give possession of δικαιοσύνη whole and complete."[81] Also of interest is Philo's claim in *De Specialibus Legibus* 2.13, where he links the Mosaic Law with all the virtues and with justice in particular: "δικαιοσύνη and every virtue are commanded by the law of our ancestors."[82] These comments reflect an understanding of righteousness as an ideal moral principle that finds its perfect, most concrete expression in the Mosaic law. In this sense, the disclosure of mysteries in our poem relates to the author's inspired understanding and presentation of the Torah's moral directives, a meaning consistent with the identifications of the poem's contents in the prologue, particularly verse 1.

I would suggest, then, that the idea of "righteousness" in the formula δικαιοσύνης μυστήρια operates simultaneously on all three of these levels. Thus we may say that the revelation of Pseudo-Phocylides' mysteries relates to the moral intention of the Torah, primarily as it promotes the knowledge and cultivation of the primary virtues, the chief of which is justice. That Torah-obedience instills the love of virtue in Philo's thought was discussed above in Chapter Two. Of course, for both Philo and Pseudo-Phocylides, understanding the divine will as expressed in the Torah and the corresponding pursuit of virtue are not simple matters of human effort or discernment but involve divine secrets revealed through a process of inspired interpretation. As we have seen, the ideas associated with Torah, virtue, wisdom, and justice could all be part of the vernacular of the mysteries.[83]

Like many of the passages surveyed above, sharing in the disclosure of Pseudo-Phocylides' mysteries not only edifies one morally, inasmuch as it 'initiates' the reader into a virtuous life informed by divine revelation, but it also ultimately endows great blessings of a more general nature. The notion that participation in mysteries has profound implications for the initiate was noted on a number of occasions above, where initiates were often promised 'life', or something similar, either in this world or the next. In the *Sentences*, such a promise is indicated by verse 1b and verses 229b–230. Both segments

---

[81] Text and translation: Colson, *Philo*, 8.98–99; cf. *De Specialibus Legibus* 4.144.

[82] Text and translation: Colson, *Philo*, 7.314–315.

[83] In light of the facts that the *Sentences*: (1) is based to some extent upon the Torah, (2) refers to itself as 'mysteries', and (3) is apparently intended for use in a religious community, Derron's (*Sentences*, 18, n. 1) observation – "Le poème a quelque chose de la révélation d'un ἱερὸς λόγος" – ought to be taken seriously. On this form of literature see Johannes Leipoldt and Siegfried Morenz, *Heilige Schriften: Betrachtungen zur Religionsgeschichte der antiken Mittelmeerwelt* (Leipzig: Otto Harrassowitz, 1953); idem, "Buch II (heilig, kultisch)," *RAC* 2 (1954) 688–717; Cerfaux, "Influence des Mystères," 71–80; West, *Orphic Poems*, s.v. hieros logos; Carsten Colpe, "Heilige Schriften," *RAC* 14 (1988) 184–223; Burkhardt, *Die Inspiration heiliger Schriften*, 101–110; Thom, *Golden Verses*, 58–59.

incorporate Homeric allusions, conveying a certain archaic and oracular aura
that heightens the revelatory character of the prologue and the epilogue.[84] In
the former, the author identifies the contents of the text as gifts of blessing,
presumably from God. Most significant is the language of verses 229b–230a:
"living by them you may achieve a good life" (τοῖα βιεῦντες ζωὴν ἐκτελέοιτ᾽
ἀγαθὴν). Underlying this promise is the presupposition that the text in some
fashion outlines for the audience a particular way of life (βίος, ζωή). This way
of living derives from participation in Pseudo-Phocylides' mysteries, which
are characterized by fairly definite moral and religious goals, goals that have
profound consequences for one's existence in the broadest sense. In conjunction with this function, the text envisions for itself also some role in the development of the recipients' social identity. In so far as it depicts a modality for
living elicited from divine disclosure, participation in Pseudo-Phocylides'
revelation, like other mysteries, has a certain role to play in individual moral
formation, resulting in a certain way of thinking and acting that helps to distinguish its participants as some sort of special community. This represents, at
least potentially, a shared and self-confirming life that serves to validate the
divine revelation and the moral formation that it engenders. In this sense the
character and function of the poem may be interpreted against the background
of the Greek conception of paideia.[85]

We have finally to consider the first line of the epilogue, verse 228, a rule on
acts of ritual purity that has presented special problems in terms of its location
and meaning: "Let there be purity of the soul where there are (ritual)
purifications of the body." With regard to the first issue, the author most likely
placed the maxim here because of its logical attraction to the reference to mysteries in verse 229. As Derron notes, the language of the mysteries characterizes all three verses of the epilogue, especially the terms ἁγνείη, καθαρμοί, and
μυστήρια.[86] This suggests that we should interpret verse 228 in light of the author's designations of the poem's contents and function found in verse 229. As

---

[84] See van der Horst, *Sentences*, 109, 261.

[85] See below, pp. 197–198.

[86] Derron, *Sentences*, 18, n. 1. Perhaps we can suppose that ἐκτελέω in v. 230 also belongs to the vernacular of the mysteries, especially in light of the importance of similar
terms with the τελ stem for the cults, such as τέλειος, τελειότης, τελειόω, τελεταί, τελέω, and
so forth. See LSJ and BAGD s.v. τέλειος, τελειόω, τελέω; Hans Hübner, "τέλειος, κτλ.,"
EWNT 3 (1983) 821–835; Paul J. Du Plessis, *ΤΕΛΕΙΟΣ: The Idea of Perfection in the New
Testament* (Uitgave: J. H. Kok N. V. Kampen, 1959) 16–20, 81–85; cf. Rigaux, "Révélation
des Mystères et Perfection," 237–262; Walter Schmithals, *Gnosticism in Corinth: An Investigation of the Letters to the Corinthians* (trans. John E. Steely; Nashville: Abingdon, 1971)
146–155. Cf., for example, Plato, *Euthydemus* 277D-E, *Phaedo* 69C; Philo, *De Abrahamo*
122, *De Cherubim* 42–43, 48–49, *De Gigantibus* 54, *De Sacrificiis Abelis et Caini* 60, *De
Specialibus Legibus* 1.319, *Legatio ad Gaium* 56; *PGM* 36.306: ... ἕως ἐλθοῦσα (ἡ δεῖνα)
ἐκτελέσῃ τὸ τῆς Ἀφροδίτης μυστήριον.

we have seen, access to the mysteries was ordinarily restricted in some way, depending on the moral or ritual worthiness of the initiate. Consistent with this feature was the prescription that the *mystes* must first be somehow purified through a ritual act as a preliminary to initiation.[87] Before the Eleusinian rites, for instance, the *mystai* were required to undergo ritual purification, first with water and then with fire.[88] As mentioned above, purifications took on special prominence in the Orphic rites as well. There, as in all mysteries, the steps taken to achieve ritual purity were seen as the means of preparing initiates for their new way of life, which itself was characterized by the ideal of purity.[89]

Significantly, verse 228 not only introduces the idea of ritual purification in association with the author's mysteries, but it does so by emphasizing the importance and priority of inner purity in the performance of such rites. Although Pseudo-Phocylides raises ritual matters only seldom in the poem, the extent to which he amplifies the ethical component of religious life at this point is in keeping with the general priorities established elsewhere. Furthermore, his application of ritual or cultic language in an ethical context echoes discussions in many and various moral texts of the ancient world.[90] Among the noteworthy witnesses to this development within the Jewish tradition is the corpus of wisdom literature,[91] with Ben Sira 34.21–35.13 representing perhaps

---

[87] See especially Parker, *Miasma*, 281–307; also Rohde, *Psyche*, 588–590, and s.v. purification; Louis Moulinier, *Le Pur et l'Impur dans la Pensée des Grecs d'Homère à Aristote* (Etudes et Commentaires 12; Paris: Klincksieck, 1952) 116–132; Burkert, *Greek Religion*, 75–84.

[88] Burkert, *Greek Religion*, 78, cf. 286; Parker, *Miasma*, 283–286; further, René Ginouvès, *Balaneutikè: Recherches sur le Bain dans l'Antiquité Grecque* (BEFAR 200; Paris: E. de Boccard, 1962) 376 ff.

[89] See above, n. 68; for example, cf. Plato, *Republic* 364E–365A (on the Orphic mysteries) and *Phaedrus* 244D–E (on the Dionysiac mysteries); also cf. Philo's requirement that participants in the Jewish mysteries be 'purified', see above, n. 49.

[90] Thus it comes as no surprise that a number of other gnomic utterances from antiquity approximate v. 228 in form and content; Derron (*Sentences*, 18, n. 2) notes Pseudo-Epicharmus, *Fragmenta* B26 (text: Diels and Kranz, *Die Fragmente der Vorsokratiker*, 1.202.15): καθαρὸν ἂν τὸν νοῦν ἔχῃς, ἅπαν τὸ σῶμα καθαρὸς εἶ. Cf. Plato, *Leges* 716E, *Phaedo* 82D; *Epistula Aristeas* 234; Philo, *De Specialibus Legibus* 3.208–209; Sextus, *Sententiae* 23: ἄριστον ἡγοῦ καθαρμὸν τὸ μηδένα ἀδικεῖν. Cf. van der Horst, *Sentences*, 258–260; Thomas, *Der jüdische Phokylides*, 195–199. Such purity rules are related also to wider discussions regarding the various requirements of cultic sacrifice, among them often righteousness; see Everett Ferguson, "Spiritual Sacrifice in Early Christianity and its Environment," *ANRW* II.23.2 (1980) 1151–1189; F. T. van Straaten, "Gifts for the Gods," *Faith, Hope and Worship: Aspects of Religious Mentality in the Ancient World* (ed. H. S. Versnel; Studies in Greek and Roman Religion 2; Leiden: E. J. Brill, 1981) 65–151; also the literature in the next note.

[91] Johannes Fichtner, *Die altorientalische Weisheit in ihrer israelitisch-jüdischen Ausprägung* (BZAW 62; Giessen: Töpelmann, 1933) 36–46; Leo G. Perdue, *Wisdom and Cult: A Critical Analysis of the Views of Cult in the Wisdom Literature of Israel and the Ancient Near East* (SBLDS 30; Missoula: Scholars Press, 1977) especially 345–362; cf.

the most developed treatment of the issue.[92] Passages of this sort critically re-formulate the concept of ritual in two closely related ways. On one hand, there is the argument that ritual is ineffectual if not motivated by spiritual conviction and guided by human reason. On the other, while refusing to eliminate ritual life altogether, these texts tend to transpose the idea of ritual from the cultic realm to the realm of everyday ethical conduct.

Likewise, while we can detect in verse 228 a certain 'spiritualization' and 'moralization' of the idea of ritual purification, it should be emphasized that Pseudo-Phocylides in no way abrogates the actual performance of these rites or nullifies their rules of purity. The text therefore apparently presupposes both the existence of certain purity rites (though what these rites consist of precisely cannot be surmised) and the validity of their rules in the somatic, as well as in the moral and spiritual, domain. Implicitly, then, Pseudo-Phocylides rejects the notion that the obligations stipulated by the Torah can be reduced to merely moral laws.[93] Instead, he maintains that the higher objective of the rites should be the purification of the ψυχή, a preparation for initiation into the mysteries of the virtuous life.[94]

By bringing the spiritual and moral implications of purification into sharper relief, Pseudo-Phocylides participates in a tradition within Hellenistic Judaism that endeavored to demonstrate a link between the observance of the ritual prescriptions of Torah and the cultivation of righteousness.[95] In *Epistula Aristeas*, for instance, the author states that Moses established rules of purity in the Torah, "for unblemished investigation and amendment of life for the sake of

---

von Rad, *Wisdom in Israel*, 186–189. Some examples: Proverbs 15.8, 27 b, 16.6, 17.1, 21.3, 27; Tobit 4.10–11; Wisdom of Solomon 18.9; Ben Sira 3.30; Sextus, *Sententiae* 23, 46 b, 47, 102, 103, 371; *Teachings of Silvanus* 104; *Papyrus Insinger* 16.11–14; cf. Qohelet 5.1–7; Philo, *De Plantatione* 30; Isocrates, *Ad Nicoclem* 20.

[92] The passage begins with an attack on abuses in offering sacrifices (34.21–27) and on insincerity in performing certain religious acts (34.28–31); afterwards there is the argument that keeping the law is the greatest form of divine worship (35.1–5) and then a depiction of how true believers sacrifice (35.6–13). The entire section is closely connected with exhortation to practice justice, especially with regard to the disadvantaged (35.14–22 a), and with a warning about God's justice, which is revealed above all in vengeance against the merciless and proud (35.22 b–26). Cf. Skehan and DiLella, *Ben Sira*, 411–423.

[93] Further see van der Horst, *Sentences*, 258–260; idem, "Pseudo-Phocylides and the New Testament," 200–202; idem, "Pseudo-Phocylides Revisited," 27–29; Berger, *Gesetzesauslegung Jesu*, 467; Heikki Räisänen, *Paul and the Law* (WUNT 29; Tübingen: J.C.B. Mohr [Paul Siebeck], 1983) 36–38.

[94] Cf. Plato, *Phaedo* 69C, where the canon of cardinal virtues is characterized as "a kind of purification" (καθαρμός τις) that prepares one for the philosophical mysteries.

[95] Jacob Neusner, *The Idea of Purity in Ancient Judaism* (SJLA 1; Leiden: E.J. Brill, 1973) 32–71; E. P. Sanders, *Jewish Law from Jesus to the Mishnah: Five Studies* (London: SCM; Philadelphia: Trinity Press International, 1990) 29–42, 134–151, 258–271; cf. Roger B. Booth, *Jesus and the Law of Purity: Tradition History and Legal History in Mark 7* (JSNTSup 13; Sheffield: JSOT, 1986) 117–154.

righteousness" (§ 144) and to keep the obedient "pure in body and soul" (§ 139).[96] Additionally, in *Antiquitates Judaicae* 18.117–118, Josephus reports on the ritual of John the Baptist; he describes how the Baptist insisted that those who participate in his baptism "must not employ it to gain pardon for whatever sins they committed, but as a consecration of the body implying that the soul was already thoroughly cleansed by right behavior."[97] Similar convictions often govern Philo's characterization of ritual purifications. In *De Decalogo* 45, for example, he remarks that the Jewish people assembled before Mt. Sinai were required to purify themselves before receiving the Law from God. As Jacob Neusner observes, all told, Philo's "interpretation of cultic and priestly purity emphasizes the spiritual or philosophical virtue symbolized by purity."[98] Likewise, in verse 228 of the *Sentences*, spiritual purity constitutes a prerequisite for initiation into the mysteries of righteousness as well as a component of the life informed by these mysteries.

In drawing this discussion to a close, we should note that the purposeful application of mystery nomenclature and conceptualities provides some corroborating evidence that Pseudo-Phocylides does not intend merely to assemble various traditional materials in his poem in the form of an anthology, but, in addition, while doing so has in mind some definite, unifying plan, complete with certain programmatic indicators as to his religious presuppositions, mode of communication, and moral agenda that would have been familiar to his intended audience. The author, in fact, goes some way in constructing a rather sophisticated program within a multicultural context that grounds the cultivation of virtue and the carrying out of moral responsibilities in his revelation of divine mysteries as mediated by wisdom and substantiated by Torah. The basis of this program corresponds with the widespread ideas of antiquity that both the meaning of God's will for human existence and the possession of virtue are not accessible merely through human effort or insight, but require initiation into divine secrets, whose revelation facilitates knowledge of God's purpose and makes the virtuous life possible. Participation in these mysteries entails a process of moral formation that prescribes for the initiate a self-confirming way of life. For Pseudo-Phocylides, this life is based upon his special

---

[96] Translation: R. J. H. Shutt, trans., "Letter of Aristeas (Third Century B.C. – First Century A.D.)," in Charlesworth, *Old Testament Pseudepigrapha*, 2.22. Cf. *Epistula Aristeas* 142, 146–148, 151, 162, 168–169.

[97] οὕτω γὰρ δὴ καὶ τὴν βάπτισιν ἀποδεκτὴν αὐτῷ φανεῖσθαι μὴ ἐπί τινων ἁμαρτάδων παραιτήσει χρωμένων, ἀλλ' ἐφ' ἁγνείᾳ τοῦ σώματος, ἅτε δὴ καὶ τῆς ψυχῆς δικαιοσύνῃ προεκκεκαθαρμένης. Text and translation: Louis H. Feldman, trans., *Josephus*, Volume 9 (LCL; London: Heinemann; Cambridge: Harvard University Press, 1965) 82–83. Cf. H. J. de Jonge in *Nederlands Theologisch Tijdschrift* 33 (1979) 247.

[98] Neusner, *The Idea of Purity*, 46. See, for example, *De Cherubim* 90–96, *De Plantatione* 162, *De Somniis* 1.209–212, *De Specialibus Legibus* 1.256–266, 269–270, *Quod Deus Sit Immutabilis* 7–8; further cf. 1QS 3.8–9, 11–14, 5.13.

revelation in the persona of a famous Greek poet and philosopher as depicted in the body of the poem. In so far as the text would have informed in some manner the beliefs and actions of its recipients, it would have been of use in establishing their moral and religious identity as a distinctive community that is assured of God's blessing.

Chapter Seven

The Literary Genre of the Poem

The formal analysis of Pseudo-Phocylides' *Sentences* conducted above allows us to make some concluding observations regarding the nature of its literary composition, its genre, and its function. It has also made it possible to shed some light on the broader matrix of ideas and methods in which the poet intended his ethical appeal to be understood. As pointed out above, in their literary assessments, modern scholars have for the most part treated the work as a gnomic anthology, even when they have not employed this particular term. According to this trend of interpretation, the *Sentences* can hardly be called a poem in the ordinary sense of the word at all, but merely a collection of individual precepts in verse grouped together here-and-there by ill-defined thematic, logical, or formal considerations. It appears, however, that the poem has been designed in a fairly sophisticated and systematic manner according to certain literary and argumentative strategies familiar from contemporaneous gnomic, paraenetic, and philosophical sources. In order to comprehend fully the author's purposes in writing, therefore, we must come to grips with the overall compositional plan that has informed the organization of the poem.

These compositional methods may be observed on a number of different levels of the text's design. They are evident, first of all, in the manner that Pseudo-Phocylides links together individual lines to form thematic clusters. Most important in this regard is the frequent employment of catchword and linkword as well as the use of similar beginnings and endings for verses. A common argumentational device involves buttressing an imperatival command or series of commands by attaching a precept or illustration by way of support and elaboration. The author also tends to juxtapose complementary or contrasting argumentative elements, both commands and reasons. On a somewhat larger scale we saw how ring composition, inclusio, introductory and summarizing statements, and various other framing and interlocking devices could be applied to help organize topical paragraphs of sayings and demarcate them from surrounding materials. A notable technique utilized within and among different paragraphs involves the association of a block of sayings whose theme is relatively general with another, related block that addresses a more specific sub-topic. Yet another technique juxtaposes a paragraph that illustrates some of the positive aspects of a subject with one that explores some of its negative ramifications. A final method involves the integration of prescriptive and descriptive sections on the same moral topic.

As for the structure of the body of the poem, we suggested that the summary of the Decalogue in verses 3–8 functions as a type of πρόθεσις (*propositio*) for the work, setting forth its basic principles and presuppositions in a succinct and formulaic manner; the main body of the poem, in turn, verses 9–227, constitutes the πίστις (*probatio*), which expands upon the πρόθεσις, indicating in concrete terms its value and implications for the recipients. This part of the poem, in turn, has been divided into two major sections, verses 9–131 and verses 132–227. The first of these contains exhortation structured according to the Canon of Cardinal Virtues: justice (verses 9–54), moderation (verses 55–96), fortitude (verses 97–121), and wisdom (verses 122–131). The ordering of the blocks within this section seems to be purposeful, especially the positioning of justice first, with moderation immediately afterwards. The utilization of such a scheme as a compositional strategy employed in conjunction with a presentation of the Torah's ethical directives finds its most significant analogue in *De Specialibus Legibus* and *De Virtutibus*, where Philo demonstrates how the Jewish laws promote the cultivation of the virtues and are actualized through them. We noted also in Chapter Two a number of other ancient gnomic and philosophical texts that have recourse to the canon as a compositional device. The organization of ethical material in the second section of the body of the *Sentences*, verses 132–227, is conducted according to the different social relationships in which an individual lives. Here, too, the arrangement of verses evidences a purposeful design as each paragraph, beginning at the periphery of social existence and moving towards the center, addresses a more specific and more familiar area of ethical conduct: how to deal with various types of social 'outsiders' (verses 132–152), the nature and importance of work (verses 153–174), and moral obligations within the household (verses 175–227). As we saw, this organizational pattern also has parallels in the ancient philosophical and gnomic literature, both on its own and in conjunction with materials structured around an analysis of the virtues. In extending his exhortation this way, Pseudo-Phocylides participates in ongoing ethical discussions of antiquity that systematically related the virtues with the observance of certain καθήκοντα towards different classes of individuals. Finally, framing the body of the poem is a coordinated prologue and epilogue that identify the author and indicate the nature of the poem's sources, ethical message, mode of communication, purpose, and intended hermeneutic.

Special attention should be paid to the interpretive and the systematic qualities of the exhortation in the body of the text. As we observed above in the inspection of Philo's *De Specialibus Legibus* and *De Virtutibus*, an inquiry of the moral principles and precepts of the Jewish law in terms of the Greek virtues – which takes place there as well as in Pseudo-Phocylides' *Sententiae* –

entails a certain shift of emphasis with reference to the nature and objectives of the ethic that is being formulated. There is, to begin with, something of a universalizing motive discernible as the author endeavors in the poem to remove or gloss over any aspects of Judaism that might be construed as particularistic, all the while synthesizing Jewish with non-Jewish materials. In this way he endeavors to situate the ethical teachings of the Torah squarely within the moral context of his Hellenistic environment. Thus we meet with a large number of trans-cultural and syncretistic features on all levels of the text's composition and message. The application of the literary and argumentative structures in our poem as described above would appear to contribute to these general objectives in a meaningful way. Second, in so far as virtue was ordinarily understood as a consistent moral disposition predicated upon critical or reasoned choices, the association made between the observance of certain moral directives informed by the commands of the Torah and the inculcation of virtue highlights the rational and character-developing qualities of the poem's individual injunctions. In ethical programs such as those articulated by Philo and Pseudo-Phocylides, there appears to be a greater focus on developing the moral character and decision-making abilities of the individual in a particular fashion than on establishing a comprehensive code of conduct or on maintaining some kind of moral conformity within a fixed ethical pattern. Third, Pseudo-Phocylides' teachings constitute a revelation of 'mysteries' inasmuch as the self-characterizations of the poem's author, source, and manner of communication reflect the widespread opinion of antiquity that the virtuous life cannot simply be had, but requires 'initiation' into holy secrets, which facilitates a true knowledge of the divine will and the divine essence of virtue. While the type of ethic that the writing projects clearly evidences universalizing features, its moral substance and standards rely extensively on the Torah, though not explicitly so, and the author's multicultural perspective permits him to critically integrate moral directives and concepts of various origins. For the initiate, a new way of life in accordance with the divine will is possible; this distinct way of thinking and acting serves as a basis of community identity, solidarity, and purpose, and holds forth the promise of divine blessings.

Of course, as noted above, moral virtue does not represent merely the potentiality or capability for making proper ethical decisions, but also entails the responsibility to act virtuously in all aspects of life as well. There is, correspondingly, a pragmatic and concrete dimension to the presentation of the virtues by Pseudo-Phocylides, as he provides for his audience in each instance a picture of the specific sorts of ethical thinking and conduct he associates with the virtue in question. Additionally, the exhortation in verses 132–227 forms an essential corollary to the teachings organized according to the virtues in the first section of the poem. Here the author demonstrates in more explicit terms how the ethical obligations that flow from the development of the various vir-tues have ramifications for one's dealings with all types of people. Of course it is not possible for him to mention all the different possible referents that the readers may encounter; it is sufficient to show in a representative fashion that moral responsibilities extend all the way from social 'outsiders' such as en-emies to those with whom one is most intimate.

It should be underscored that the gnomic style is especially well suited to ethical and rhetorical tasks such as those described above. On account of the subjective, concrete, and paradigmatic qualities of gnomic utterances, their appropriate interpretation and application often require a special sort of moral and rational response on the part of the recipient. Gnomic sayings are not moral 'laws' or 'rules'. The gnomic style does not assume a hermeneutic of mere obedience, but rather promotes a certain degree of intellectual reflection, ethical criticism, and personal creativity as individuals make sense of wisdom sayings for themselves in their daily moral judgments. On the other hand, the subject matter and point of reference for most gnomic sayings is quite specific and pragmatic in orientation, encouraging the reader to put their advice to work in actual situations of life; hence the gnomic style suits a program em-phasizing moral action as much as one emphasizing moral reflection. We should also take note of the fact that gnomic paraenesis represents a truly in-ternational mode of communication, one that characterizes most every culture of antiquity. No doubt this feature was not overlooked by the author of our poem, who apparently sought a literary style that would help him cut across traditional ethical and cultural boundaries.

The formal observations made in this investigation of the *Sentences* also al-low us to make some more specific suggestions in the matter of its literary genre. The compositional features of the poem as delineated above suggest the possibility of generic connections with all three of the prominent gnomic gen-res surveyed in Chapter One: wisdom instruction, gnomologia, and gnomic poetry. The designation wisdom instruction, though, seems to be the most problematic; the *Sentences* is written in Greek verses ascribed to a famous Greek poet and lacks the introductory devices and the narrative or argumenta-tive elements ordinarily associated with the instructional materials. It is inter-esting, however, that our poem is, like many wisdom instructions, of (most likely) Egyptian provenance, and some degree of influence or interaction should not be ruled out altogether.

Turning to the other two possibilities, it is clear that the work is not an an-thology or collection of wisdom sentences either, but rather it manifests evi-dence of a careful and sustained literary structure. For this reason, the term gnomic poem seems a more appropriate designation for the text's literary genre than gnomologium. As I have discussed in Chapter One, gnomic poetry was a fairly prevalent secondary genre in antiquity, both in Jewish and Greco-

Roman literature. The regular characteristics of these texts are: 1) they are poetic, 2) they make use of gnomic sayings, 3) their content is ethical and their tone frequently didactic, suggesting some connection with moral education, and 4) they manifest some type of coherent design or pattern of argumentation. As the investigation above has indicated, our poem exhibits these characteristics, too. That it also bears comparison with certain (mostly Greek) gnomic poems, such as Hesiod's *Opera et Dies*, the *Carmen Aureum*, the *Comparatio Menandri et Philistionis*, and some of the longer pieces in Ben Sira and the Theognidea, tends to corroborate this identification. At the same time, the *Sententiae*, like most gnomic poems, displays significant formal and material features that are familiar from sources that generically lie outside the realm of gnomic poetry; among the texts most germane for comparative reasons are the *Sentences* of Syriac Menander, *Papyrus Insinger*, Pseudo-Isocrates' *Ad Demonicum*, and Isocrates' *Ad Nicoclem*.

The designation gnomic poem also offers certain advantages over some of the other recently proposed literary categorizations.[1] The description of the *Sentences* as a wisdom poem, for instance, is of some value in so far as it correctly situates the work within the corpus of ancient sapiential literature, particularly Jewish wisdom literature. The term, however, is in its usual sense very broad in scope and may be applied to materials that differ considerably in composition and content. Not all poems of this sort make use of gnomic sayings either.[2] Similarly, the designation didactic poem is useful because it highlights the pedagogical and argumentative tone of the work and its connections with a broader spectrum of instructional texts. It should be noted, however, that this designation also reflects a very broad literary category. Didactic poets may deal with an array of technical subjects other than ethics (farming or astronomy, for instance) and they do not necessarily avail themselves of the gnomic style, while gnomic poems are by definition ethically oriented and contain maxims.[3] Therefore the categorizations of the *Sentences* as either a wisdom poem or a didactic poem do have some merit, but in so far as gnomic poetry constitutes a more specific sub-genre that intersects both of these categories formally and functionally, approaching our text as a gnomic poem provides a

---

[1] See especially van der Horst, *Sentences*, 77–78; idem, "Pseudo-Phocylides Revisited," 15.

[2] See, for example, Hartmut Gese, "Weisheitsdichtung," *RGG³* 6 (1962) 1577–1581; van der Horst, *Sentences*, 77–78; Wilson, *Love Without Pretense,* 56–61.

[3] On didactic poetry in antiquity see Bielohlawek, *Hypotheke und Gnome*, passim; R. A. B. Myers, "Didactic Poetry," *OCD* (1949) 277–278; Alister Cox, "Didactic Poetry," *Greek and Latin Literature: A Comparative Study* (ed. John Higginbotham; London: Methuen, 1969) 124–161; Bernd Effe, *Dichtung und Lehre: Untersuchung zur Typologie des antiken Lehrgedichts* (Zetemata 69; München: C.H. Beck, 1977); Michael von Albrecht, "Didaktische Poesie," *KP* 2 (1967) 4–6; van der Horst, *Sentences*, 78; Thom, *Golden Verses,* 51–52.

more accurate and more descriptive angle for investigating its literary character and its connections with other types of texts.

Within the basic formal parameters outlined above, gnomic poems could perform any number of different functions. So while the designation gnomic poem adequately describes the form and tone of our text, it may be possible additionally to associate it with another literary genre that describes its actual function(s) in more specific and accurate terms. For this reason we may think of gnomic poetry as a primary or 'host' genre that can accommodate complementary or secondary genres which may be reckoned as more determinative for interpreting a text's intended purpose. So, to take one example, the *Carmen Aureum* may be classified as both a gnomic poem (a designation relating particularly but not exclusively to its formal characteristics) and, as Thom has argued, a ἱερὸς λόγος (a designation referring more to the text's function but taking into account formal qualities as well).[4] Thom's literary and rhetorical analysis of the text, demonstrating its integrated composition and coherent argument, lends weight to both of these generic identifications.

On the other hand, a central function for Pseudo-Phocylides' *Sentences*, already well documented by modern scholars, is evidenced by the author's attempt to construct some type of summary of the Jewish law for a Hellenistic-Jewish audience. As van der Horst writes, recent studies "have made abundantly clear that the characteristics of our poem, such as pseudonymity, the omission of anything exclusively Jewish (circumcision, shabbath, kashrut, etc.), and the incorporation of originally non-biblical commandments, can all be explained on the assumption that the author wrote a kind of compendium of *misvot* for daily life which could help Jews in a thoroughly Hellenistic environment to live as Jews without having to abandon their interest in Greek culture."[5] The presence of a systematic literary and argumentative design in the *Sentences*, as documented above, leads us to the further question of whether it conforms to any particular literary genre along with gnomic poetry with respect to this summarizing function. Such a discussion would also need to take into account the text's probable school setting, as noted in the Introduction.[6]

---

[4] Thom, *Golden Verses*, 49–59.

[5] Van der Horst, "Pseudo-Phocylides Revisited," 16. Cf. Crouch, *Colossian Haustafel*, 84–101; Walter, *Poetische Schriften*, 185–193. Similar, too, is Niebuhr's characterization of Pseudo-Phocylides' *Sentences* and comparable Hellenistic-Jewish summaries as 'katechismusartig'(*Gesetz und Paränese*, 5–72 and passim), though it is debatable to what extent the term catechism is appropriate and useful for the analysis of such materials. Strictly speaking, it seems to be accurate only in the description of later Christian texts. See, for example, Klein, *Der älteste christliche Katechismus*, passim; André Turck, *Evangélisation et Catéchèse aux Deux Premiers Siècles* (Paris: Cerf, 1962); idem, "Catéchein et Catéchesis chez les Premiers Pères," *RSPT* 47 (1963) 361–372; Georg Kretschmar and Karl Hauschildt, "Katechumenat, Katechumenen," *TRE* 18 (1988) 1–14.

[6] See above, pp. 6–7.

One possibility, recently offered by Hans Dieter Betz, is that the poem belongs to the category of ἐπιτομή.[7] In drawing our study to a close, the appropriateness of this proposed classification will be examined.

Before outlining some of the essential characteristics of epitomic literature, two caveats are in order. First, this genre has not been extensively studied in modern times and so a number of questions continue to be unanswered in the matter of its basic features.[8] A related difficulty emerges from the fact that the authors of epitomes do not always refer to their works as such, and so the classification of some of the texts – including many of those mentioned below – remains tentative until more thorough critical investigations have been conducted. Second, epitomes encompass a very diverse body of literature, both in terms of their contents and the types of material that could be incorporated in them. Authors could in fact compile epitomes in such diverse areas of study as history, geography, or medicine. The comments below will focus on those epitomes that are philosophical and religious in nature, since these works constitute the closest analogues to the *Sentences*, though the observations made about them apply generally to other categories of epitomes as well.

In a provisional way, then, the following texts are proposed as candidates for the genre of religious or philosophical epitome: from the Greco-Roman world, Epicurus' *Epistles* to Herodotus, Pythocles, and Menoeceus, and the *Kyriai Doxai*,[9] Epictetus' *Encheiridion*, the Pythagorean ἀκούσματα,[10] the *Carmen Aureum*, the *Epitome* of Hierocles, the *Epitome* of Arius Dydimus, the *De Virtutibus et Vitiis* of Pseudo-Aristotle, Porphyry's *Ad Marcellam*,[11] and

---

[7] Hans Dieter Betz, *A Commentary on the Sermon on the Mount and the Sermon on the Plain* (Hermeneia; Philadelphia: Fortress, forthcoming) 'Main Introduction: D. The Literary Genre'.

[8] In addition to Betz's *Sermon on the Mount* commentary see Eduard von Wölfflin, "Epitome," *Archiv für lateinische Lexikographie und Grammatik* 12 (1902) 333–344; Henricus Bott, *De Epitomis Antiquis* (Marburg: Hamel, 1920); Marco Galdi, *L'Epitome nella Letteratura Latina* (Napoli: P. Federico and G. Ardia, 1922) especially 1–16; Norman W. DeWitt, *Epicurus and His Philosophy* (Minneapolis: University of Minnesota Press, 1954) 111–113; Ilona Opelt, "Epitome," *RAC* 5 (1962) 944–973; Hans Dieter Betz, "The Sermon on the Mount (Matthew 5.3–7.27): Its Literary Genre and Function," *JR* 59 (1979) 285–297 [reprint, idem, *Essays on the Sermon on the Mount* (trans. L. L. Welborn; Philadelphia: Fortress, 1985) 1–16]; Malherbe, *Moral Exhortation*, 85–104.

[9] In Diogenes Laertius, *Vitae Philosophorum* 10.35–154.

[10] In Iamblichus, *De Vita Pythagorica* 18.80–87; Porphyry, *Vita Pythagorae* 42; Plutarch, *De Liberis Educandis* 12D-F; Diogenes Laertius, *Vitae Philosophorum* 8.17–18; cf. Armand Delatte, *Etudes sur la Littérature Pythagoricienne* (Paris: Champion, 1915) 271–312; Dillon and Hershbell, *Iamblichus*, 104–111; Johan C. Thom, "The Semantic Universe of the Pythagorean Akousmata," *AARSBLA* (ed. Eugene H. Lovering and Barbara S. Yoshioka; Atlanta: Scholars Press, 1991) 21.

[11] On the *Ad Marcellam* as an epitome see Kathleen O'Brien Wicker, *Porphyry the Philosopher: To Marcella* (SBLTT 28, Graeco-Roman Religion Series 10; Atlanta: Scholars Press, 1987) 11, with nn. 68 and 72; while she personally rejects this identification, some of

the Prologue to the *Dicta Catonis*;[12] from ancient Egypt, *Papyrus Louvre* 2414;[13] from Hellenistic Judaism and early Christianity, Philo's *Hypothetica* 8.7.1–20 (preserved in Eusebius' *Praeparatio Evangelica*), Josephus' *Contra Apionem* 2.190–219, the *Epitome* of Syriac Menander, the *Sermon on the Mount* (Matthew 5.3–7.27) and the *Sermon on the Plain* (Luke 6.20b–49), *Didache* 1.1–6.2, and the *Epistle of Barnabas* 18.1–21.1.[14] Also, a number of rabbinic texts are in the nature of epitomes, especially *Pirke 'Avot*, the *'Avot de Rabbi Nathan*, *Derek Eretz Rabbah*, and *Derek Eretz Zuta*.[15] While isolating those features that are shared by even these religious and philosophical epitomes presents a formidable task, the following observations at least can be made.

To begin with, the epitomic genre originated and initially developed in the Greek-speaking world, but by the Hellenistic era the compilation of such forms had grown to become a cross-cultural phenomenon and potential candidates for the genre can be located in Egyptian, Jewish, and Jewish-Christian literature as well. The employment of a genre essentially Greek in provenance and character in the *Sentences* corresponds with the fundamental features and objectives evident throughout the poem, whose author consistently formulates

---

her descriptions of the epistle would corroborate my classification, for example, "[the epistle] contains a summary of important Neoplatonic doctrines which constitute the foundation for the practice of the philosophical life." (*op cit.*, p. 1).

[12] See Otto Skutsch, "Dicta Catonis," *PW* 5.1 (1903) 358–370.

[13] For translation and notes see Lichtheim, *Late Egyptian Wisdom*, 93–100; as she observes, this fragmentary Demotic text, written near the middle of the second century B.C., contains a number of brief thematic units on basic topics in outline form. The extensive parallels between *Papyrus Louvre 2414* and the older and much longer Instructions of Ankhsheshonqy indicate that the scribe drew from either this instruction or a common source for excepts for his work.

[14] There is widespread agreement that the 'Two Ways' teaching shared by *Didache* 1.1–6.2 and the *Epistle of Barnabas* 18.1–21.1 depends upon a Jewish manual of some sort that also has a close relationship with the *Doctrina Apostolorum*. Critics also generally recognize some connection between this source and 1QS 3.13–4.26. See Jean-Paul Audet, "Affinités Littéraires et Doctrinales du 'Manuel de Discipline'," *RB* 59 (1952) 219–238 and 60 (1953) 41–82; idem, *La Didachè* (EBib; Paris: Gabalda, 1958) 121–163; Leslie W. Barnard, "The Dead Sea Scrolls, Barnabas, the Didache, and the Later History of the 'Two Ways'," *Studies in the Apostolic Fathers and Their Background* (New York: Schocken, 1966) 87–107 [originally in *SJT* 13 (1960) 45–59]; Stanislas Giet, *L'Enigme de la Didache* (PFLUS 149; Paris: Ophrys, 1970) 39–170; Klaus Wengst, *Tradition und Theologie des Barnabasbriefes* (AKG 42; Berlin and New York: de Gruyter, 1971) 58–67; Niederwimmer, *Die Didache*, 48–64.

[15] See Marcus van Loopik, *The Ways of the Sages and the Way of the World: The Minor Tractates of the Babylonian Talmud: Derekh Eretz Rabbah, Derekh Eretz Zuta, Pereq ha-Shalom* (TSAJ 26; Tübingen: J.C.B. Mohr [Paul Siebeck], 1991); Jacob Neusner, *Form-Analytical Comparison in Rabbinic Judaism: Structure and Form in The Fathers and The Fathers According to Rabbi Nathan* (University of South Florida Studies in the History of Judaism 45; Atlanta: Scholars Press, 1992). See also above, p. 35, n. 18.

his message in terms that would be intelligible to a thoroughly Hellenized audience. At the same time, as the list above suggests, Pseudo-Phocylides was not the only Jewish author to adopt this genre for his own purposes.

As a rule, an epitome constitutes a secondary or derivative work in so far as it represents a compilation in some way based upon one or more previous sources, which may be either written or oral. Occasionally, authors epitomized not a single text but the teachings of an entire philosophical system or one of its broader areas of study.[16] Thus we may think of an epitome as a condensed and more selective version of the work(s) it draws on. The epitome purports to summarize the larger source in a type of compendium, presenting its essential principles, ideas, and objectives in an abridged and more accessible form. In this respect, the *Sentences* may be considered an epitome of the Mosaic law, though to the extent that it concentrates on the ethical aspects of the Torah and readily draws from non-Jewish sources of wisdom it is more accurate to treat it as an epitome derived from a wider pool of authoritative ethical teachings judged to be of value for the Hellenistic Jews who comprised Pseudo-Phocylides' audience. Hence, in terms of its relationship to the Torah, our poem exhibits a highly selective principle of selection, while on the other hand the author's moral horizons are more far-ranging, as he borrows extensively from Hellenistic-Jewish and pagan sources. A significant objective evident in this epitomizing activity emerges in the programmatic linkage of moral obligations familiar from the Torah with some of the central concepts and strategies of Hellenistic ethics, with a view to the actualization of the resulting ethical program as it is summarized by the poem.

The precise methods employed by authors in epitomizing previous texts vary considerably. Although an epitomizer endeavors to sum up the seminal ideas of another author or work, he does more than simply assemble direct quotations or excerpts. In truth, for the majority of cases, a great deal of interpretation and creativity is evident in the selection, formulation, and arrangement of the different elements of an epitome. Authors also felt free to abbreviate or to expand the sources with which they were working, and would even introduce new or foreign materials that they deemed to be compatible with the intentions of the original work or author. So besides the changes necessitated by its compressed form and style, an epitome often differed materially and structurally from its previous work. It should also be noted that while epitomes often operate at a fairly general level of abstraction, concentrating on basic principles and formulations, they can also include quite specific recommendations, concrete illustrations offered by way of example, and even digressions.

---

[16] The *Epistles* of Epicurus to Herodotus, Pythocles, and Menoecus, for instance, summarize the master's teachings on physics, celestial phenomena, and ethics respectively.

In conjunction with this, all epitomes are characterized by the application of some systematic design or comprehensive argument for organizing their materials. This design is not necessarily identical with that of the original work, and so epitomes should not be confused with mere outlines. To the extent that it is not simply a haphazard anthology of passages gleaned from a previous text, an epitome is distinguished structurally from a gnomologium, although both genres often make use of similar constituent elements, among them especially gnomic sayings. The differences can be observed fairly readily by comparing the works of those authors to whom both an epitome and a gnomologium have been attributed, for example, Epicurus, Epictetus, and Syriac Menander.[17] The materials of an epitome, in contrast to those of a gnomologium, have been carefully integrated into a coherent literary and rhetorical scheme, and they must be interpreted within this larger context.

At this point we can mention a number of more specific formal considerations that tend to corroborate the generic classification of the *Sentences* proposed by Betz and the observations made so far:

(1) Like a number of other epitomes, in Pseudo-Phocylides' poem the most fundamental principles of the text's instruction are formulaically stated near the beginning, verses 3–8, a summary of the Decalogue, which creates an ideational and hermeneutical foundation for the remainder of the poem. Comparable strategies are evident in Epicurus' *Kyriai Doxai* and *Epistle to Herodotus*, both of which (as Betz has noted) open with the *tetrapharmakos*, "fourfold medicine", which enunciates the basic concepts underlying everything else.[18] In Chapter Three, we saw how the introduction to the *Carmen Aureum* is formulated in a manner akin to the *Sentences*, making use of the so-called Canon of Two Virtues and alluding to a number of 'unwritten laws'.[19]

(2) All the Jewish and Jewish-Christian epitomes listed above, as well as Pseudo-Phocylides' *Sententiae*, are at least to some extent based upon the ethi-

---

[17] Contrast Epicurus' *Kyriai Doxai* and *Gnomologium Vaticanum*, Epictetus' *Encheiridion* and *Gnomologium Epictetum*, Syriac Menander's *Epitome* and *Sentences*. A similar type of connection exists between the Prologue to the *Dicta Catonis* and the anthology of sayings itself. Perhaps the same may be said of the relationship between the Sermon on the Mount and the Sermon on the Plain, on one hand, and the synoptic sayings source Q, on the other, though modern scholarship has yet to clarify fully the exact nature of this relationship.

[18] See Betz, *op. cit.*; he also refers to Epictetus, *Encheiridion* 1.1.3; cf. *Carmen Aureum* 1–8, with Thom, *Golden Verses*, 82–104. Also cf. Epicurus' use of πρῶτα in Diogenes Laertius, *Vitae Philosophorum* 10.37, 85, and 123 with Pseudo-Phocylides, *Sententiae* 8. Vermes ("A Summary of the Law," 290) notes that Josephus' summary of the Torah in *Antiquitates Judaicae* 3.90–286 (which is in the nature of an epitome) begins with a discussion of the Decalogue; cf. Thomas, *Der jüdische Phokylides*, 413–415.

[19] Also cf. the use of 'unwritten laws' in Philo, *Hypothetica* 8.7.6–8. Both the Sermon on the Mount and the Sermon on the Plain also appear to have placed their most fundamental principles up front, see Matthew 5.3–10, Luke 6.20b–26.

cal teachings of the Torah, and so undertake to summarize and interpret it according to the epitomizer's particular literary, rhetorical, and moral objectives. Most pertinent for comparative reasons is the sort of 'Gesetzesepitome' that finds expression in Philo's *Hypothetica* 8.7.1–20 and Josephus' *Contra Apionem* 2.190–219, texts whose contents evidence substantial parallels with our poem.[20] The introductory remarks that Eusebius provides for Philo's *Hypothetica* 8.7.1–20 are especially instructive for understanding the nature of its literary genre: ταῦτ᾽ εἰπὼν ἐπιτέμνεται τὴν ἐκ τῶν Μωσέως νόμων καταβεβλημένην τῷ Ἰουδαίων ἔθνει πολιτείαν, γράφων οὕτως· ("After saying these things, he [Philo] made an epitome of the civic life established for the nation of Jews out of the laws of Moses, writing as follows ...").[21] The use of the verb ἐπιτέμνειν ("to cut," "to abridge," "to epitomize") serves as an indication that Eusebius understood Philo to be compiling an epitome of the Mosaic law; furthermore, Philo created this epitome with a specific theme or aspect of the Torah in mind, that is, the civic, or social, life of the Jewish people. While no similar designation occurs in Josephus' *Contra Apionem* 2.190–219, the large number of material, formal, and structural similarities that it exhibits with Philo's *Hypothetica* suggest that it may be suitably included within this generic classification as well. Pseudo-Phocylides' *Sententiae*, likewise, shares a great deal with both of these texts in terms of content, scope, and form, and even may have drawn from the same traditional source known independently by their authors. Additionally, in formulating their summaries of the Jewish law all three authors tend to minimize the ritual obligations of Judaism while integrating non-biblical materials into their instruction. Of course, each text also displays its own unique features. The *Sententiae* is distinguished from the other epitomes in that different compositional standards are observed in the ordering of its materials and that the whole text is cast in the form of a gnomic poem.

(3) The two chief principles of organization employed by Pseudo-Phocylides in arranging the verses of his poem, the Canon of Cardinal Virtues and the different relationships in which one lives, have some parallels in the epitomic literature. To begin with, we should remember that some of the Stoic summaries of ethics, among them the *Epitome* of Arius Didymus, make reference to both the Canon of Cardinal Virtues and the καθήκοντα-scheme in organizing their ethical teachings. As for the use of the καθήκοντα-scheme in particular, the connections between our poem and the *Epitome* of Hierocles

---

[20] See Crouch, *Colossian Haustafel*, 84–101; Küchler, *Weisheitstraditionen*, 207–235; Niebuhr, *Gesetz und Paränese*, 31–72; cf. above, p. 7, n. 22 and p. 123, n. 10. Cf. also Josephus' summaries of the Torah in *Antiquitates Judaicae* 3.90–286 and 4.196–301.

[21] Eusebius, *Praeparatio Evangelica* 8.6.10 (357 c 3–5); text: E. H. Gifford, ed., *Eusebii Pamphili Evangelicae Praeparationis*, Volume 1 (Oxford: Oxford University Press, 1903) 455; my translation.

have already been documented in Chapter Five.[22] With respect to the use of the Canon, both the authors of the *De Virtutibus et Vitiis* and the *Carmen Aureum* arrange their materials according to some kind of presentation of the virtues.

Although the author of *De Virtutibus et Vitiis* no where explicitly identifies his treatise as a philosophical epitome, the fact that the work demonstrates a highly structured design, a telegraphic style, and a relatively abstract level of discussion (consisting almost entirely of basic assertions, lists, and definitions) lends some weight to this proposed classification. This text, like the *Sententiae*, relies extensively on an analysis of the virtues as a literary scheme, though here the number and identity of the virtues differ and the discussion is more analytical and less exhortatory than in our poem. Another distinction of the *De Virtutibus et Vitiis* shows up in its cataloguing of corresponding vices as well as virtues; however, this is to some degree paralleled by Pseudo-Phocylides, who on certain occasions examines opposing sides of the same ethical theme.

More germane for comparative reasons is the *Carmen Aureum*, which provides us with an important example of a text that appears to be identifiable in terms of genre both as a gnomic poem and as an epitome, much in the same way as our *Sentences*. Like Pseudo-Phocylides, its author demonstrates a concern with teaching virtue, availing himself of the Platonic canon as a compositional device for arranging a major block of exhortation at an early point in the poem, verses 9–20. Also like Pseudo-Phocylides, the author of the *Carmen Aureum* utilizes certain mystery conceptualities as a vehicle for indicating the origin of the poem's instruction on virtue in divine revelation.[23] By the same token, this text differs from the *Sentences* in its Pythagorean

---

[22] See above, pp. 120–121.

[23] Thom, *Golden Verses*, 197–200, 210–215. Further cf. Josephus, *Contra Apionem* 2.188–189, comments that come at the end of the introduction to his epitome of the Law in 2.190–219:

τίς ἂν οὖν ἀρχὴ γένοιτο ταύτης ὁσιωτέρα; τίς δὲ τιμὴ θεῷ μᾶλλον ἁρμόζουσα, παντὸς μὲν τοῦ πλήθους κατεσκευασμένου πρὸς τὴν εὐσέβειαν, ἐξαίρετον δὲ τὴν ἐπιμέλειαν τῶν ἱερέων πεπιστευμένων, ὥσπερ δὲ τελετῆς τινος τῆς ὅλης πολιτείας οἰκονομουμένης; ἃ γὰρ ὀλίγων ἡμερῶν ἀριθμὸν ἐπιτηδεύοντες ἄλλοι φυλάττειν οὐ δύνανται, μυστήρια καὶ τελετὰς ἐπονομάζοντες, ταῦτα μεθ' ἡδονῆς καὶ γνώμης ἀμεταθέτου φυλάττομεν ἡμεῖς διὰ τοῦ παντὸς αἰῶνος.

"Could there be a more saintly government than that? Could God be more worthily honoured than by such a scheme, under which religion is the end and aim of the training of the entire community, the priests are entrusted with the special charge of it, and the whole administration of the state resembles some rite of initiation? Practices which, under the name of mysteries and rites of initiation, other nations are unable to observe for but a few days, we maintain with delight and unflinching determination all our lives."

Text and translation: H. St. J. Thackeray, trans., *Josephus,* Volume 1 (LCL; Cambridge: Harvard University Press; London: Heinemann, 1926) 368–369.

bent, though, like our poem, its author also felt free to absorb outside materials and presents a rather eclectic message. As Thom observes, some ancient commentators characterized the *Carmen Aureum* as an epitome of the Pythagorean way of life.[24] According to Hierocles of Alexandria, for instance, the *Carmen Aureum* represents "an epitome of the more important doctrines" (τῶν κεφαλαιωδεστέρων ... δογμάτων ἐπιτομή) of philosophy as well as a παιδευτικὴ στοιχείωσις ("elementary teaching") – a description that implies also some connection with the objectives of philosophical paideia.[25]

As we will see in some more detail below, language of the sort employed by Hierocles occurs regularly whenever ancient epitomizers or commentators make some attempt to describe an epitome or to explain what it is intended to accomplish (compare, for example, the prologue of Epicurus' *Epistle to Herodotus*, cited below on pp. 193 and 195). Although it is limited, there is some evidence that comparable language was applied also in ancient characterizations of the poetry of Phocylides of Miletus, and this may furnish another clue as to Pseudo-Phocylides' choice of pseudonym. In their evaluations of the work of the original Phocylides, ancient writers were quick to praise his ability to articulate succinctly some beneficial moral observation or to render a striking point of advice relating to human life.[26] Of special interest in this regard is the Suda's observation that some of Phocylides of Miletus' poems were entitled Κεφάλαια, "Main Points" or "Principal Matters", a term that brings to mind Hierocles' choice of κεφαλαιώδης in portraying the *Carmen Aureum* as a philosophical epitome.[27] While this term appears nowhere as a title in Phocylides' (or Pseudo-Phocylides') extant poetry, the witness of the Suda raises the possibility that some (or all) of Phocylides' works were well known in antiquity for their summarization of essential points, presumably of ethical matters. If Phocylides of Miletus was indeed noted as a gnomic poet with an ability to summarize principal matters of ethical conduct, he would have made an ideal candidate for imitation for a Hellenized Jewish author who sought to compose a summary of ethical teachings in the form of a gnomic poem.

(4) It should be emphasized that the employment of the gnomic style is crucial for the sort of ethical program articulated by Pseudo-Phocylides and in this regard it is comparable to nearly all the epitomes listed above. Generally speaking, gnomic sayings are to a significant degree paradigmatic and underdetermined, and so they place certain demands upon the rational abilities of the reader to interpret and apply them in various ethical situations beyond

---

[24] Thom, *Golden Verses*, 3–4, 50, 57.

[25] Text and translation: Thom, *Golden Verses*, 3–4.

[26] See the material assembled by van der Horst, *Sentences*, 59–63.

[27] Cf. Isocrates, *Ad Nicoclem* 9, *Nicocles* 62; Pseudo-Aristotle, *Magna Moralia*, 2.9.1; von Arnim, *Stoicorum Veterum Fragmenta*, 2.75.16, 3.69.8 ff., 3.73.2; LSJ s.v. κεφάλαιος, κεφαλαιόω, κεφαλαιώδης, κεφαλαίωμα, κεφαλαίωσις.

those that are ordinarily associated with obeying specific orders or legal injunctions. At the same time, although they represent themselves as timeless, authoritative ethical demands, gnomic sayings are by nature limited and subjective, and so they allow for greater interpretive freedom and flexibility on the part of those who use them. It should also be noted that gnomic sayings are for the most part quite specific and practical in their level of argumentation and so invite concrete ethical responses and the formation of responsible strategies for ethical conduct and decision-making.[28] In all of these respects, the gnomic style was an appropriate mode of communication for the ancient epitomizers.

(5) A number of epitomes conclude with a promise of rewards to be conferred upon the obedient reader similar in formulation and purpose to Pseudo-Phocylides, *Sentences* 228–230. The epilogue attached to Epicurus' *Epistle to Menoeceus*, for instance, holds forth for the dutiful student the possibility of living "as a god" and enjoying "immortal blessings":[29]

ταῦτα οὖν καὶ τὰ τούτοις συγγενῆ μελέτα πρὸς σεαυτὸν ἡμέρας καὶ νυκτὸς πρός τε τὸν ὅμοιον σεαυτῷ, καὶ οὐδέποτε οὔθ᾽ ὕπαρ οὔτ᾽ ὄναρ διαταραχθήσῃ, ζήσεις δὲ ὡς θεὸς ἐν ἀνθρώποις. οὐθὲν γὰρ ἔοικε θνητῷ ζῴῳ ζῶν ἄνθρωπος ἐν ἀθανάτοις ἀγαθοῖς.

So exercise yourself in these and kindred (teachings) day and night both by yourself and with one who is similar to yourself, and then never, either in waking or in dream, will you be confounded, but you will live as a god among mortals. For a person living in the midst of immortal blessings has no semblance of mortal life.

By contrast, the author of the *Epistle of Barnabas* 18.1–21.1 has formulated the conclusion to his summary antithetically, promising entry into the kingdom of God to those who learn and obey the Lord's "ordinances" but condemning those who fail in these matters to death:[30]

καλὸν οὖν ἐστιν μαθόντα τὰ δικαιώματα τοῦ κυρίου, ὅσα γέγραπται, ἐν τούτοις περιπατεῖν. ὁ γὰρ ταῦτα ποιῶν ἐν τῇ βασιλείᾳ τοῦ θεοῦ δοξασθήσεται· ὁ ἐκεῖνα ἐκλεγόμενος μετὰ τῶν ἔργων αὐτοῦ συναπολεῖται·

So it is good to learn the ordinances of the Lord, as many as have been written, and in them to conduct one's life. For the one doing these things will be glorified in the kingdom of God, while the one choosing the other things (that is, the Way of Darkness) will perish together with his works.

---

[28] Wilson, *Love Without Pretense*, 11–24.

[29] Diogenes Laertius, *Vitae Philosophorum* 10.135; text: R. D. Hicks, trans., *Diogenes Laertius: Lives of the Eminent Philosophers* (LCL; 2 vols.; London: Heinemann; New York: G. P. Putnam's Sons, 1925) 2.658–659; my translation. Cf. *Carmen Aureum* 65–71, with Thom, *Golden Verses*, 199–215.

[30] *Epistle of Barnabas* 21.1; text: Klaus Wengst, *Schriften des Urchristentums: Didache (Apostellehre), Barnabasbrief, Zweiter Klemensbrief, Schriften an Diognet* (München: Kösel-Verlag, 1984) 192; my translation.

A third illustration comes from Josephus' summary of the Torah in *Contra Apionem* 2.190–219. In an epilogue comparable to those above, he assures the reader that to those who are obedient to the Law, even unto death, God grants "a renewed existence" and "the gift of a better life":[31]

τοῖς μέντοι γε νομίμως βιοῦσι γέρας ἐστὶν οὐκ ἄργυρος οὐδὲ χρυσός, οὐ κοτίνου στέφανος ἢ σελίνου καὶ τοιαύτη τις ἀνακήρυξις, ἀλλ᾽ αὐτὸς ἕκαστος αὑτῷ τὸ συνειδὸς ἔχων μαρτυροῦν πεπίστευκεν, τοῦ μὲν νομοθέτου προφητεύσαντος, τοῦ δὲ θεοῦ τὴν πίστιν ἰσχυρὰν παρεσχηκότος, ὅτι τοῖς τοὺς νόμους διαφυλάξασι κἂν εἰ δέοι θνήσκειν ὑπὲρ αὐτῶν προθύμως ἀποθανοῦσι δέδωκεν ὁ θεὸς γενέσθαι τε πάλιν καὶ βίον ἀμείνω λαβεῖν ἐκ περιτροπῆς.

For those, on the other hand, who live in accordance with our laws the prize is not silver or gold, no crown of wild olive or of parsley with any such public mark of distinction. No; each individual, relying on the witness of his own conscience and the lawgiver's prophecy, confirmed by the sure testimony of God, is firmly persuaded that to those who observe the laws and, if they must needs die for them, willingly meet death, God has granted a renewed existence and in the revolution of the ages the gift of a better life.

Besides the motif of blessing, all three of the epilogues indicate in some manner the divine source or divine nature of the instruction conveyed by the epitome, reinforcing the authority with which the author speaks (compare Pseudo-Phocylides, *Sentences* 1–2, 229–230). In each case, the epitomizer demonstrates some effort to focus the recipients' attention on the importance of learning and practicing the specific directives of the epitome. As with most epitomes, the writers attach a great deal of significance to the actualization of the religious or philosophical system that their respective texts summarize and promote. The purpose of each work is to inform and direct the readers' way of life and moral outlook in a manner that is in conformity with the divine will (compare the use of ζήσεις, περιπατεῖν, and βιοῦσι in the citations above with Pseudo-Phocylides, *Sentences* 229 b–230).[32]

Turning now to the question of function, philosophical and religious epitomes generally operated on at least two different levels. These texts appear to have been designed primarily for students who had already made significant progress in their education within the philosophical or religious system. For them, an epitome was of value for inculcating the principle doctrines of an area of study in a convenient and orderly manner and for putting these doctrines to work in their everyday inquiries and conduct. In this manner, the regular use of epitomes facilitated a carefully devised educational process as well as a blueprint for moral action and responsibility. By means of such handbooks, students were able to internalize the ethos of the philosophical or reli-

---

[31] Josephus, *Contra Apionem* 2.217 b–218; text and translation: Thackeray, *Josephus*, 380–381.

[32] The conclusions to the Sermon on the Mount and the Sermon on the Plain are comparable in function; see Matthew 7.24–27, Luke 6.46–49.

gious system and to participate actively as one of its adherents without having studied all of its writings. The prologue to Epicurus' *Epistle to Herodotus*, which summarizes the philosopher's teachings on physics, offers some insight on these basic procedures:[33]

τοῖς μὴ δυναμένοις, ὦ 'Ηρόδοτε, ἕκαστα τῶν περὶ φύσεως ἀναγεγραμμένων ἡμῖν ἐξακριβοῦν μηδὲ τὰς μείζους τῶν συντεταγμένων βίβλους διαθρεῖν ἐπιτομὴν τῆς ὅλης πραγματείας εἰς τὸ κατασχεῖν τῶν ὁλοσχερωτάτων γε δοξῶν τὴν μνήμην ἱκανῶς αὐτὸς παρεσκεύασα, ἵνα παρ' ἑκάστους τῶν καιρῶν ἐν τοῖς κυριωτάτοις βοηθεῖν αὑτοῖς δύνωνται, καθ' ὅσον ἂν ἐφάπτωνται τῆς περὶ φύσεως θεωρίας. καὶ τοὺς προβεβηκότας δὲ ἱκανῶς ἐν τῇ τῶν ὅλων ἐπιβλέψει τὸν τύπον τῆς ὅλης πραγματείας τὸν κατεστοιχειωμένον δεῖ μνημονεύειν· τῆς γὰρ ἀθρόας ἐπιβολῆς πυκνὸν δεόμεθα, τῆς δὲ κατὰ μέρος οὐχ ὁμοίως.

For those who are unable to study carefully all my physical writings or to go into the longer treatises at all, I have myself prepared an epitome of the whole system, Herodotus, to preserve in the memory enough of the principal doctrines, to the end that on every occasion they may be able to aid themselves on the most important points, so far as they take up the study of Physics. Those who have made some advance on the survey of the entire system ought to fix in their minds under the principal headings an elementary outline of the whole treatment of the subject. For a comprehensive view is often required, the details but seldom.

As his comments suggest, Epicurus intended the epitome to serve as a pedagogical tool and as a vehicle for self-help and self-advancement. Instruction in the teachings of the epitome also created an opportunity for providing students with 'the big picture', as it were, so that they might not become mired in details or lose sight of the broader philosophical themes and objectives of the system.

There exists, accordingly, an emphasis in the epitomic literature on continuous practice, training, and meditation, so that students might properly develop as functioning members of the group and validate its essential principles in their own lives. This appeal from the *Epistle to Menoeceus* is typical: ἃ δέ σοι συνεχῶς παρήγγελλον, ταῦτα καὶ πρᾶττε καὶ μελέτα, στοιχεῖα τοῦ καλῶς ζῆν ταῦτ' εἶναι διαλαμβάνων ("Those things which without ceasing I have declared unto thee, those do and exercise thyself therein, holding them to be the elements of right life.").[34] Mere knowledge of the epitome's contents is not enough; the text possesses a clear practical function, and, to be successful, the students must put its precepts into effect in their everyday judgments and behavior. In this way the teachings of the epitome play a positive role in shaping one's life in its entirety (compare the phrase καλῶς ζῆν in the citation above with Pseudo-Phocylides, *Sentences* 229 b–230).

---

[33] Diogenes Laertius, *Vitae Philosophorum* 10.35; text and translation: Hicks, *Diogenes Laertius*, 2.564–567.

[34] Diogenes Laertius, *Vitae Philosophorum* 10.123; text and translation: Hicks, *Diogenes Laertius*, 2.648–649.

On the other hand, along with the utility they afforded advanced students, it appears that epitomes could also be of some value for introducing new or prospective students to the teachings of a complex system of beliefs or area of study. This is true especially in so far as epitomes were considered less intimidating and more easily digested than full-blown philosophical tractates. The epilogue to Epicurus' *Epistle to Herodotus* indicates the manner in which an epitomizer might have a dual audience in mind:[35]

> τοιαῦτα γάρ ἐστιν, ὥστε καὶ τοὺς κατὰ μέρος ἤδη ἐξακριβοῦντας ἱκανῶς ἢ καὶ τελείως, εἰς τὰς τοιαύτας ἀναλύοντας ἐπιβολάς, τὰς πλείστας τῶν περιοδειῶν ὑπὲρ τῆς ὅλης φύσεως ποιεῖσθαι· ὅσοι δὲ μὴ παντελῶς τῶν ἀποτελουμένων εἰσίν, ἐκ τούτων καὶ κατὰ τὸν ἄνευ φθόγγων τρόπον τὴν ἅμα νοήματι περίοδον τῶν κυριωτάτων πρὸς γαληνισμὸν ποιοῦνται.

> It (that is, the epitome) is of such a sort that those who are already tolerably, or even perfectly, well acquainted with the details can, by analysis of what they know into such elementary perceptions as these, best prosecute their researches into physical science as a whole; while those, on the other hand, who are not altogether entitled to rank as mature students can in silent fashion and as quick as thought run over the doctrines most important for their peace of mind.

To the extent that they could operate as tools for introducing the uninitiated to a new way of life in a systematic fashion, religious and philosophical epitomes overlap in terms of their function with sources familiar from the so-called protreptic literature, and in fact the epitomic and protreptic materials do share a number of basic features with regard to form and purpose.[36]

Although it is safe to say the authors of epitomes would have normally anticipated that dutiful students would eventually memorize the contents of these manuals, this accomplishment by no means completed the educational process associated with these texts or exhausted the benefits that they could bestow. This thought is expressed plainly, for example, in the second paragraph of the

---

[35] Diogenes Laertius, *Vitae Philosophorum* 10.83; text and translation: Hicks, *Diogenes Laertius*, 2.612–613.

[36] On protreptic literature see especially Mark D. Jordan, "Ancient Philosophic Protreptic and the Problem of Persuasive Genres," *Rhetorica* 4 (1986) 309–333; also Burgess, "Epideictic Literature," s.v. προτρεπτικὸς λόγος; Konrad Gaiser, *Protreptik und Paränese bei Plato: Untersuchungen zur Form des platonischen Dialogs* (TBAW 40; Stuttgart: W. Kohlhammer, 1959); A. J. Festugière, *Les Trois 'Protreptiques' bei Platon: Euthydème, Phédon, Epinomis* (Bibliothèque d'Histoire de la Philosophie; Paris: J. Vrin, 1973); Leo G. Perdue, "The Social Character of Paraenesis and Paraenetic Literature," *Semeia* 50 (1990) 23–24; John G. Gammie, "Paraenetic Literature: Toward the Morphology of a Secondary Genre," *Semeia* 50 (1990) 43–44, 52–55, 57; David E. Aune, "Romans as a Logos Protreptikos in the Context of Ancient Religious and Philosophical Propaganda," *Paulus und das antike Judentum* (ed. Martin Hengel and Ulrich Heckel; WUNT 58; Tübingen: J.C.B. Mohr [Paul Siebeck], 1991) 91–124; Wilson, *Love Without Pretense*, 53.

prologue for Epicurus' *Epistle to Herodotus* (a continuation of the excerpt cited above on p. 193):[37]

βαδιστέον μὲν οὖν καὶ ἐπ' ἐκεῖνα συνεχῶς, ἐν ‹δὲ› τῇ μνήμῃ τὸ τοσοῦτο ποιητέον, ἀφ' οὗ ἥ τε κυριωτάτη ἐπιβολὴ ἐπὶ τὰ πράγματα ἔσται καὶ δὴ καὶ τὸ κατὰ μέρος ἀκρίβωμα πᾶν ἐξευρήσεται, τῶν ὁλοσχερωτάτων τύπων εὖ περιειλημμένων καὶ μνημονευομένων· ἐπεὶ καὶ τῷ τετελεσιουργημένῳ τοῦτο κυριώτατον τοῦ παντὸς ἀκριβώματος γίνεται, τὸ ταῖς ἐπιβολαῖς ὀξέως δύνασθαι χρῆσθαι, ἑκάστων πρὸς ἁπλᾶ στοιχειώματα καὶ φωνὰς συναγομένων. οὐ γὰρ οἷόν τε τὸ πύκνωμα τῆς συνεχοῦς βραχέων φωνῶν ἅπαν ἐμπεριλαβεῖν ἐν αὐτῷ τὸ καὶ κατὰ μέρος ἂν ἐξακριβωθέν.

To the former, then – the main heads (that is, the principal headings outlined in the epitome) – we must continually return, and must memorize them so far as to get a valid conception of the facts, as well as the means of discovering all the details exactly when once the general outlines are rightly understood and remembered; since it is the privilege of the mature student to make a ready use of his conceptions by referring every one of them to elementary facts and simple terms. For it is impossible to gather up the results of continuous diligent study of the entirety of things, unless we can embrace in short formulas and hold in mind all that might have been accurately expressed even to the minutest detail.

As Epicurus indicates, memorizing an epitome is not only a way of achieving a correct comprehension of its subject matter, but also entails a certain heuristic process, as the student is encouraged to discover the details of the philosophical system and their relationship with the more essential precepts. Thus an epitome can foster additional learning and research; in this capacity it serves a certain referential function as well. Furthermore, an epitome affords advanced students a mechanism for relating their own conceptions and experiences to the authoritative teachings of the philosophical system. All in all, an epitome consistently keeps the end of its educational procedure in view as it facilitates the process of consolidating the significant results of an individual's ongoing studies and discoveries within the context of the system. Betz's comments on the function of the Sermon on the Mount (SM) in this regard may be aptly applied to other religious and philosophical epitomes as well:[38]

The literary genre of the SM is that of an epitome presenting the theology of Jesus in a systematic fashion. The epitome is a composition carefully designed out of sayings of Jesus grouped according to thematic points of doctrine considered to be of primary importance. Correspondingly, its function is to provide the disciples of Jesus with the necessary tools for becoming a Jesus theologian ... The SM is not law to be obeyed, but theology to be intellectually appropriated and internalized, in order then to be creatively developed and implemented in concrete situations of life.

Generally speaking, the hermeneutic that an epitome recommends for itself is predicated upon the development of the critical abilities and moral character

---

[37] Diogenes Laertius, *Vitae Philosophorum* 10.36; text and translation: Hicks, *Diogenes Laertius*, 2.566–567.

[38] Betz, *Essays*, 15–16.

of the individual. While it promotes a particular way of life or a particular type of approach to dealing with philosophical or religious issues, the educational process associated with an epitome welcomes the initiatives and creativity of mature adherents as they themselves become purveyors of new wisdom.

Most of the observations made above concerning the function of the epitomic literature may be brought to bear, mutatis mutandis, on the interpretation of Pseudo-Phocylides' *Sentences*. Our investigation suggests that this text is a gnomic poem that epitomizes those ethical teachings deemed essential for the Jewish way of life, particularly as it is experienced in a fully Hellenistic milieu. As such, it summarizes what the author understands as the principal doctrines and characteristics of this teaching in a systematic fashion, with a view to providing the reader with a framework for learning its essential points, inculcating the ethos of its moral agenda, and applying its ideas in concrete situations of life. In conjunction with this summarizing function, Pseudo-Phocylides sketches a picture of the wide-ranging ethical qualities and objectives of the Torah and other pertinent ethical sources as they pertain to the cultivation of virtue and the observation of moral obligations in different areas of life. There is, at the same time, a clear emphasis on the actualization of these objectives, as the author stipulates the sorts of ethical responsibilities and priorities the reader must acknowledge. In this way the text is of use in establishing an ethical program or policy for the audience. The *Sentences* therefore represents a pedagogical tool meant to facilitate a carefully planned educational process and to promote a particular type of understanding of the Jewish way of life. This is a way of life that generally seeks assimilation to the Hellenistic culture, camouflaging its peculiarly Jewish features while appropriating Greek ideas and methods, but still understands the moral standards and specific moral commands of the Torah as somehow central or guiding for the self-understanding and conduct of Jewish people. Judaism and Hellenism, then, are not irreconcilable according to Pseudo-Phocylides, but the Torah can be expressed and experienced through wisdom, even (or especially) Greek wisdom. This not only implies that for the author the moral stipulations of the Torah and the ideals of Greek wisdom are in agreement, and had been recognized and promoted as such centuries earlier by a revered Greek poet and philosopher, but also suggests something of a critique of the latter's moral tradition. Implicit in the poem's appeal is the argument that Greek wisdom, at least as it is appropriated and interpreted by the author's Jewish audience, can be "improved" – undergirded by revelational authority and informed by the moral content and principles of the Mosaic law.

So we can observe how in compiling his epitome Pseudo-Phocylides undertakes a special kind of interpretive conversation not only with the authoritative texts of his own tradition, but with those of other traditions as well. The critical appropriation of disparate types of sources and the subsequent reconstruction of a new ethical program within a multicultural context based upon these sources involves more on his part than identifying common ground or setting similar materials side-by-side for comparison. It has as its task the reflective and synthetic restructuring of ethical norms, strategies, and objectives, as well as the formulation of creative modalities for articulating this new structure in a rhetorically effective manner. For Pseudo-Phocylides, this restructuring is predicated upon his special revelation of God's "mysteries of righteousness" mediated by *sophia*. Although its ethos is clearly Torah centered, the expression of this revelation takes the shape of a gnomic poem written in a classical Greek dialect and style, it is attributed to a famous Greek poet of ages past, and it has been organized according to distinctively Hellenistic literary structures. The manner of appeal to a higher source of revelation for moral guidance and the corresponding shape assumed by the work reflects the author's search for a deeper and more universal foundation for articulating an ethic that the Mosaic law shares with the surrounding Greco-Roman culture.

The potential of this moral and social program, however, is not at all exhausted by the material of the epitome itself. In this respect the *Sentences* functions in a referential or heuristic manner as well. Like all epitomes, our poem is a literary condensation whose contents are representative of the sources upon which it draws; in this case the epitomizer depends primarily upon the Mosaic law, but he also borrows from and integrates certain Jewish and pagan traditions that are deemed compatible, as well as similarly valuable. As part of its intended educational procedure, the epitome encourages the reader to study these traditions in greater detail, providing criteria for relating further learning to the principle objectives of the ethical program. This procedure fosters the development of the moral character and critical abilities of the reader – especially in so far as it focuses on the role of the Torah in the cultivation of the virtues – as well as the recognition of the individual's moral responsibilities within a multicultural environment.

In so far as the *Sentences*, like philosophical and religious epitomes generally, possesses an educational agenda and aims at the social, moral, and intellectual instruction of its 'students' in the broadest sense, its function should be understood against the background of the Greek ideal of paideia.[39] In this re-

---

[39] See, especially Werner Jaeger, *Paideia: The Ideals of Greek Culture* (trans. Gilbert Highet; 3 vols.; New York: Oxford University Press, 1942–44); also, idem, *Early Christianity and Greek Paideia* (London: Oxford University Press, 1961); Martin P. Nilsson, *Die hellenistische Schule* (München: Beck, 1955); Marrou, *History of Education*, especially 95–164, 267–308; Paul Blomenkamp, "Erziehung," *RAC* 6 (1966) 502–559; Georg Betram, "παιδεύω, κτλ.," *TDNT* 5 (1967) 596–625; M. L. Clarke, *Higher Education in the Ancient World* (London: Routledge and Kegan Paul, 1971) 55–108; Spicq, *Notes*, 2.639–641; Gerard Verbeke, *Moral Education in Aristotle* (Washington, D.C.: University Press of America, 1990).

gard, our categorization of the poem as an epitome is consistent with and rein-
forces the school-book theory of van der Horst mentioned (and endorsed)
above.[40] The evidence considered above suggests the likelihood of some type
of school setting for our poem, and underscores the need for understanding the
Sentences' possible social functions within the broader context of moral and
religious education both within the communities of Second Temple Judaism
and in Greco-Roman society at large.[41] It should be underscored that one special concern of paideia in antiquity, particularly in the Socratic tradition, was
the development of a correct understanding concerning the nature and practice
of virtue, which, as we saw above, is a prominent element in the instruction of
the *Sentences*. From the very beginning of Greek civilization, the development
of moral virtue was closely connected with the goals of education. In *Leges*
653A–C, for instance, Plato effectively defines paideia as training in *arete*.[42]
Timaeus Locrus (first century A.D.) takes a similar stand when he argues that
the four primary virtues, with which the soul must be in harmony for a prosperous life, have their beginnings in nature but have their intermediate and final parts in care through paideia and philosophy respectively.[43] Hellenistic
Jews also made the connection between paideia and virtue. In 4 Maccabees
5.23–24, for instance, the author describes how Torah teaches the different
virtues to the obedient through paideia.[44] According to Philo, paideia, which is
connected with the Law, characterizes the initiation of the life according to
virtue, with the cardinal virtues constituting the essential elements of paideia
itself. This process of instruction represents a mechanism for cleansing the
soul of the dutiful student (compare Pseudo-Phocylides, *Sentences* 228).[45]

---

[40] See above, pp. 6–7.

[41] The literature is extensive; see, for instance, Nathan Drazin, *The History of Jewish Education from 515 B.C. to 220 C.E.* (Johns Hopkins University Studies in Education; Baltimore: Johns Hopkins University Press, 1940); Eliezer Ebner, *Elementary Education in Ancient Israel During the Tannaitic Period: 10–220 C.E.* (New York: Bloch, 1956); Walter H. Wagner, "Philo and Paideia," *Cithara* 10 (1971) 53–64; Thomas Conley, *'General Education' in Philo of Alexandria* (Center for Hermeneutical Studies in Hellenistic and Modern Culture 15; Berkeley: The Center, 1975); Shmuel Safrai, "Education and the Study of Torah," *The Jewish People in the First Century: Historical Geography, Political History, Social, Cultural and Religious Life and Institutions,* Volume 2 (ed. idem and M. Stern; CRINT 1.2; Assen: van Gorcum, 1976) 945–970; Gerhard Delling, *Die Bewältigung der Diasporasituation durch das hellenistische Judentum* (Göttingen: Vandenhoeck & Ruprecht, 1987).

[42] Text and translation: R. G. Bury, trans., *Plato: Laws* (LCL; 2 vols.; London: Heinemann; Cambridge: Harvard University Press, 1926) 1.88–91.

[43] Text: Thesleff, *Pythagorean Texts*, 203–225, especially 222–224; cf. Richard Harder, "Timaios 4," *PW* 6A (1937) 1203–1226; Mott, "Greek Ethics," 30–35.

[44] σωφροσύνην τε γὰρ ἡμᾶς ἐκδιδάσκει ὥστε πασῶν τῶν ἡδονῶν καὶ ἐπιθυμιῶν κρατεῖν καὶ ἀνδρείαν ἐξασκεῖ ὥστε πάντα πόνον ἑκουσίως ὑπομένειν καὶ δικαιοσύνην παιδεύει ὥστε διὰ πάντων τῶν ἠθῶν ἰσονομεῖν καὶ εὐσέβειαν ἐκδιδάσκει ὥστε μόνον τὸν ὄντα θεὸν σέβειν μεγαλοπρεπῶς.

[45] *De Abrahamo* 24–25, *De Agricultura* 18, *De Fuga et Inventione* 183, *De Mutatione Nominum* 228–229, *De Somniis* 1.49, 2.73; also cf. *De Agricultura* 44, *De Congressu*

A crucial feature that we can discern in the tradition of paideia in antiquity is the opinion that there is a higher principle underlying virtue that is beyond the grasp of ordinary human perception or effort. In order to cultivate the virtues in any truly effective way, paideia necessarily entails inquiry into the essence or origin of virtue, which is divine. Thus paideia involves more than merely conveying doctrinal information or moral guidelines (though it does do these things); it relies upon the special insight that comes through divine revelation. For a Greek philosopher like Plato, this means knowledge of the Good; for Pseudo-Phocylides this means primarily access to the θεοῦ βουλεύματα and the δικαιοσύνης μυστήρια, terms that refer especially to the moral commands of Torah, whose interpretation and presentation in the poem is mediated through *sophia*. The revelation that this involves guides personal moral formation, facilitating the cultivation of virtue and the observance of moral obligations of varying characteristics and origins. In so far as this revelation educates and molds the individual in a fundamental manner, fostering a specific way of thinking and acting, the educational process associated with it is also inherently communal in nature. Like other epitomes, the *Sentences* outlines a special, self-confirming way of life derived from the author's special insights and moral principles that helps to create a foundation for community formation, identity, and purpose. The poem, inasmuch as it contributes to the community's self-expression and development, constitutes a means for inviting its recipients to share in the body of knowledge and beliefs that it represents and to participate in the new way of life informed by these ideas.

Eruditionis Causa 12, 22, *De Ebrietate* 23, 80, 137, 224, *De Fuga et Inventione* 52, 137, *De Plantatione* 126, 137–138, *De Posteritate Caini* 118, 130, *De Sacrificiis Abelis et Caini* 43, *De Specialibus Legibus* 2.29, *Legum Allegoriae* 2.89–90, 3.244, *Quis Rerum Divinarum Heres Sit* 274, *Quod Deteris Potiori Insidiari Soleat* 66, 77. Further cf. Mott, "Greek Ethics," 30–35.

Bibliography

Primary Sources

Ahiqar
  Frederick C. Conybeare, J. R. Harris, and A. S. Lewis. *The Story of Ahikar from Aramaic, Syriac, Arabic, Ethiopic, Old Turkish, Greek and Slavonic Versions.* 2nd ed. Cambridge: Cambridge University Press, 1913.
  James M. Lindenberger. *The Aramaic Proverbs of Ahiqar.* Baltimore and London: Johns Hopkins University Press, 1983.
  –. trans. "Ahiqar (Seventh to Sixth Century B.C.)," in Charlesworth, *Old Testament Pseudepigrapha*, 2.479–507.
Amenemope
  Miriam Lichtheim, trans. *Ancient Egyptian Literature: A Book of Readings.* 3 vols. Berkeley, Los Angeles, London: University of California Press, 1975–1980. 2.146–163.
Ankhsheshonqy
  Miriam Lichtheim. *Late Egyptian Wisdom Literature in the International Context: A Study of Demotic Instructions.* OBO 52. Freiburg: Universitätsverlag; Göttingen: Vandenhoeck & Ruprecht, 1983. 66–92.
Anthologia Graeca
  Andrew S. F. Gow and Denys L. Page, eds. *The Greek Anthology: Hellenistic Epigrams.* 2 vols. Cambridge: Cambridge University Press, 1965.
  –. eds. *The Greek Anthology: The Garland of Philip and Some Contemporary Epigrams.* 2 vols. Cambridge: Cambridge University Press, 1968.
  Denys L. Page, ed. *Further Greek Epigrams.* Cambridge: Cambridge University Press, 1981.
Aristotle *Ethica Eudemia*
  R. R. Walzer and J. M. Mingay, eds. *Aristotelis: Ethica Eudemia.* OCT. Oxford: Clarendon, 1991.
Aristotle *Ethica Nicomachea*
  I. Bywater, ed. *Aristotelis: Ethica Nicomachea.* OCT. Oxford: Clarendon, 1894. Reprint, 1962.
Aristotle *Protrepticus*
  Ingemar Düring. *Aristotle's Protrepticus: An Attempt at Reconstruction.* Studia Graeca et Latina Gothoburgensia 12. Göteborg: Elanders Boktryckeri Aktiebolag, 1961.
Aristotle *Rhetorica*
  Rudolf Kassel, ed. *Aristotelis: Ars Rhetorica.* Berlin and New York: de Gruyter, 1976.
Babrius ΜΥΘΙΑΜΒΟΙ
  Otto Crusius, ed. *Babrii Fabulae Aesopeae.* BT. Leipzig: Teubner, 1897.
  Ben E. Perry, trans. *Babrius and Phaedrus.* LCL. Cambridge: Harvard University Press; London: Heinemann, 1984.
Barnabas, Epistle of
  Klaus Wengst, ed. *Schriften des Urchristentums: Didache (Apostellehre), Barnabasbrief, Zweiter Klemensbrief, Schriften an Diognet.* München: Kösel-Verlag, 1984.

Ben Sira
Joseph Ziegler, ed. *Sapientia Iesu Filii Sirach.* Septuaginta, Vetus Testamentum Graecum 12.2. Göttingen: Vandenhoeck & Ruprecht, 1965.
Patrick W. Skehan and Alexander A. DiLella. *The Wisdom of Ben Sira: A New Translation with Notes.* AB 39. Garden City, New York: Doubleday, 1987.
Carmen Aureum
Douglas Young, ed. *Theognis.* BT. 2nd ed. Leipzig: Teubner, 1971. 86–94.
Johan C. Thom. *The Golden Verses of Pythagoras: A Critical Investigation of its Literary Composition and Religio-historical Significance.* Ph.D. Dissertation, University of Chicago, 1989. 69–79.
Cercidas of Megalopolis and the *Cercidea*
A. D. Knox, trans. *Herodes, Cercidas, and the Greek Choliambic Poets.* LCL. Cambridge: Harvard University Press; London: Heinemann, 1967. 189–239.
Chares ΓΝΩΜΑΙ
Douglas Young, ed. *Theognis.* BT. 2nd ed. Leipzig: Teubner, 1971. 113–118.
Cicero *De Officiis*
Walter Miller, trans. *Cicero: De Officiis.* LCL. Cambridge: Harvard University Press; London: Heinemann, 1961.
Comparatio Menandri et Philistionis
Siegfried Jaekel, ed. *Menandri Sententiae.* BT. Leipzig: Teubner, 1964. 87–120.
Counsels of Wisdom
W. G. Lambert, ed. *Babylonian Wisdom Literature.* Oxford: Clarendon, 1960. 96–107.
Crates of Thebes
Hermann Diels, ed. *Poetarum Philosophorum Fragmenta.* Berlin: Weidmann, 1901. 207–223.
Ernst Diehl, ed. *Anthologia Lyrica Graeca.* 3rd ed. 4 vols. Leipzig: Teubner, 1958. 1.120–126.
Demetrius *De Elocutione*
W. Rhys Roberts (with W. Hamilton Fyfe), trans. *Aristotle: The Poetics. "Longinus": On the Sublime. Demetrius: On Style.* LCL. 2nd ed. Cambridge: Harvard University Press; London: Heinemann, 1932. 257–487.
Derek Eretz Rabbah, Derek Eretz Zuta
M. Ginsberg, trans. *Hebrew-English Edition of the Babylonian Talmud: Minor Tractates.* ed. Abraham Cohen. London: Soncino, 1984. 55b–59a.
Marcus van Loopik. *The Ways of the Sages and the Way of the World: The Minor Tractates of the Babylonian Talmud: Derekh Eretz Rabbah, Derekh Eretz Zuta, Pereq ha-Shalom.* TSAJ 26. Tübingen: J.C.B. Mohr (Paul Siebeck), 1991.
Dicta Catonis
J. Wight Duff and Arnold M. Duff, trans. *Minor Latin Poets.* LCL. 2nd ed. Cambridge: Harvard University Press; London: Heinemann, 1935. 592–629.
Didache
Cyril C. Richardson, ed. *Early Christian Fathers.* LCC 1. Philadelphia: Westminster, 1953. 161–179.
Klaus Wengst, ed. *Schriften des Urchristentums: Didache (Apostellehre), Barnabasbrief, Zweiter Klemensbrief, Schriften an Diognet.* München: Kösel-Verlag, 1984. 66–91.
Kurt Niederwimmer. *Die Didache.* Kommentar zu den Apostolischen Vätern 1. Göttingen: Vandenhoeck & Ruprecht, 1989.
Diodorus Siculus *Bibliotheca Historica*
C. H. Oldfather, et al., trans. *Diodorus of Sicily.* LCL. 12 vols. Cambridge: Harvard University Press; London: Heinemann, 1933–1967.
Diogenes Laertius *Vitae Philosophorum*
R. D. Hicks, trans. *Diogenes Laertius: Lives of the Eminent Philosophers.* LCL. 2 vols. London: Heinemann; New York: G. P. Putnam's Sons, 1925.

1 Enoch

    Matthew Black. *The Book of Enoch, or 1 Enoch.* SVTP 7. Leiden: E.J. Brill, 1985.

    E. Isaac, trans. "1 (Ethiopic Apocalypse of) Enoch (Second Century B.C. – First Century A.D.)," in Charlesworth, *Pseudepigrapha*, 1.5–89.

Epictetus

    William A. Oldfather, trans. *Epictetus.* LCL. 2 vols. New York: G. P. Putnam's Sons; London: Heinemann, 1926, 1928.

Epistula Aristeas

    Moses Hadas, ed. *Aristeas to Philocrates (Letter of Aristeas).* Jewish Apocryphal Literature, Dropsie College Edition. New York: Harper & Brothers, 1951.

    R. J. H. Shutt, trans. "Letter of Aristeas (Third Century B.C. – First Century A.D.)," in Charlesworth, *Pseudepigrapha*, 2.7–34.

Fragments of Pseudonymous Hellenistic-Jewish Philosophical and Poetic Texts

    Albert-Marie Denis, ed. *Fragmenta Pseudepigraphorum Quae Supersunt Graeca.* PVTG 3. Leiden: E.J. Brill, 1970. 161–174.

    Harold W. Attridge, trans. "Fragments of Pseudo-Greek Poets (Third to Second Century B.C.)," in Charlesworth, *Old Testament Pseudepigrapha*, 2.821–830.

    Nikolaus Walter. *Poetische Schriften.* JSHRZ 4.3. Gütersloh: Mohn, 1983. 244–276.

Gnomologium Democrateum

    Hermann Diels and Walter Kranz, eds. *Die Fragmente der Vorsokratiker.* 6th ed. 3 vols. Berlin: Weidmann, 1951–52. 2.153–165 (B35–115).

Gnomologium Epictetum

    Heinrich Schenkl, ed. *Epicteti Dissertationes ab Arriano Digestae.* BT. 2nd ed. Stuttgart: Teubner, 1916. Reprint, 1965. 476–492.

Gnomologium Vaticanum

    Cyril Bailey, ed. *Epicurus: The Extant Remains.* Oxford: Clarendon, 1926. Reprint, Westport, CT: Hyperion, 1979. 106–119.

    Graziano Arrighetti, ed. *Epicuro: Opere.* Biblioteca di Cultura Filosofica 41. 2nd ed. Torino: Einaudi, 1983. 139–157.

Heraclitus

    Charles H. Kahn. *The Art and Thought of Heraclitus: An Edition of the Fragments with Translation and Commentary.* Cambridge and New York: Cambridge University Press, 1979.

Herodes

    A. D. Knox, trans. *Herodes, Cercidas, and the Greek Choliambic Poets.* LCL. Cambridge: Harvard University Press; London: Heinemann, 1967. 80–175.

    I. C. Cunningham, ed. *Herodae Mimiambi.* BT. Leipzig: Teubner, 1987.

Hesiod *Opera et Dies*

    Martin L. West. *Hesiod: Works and Days.* Oxford: Clarendon, 1978.

Iamblichus *De Vita Pythagorica*

    John Dillon and Jackson Hershbell, eds. *Iamblichus: On the Pythagorean Way of Life. Text, Translation, and Notes.* SBLTT 29, Graeco-Roman Religion Series 11. Atlanta: Scholars Press, 1991.

Isocrates and Pseudo-Isocrates

    George Norlin, trans. *Isocrates.* LCL. 2 vols. Cambridge: Harvard University Press; London: Heinemann, 1928, 1929.

    Stephen Usher. *Isocrates: Panegyricus and To Nicocles.* Greek Orators 3. Warminster: Aris & Phillips, 1990.

Joseph and Aseneth

    Marc Philonenko, ed. *Joseph et Aséneth: Introduction, Texte Critique, Traduction et Notes.* SPB 13. Leiden: E.J. Brill, 1968.

Josephus

    H. St. J. Thackeray, Ralph Marcus, and Louis H. Feldman, trans. *Josephus.* LCL. 10 vols. Cambridge: Harvard University Press; London: Heinemann, 1926–65.

Leonidas of Tarentum
Andrew S. F. Gow and Denys L. Page, eds. *The Greek Anthology: Hellenistic Epigrams*. 2 vols. Cambridge: Cambridge University Press, 1965. 1.107–139.

4 Maccabees
H. Anderson, trans. "4 Maccabees (First Century A.D.)," in Charlesworth, *Pseudepigrapha*, 2.531–564.

Menander *Sententiae*
Siegfried Jaekel, ed. *Menandri Sententiae*. BT. Leipzig: Teubner, 1964. 33–83.

Menander *Sententiae* (Syriac)
T. Baarda, trans. "The Sentences of the Syriac Menander (Third Century A.D.)," in Charlesworth, *Pseudepigrapha*, 2.583–606.

Menander Rhetor
D. A. Russell and N. G. Wilson. *Menander Rhetor*. Oxford: Clarendon, 1981.

Moschion *Sententiae* and *Hypothekai*
Heinrich Schenkl, ed. *Epicteti Dissertationes ab Arriano Digestae*. BT. 2nd ed. Stuttgart: Teubner, 1916. Reprint, 1965. 493–496.

Musonius Rufus
Cora E. Lutz. *Musonius Rufus: 'The Roman Socrates'*. YCS 10. New York: Yale University Press, 1942.

Odes of Solomon
James H. Charlesworth, trans. "Odes of Solomon (Late First to Early Second Century A.D.)," in Charlesworth, *Old Testament Pseudepigrapha*, 2.725–771.

Orphica
Nikolaus Walter. *Poetische Schriften*. JSHRZ 4.3. Gütersloh: Mohn, 1983. 217–243.
M. Lafargue, trans. "Orphica (Second Century B.C. – First Century A.D.)," in Charlesworth, *Old Testament Pseudepigrapha*, 2.795–801.

Ovid *Amores*
Grant Showerman, trans. *Ovid: Heroides and Amores*. LCL. 2nd ed. Cambridge: Harvard University Press; London: Heinemann, 1977. 313–511.

Papyrus Insinger
Miriam Lichtheim. *Late Egyptian Wisdom Literature in the International Context: A Study of Demotic Instructions*. OBO 52. Freiburg: Universitätsverlag; Göttingen: Vandenhoeck & Ruprecht, 1983. 197–234.

Papyrus Louvre 2414
Miriam Lichtheim. *Late Egyptian Wisdom Literature in the International Context: A Study of Demotic Instructions*. OBO 52. Freiburg: Universitätsverlag; Göttingen: Vandenhoeck & Ruprecht, 1983. 93–106.

Parmenides of Elea
Leonardo Tarán. *Parmenides: A Text with Translation, Commentary, and Critical Essays*. Princeton: Princeton University Press, 1965.
David Gallop. *Parmenides of Elea: Fragments*. Phoenix Sup. 18. Toronto: University of Toronto Press, 1984.

Philo
Francis H. Colson, George H. Whitaker, and Ralph Marcus, trans. *Philo*. LCL. 12 vols. New York: G. P. Putnam's Sons; London: Heinemann, 1929–1962.

Philodemus of Gadara
Andrew S. F. Gow and Denys L. Page, eds. *The Greek Anthology: The Garland of Philip and Some Contemporary Epigrams*. 2 vols. Cambridge: Cambridge University Press, 1968. 1.351–369.

Phocylides of Miletus
J. M. Edmonds, trans. *Elegy and Iambus*. LCL. 2 vols. London: Heinemann; New York: G. P. Putnam's Sons, 1931. 1.172–181.

Bruno Gentili and Carolus Prato, eds. *Poetarum Elegiacorum Testimonia et Fragmenta.* BT. 2 vols. Leipzig: Teubner, 1979, 1985. 1.135–140.

Phoenix of Colophon

Gustav A. Gerhard. *Phoinix von Kolophon: Texte und Untersuchungen.* Leipzig and Berlin: Teubner, 1909.

A. D. Knox, trans. *Herodes, Cercidas, and the Greek Choliambic Poets.* LCL. Cambridge: Harvard University Press; London: Heinemann, 1967. 242–263.

Pirke 'Avot

R. Travers Herford, ed. *Pirke Aboth. The Ethics of the Talmud: Sayings of the Fathers.* New York: Jewish Institute of Religion, 1945. Reprint, New York: Schocken, 1962.

Plato *Opera*

J. Burnet, ed. *Platonis Opera.* OCT. 5 vols. Oxford: Clarendon, 1900–07. Reprint, 1967.

Plato *Republic*

Paul Shorey, trans. *Plato: The Republic.* LCL. 2 vols. Cambridge: Harvard University Press; London: Heinemann, 1930, 1935.

Plutarch *Moralia*

Frank Cole Babbitt, et al., trans. *Plutarch's Moralia.* LCL. 15 vols. Cambridge: Harvard University Press; London: Heinemann, 1927–69.

Pseudepigrapha

James H. Charlesworth, ed. *The Old Testament Pseudepigrapha.* 2 vols. Garden City, New York: Doubleday, 1983, 1985.

Pseudo-Aristotle *De Virtutibus et Vitiis*

H. Rackham, trans. *Aristotle: The Athenian Constitution, The Eudemian Ethics, On Virtues and Vices.* LCL. Cambridge: Harvard University Press; London: Heinemann, 1961. 484–503.

Pseudo-Aristotle *Rhetorica ad Alexandrum*

Harris Rackham, trans. *Aristotle: Rhetorica ad Alexandrum.* LCL. Cambridge: Harvard University Press; London: Heinemann, 1938.

Pseudo-Cicero *Rhetorica ad Herennium*

Harry Caplan, trans. *[Cicero]: Rhetorica ad Herennium.* LCL. Cambridge: Harvard University Press; London: Heinemann, 1954.

Pseudo-Periktione

Holger Thesleff, ed. *The Pythagorean Texts of the Hellenistic Period.* Acta Academiae Aboensis A.30.1. Åbo: Åbo Akademi, 1965. 142–146.

Pseudo-Phocylides *Sentences*

Douglas Young, ed. *Theognis.* BT. 2nd ed. Leipzig: Teubner, 1971. 95–112.

Pieter W. van der Horst. *The Sentences of Pseudo-Phocylides: With Introduction and Commentary.* SVTP 4. Leiden: E.J. Brill, 1978.

–. trans. "Pseudo-Phocylides (First Century B.C. – First Century A.D.)," in Charlesworth, *Pseudepigrapha,* 2.565–582.

Nikolaus Walter. *Poetische Schriften.* JSHRZ 4.3. Gütersloh: Mohn, 1983. 182–216.

Pascale Derron. *Pseudo-Phocylide: Sentences.* Budé. Paris: Société d'Edition 'Les Belles Lettres', 1986.

Ptahhotep

William K. Simpson, et al., trans. *The Literature of Ancient Egypt: An Anthology of Stories, Instructions, and Poetry.* 2nd ed. New Haven and London: Yale University Press, 1973. 159–176.

Publilius Syrus *Sententiae*

J. Wight Duff and Arnold M. Duff, trans. *Minor Latin Poets.* LCL. 2nd ed. Cambridge: Harvard University Press; London: Heinemann, 1935. 3–111.

Quintilian *Institutio Oratoria*

Harold E. Butler, trans. *The Institutio Oratoria of Quintilian.* LCL. 4 vols. New York: G. P. Putnam's Sons; London: Heinemann, 1921–22.

Qumran Library
  Geza Vermes, trans. *The Dead Sea Scrolls in English*. 3rd ed. London: Penguin, 1987.
Secundus
  Ben E. Perry, ed. *Secundus the Silent Philosopher*. APA Philological Monographs 22.
  Ithaca: Cornell University Press, 1964.
Septuagint
  Alfred Rahlfs, ed. *Septuaginta*. 7th ed. 2 vols. Stuttgart: Württemberische Bibelanstalt,
  1962.
Sextus *Sententiae*
  Henry Chadwick, ed. *The Sentences of Sextus: A Contribution to the Early Christian
  History of Ethics*. TextsS 5. Cambridge: Cambridge University Press, 1959.
  Richard A. Edwards and Robert A. Wild, eds. *The Sentences of Sextus*. SBLTT 22.
  Chico, CA: Scholars Press, 1981.
Sextus Empiricus
  R. G. Bury, trans. *Sextus Empiricus*. LCL. 4 vols. Cambridge: Harvard University Press;
  London: Heinemann, 1933–1949.
Silvanus
  Malcolm L. Peel and Jan Zandee, trans. "The Teachings of Silvanus (VII, 4)," *The Nag
  Hammadi Library in English*. ed. James M. Robinson. 3rd ed. San Francisco: Harper
  & Row, 1988. 346–361.
Stobaeus
  Otto Hense, ed. *Johannis Stobaei Anthologium*. 5 vols. Berlin: Weidmann, 1884–1912.
  Reprint, 1958.
Stoic Philosophers
  Hans F. A. von Arnim, ed. *Stoicorum Veterum Fragmenta*. 4 vols. Leipzig: Teubner,
  1905–1924.
Testaments of the Twelve Patriarchs
  Marinus de Jonge, ed. (with Harm W. Hollander, H. J. de Jonge, Th. Korteweg) *The Tes-
  taments of the Twelve Patriarchs: A Critical Edition of the Greek Text*. PVTG 1.2.
  Leiden: E.J. Brill, 1978.
  Harm W. Hollander and Marinus de Jonge. *The Testaments of the Twelve Patriarchs: A
  Commentary*. SVTP 8. Leiden: E.J. Brill, 1985.
  H. C. Kee, trans. "Testaments of the Twelve Patriarchs (Second Century B.C.)," in Char-
  lesworth, *Pseudepigrapha*, 1.775–828.
Theognis and the *Theognidea*
  Martin L. West, ed. *Iambi et Elegi Graeci ante Alexandrum Cantati*. OCT. 2 vols. Ox-
  ford: Clarendon, 1971–72. 1.172–241.
  Douglas Young, ed. *Theognis*. BT. 2nd ed. Leipzig: Teubner, 1971. 1–85.
Timon of Phlius
  Hermann Diels, ed. *Poetarum Philosophorum Fragmenta*. Berlin: Weidmann, 1901.
  173–206.
Wisdom of Solomon
  David Winston. *The Wisdom of Solomon*. AB 43. Garden City, New York: Doubleday,
  1979.
Xenophon
  E. C. Marchant, ed. *Xenophontis Opera Omnia*. OCT. 5 vols. Oxford: Clarendon, 1900–
  1921. Reprint, 1961–1971.
Zenobius
  Ernst L. Leutsch and F. G. Schneidewin, eds. *Corpus Paroemiographorum Graecorum*.
  2 vols. Göttingen: Vandenhoeck & Ruprecht, 1839–51. Reprint (with third volume),
  Hildesheim: G. Olms, 1958. 1.1–175.
  Winfried Bühler, ed. *Griechische Sprichwörter: Zenobii Athoi Proverbia*. 4 vols. Göttin-
  gen: Vandenhoeck & Ruprecht, 1982.

Secondary Sources

Adcock, F. E. "Literary Tradition and Early Greek Code Makers," *Cambridge Historical Journal* 2 (1927) 95–109.

Adkins, Arthur W. H. *Merit and Responsibility: A Study in Greek Values.* Oxford: Oxford University Press, 1960. Reprint, Midway Reprints; Chicago: University of Chicago Press, 1975.

Ahlert, P., and Wilhelm Kroll. "Phokylides," *PW* 20.1 (1941) 503–510.

Ahrens, Ernst. *Gnomen in griechischer Dichtung: Homer, Hesiod, Aeschylus.* Würzburg: Triltsch, 1937.

Alderink, Larry J. *Creation and Salvation in Ancient Orphism.* American Classical Studies 8. Chico, CA: APA, 1981.

Alster, Brendt. *The Instructions of Shuruppak: A Sumerian Proverb Collection.* Copenhagen: Akademisk Forlag, 1974.

–. *Studies in Sumerian Proverbs.* Copenhagen: Akademisk Forlag, 1975.

Aly, Wolfgang. "Theognis," *PW* 5.A2 (1934) 1972–1984.

Amand, David. *Fatalisme et Liberté dans l'Antiquité Grecque.* Recueil de Travaux d'Histoire et de Philologie 3.19. Amsterdam: Adolf M. Hakkert, 1973.

Amir, Yehoshua. *Die hellenistische Gestalt des Judentums bei Philon von Alexandria.* Forschungen zum jüdisch-christlichen Dialog 5. Neukirchen: Neukirchener Verlag, 1983.

–. "Authority and Interpretation of Scripture in the Writings of Philo," in Mulder, *Mikra*, 421–453.

–. "The Decalogue according to Philo," *The Ten Commandments in History and Tradition.* ed. Ben-Zion Segal and Gershon Levi. Jerusalem: Magnes, 1990. 121–160.

Amstutz, Joseph. *ΑΠΛΟΤΗΣ: Eine begriffsgeschichtliche Studie zum jüdisch-christlichen Griechisch.* Theophaneia, Beiträge zur Religions- und Kirchengeschichte des Altertums 19. Bonn: Peter Hanstein, 1968.

Asmis, Elizabeth. "Philodemus' Epicureanism," *ANRW* II.36.4 (1990) 2369–2406.

Audet, Jean-Paul. "La Sagesse de Ménandre l'Egyptien," *RB* 59 (1952) 55–81.

–. "Affinités Littéraires et Doctrinales du 'Manuel de Discipline'," *RB* 59 (1952) 219–238 and 60 (1953) 41–82.

–. *La Didachè.* EBib. Paris: Gabalda, 1958.

Aune, David E. "Romans as a Logos Protreptikos in the Context of Ancient Religious and Philosophical Propaganda," *Paulus und das antike Judentum.* ed. Martin Hengel and Ulrich Heckel. WUNT 58. Tübingen: J.C.B. Mohr (Paul Siebeck), 1991. 91–124.

Baasland, Ernst. "Der Jakobusbrief als neutestamentliche Weisheitsschrift," *ST* 36 (1982) 119–139.

–. "Literarische Form, Thematik und geschichtliche Einordnung des Jakobusbriefes," *ANRW* II.25.5 (1988) 3646–3684.

Balch, David L. "Two Apologetic Encomia: Dionysius on Rome and Josephus on the Jews," *JSJ* 13 (1982) 102–122.

–. "Household Codes," *Greco-Roman Literature and the New Testament.* ed. David E. Aune. Atlanta: Scholars Press, 1988. 25–50.

Baltes, Matthias. "Die Todesproblematik in der griechischen Philosophie," *Gymnasium* 95 (1988) 97–128.

Barley, Nigel. "A Structural Approach to the Proverb and Maxim with Special Reference to the Anglo-Saxon Corpus," *Proverbium* 20 (1972) 737–750.

Barnard, Leslie W. *Studies in the Apostolic Fathers and Their Background.* New York: Schocken, 1966.

Barnes, J. "A New Gnomologium, with Some Remarks on Gnomic Anthologies," *CQ* 44 (1950) 126–137 and 45 (1951) 1–19.

Barnes, Jonathan. *The Presocratic Philosophers*. 2 vols. London: Routledge and Kegan Paul, 1979.

–. "Aphorism and Argument," in Robb, *Language and Thought* , 91–109.

Bartlett, John R. "Revelation and the Old Testament," *Witness to the Spirit: Essays on Revelation, Spirit, Redemption*. ed. Wilfrid Harrington. Proceedings of the Irish Biblical Association 3. Dublin: Irish Biblical Association; Manchester: Koinonia, 1979. 11–31.

Battistone, Joseph J. *An Examination of the Literary and Theological Background of the Wisdom Passage of the Book of Baruch*. Ph.D. Dissertation, Duke University, 1968.

Bauckmann, E. G. "Die Proverbien und die Sprüche des Jesus Sirach: Eine Untersuchung zum Strukturwandel der Israelitischen Weisheitslehre," *ZAW* 72 (1960) 33–63.

Baumgartner, W. "Die literarischen Gattungen in der Weisheit des Jesus Sirach," *ZAW* 34 (1914) 161–198.

Benz, Ernst. *Das Todesproblem in der stoischen Philosophie*. TBAW 7. Stuttgart: W. Kohlhammer, 1929.

Berger, Klaus. *Die Gesetzesauslegung Jesu. Ihr historischer Hintergrund im Judentum und im Alten Testament I: Markus und Parallelen*. WMANT 40. Neukirchen-Vluyn: Neukirchener Verlag, 1972.

–. *Formgeschichte des Neuen Testaments*. Heidelberg: Quelle & Meyer, 1984.

–. "Hellenistische Gattungen im Neuen Testament," *ANRW* II.25.2 (1984) 1031–1432.

Bernays, Jacob. *Gesammelte Abhandlungen*. ed. Hermann Usener. 2 vols. Berlin: Wilhelm Hertz, 1885.

Betram, Georg. "παιδεύω, κτλ.," *TDNT* 5 (1967) 596–625.

–. "ὕβρις, κτλ.," *TDNT* 8 (1972) 295–307.

–. "ὑπερήφανος, ὑπερηφανία," *TDNT* 8 (1972) 525–529.

Betz, Hans Dieter. *Galatians: A Commentary on Paul's Letter to the Churches in Galatia*. Hermeneia. Philadelphia: Fortress, 1979.

–. *Essays on the Sermon on the Mount*. trans. L. L. Welborn. Philadelphia: Fortress, 1985.

–. "Christianity as Religion: Paul's Attempt at Definition in Romans," *JR* 71 (1991) 315–344.

–. *A Commentary on the Sermon on the Mount and the Sermon on the Plain*. Hermeneia. Philadelphia: Fortress, forthcoming.

Betz, Hans Dieter, ed. *Plutarch's Theological Writings and Early Christian Literature*. SCHNT 3. Leiden: E.J. Brill, 1975.

–. *Plutarch's Ethical Writings and Early Christian Literature*. SCHNT 4. Leiden: E.J. Brill, 1978.

Betz, Otto. *Offenbarung und Schriftforschung in der Qumransekte*. WUNT 6. Tübingen: J.C.B. Mohr (Paul Siebeck), 1960.

Biale, Rachel. *Women and Jewish Law: An Exploration of Women's Issues in Halakhic Sources*. New York: Schocken, 1984.

Bianchi, Ugo. *The Greek Mysteries*. Iconography of Religions 17.3. Leiden: E.J. Brill, 1976.

–. "The Religio-Historical Question of the Mysteries of Mithra," *Mysteria Mithrae*. EPRO 80. Leiden: E.J. Brill, 1979. 3–60.

Bianchi, Ugo, ed. *La Tradizione dell'Enkrateia: Motivazioni Ontologiche e Protologiche*. Rome: Edizioni dell'Ateneo, 1985.

Bielohlawek, Karl. *Hypotheke und Gnome: Untersuchungen über die griechische Weisheitsdichtung der vorhellenistischen Zeit*. Philologus Sup. 32.3. Leipzig: Dieterich'sche Verlagsbuchhandlung, 1940.

Bieritz, Karl-Heinrich, and Christoph Kähler. "Haus III," *TRE* 14 (1985) 478–492.

Bischoff, Heinrich. *Gnomen Pindars*. Würzburg: Triltsch, 1938.

Blenkinsopp, Joseph. *Prophecy and Canon: A Contribution to the Study of Jewish Origins*. University of Notre Dame Center for the Study of Judaism and Christianity in Antiquity 3. Notre Dame and London: University of Notre Dame Press, 1977.

Blomenkamp, Paul. "Erziehung," *RAC* 6 (1966) 502–559.

Bockmuehl, Markus N. A. *Revelation and Mystery in Ancient Judaism and Pauline Christianity*. WUNT 2.36. Tübingen: J.C.B. Mohr (Paul Siebeck), 1990.

Bolkestein, Hendrik. *Wohltätigkeit und Armenpflege im vorchristlichen Altertum: Ein Beitrag zum Problem "Moral und Gesellschaft"*. Utrecht: A. Oosthoeck, 1939.

Bolkestein, Hendrik, and W. Schwer. "Almosen," *RAC* 1 (1950) 301–307.

Bolkestein, Hendrik, and A. Kalsbach. "Armut I," *RAC* 1 (1950) 698–705.

Booth, Roger B. *Jesus and the Law of Purity: Tradition History and Legal History in Mark 7*. JSNTSup 13. Sheffield: JSOT, 1986.

Bornkamm, Günther. "Heuchelei," *RGG³* 3 (1959) 305–306.

–. "μυστήριον, μυέω," *TDNT* 4 (1967) 802–828.

Bott, Henricus. *De Epitomis Antiquis*. Marburg: Hamel, 1920.

Bowie, Ewen L. "Greek Sophists and Greek Poetry in the Second Sophistic," *ANRW* II.33.1 (1989) 209–258.

Bowra, Cecil M. "The Proem of Parmenides," *CP* 32 (1937) 97–112.

–. "Aristotle's Hymn to Virtue," *CQ* 32 (1938) 182–189.

Braumann, Georg, and Colin Brown. "Child," *NIDNTT* 1 (1986) 280–291.

Bréhier, Emile. *Les Idées Philosophiques et Religieuses de Philon d'Alexandrie*. Etudes de Philosophie Médiévale 8. 2nd ed. Paris: J. Vrin, 1925.

Breitenstein, Urs. *Beobachtungen zu Sprache, Stil und Gedankengut des vierten Makkabäerbuchs*. 2nd ed. Basel and Stuttgart: Schwabe, 1978.

Brown, Colin, Ulrich Falkenroth, and Wilhelm Mundle. "Patience," *NIDNTT* 2 (1986) 764–776.

Brunner, Helmut. *Altägyptische Erziehung*. Wiesbaden: Otto Harrassowitz, 1957.

–. "Erziehung," *LÄ* 2 (1977) 22–27.

–. "Lehren," *LÄ* 3 (1980) 964–968.

–. "Lehre des Ptahhotep," *LÄ* 3 (1980) 989–991.

–. *Altägyptische Weisheit: Lehren für das Leben*. Die Bibliothek der Alten Welt. Zürich and München: Artemis, 1988.

Brunt, P. A. "Aspects of the Social Thought of Dio Chrysostom and the Stoics," *PCPS* 19 (1973) 9–34.

Buffière, Felix. *Eros Adolescent: La Pédérastie dans la Grèce Antique*. Paris: Société d'Edition 'Les Belles Lettres', 1980.

Bultmann, Rudolf. "ἔλεος, κτλ.," *TDNT* 2 (1964) 477–487.

–. "θάνατος, κτλ.," *TDNT* 3 (1965) 7–25.

–. *The History of the Synoptic Tradition*. trans. John Marsh. 2nd ed. Oxford: Blackwell, 1968.

Burgess, Theodore. "Epideictic Literature," *University of Chicago Studies in Classical Philology* 3 (1902) 89–261.

Burke, David G. *The Poetry of Baruch: A Reconstruction and Analysis of the Original Hebrew Text of Baruch 3.9–5.9*. SBLSCS 10. Chico, CA: Scholars Press, 1982.

Burkert, Walter. "Craft Versus Sect: The Problem of Orphics and Pythagoreans," *Jewish and Christian Self-Definition*, Volume 3: *Self-Definition in the Greco-Roman World*. ed. Ben F. Meyer and E. P. Sanders. Philadelphia: Fortress, 1982. 1–22.

–. *Greek Religion*. trans. John Raffan. Cambridge: Harvard University Press, 1985.

Burkhardt, Helmut. *Die Inspiration heiliger Schriften bei Philo von Alexandrien*. Giessen: Brunnen, 1988.

Carras, George P. "Philo's Hypothetica, Josephus' Contra Apionem and the Question of Sources," *SBLSP* 29. ed. David J. Lull. Atlanta: Scholars Press, 1990. 431–450.

Cavallin, Hans C. C. *Life After Death: Paul's Argument for the Resurrection of the Dead in 1 Corinthians 15*, Part 1: *An Enquiry into the Jewish Background*. ConBNT 7.1. Lund: Gleerup, 1974.

–. "Leben nach dem Tode im Spätjudentum und im frühen Christentum: I. Spätjudentum," *ANRW* II.19.1 (1979) 240–345.

Cerfaux, Lucien. "Influence des Mystères sur le Judaïsme Alexandrin avant Philon," *Recueil Lucien Cerfaux: Etudes d'Exégèse et d'Histoire Religieuse de Monseigneur Cerfaux à l'Occasion de son Soixante-Dixième Anniversaire.* BETL 6–7. 2 vols. Gembloux: Duculot, 1954. 1.65–112.

Chadwick, Henry. "Enkrateia," *RAC* 5 (1965) 343–365.

–. "Florilegium," *RAC* 7 (1969) 1131–1160.

Charlesworth, James H. *The Pseudepigrapha and Modern Research, with a Supplement.* SBLSCS 7. 2nd ed. Ann Arbor, MI: Scholars Press, 1981.

–. "Jewish Hymns, Odes, and Prayers (ca. 167 BCE–135 CE)," in Kraft and Nickelsburg, *Early Judaism and its Modern Interpreters,* 411–436.

Chernus, Ira. *Mysticism in Rabbinic Judaism: Studies in the History of Midrash.* SJ 11. Berlin and New York: de Gruyter, 1982.

Christ, Felix. "Das Leben nach dem Tode bei Pseudo-Phokylides," *TZ* 31 (1975) 140–149.

Christiansen, Irmgard. *Die Technik der allegorischen Auslegungswissenschaft bei Philo von Alexandrien.* BGBH 7. Tübingen: J.C.B. Mohr (Paul Siebeck), 1969.

Clarke, M. L. *Higher Education in the Ancient World.* London: Routledge and Kegan Paul, 1971.

Classen, C. J. "Der platonisch-stoische Kanon der Kardinaltugenden bei Philon, Clemens Alexandrinus und Origenes," *Kerygma und Logos: Beiträge zu den geistesgeschichtlichen Beziehungen zwischen Antike und Christentum. Festschrift für Carl Andresen zum 70. Geburtstag.* ed. Adolf M. Ritter. Göttingen: Vandenhoeck & Ruprecht, 1979. 68–88.

Cohen, Naomi G. "The Jewish Dimension of Philo's Judaism: An Elucidation of de Spec. Leg. IV 132–150," *JJS* 38 (1987) 165–186.

Collins, Adela Yarbro. *The Beginning of the Gospel: Probings of Mark in Context.* Minneapolis: Fortress, 1992.

Collins, John J. "Jewish Apocalyptic Against its Hellenistic Near Eastern Environment," *BASOR* 220 (1975) 27–36.

–. *Between Athens and Jerusalem: Jewish Identity in the Hellenistic Diaspora.* New York: Crossroad, 1983.

Colpe, Carsten. "Heilige Schriften," *RAC* 14 (1988) 184–223.

Conley, Thomas. *'General Education' in Philo of Alexandria.* Center for Hermeneutical Studies in Hellenistic and Modern Culture 15. Berkeley: The Center, 1975.

Cornford, F. M. "Psychology and Social Structure in the Republic of Plato," *CQ* 6 (1912) 246–265.

Cousin, Jean. *Etudes sur Quintilian.* 2 vols. Paris: Boivin, 1935–1936. Reprint, Amsterdam: Schippers, 1967.

Cox, Alister. "Didactic Poetry," *Greek and Latin Literature: A Comparative Study.* ed. John Higginbotham. London: Methuen, 1969. 124–161.

Cremer, Friedrich W. *Die Chaldäischen Orakel und Jamblich De Mysteriis.* Beiträge zur klassischen Philologie 26. Meisenheim: A. Hein, 1969.

Crenshaw, James L. "Wisdom," in Hayes, *Old Testament Form Criticism,* 225–264.

–. *Old Testament Wisdom: An Introduction.* Atlanta: John Knox, 1981.

Crenshaw, James L., ed. *Studies in Ancient Israelite Wisdom.* Library of Biblical Studies. New York: KTAV, 1976.

Crossan, John D., ed. *Semeia 17: Gnomic Wisdom.* Chico, CA: Scholars Press, 1980.

Crossett, John M. "Aristotle as a Poet: The Hymn to Hermeias," *Philological Quarterly* 46 (1967) 145–155.

Crouch, James E. *The Origin and Intention of the Colossian Haustafel.* FRLANT 2.109. Göttingen: Vandenhoeck & Ruprecht, 1972.

Crüsemann, Frank. *Studien zur Formgeschichte von Hymnus und Danklied in Israel.* WMANT 32. Neukirchen-Vlyun: Neukirchener Verlag, 1969.

Davids, Peter H. "The Epistle of James in Modern Discussion," *ANRW* II.25.5 (1988) 3621–3645.

Davies, Stevan L. *The Gospel of Thomas and Christian Wisdom*. New York: Seabury, 1983.

Delatte, Armand. *Etudes sur la Littérature Pythagoricienne*. Paris: Champion, 1915.

Delhaye, Philippe. "Florilèges Mediévaux d'Ethique," *DSp* 5 (1964) 460–475.

Delling, Gerhard. "Ehebruch, Ehegesetze, Ehehindernisse, Eheleben, Ehescheidung, Eheschliessung," *RAC* 4 (1959) 666–730.

–. "πλεονέκτης, πλεονεκτέω, πλεονεξία," *TDNT* 6 (1968) 266–274.

den Boer, W. *Private Morality in Greece and Rome: Some Historical Aspects*. Mnemosyne Sup. 57. Leiden: E.J. Brill, 1979.

Denis, Albert-Marie. *Introduction aux Pseudépigraphes Grecs d'Ancien Testament*. SVTP 1. Leiden: E.J. Brill, 1970.

Derron, Pascale. "Inventaire des Manuscrits du Pseudo-Phocylide," *Revue d'Histoire des Textes* 10 (1980) 237–247.

Deselaers, Paul. *Das Buch Tobit: Studien zu seiner Entstehung, Komposition und Theologie*. OBO 43. Göttingen: Vandenhoeck & Ruprecht, 1982.

Devereux, Daniel. "Courage and Wisdom in Plato's Laches," *JHP* 15 (1977) 129–141.

DeWitt, Norman W. *Epicurus and His Philosophy*. Minneapolis: University of Minnesota Press, 1954.

Dibelius, Martin. *James: A Commentary on the Epistle of James*. rev. Heinrich Greeven. Hermeneia. Philadelphia: Fortress, 1975.

Dibelius, Martin, and Hans Conzelmann. *The Pastoral Epistles*. Hermeneia. Philadelphia: Fortress, 1972.

Dietrich, Bernard C. *Death, Fate and the Gods: The Development of a Religious Idea in Greek Popular Belief and in Homer*. University of London Classical Studies 3. rev. ed. London: Athlone, 1967.

Dietrich, Ernst L. "Die 'Religion Noahs', ihre Herkunft und ihre Bedeutung," *ZRGG* 1 (1948) 301–315.

Dihle, Albrecht. *Der Kanon der zwei Tugenden*. Arbeitsgemeinschaft für Forschung des Laudes Nordrhein-Westfalen, Reihe: Geisteswissenschaften, Heft 44. Cologne and Opladen: Westdeutscher Verlag, 1968.

–. "Gerechtigkeit," *RAC* 10 (1978) 236–289.

Dillon, John. "The Platonizing of Mithra," *Journal of Mithraic Studies* 2 (1977) 79–85.

Dimant, Devorah. "Use and Interpretation of Mikra in the Apocrypha and Pseudepigrapha," in Mulder, *Mikra,* 379–419.

Dölger, Franz J. "Das Lebensrecht des ungeborenen Kindes und die Fruchtabtreibung in der Bewertung der heidnischen und christlichen Antike," *Antike und Christentum: Kultur- und religionsgeschichtliche Studien*, Volume 4. Münster: Aschendorff, 1934. Reprint, 1975. 1–61.

Dörrie, Heinrich. "Krates 2," *KP* 3 (1969) 327–328.

–. "Timon 3," *KP* 5 (1975) 847.

Dover, Kenneth J. *Greek Popular Morality in the Time of Plato and Aristotle*. Berkeley: University of California Press, 1974.

Downey, Glanville. "Philanthropia in Religion and Statescraft in the Fourth Century After Christ," *Historia* 4 (1955) 199–208.

Drazin, Nathan. *The History of Jewish Education from 515 B.C. to 220 C.E.* Johns Hopkins University Studies in Education. Baltimore: Johns Hopkins University Press, 1940.

Dudley, Donald R. *A History of Cynicism*. London: Methuen, 1937. Reprint, Hildesheim: Olms, 1967.

Du Plessis, Paul J. *ΤΕΛΕΙΟΣ: The Idea of Perfection in the New Testament*. Uitgave: J. H. Kok N. V. Kampen, 1959.

Dyck, A. R. "The Plan of Panaetius' ΠΕΡΙ ΤΟΥ ΚΑΘΗΚΟΝΤΟΣ," *AJP* 100 (1979) 408–416.

–. "Notes on the Composition, Text and Sources of Cicero's De Officiis," *Hermes* 112 (1984) 215–227.

Ebner, Eliezer. *Elementary Education in Ancient Israel During the Tannaitic Period: 10–220 C.E.* New York: Bloch, 1956.

Edelstein, Ludwig. *The Meaning of Stoicism.* Martin Classical Lectures 21. Cambridge: Harvard University Press, 1966.

Effe, Bernd. *Dichtung und Lehre: Untersuchung zur Typologie des antiken Lehrgedichts.* Zetemata 69. München: C. H. Beck, 1977.

Eitrem, Samson. "Moira," *PW* 15.2 (1932) 2449–2497.

Elsas, Christoph. "Das Judentum als philosophische Religion bei Philo von Alexandrien," *Altes Testament – Frühjudentum – Gnosis: Neue Studien zu 'Gnosis und Bibel'.* ed. Karl-Wolfgang Tröger. Gutersloh: Gerd Mohn, 1980. 195–220.

Else, Gerald F. *The Structure and Date of Book Ten of Plato's Republic.* AHAW.PH 3. Heidelberg: Carl Winter, 1972.

–. *Plato and Aristotle on Poetry.* Chapel Hill: University of North Carolina Press, 1986.

Elter, Anton. *Gnomologiorum Graecorum Historia Atque Origine.* 9 parts plus 2-part supplement. Bonn: C. George, 1893–1897.

Emminger, Kurt. "Ps-Isokrates πρὸς Δημόνικον," *Jahrbücher für Philologie und Pädagogik* B 27 (1902) 373–442.

Engberg-Pedersen, Troels. *Aristotle's Theory of Moral Insight.* Oxford: Clarendon, 1983.

Epstein, Louis M. *Sex Laws and Customs in Judaism.* New York: Bloch, 1948.

Erskine, Andrew. *The Hellenistic Stoa: Political Thought and Action.* Ithaca: Cornell University Press, 1990.

Esser, Hans-Helmut. "Mercy," *NIDNTT* 2 (1986) 593–601.

Falk, Ze'ev W. *Introduction to Jewish Law of the Second Commonwealth.* AGJU 11. 2 vols. Leiden: E.J. Brill, 1972, 1978.

Fallon, F. T., and Ron Cameron. "The Gospel of Thomas: A Forschungsbericht and Analysis," *ANRW* II.25.6 (1988) 4195–4251.

Fedeli, Paolo. "Il 'De Officiis' di Cicerone: Problemi e Atteggiamenti della Critica Moderna," *ANRW* 1.4 (1973) 357–427.

Feldman, David M. *Birth Control in Jewish Law: Marital Relations, Contraception and Abortion as Set Forth in the Classic Texts of Jewish Law.* 2nd ed. New York: Schocken, 1974.

Ferguson, Everett. "Spiritual Sacrifice in Early Christianity and its Environment," *ANRW* II.23.2 (1980) 1151–1189.

Ferguson, John. *Moral Values in the Ancient World.* London: Methuen, 1958.

Festugière, A. J. *Les Trois 'Protreptiques' bei Platon: Euthydème, Phédon, Epinomis.* Bibliothèque d'Histoire de la Philosophie. Paris: J. Vrin, 1973.

Festugière, A. M. "ΥΠΟΜΟΝΗ dans la Tradition Grecque," *RSR* 30 (1931) 477–486.

Fichtner, Johannes. *Die altorientalische Weisheit in ihrer israelitisch-jüdischen Ausprägung.* BZAW 62. Giessen: Töpelmann, 1933.

Fiedler, Martin. "Δικαιοσύνη in der diaspora-jüdischen und intertestamentarischen Literatur," *JSJ* 1 (1970) 120–143.

Fiedler, Peter. "Haustafel," *RAC* 13 (1986) 1063–1073.

Fieger, Michael. *Das Thomasevangelium: Einleitung, Kommentar, und Systematik.* NTAbh 22. Münster: Aschendorff, 1991.

Figueira, Thomas J., and Gregory Nagy, eds. *Theognis of Megara: Poetry and the Polis.* Baltimore and London: Johns Hopkins University Press, 1985.

Finegan, Jack. *The Archaeology of the New Testament.* Princeton: Princeton University Press, 1969.

Finkel, Asher. "Gerechtigkeit II. Judentum," *TRE* 12 (1984) 411–414.

Finkelstein, Louis. "Introductory Study to Pirke Aboth," *JBL* 57 (1938) 13–50. Reprint, idem, *Pharisaism in the Making.* New York: KTAV, 1972. 121–158.

Fiore, Benjamin. *The Function of Personal Example in the Socratic and Pastoral Epistles.* AnBib 105. Rome: Biblical Institute Press, 1986.

Fiorenza, Elisabeth Schüssler. "Wisdom Mythology and the Christological Hymns of the New Testament," in Wilken, *Aspects of Wisdom*, 14–41.

Fischel, Henry A. "The Transformation of Wisdom in the World of Midrash," in Wilken, *Aspects of Wisdom*, 67–101.

Fischer, Ulrich. *Eschatologie und Jenseitserwartung im hellenistischen Diasporajudentum.* BZNW 44. Berlin: de Gruyter, 1978.

Fishbane, Michael. "Revelation and Tradition: Aspects of Inner-Biblical Exegesis," *JBL* 99 (1980) 343–361.

–. *Biblical Interpretation in Ancient Israel.* Oxford: Clarendon, 1985.

–. "Inner Biblical Exegesis: Types and Strategies in Ancient Israel," *Midrash and Literature.* ed. Geoffrey H. Hartman and Sanford Budick. New Haven and London: Yale University Press, 1986. 19–37.

–. "Use, Authority and Interpretation of Mikra at Qumran," in Mulder, *Mikra*, 339–377.

Fisher, N. R. E. "Hybris and Dishonour," *Greece and Rome* 23 (1976) 177–193.

–. *Hybris: Study in Values.* Warminster: Aris & Phillips, n.d.

Ford, Andrew L. "The Seal of Theognis: The Politics of Authorship in Archaic Greece," in Figueira and Nagy, *Theognis of Megara*, 82–95.

Forschner, Maximilian. *Die stoische Ethik: Über den Zusammenhang von Natur-, Sprach- und Moralphilosophie im altstoischen System.* Stuttgart: Klett-Cotta, 1981.

Fortenbaugh, William W., ed. *On Stoic and Peripatetic Ethics: The Work of Arius Didymus.* Rutgers University Studies in Classical Humanities 1. New Brunswick, NJ and London: Transaction Books, 1983.

Fraenkel, Jozua J. *Hybris.* Utrecht: P. den Boer, 1941.

Frank, Karl Suso. "Habsucht (Geiz)," *RAC* 13 (1986) 227–238.

Fränkel, Hermann. "Studies in Parmenides," *Studies in Presocratic Philosophy.* ed. R. E. Allen and David J. Furley. International Library of Philosophy and Scientific Method. 2 vols. New York: Humanities Press, 1970, 1975. 2.1–47.

Franzmann, Majella. *The Odes of Solomon: An Analysis of the Poetical Structure and Form.* NTOA 20. Freiburg (Schweiz): Universitätsverlag; Göttingen: Vandenhoeck & Ruprecht, 1991.

Frey, J.-B. "La Révélation d'après les Conceptions Juives au Temps de Jésus-Christ," *RB* 13 (1916) 472–510.

Friedländer, P. "ΥΠΟΘΗΚΑΙ," *Hermes* 48 (1913) 558–616.

Gabrion, Hervé. "L'Interprétation de l'Ecriture dans la Littérature de Qumrân," *ANRW* II.19.1 (1979) 779–848.

Gaiser, Konrad. *Protreptik und Paränese bei Plato: Untersuchungen zur Form des platonischen Dialogs.* TBAW 40. Stuttgart: W. Kohlhammer, 1959.

Galdi, Marco. *L'Epitome nella Letteratura Latina.* Napoli: P. Federico and G. Ardia, 1922.

Gammie, John G. "The Septuagint of Job: Its Poetic Style and Relationship to the Septuagint of Proverbs," *CBQ* 49 (1987) 14–31.

–. "Paraenetic Literature: Toward the Morphology of a Secondary Genre," *Semeia* 50 (1990) 41–77.

Gammie, John G., Walter R. Brueggemann, W. Lee Humphreys, and James M. Ward, eds. *Israelite Wisdom: Theological and Literary Essays in Honor of Samuel Terrien.* New York: Union Theological Seminary; Missoula: Scholars Press, 1978.

Garland, Robert. *The Greek Way of Death.* Ithaca: Cornell University Press, 1985.

Gärtner, Hans Armin. *Cicero und Panaitios: Beobachtungen zu Ciceros De Officiis.* Heidelberg: Carl Winter, 1974.

Gauthier, René-Antonin. *Magnanimité: L'Idéal de la Grandeur dans la Philosophie Païenne et dans la Théologie Chrétienne.* Bibliothèque Thomiste 28. Paris: J. Vrin, 1951.

Gemser, Berend. "The Instructions of 'Onchsheshonqy' and Biblical Wisdom Literature," *VTSup* 7 (1960) 102–128. Reprint, Crenshaw, *Studies*, 134–160.

–. *Sprüche Salomos*. HAT 1.16. 2nd ed. Tübingen: J.C.B. Mohr (Paul Siebeck), 1963.

Georgi, Dieter. *Die Gegner des Paulus in 2.Korintherbrief*. WMANT 11. Neukirchen-Vluyn: Neukirchener Verlag, 1964.

Gerhard, Gustav A. *Phoinix von Kolophon: Texte und Untersuchungen*. Leipzig: Teubner, 1909.

–. *ΧΑΡΗΤΟΣ ΓΝΩΜΑΙ*. SHAW.PH 3.13. Heidelberg: Carl Winter, 1912.

Gerleman, Gillis. "The Septuagint Proverbs as a Hellenistic Document," *OTS* 8 (1950) 15–27.

–. "Studies in the Septuagint: Religion and Ethics in the LXX Proverbs," *LUÅ* 1.52.3 (1956) 36–63.

Gerstenberger, Erhard. "Psalms," in Hayes, *Form Criticism*, 179–223.

Gese, Hartmut. "Weisheit," *RGG³* 6 (1962) 1574–1577.

–. "Weisheitsdichtung," *RGG³* 6 (1962) 1577–1581.

Gielen, Marlis. *Tradition und Theologie neutestamentlicher Haustafelethik: Ein Beitrag zur Frage einer christlichen Auseinandersetzung mit gesellschaftlichen Normen*. BBB 75. Frankfurt am Main: Hain, 1990.

Giesen, Heinz. "ὑπόκρισις, ὑποκριτής," *EWNT* 3 (1983) 963–966.

Giet, Stanislas. *L'Enigme de la Didache*. PFLUS 149. Paris: Ophrys, 1970.

Gigon, Olof. "Bemerkungen zu Cicero De Officiis," *Politeia und Respublica: Beiträge zum Verständnis von Politik, Recht und Staat in der Antike. Dem Andenken Rudolf Starks gewidmet*. ed. Peter Steinmetz. Palingensia 4. Wiesbaden: Franz Steiner, 1969. 267–278.

–. "Phronesis und Sophia in der Nikomachischen Ethik des Aristotles," *Kephalaion: Studies in Greek Philosophy and its Continuation Offered to Professor Cornelia J. de Vogel*. ed. Jaap Mansfeld and Lambertus M. de Rijk. Assen: van Gorcum, 1975. 91–104.

Gilbert, Maurice. "L'Eloge de la Sagesse (Siracide 24)," *RTL* 5 (1974) 326–348.

–. "Le Discours de la Sagesse en Proverbes 8: Structure et Cohérence," *La Sagesse de l'Ancien Testament*. ed. idem. BETL 51. Leuven: Leuven University Press; Gembloux: Duculot, 1979. 202–218.

–. "Wisdom Literature," *Jewish Writings of the Second Temple Period*. ed. Michael E. Stone. CRINT 2.2. Assen: van Gorcum; Philadelphia: Fortress, 1984. 283–324.

Ginouvès, René. *Balaneutikè: Recherches sur le Bain dans l'Antiquité Grecque*. BEFAR 200. Paris: E. de Boccard, 1962.

Ginzberg, Louis. *The Legends of the Jews*. 7 vols. Philadelphia: Jewish Publication Society, 1909–1938.

Giusta, Michelangelo. *I Dossografi di Etica*. 2 vols. Turin: Giappichelli, 1964, 1967.

Goldenberg, Robert. "Gnade II. Judentum," *TRE* 13 (1984) 465–467.

Gooch, P. W. "The Relation Between Wisdom and Virtue in Phaedo 69A–C3," *JHP* 12 (1974) 153–159.

Goodenough, E. R. *By Light, Light: The Mystic Gospel of Hellenistic Judaism*. New Haven: Yale University Press, 1935.

–. "Literal Mystery in Hellenistic Judaism," *Quantulacumque: Studies Presented to Kirsopp Lake*. ed. Robert P. Casey, Silva Lake, and Agnes K. Lake. London: Christophers, 1937. 227–241.

Gorden, E. I., and T. Jacobsen. *Sumerian Proverbs*. Philadelphia: University Museum of the University of Pennsylvania, 1959.

Görler, Woldemar. *Menandrou Gnomai*. Berlin: Freie Universität Berlin, 1963.

Greene, William C. *Moira: Fate, Good, and Evil in Greek Thought*. Cambridge: Harvard University Press, 1948.

Gregg, Robert C. *Consolation Philosophy: Greek and Christian Paideia in Basil and the Two Gregories*. Patristic Monograph Series 3. Cambridge, MA: Philadelphia Patristic Foundation, 1975.

Grimaldi, William M. A. *Aristotle, Rhetoric I: A Commentary*. New York: Fordham University Press, 1980.

Griswold, Charles L. *Self-Knowledge in Plato's Phaedrus*. New York and London: Yale University Press, 1986.

Grumach-Shirun, Irene. "Lehre des Amenemope," *LÄ* 3 (1980) 971–974.

Grundmann, Walter. "ἐγκράτεια, κτλ.," *TDNT* 2 (1964) 339–342.

–. "καρτερέω, κτλ.," *TDNT* 3 (1965) 617–620.

Guglielmi, Waltrand. "Sprichwort," *LÄ* 5 (1984) 1219–1222.

Gundel, Wilhelm. "Heimarmene," *PW* 7.2 (1912) 2622–2645.

Gunkel, Hermann, and Joachim Begrich. *Einleitung in die Psalmen: Die Gattungen der religiösen Lyrik Israels*. HKATSup 2.19. Göttingen: Vandenhoeck & Ruprecht, 1933.

Gutas, Dimitri. *Greek Wisdom Literature in Arabic Translation: A Study of the Graeco-Arabic Gnomologia*. AOS 60. New Haven: American Oriental Society, 1975.

Guthrie, William K. C. *Orpheus and Greek Religion: A Study of the Orphic Movement*. 2nd ed. New York: Norton, 1967.

Guttmann, Michael. *Das Judentum und seine Umwelt*. Berlin: Philo Verlag, 1927.

Haag, Herbert. "Révélation I. Ancien Testament," *DBSup* 56 (1982) 586–600.

Hadot, Pierre. "Fürstenspiegel," *RAC* 8 (1972) 555–632.

Hägglund, Bengt. "Gerechtigkeit VII. Ethisch," *TRE* 12 (1984) 440–443.

Harder, Richard. "Timaios 4," *PW* 6A (1937) 1203–1226.

Hardie, W. F. R. *Aristotle's Ethical Theory*. 2nd ed. Oxford: Clarendon, 1980.

Harvey, Anthony E. "The Use of Mystery Language in the Bible," *JTS* 31 (1980) 320–336.

–. *Strenuous Commands: The Ethic of Jesus*. London: SCM; Philadelphia: Trinity Press International, 1990.

Hauck, Friedrich. "ἑκών, κτλ.," *TDNT* 2 (1964) 469–470.

–. "ὑπομένω, ὑπομονή," *TDNT* 4 (1967) 581–588.

–. "πένης, πενιχρός," *TDNT* 6 (1968) 37–40.

Hauck, Friedrich, and Ernst Bammel. "πτωχός, κτλ.," *TDNT* 6 (1968) 885–915.

Hayes, John H., ed. *Old Testament Form Criticism*. Trinity University Monograph Series in Religion. San Antonio: Trinity University Press, 1974.

Hecht, Richard D. "Preliminary Issues in the Analysis of Philo's De Specialibus Legibus," *Studia Philonica* 5 (1978) 1–55.

–. "Scripture and Commentary in Philo," *SBLSP* 20. ed. Kent H. Richards. Chico: Scholars Press, 1981. 129–164.

Hegermann, Harald. *Die Vorstellung vom Schöpfungsmittler im hellenistischen Judentum und Urchristentum*. TU 82. Berlin: Akademie-Verlag, 1961.

Heilmann, Willibald. *Ethische Reflexion und römische Lebenswirklichkeit in Ciceros Schrift De Officiis: Ein literatursoziologischer Versuch*. Palingensia 17. Wiesbaden: Franz Steiner, 1982.

Hengel, Martin. "Anonymität, Pseudepigraphie und 'literarische Fälschung' in der jüdisch-hellenistischen Literatur," *Foundation Hardt pour l'Etude de l'Antiquité Classique, Entretiens* 18 (1972) 231–329.

–. *Judaism and Hellenism: Studies in their Encounter in Palestine during the Early Hellenistic Period*. trans. John Bowden. 2 vols. Philadelphia: Fortress, 1974.

Hense, Otto. "Chares und Verwandtes," *RMP* 72 (1917–18) 14–34.

Hermisson, Hans-Jürgen. *Studien zur israelitischen Spruchweisheit*. WMANT 28. Neukirchen-Vlyun: Neukirchener Verlag, 1968.

–. "Observations on the Creation Theology in Wisdom," in Gammie, *Israelite Wisdom*, 43–57.

Herms, Eilert. "Humanität," *TRE* 15 (1986) 661–682.

Hirzel, Rudlof. *ΑΓΡΑΦΟΣ ΝΟΜΟΣ*. ASGW.PH 20.1. Leipzig: Teubner, 1900.

Hock, Ronald F., and Edward N. O'Neil. *The Chreia in Ancient Rhetoric*, Volume I: *The Progymnasmata*. SBLTT 27, Graeco-Roman Religion Series 9. Atlanta: Scholars Press, 1986.

Hollander, Harm W. "μακροθυμία, κτλ.," *EDNT* 2 (1991) 380–381.

Hoppe, Rudolf. *Der theologische Hintergrund des Jakobusbriefes.* FB 28. Würzburg: Echter Verlag, 1977.

Horna, Konstantin. "Gnome, Gnomendichtung, Gnomologien," *PWSup* 6 (1935) 74–87.

Hornung, Erik, and Othmar Keel, eds. *Studien zu altägyptischen Lebenslehren.* OBO 28. Freiburg (Schweiz): Universitätsverlag; Göttingen: Vandenhoeck & Ruprecht, 1979.

Horst, Johannes. "μακροθυμία, κτλ.," *TDNT* 4 (1967) 374–387.

Hübner, Hans. "τέλειος, κτλ.," *EWNT* 3 (1983) 821–835.

Ibscher, Gred. *Der Begriff des Sittlichen in der Pflichtenlehre des Panaitios: Ein Beitrag zur Erkenntnis der mittleren Stoa.* München: R. Oldenbourg, 1934.

Irwin, Terence. *Plato's Moral Theory: The Early and Middle Dialogues.* Oxford: Clarendon, 1977.

Jackson, F. J. Foakes, and Kirsopp Lake. *The Beginnings of Christianity: The Acts of the Apostles.* 5 vols. London: Macmillan, 1920–1933. Reprint, Grand Rapids: Baker Book House, 1979.

Jaeger, Werner. *Paideia: The Ideals of Greek Culture.* trans. Gilbert Highet. 3 vols. New York: Oxford University Press, 1942–44.

–. *The Theology of the Early Greek Philosophers.* Oxford: Clarendon, 1947. Reprint, Westport, CN: Greenwood, 1980.

–. *Early Christianity and Greek Paideia.* London: Oxford University Press, 1961.

Jansen, Ludin H. *Die spätjüdische Psalmendichtung. Ihr Entstehungskreis und ihr "Sitz im Leben": Eine literaturgeschichtlich-soziologische Untersuchung.* SNVAO 2.3. Oslo: Jacob Dybwad, 1937.

Jastram, Daniel N. "Philo's Concept of Generic Virtue," *SBLSP* 30. ed. Eugene H. Lovering. Atlanta: Scholars Press, 1991. 323–347.

Jellicoe, Sidney. *The Septuagint and Modern Study.* Oxford: Clarendon, 1968.

Joachim, H. H. *Aristotle: The Nicomachean Ethics.* Oxford: Clarendon, 1951.

Johnson, Luke T. "The Use of Leviticus 19 in the Letter of James," *JBL* 101 (1982) 391–401.

–. "James 3.13–4.10 and the *Topos* ΠΕΡΙ ΦΘΟΝΟΥ," *NovT* 25 (1983) 327–347.

Jones, Christopher P. *The Roman World of Dio Chrysostom.* Loeb Classical Monographs. Cambridge and London: Harvard University Press, 1978.

Jordan, Mark D. "Ancient Philosophic Protreptic and the Problem of Persuasive Genres," *Rhetorica* 4 (1986) 309–333.

Kabiersch, Jürgen. *Untersuchungen zum Begriff der Philanthropia bei dem Kaiser Julian.* KPS 21. Wiesbaden: Otto Harrassowitz, 1960.

Kahn, Charles H. "Arius as Doxographer," in Fortenbaugh, *Ethics,* 3–13.

Kamlah, Ehrhard. "Frömmigkeit und Tugend: Die Gesetzesapologie des Josephus in c Ap 2, 145–195," *Josephus-Studien. Untersuchungen zu Josephus, dem antiken Judentum und dem Neuen Testament: Otto Michel zum 70. Geburtstag gewidmet.* ed. Otto Betz, Klaus Haacker, and Martin Hengel. Göttingen: Vandenhoeck & Ruprecht, 1974. 220–232.

Kasher, Rimon. "The Interpretation of Scripture in Rabbinic Literature," in Mulder, *Mikra,* 547–594.

Kassel, Rudolf. *Untersuchungen zur griechischen und römischen Konsolationsliteratur.* Zetemata 18. München: C.H. Beck, 1958.

Kayatz, Christa. *Studien zu Proverbien 1–9: Eine form- und motivgeschichtliche Untersuchung unter Einbeziehung ägyptischen Vergleichsmaterials.* WMANT 22. Neukirchen-Vluyn: Neukirchener Verlag, 1966.

Kennedy, George A. *The Art of Persuasion in Greece.* History of Rhetoric 1. Princeton: Princeton University Press, 1963.

–. *The Art of Rhetoric in the Roman World.* History of Rhetoric 2. Princeton: University of Princeton Press, 1972.

Keydell, Rudolf. "Herodas," *KP* 2 (1967) 1090.

–. "Leonidas 9," *KP* 3 (1969) 567–568.

–. "Phokylides," *KP* 4 (1971) 298–299.

Kidd, I. G. "Moral Actions and Rules in Stoic Ethics," *The Stoics*. ed. John M. Rist. Berkeley and Los Angeles: University of California Press, 1978. 247–258.

Kindstrand, Jan F. "The Cynics and Heraclitus," *Eranos* 82 (1984) 149–178.

Kitchen, Kenneth A. "Basic Literary Forms and Formulations of Ancient Instructional Writing in Egypt and Western Asia," in Hornung and Keel, *Studien*, 235–282.

Klauser, Theodor. "Apophthegma," *RAC* 1 (1950) 545–550.

Klein, Gottlieb. *Der älteste christliche Katechismus und die jüdische Propagandaliteratur.* Berlin: Reimer, 1909.

Kloppenborg, John S. *The Formation of Q: Trajectories in Ancient Wisdom Collections.* Studies in Antiquity and Christianity. Philadelphia: Fortress, 1987.

Kötting, Bernhard. "Digamus," *RAC* 3 (1957) 1016–1024.

Kraft, Robert A., and George W. E. Nickelsburg, eds. *Early Judaism and its Modern Interpreters.* SBLBMI 2. Philadelphia: Fortress; Atlanta: Scholars Press, 1986.

Kranz, Walther. "Sphragis: Ichform und Namensiegel als Eingangs- und Schluszmotiv antiker Dichtung," *RMP* 104 (1961) 3–46, 97–124. Reprint, idem, *Studien zur Antiken Literatur und ihrem Nachwirken: Kleine Schriften.* ed. Ernst Vogt. Bibliothek der klassischen Altertumswissenschaften 1.3. Heidelberg: Carl Winter, 1967. 27–78.

Krause, Jutta. *ΑΛΛΟΤΕ ΑΛΛΟΣ: Untersuchungen zum Motiv des Schicksalswechsels in der griechischen Dichtung bis Euripides.* Tuduv Studies, Reihe Kulturwissenschaften 4. München: Tuduv-Verlagsgesellschaft, 1976.

Krauss, Samuel. "Les Préceptes des Noachides," *REJ* 47 (1903) 32–40.

Kretschmar, Georg, and Karl Hauschildt. "Katechumenat, Katechumenen," *TRE* 18 (1988) 1–14.

Krikmann, Arvo. "On Denotative Indefiniteness of Proverbs," *Proverbium: Yearbook of International Proverb Scholarship* 1 (1984) 47–91.

Krischer, Tilman. "Die logischen Formen der Priamel," *Grazer Beiträge* 2 (1974) 79–91.

Kröhling, Walter. *Die Priamel (Beispielreihung) als Stilmittel in der griechisch-römischen Dichtung, nebst einen Nachwort: Die altorientalische Priamel, von Franz Dornseiff.* GBLS 10. Greifswald: Hans Dallmeyer, 1935.

Kroll, Wilhelm. "Rhetorica V," *Philologus* 90 (1935) 206–215.

Küchler, Max. *Frühjüdische Weisheitstraditionen: Zum Fortgang weisheitlichen Denkens im Bereich des frühjüdischen Jahweglaubens.* OBO 26. Freiburg (Schweiz): Universitätsverlag; Göttingen: Vandenhoeck & Ruprecht, 1979.

Kunsemüller, Otto. *Die Herkunft der platonischen Kardinaltugenden.* Erlangen: Gutenberg, 1935.

Kurfuss, Anton. "Das Mahngedicht des sogenannten Phokylides im zweiten Buch der Oracula Sybyllina," *ZNW* 38 (1939) 171–181.

Labowsky, Lotte. *Die Ethik des Panaitios: Untersuchungen zur Geschichte des Decorum bei Cicero und Horaz.* Leipzig: F. Meiner, 1934.

Lachmann, Rainer. "Kind," *RAC* 18 (1989) 156–176.

Lang, Bernhard. *Die weisheitliche Lehrrede: Eine Untersuchung von Sprüche 1–7.* SBS 54. Stuttgart: KBW, 1972.

–. "Schule und Unterricht im alten Israel," *La Sagesse de l'Ancient Testament.* ed. Maurice Gilbert. BETL 51. Leuven: Leuven University Press; Gembloux: Duculot, 1979. 186–201.

Larcher, Chrysostome. *Etudes sur le Livre de la Sagesse.* Paris: Gabalda, 1969.

–. *Le Livre de la Sagesse ou la Sagesse de Salomon.* EBib 1, 3, 5. 3 vols. Paris: Gabalda, 1983–1985.

Lattke, Michael. *Hymnus: Materialien zu einer Geschichte der antiken Hymnologie.* NTOA 19. Freiburg (Schweiz): Universitätsverlag; Göttingen: Vandenhoeck & Ruprecht, 1991.

Lausberg, Heinrich. *Handbuch der literarischen Rhetorik.* 2nd ed. München: Hueber, 1973.

Lease, Gary. "Mithraism and Christianity: Borrowings and Transformations," *ANRW* II.23.2 (1980) 1306–1332.
–. "Jewish Mystery Cults since Goodenough," *ANRW* II.20.2 (1987) 858–880.
Lee, Thomas R. *Studies in the Form of Sirach 44–50*. SBLDS 75. Atlanta: Scholars Press, 1986.
Leipoldt, Johannes, and Siegfried Morenz. *Heilige Schriften: Betrachtungen zur Religionsgeschichte der antiken Mittelmeerwelt*. Leipzig: Otto Harrassowitz, 1953.
–. "Buch II (heilig, kultisch)," *RAC* 2 (1954) 688–717.
Lerner, M. B. "The Tractate Avot," in Safrai, *The Literature of the Sages*, 262–281.
–. "Avot de-R. Natan," in Safrai, *The Literature of the Sages*, 369–379.
–. "The Tractates Derekh Erets," in Safrai, *The Literature of the Sages*, 379–389.
Lewis, Philip E. "The Discourse of the Maxim," *Diacritics* 2 (1972) 41–48.
Lichtheim, Miriam. "Observations on Papyrus Insinger," in Hornung and Keel, *Studien*, 284–305.
Lilla, S. "Middle Platonism, Neoplatonism and Jewish-Alexandrine Philosophy in the Terminology of Clement of Alexandria's Ethics," *AISP* 3 (1962) 3–36.
Lohse, Eduard. *Theological Ethics of the New Testament*. Minneapolis: Fortress, 1991. Originally, *Theologische Ethik des Neuen Testaments*. Stuttgart: W. Kohlhammer, 1988.
Long, Anthony A. "Timon of Phlius: Pyrrhonist and Satirist," *PCPS* 204 (1978) 68–91.
–. "Arius Didymus and the Exposition of Stoic Ethics," in Fortenbaugh, *Ethics*, 41–65.
–. *Hellenistic Philosophy: Stoics, Epicureans, Sceptics*. 2nd ed. New York: Scribner's, 1986.
Long, Anthony A., ed. *Problems in Stoicism*. London: Athlone, 1971.
Luck, Ulrich. "φιλανθρωπία, φιλανθρώπως," *TDNT* 9 (1974) 107–112.
–. "Die Theologie des Jakobusbriefes," *ZTK* 81 (1984) 1–30.
Lutz, Cora E. *Musonius Rufus: 'The Roman Socrates'*. YCS 10. New York: Yale University Press, 1942.
MacDowell, Douglas M. "Hybris in Athens," *Greece and Rome* 23 (1976) 14–31.
Mack, Burton L. *Logos und Sophia: Untersuchungen zur Weisheitstheologie im hellenistischen Judentum*. SUNT 10. Göttingen: Vandenhoeck & Ruprecht, 1973.
–. "Philo Judaeus and Exegetical Traditions in Alexandria," *ANRW* II.21.1 (1984) 227–271.
–. *Wisdom and the Hebrew Epic: Ben Sira's Hymn in Praise of the Fathers*. Chicago Studies in the History of Judaism. Chicago and London: University of Chicago Press, 1985.
Mack, Burton L., and Roland E. Murphy. "Wisdom Literature," in Kraft and Nickelsburg, *Early Judaism and its Modern Interpreters*, 371–410.
MacMullen, Ramsay. *Roman Social Relations, 50 B.C. to A.D. 284*. New Haven and London: Yale University Press, 1974.
–. *Paganism in the Roman Empire*. New Haven and London: Yale University Press, 1981.
Maier, Johann. "Armut IV. Judentum," *TRE* 4 (1979) 80–85.
Malgarini, Alessandra B. "ΑΡΧΑΙΩΝ ΦΙΛΟΣΟΦΩΝ ΓΝΩΜΑΙ ΚΑΙ ΑΠΟΦΘΕΓΜΑΤΑ in un Manoscritto di Patmos," *Elenchos* 5 (1984) 153–200.
Malherbe, Abraham J. *Social Aspects of Early Christianity*. 2nd ed. Philadelphia: Fortress, 1983.
–. *Moral Exhortation: A Greco-Roman Sourcebook*. LEC 4. Philadelphia: Westminster, 1986.
Marböck, Johann. *Weisheit im Wandel: Untersuchungen zur Weisheitstheologie bei Ben Sira*. BBB 37. Bonn: Hanstein, 1971.
–. "Gesetz und Weisheit: Zum Verstandnis des Gesetzes bei Jesus Sira," *BZ* 20 (1976) 1–21.
Marrou, Henri I. *A History of Education in Antiquity*. trans. George Lamb. London and New York: Sheed and Ward, 1956.
Martin, Hubert, and Jane E. Phillips. "Consolatio ad Uxorem (Moralia 608A–612B)," in Betz, *Plutarch's Ethical Writings*, 394–441.
Martin, Josef. *Antike Rhetorik: Technik und Methode*. HAW 2.3. München: Beck, 1974.

McKane, William. *Proverbs: A New Approach*. OTL. Philadelphia: Westminster, 1970.
–. "Functions of Language and Objectives of Discourse According to Proverbs 10–30," *La Sagesse de l'Ancien Testament*. ed. Maurice Gilbert. BETL 51. 2nd ed. Leuven: Leuven University Press, 1990. 166–185.
Meade, David G. *Pseudonymity and Canon: An Investigation into the Relationship of Authorship and Authority in Jewish and Earliest Christian Tradition*. WUNT 39. Tübingen: J.C.B. Mohr (Paul Siebeck), 1986.
Meeks, Wayne A. "The Circle of Reference in Pauline Morality," *Greeks, Romans, and Christians: Essays in Honor of Abraham J. Malherbe*. ed. David L. Balch, Everett Ferguson, and Wayne A. Meeks. Minneapolis: Fortress, 1990. 305–317.
Mees, Michael. "Die Bedeutung der Sentenzen und ihrer auxesis für die Formung der Jesusworte nach Didaché 1,3b–2,1," *Vetera Christianorum* 8 (1971) 55–76.
Meilaender, Gilbert C. *The Theory and Practice of Virtue*. Notre Dame: Notre Dame University Press, 1984.
Merkelbach, Reinhold. *Mithras*. Königstein/Ts.: Anton Hain, 1984.
Merklein, Helmut. "πτωχός, κτλ.," *EWNT* 3 (1983) 466–472.
Metzger, Bruce M. "A Classified Bibliography of the Graeco-Roman Mystery Religions 1924–1973 with a Supplement 1974–1977," *ANRW* II.17.3 (1984) 1259–1423.
Meyer, Marvin W. *The Gospel of Thomas: The Hidden Sayings of Jesus*. San Francisco: Harper & Row, 1992.
Meyer, Marvin W., ed. *The Ancient Mysteries: A Sourcebook*. San Francisco: Harper & Row, 1987.
Meyer, Wilhelm. "Die athenische Spruchrede des Menander und Philistion," *ABAW* 19 (1891) 227–295.
Michel, Diethelm. "Armut II. Altes Testament," *TRE* 4 (1979) 72–76.
Milobenski, Ernst. *Der Neid in der griechischen Philosophie*. KPS 29. Wiesbaden: Otto Harrassowitz, 1964.
Moore, Carey A. *Daniel, Esther, and Jeremiah: The Additions. A New Translation with Introduction and Commentary*. AB 44. Garden City, New York: Doubleday, 1977.
Mott, Stephen C. "Greek Ethics and Christian Conversion: The Philonic Background of Titus 2.10–14 and 3.3–7," *NovT* 20 (1978) 22–48.
Moulinier, Louis. *Le Pur et l'Impur dans la Pensée des Grecs d'Homère à Aristote*. Etudes et Commentaires 12. Paris: Klincksieck, 1950.
Mourelatos, Alexander P. D. *The Route of Parmenides: A Study of Word, Image, and Argument in the Fragments*. New Haven and London: Yale University Press, 1970.
–. "Some Alternatives in Interpreting Parmenides," *The Monist* 62 (1979) 3–14.
Mowinckel, Sigmund. "Psalms and Wisdom," *Wisdom in Israel and in the Ancient Near East: Presented to Professor Harold Henry Rowley*. ed. Martin Noth and D. Winton Thomas. VTSup 3. Leiden: E.J. Brill, 1955. 205–224.
–. *The Psalms in Israel's Worship*. 2 vols. Nashville: Abingdon, 1962.
Mulder, Martin Jan, ed. *Mikra: Text, Translation, Reading and Interpretation of the Hebrew Bible in Ancient Judaism and Early Christianity*. CRINT 2.1. Assen and Maastricht: van Gorcum; Philadelphia: Fortress, 1988.
Munch, P. A. "Die jüdischen 'Weisheitspsalmen' und ihr Platz im Leben," *AnOr* 15 (1937) 112–140.
Murphy, Roland E. "A Consideration of the Classification 'Wisdom Psalms'," *VTSup* 9 (1962) 156–167. Reprint, Crenshaw, *Studies*, 456–467.
–. *The Forms of the Old Testament Literature*, Volume 13: *Wisdom Literature*. Grand Rapids: Eerdmans, 1981.
Murray, O. "Philodemus on the Good King according to Homer," *JRS* 55 (1965) 161–182.
Mußner, Franz. *Der Jakobusbrief*. HTKNT 13.1. 3rd ed. Freiburg, Basel, Wien: Herder, 1975.
Myers, R. A. B. "Didactic Poetry," *OCD* (1949) 277–278.

Nagy, Gregory. "Theognis and Megara: A Poet's Vision of his City," in Figueira and Nagy, *Theognis*, 22–81.

Neri, Valerio. "Dei, Fato e Divinazione nella Letteratura Latina del I sec. d.C.," *ANRW* II.16.3 (1986) 1974–2051.

Neumann, Gerhard, ed. *Der Aphorismus: Zur Geschichte, zu den Formen und Möglichkeiten einer literarischen Gattung.* WdF 356. Darmstadt: Wissenschaftliche Buchgesellschaft, 1976.

Neusner, Jacob. "Types and Forms of Ancient Jewish Literature: Some Comparisons," *HR* 11 (1971–72) 354–390.

–. *The Idea of Purity in Ancient Judaism.* SJLA 1. Leiden: E.J. Brill, 1973.

–. *Form-Analytical Comparison in Rabbinic Judaism: Structure and Form in The Fathers and The Fathers According to Rabbi Nathan.* University of South Florida Studies in the History of Judaism 45. Atlanta: Scholars Press, 1992.

Neustadt, Ernst. "Der Zeushymnos des Kleanthes," *Hermes* 66 (1931) 387–401.

Nickelsburg, George W. E. *Resurrection, Immortality and Eternal Life in Intertestamental Judaism.* HTS 26. Cambridge: Harvard University Press, 1972.

Niebuhr, Karl-Wilhelm. *Gesetz und Paränese: Katechismusartige Weisungsreihen in der frühjüdischen Literatur.* WUNT 2.28. Tübingen: J.C.B. Mohr (Paul Siebeck), 1987.

Niederstrasser, H. *Kerygma und Paideia: Zum Problem der erziehenden Gnade.* Stuttgart: Evangelisches Verlagswerk, 1967.

Nilsson, Martin P. *Die hellenistische Schule.* München: Beck, 1955.

Nock, Arthur Darby. *Essays on Religion and the Ancient World.* ed. Zeph Stewart. 2 vols. Cambridge: Harvard University Press, 1972.

Norden, Eduard. *Agnostos Theos: Untersuchungen zur Formengeschichte religiöser Rede.* Leipzig and Berlin: Teubner, 1913. Reprint, Darmstadt: Wissenschaftliche Buchgesellschaft, 1956.

North, Helen. "Pindar, Isthmian, 8, 24–28," *AJP* 69 (1948) 304–308.

–. "Canons and Hierarchies of the Cardinal Virtues in Greek and Latin Literature," *The Classical Tradition: Literary and Historical Studies in Honor of Harry Caplan.* ed. Luitpold Wallach. Ithaca: Cornell University Press, 1966. 165–183.

–. *Sophrosyne: Self-Knowledge and Self-Restraint in Greek Literature.* CSCP 35. Ithaca: Cornell University Press, 1966.

Nussbaum, Martha C. "Mortal Immortals: Lucretius on Death and the Voice of Nature," *PPR* 50 (1989) 303–351.

Oepke, Albrecht. "Auferstehung II (des Menschen)," *RAC* 1 (1950) 930–938.

–. "Ehe," *RAC* 4 (1959) 650–666.

–. "παῖς, παιδίον, κτλ.," *TDNT* 5 (1967) 636–654.

Opelt, Ilona. "Epitome," *RAC* 5 (1962) 944–973.

Parker, Robert. *Miasma: Pollution and Purification in Early Greek Religion.* Oxford: Clarendon, 1983.

Patte, Daniel, ed. *Semeia 29. Kingdom and Children: Aphorism, Chreia, Structure.* Chico, CA: Scholars Press, 1983.

Patzer, Harald. *Gesammelte Schriften.* Stuttgart: Steiner, 1985.

Peel, Malcolm L., and Jan Zandee. "The Teachings of Silvanus from the Library of Nag Hammadi," *NovT* 14 (1972) 294–311.

Pelletier, A. "La Philanthropia de Tous les Jours chez les Ecrivains Juifs Hellénisés," *Paganisme, Judaïsme, Christianisme: Influences et Affrontements dans le Monde Antique. Mélanges Offerts à Marcel Simon.* Paris: Editions E. de Boccard, 1978. 35–44.

Pépin, Jean. "Remarques sur la Théorie de l'Exégèse Allégorique chez Philon," *Philon d'Alexandrie: Lyon 11–15 Septembre 1966.* Colloques Nationaux du Centre National de la Recherche Scientifique. Paris: Editions du Centre National de la Recherche Scientifique, 1967. 131–167.

–. *Myth et Allégorie: Les Origines Grecques et les Contestations Judéo-Chrétiennes.* 2nd ed. Paris: Etudes Augustiniennes, 1976.

Perdue, Leo G. *Wisdom and Cult: A Critical Analysis of the Views of Cult in the Wisdom Literature of Israel and the Ancient Near East.* SBLDS 30. Missoula: Scholars Press, 1977.

–. "Liminality as the Social Setting of Wisdom Instructions," *ZAW* 93 (1981) 114–126.

–. "The Social Character of Paraenesis and Paraenetic Literature," *Semeia* 50 (1990) 5–39.

Peretti, Aurelio. *Teognide nella Tradizione Gnomolica.* Classici e Orientali 4. Pisa: Libreria Goliardiea, 1953.

–. "Calchi Gnomici nella Silloge Teognidea," *Maia* 8 (1956) 197–217.

Petuchowski, Jakob J. "Judaism as 'Mystery' – The Hidden Agenda?" *HUCA* 52 (1981) 141–152.

–. "Zur rabbinischen Interpretation des Offenbarungsglaubens," *Offenbarung im jüdischen und christlichen Glaubenverständnis.* ed. idem and Walter Strolz. QD 92. Freiburg: Herder, 1981. 72–86.

Piper, Ronald A. *Wisdom in the Q-Tradition: The Aphoristic Teaching of Jesus.* SNTSMS 61. Cambridge: Cambridge University Press, 1989.

Pohlenz, Max. "Tò πρέπον: Ein Beitrag zur Geschichte des griechischen Geistes," *Nachrichten von der Gesellschaft der Wissenschaften zu Göttingen; Philologisch-historische Klasse.* Berlin: Weidmannsche Buchhandlung, 1933. 53–92.

–. *Antikes Führertum: Cicero De Officiis und das Lebensideal des Panaitios.* Neue Wege zur Antike 2.3. Leipzig and Berlin: Teubner, 1934. Reprint, Amsterdam: Adolf M. Hakkert, 1967.

–. "Kleanthes' Zeushymnus," *Hermes* 75 (1940) 117–123.

–. *Die Stoa: Geschichte einer geistigen Bewegung.* 2nd ed. 2 vols. Göttingen: Vandenhoeck & Ruprecht, 1959.

Powell, J. U., and E. A. Barber. *New Chapters in the History of Greek Literature.* Oxford: Clarendon, 1921.

Praechter, Karl. *Hierokles der Stoiker.* Leipzig: Dieterich'sche Verlags-Buchhandlung, 1901.

Préaux, Claire. "L'Image du Roi de l'Epoque Hellenistique," *Images of Man in Ancient and Medieval Thought: Studia Gerardo Verbeke ab Amicis et Collegis Dicata.* ed. F. Bossier, et al. Symbolae, Facultatis Litterarum et Philosophiae Lovaniensis A.1. Louvain: University of Louvain Press, 1976. 53–76.

Preuß, Horst D. "Barmherzigkeit I. Altes Testament," *TRE* 5 (1980) 215–224.

Procope, J. F. "Quiet Christian Courage: A Topic in Clemens Alexandrinus and its Philosophical Background," *Studia Patristica* 15 (1984) 489–494.

Prümm, Karl. "Mystères," *DBSup* 6 (1960) 1–225.

Puelma, Mario. "Der Dichter und die Wahrheit in der griechischen Poetik von Homer bis Aristoteles," *Museum Helveticum* 46 (1989) 65–100.

Race, William H. *The Classical Priamel from Homer to Boethius.* Mnemosyne Sup. 74. Leiden: E.J. Brill, 1982.

Radl, Walter. "ὑπομονή," *EWNT* 3 (1983) 969–971.

Räisänen, Heikki. *Paul and the Law.* WUNT 29. Tübingen: J.C.B. Mohr (Paul Siebeck), 1983.

Ratschow, Carl H., et al. "Ehe, Eherecht, Ehescheidung," *TRE* 9 (1982) 308–362.

Reese, James M. *Hellenistic Influence in the Book of Wisdom and its Consequences.* AnBib 41. Rome: Biblical Institute Press, 1970.

Reicke, Bo. *Die Zehn Worte in Geschichte und Gegenwart: Zählung und Bedeutung der Gebote in den verschiedenen Konfessionen.* BGBE 13. Tübingen: J.C.B. Mohr (Paul Siebeck), 1973.

Reinmuth, Eckart. *Geist und Gesetz: Studien zu Voraussetzungen und Inhalt der paulinischen Paränese.* ThA 44. Berlin: Evangelische Verlagsanstalt, 1985.

Renehan, Robert. "The Greek Philosophic Background of Fourth Maccabees," *RMP* 115 (1972) 223–238.

Requadt, Paul. "Das Aphoristische Denken," in Neumann, *Der Aphorismus,* 331–377.

Reventlow, Henning G. "Gnade I. Altes Testament," *TRE* 13 (1984) 459–464.

Richard, Marcel. "Florilèges Grecs," *DSp* 5 (1964) 475–512.

Richter, Wolfgang. *Recht und Ethos: Versuch einer Ortung des weisheitlichen Mahnspruches.* SANT 15. München: Kösel, 1966.

Rickenbacher, O. *Weisheitsperikopen bei Ben Sira.* OBO 1. Freiburg (Schweiz): Universitätsverlag; Göttingen: Vandenhoeck & Ruprecht, 1973.

Riedweg, Christoph. *Mysterienterminologie bei Platon, Philon und Klemens von Alexandrien.* UaLG 26. Berlin and New York: de Gruyter, 1987.

Rigaux, Béda. "Révélation des Mystères et Perfection à Qumran et dans le Nouveau Testament," *NTS* 4 (1958) 237–262.

Rist, John M. *Stoic Philosophy.* Cambridge: Cambridge University Press, 1969.

–. *Human Value: A Study in Ancient Philosophical Ethics.* Philosophia Antiqua 40. Leiden: E.J. Brill, 1982.

Robb, Kevin, ed. *Language and Thought in Early Greek Philosophy.* La Salle, IL: Hegeler Institute, 1983.

Robinson, James M. "LOGOI SOPHON: On the Gattung of Q," *Trajectories through Early Christianity.* ed. idem and Helmut Koester. Philadelphia: Fortress, 1971. 71–113. Also in *The Future of Our Religious Past: Essays in Honor of Rudolf Bultmann.* ed. idem. New York, Evanston, San Francisco: Harper & Row, 1971. 84–130.

Robinson, T. M. *Plato's Psychology.* Phoenix Sup. 8. Toronto: University of Toronto Press, 1970.

Rochaise, Henri-Marie. "Florilèges Latins," *DSp* 5 (1964) 435–460.

Rodes, Robert E. "On Law and Virtue," *Virtue: Public and Private.* ed. Richard J. Neuhaus. The Encounter Series 1. Grand Rapids: Eerdmans, 1986. 30–42.

Rohde, Erwin. *Psyche: The Cult of Souls and Belief in Immortality Among the Greeks.* trans. W. B. Hillis. New York: Arno, 1972.

Rorty, Amélie O., ed. *Essays on Aristotle's Ethics.* Major Thinkers Series 2. Berkeley, Los Angeles, London: University of California Press, 1980.

Rosenkranz, Bernhard. "Die Struktur der Pseudo-Isokrateischen Demonicea," *Emerita* 34 (1966) 95–129.

Rosenthal, Franz. "Sedaka, Charity," *HUCA* 23 (1950–51) 411–430.

Roth, Wolfgang. "On the Gnomic-Discursive Wisdom of Jesus Ben-Sirach," *Semeia* 17 (1980) 59–79.

Rowe, Christopher J. "Justice and Temperance in Republic IV," *Arktouros: Hellenic Studies Presented to Bernard M. W. Knox.* ed. Glen W. Bowersock, Walter Burkert and Michael C. J. Putnam. Berlin and New York: de Gruyter, 1979. 336–344.

Rudberg, Gunnar. "Zur Diogenes-Tradition," *Symbolae Osloenses* 14 (1935) 22–43.

Rudolph, Kurt. "Mystery Religions," *The Encyclopedia of Religion*, Volume 10. ed. Mircea Eliade. New York and London: Macmillan, 1987. 230–239.

Rupprecht, Karl. "Paroimiographoi," *PW* 18.4 (1949) 1735–1778.

Rzach, Alois. "Hesiodos," *PW* 8.1 (1912) 1167–1240.

Safrai, Shmuel. "Education and the Study of Torah," *The Jewish People in the First Century: Historical Geography, Political History, Social, Cultural and Religious Life and Institutions*, Volume 2. ed. idem and M. Stern. CRINT 1.2. Assen: van Gorcum, 1976. 945–970.

Safrai, Shmuel, ed. *The Literature of the Sages,* First Part: *Oral Tora, Halakha, Mishna, Tosefta, Talmud, External Tractates.* CRINT 2.3.1. Assen, Maastricht: van Gorcum; Philadelphia: Fortress, 1987.

Sahlin, Harald. "Die drei Kardinalsünden und das Neue Testament," *ST* 24 (1970) 93–112.

Saldarini, Anthony J. *The Fathers According to Rabbi Nathan (Abot de Rabbi Nathan): Version B.* SJLA 11. Leiden: E.J. Brill, 1975.

–. *Scholastic Rabbinism: A Literary Study of the Fathers According to Rabbi Nathan.* BJS 14. Chico, CA: Scholars Press, 1982.

Sandbach, F. H. *The Stoics.* Ancient Culture and Society. New York: W. W. Norton & Co., 1975.

Sanders, E. P. *Jewish Law from Jesus to the Mishnah: Five Studies.* London: SCM; Philadelphia: Trinity Press International, 1990.

Sanders, Jack T. *Ben Sira and Demotic Wisdom.* SBLMS 28. Chico, CA: Scholars Press, 1983.

Sandmel, Samuel. "Virtue and Reward in Philo," *Essays in Old Testament Ethics: J. Philip Hyatt, In Memoriam.* ed. James L. Crenshaw and John T. Willis. New York: KTAV, 1974. 215–223.

Sänger, Dieter. *Antikes Judentum und die Mysterien: Religionsgeschichtliche Untersuchungen zu Joseph und Aseneth.* WUNT 2.5. Tübingen: J.C.B. Mohr (Paul Siebeck), 1980.

Santas, Gerasimos. "Socrates at Work on Virtue and Knowledge in Plato's Laches," *Review of Metaphysics* 22 (1969) 433–460.

Scharbert, Josef. "Gerechtigkeit I. Altes Testament," *TRE* 12 (1984) 404–411.

Schmid, Hans H. *Wesen und Geschichte der Weisheit: Eine Untersuchung zur altorientalischen und israelitischen Weisheitsliteratur.* BZAW 101. Berlin: Töpelmann, 1966.

Schmid, Ulrich. *Die Priamel der Werte im Griechischen von Homer bis Paulus.* Wiesbaden: Otto Harrassowitz, 1964.

Schmid, Walter T. "Socratic Moderation and Self-Knowledge," *JHP* 21 (1983) 349–358.

–. *On Manly Courage: A Study of Plato's Laches.* Philosophical Explorations. Carbondale, IL: Southern Illinois University Press, 1992.

Schmidt, Leopold. *Die Ethik der alten Griechen.* 2 vols. Berlin: W. Hertz, 1882. Reprint, Stuttgart: Friedrich Frommann, 1964.

Schmitz, Otto, and Gustav Stählin. "παρακαλέω, παράκλησις," *TDNT* 5 (1967) 773–799.

Schnabel, Eckhard J. *Law and Wisdom from Ben Sira to Paul: A Tradition Historical Enquiry into the Relation of Law, Wisdom, and Ethics.* WUNT 2.16. Tübingen: J.C.B. Mohr (Paul Siebeck), 1985.

Schneider, Carl. "Eros," *RAC* 6 (1966) 306–311.

Schoedel, William R. "Jewish Wisdom and the Formation of the Christian Ascetic," in Wilken, *Aspects of Wisdom,* 169–199.

Scholem, Gershom G. "Revelation and Tradition as Religious Categories in Judaism," *The Messianic Idea in Judaism and Other Essays on Jewish Spirituality.* New York: Schocken, 1971. 282–303.

Schrenk, Gottlob. "δικαιοσύνη," *TDNT* 2 (1964) 192–210.

Schrey, Heinz-Horst. "Geduld," *TRE* 12 (1984) 139–144.

Schröder, Heinrich O. "Fatum (Heimarmene)," *RAC* 7 (1969) 524–636.

Schubart, W. "Das Königsbild des Hellenismus," *Die Antike* 13 (1937) 272–288.

Schürer, Emil, et al. *The History of the Jewish People in the Age of Jesus Christ,* Volume 3, Part 1. 2nd ed. Edinburgh: T. & T. Clark, 1986.

Schwarzschild, Steven S., and Saul Berman. "Noachide Laws," *EncJud* 12 (1971) 1189–1191.

Scott, R. B. Y. "Solomon and the Beginnings of Wisdom in Israel," *Wisdom in Israel and in the Ancient Near East: Presented to Professor Harold Henry Rowley.* ed. Martin Noth and D. Winton Thomas. VTSup 3. Leiden: E.J. Brill, 1955. 262–279. Reprint, Crenshaw, *Studies,* 84–101.

Seeberg, Alfred. *Die beiden Wege und das Aposteldekret.* Leipzig: A. Deichert, 1906.

Segal, Charles. *Lucretius on Death and Anxiety: Poetry and Philosophy in De Rerum Natura.* Princeton: Princeton University Press, 1990.

Sharples, R. W. *Alexander of Aphrodisias, On Fate: Text, Translation, and Commentary.* Duckworth Classical Editions. London: Duckworth, 1983.

Sheppard, Gerald T. "Wisdom and Torah: The Interpretation of Deuteronomy Underlying Sirach 24.23," *Biblical and Near Eastern Studies: Essays in Honor of William S. LaSor.* ed. Gary A. Tuttle. Grand Rapids: Eerdmans, 1978. 166–176.

–. *Wisdom as a Hermeneutical Construct: A Study in the Sapientializing of the Old Testament*. BZAW 151. Berlin and New York: de Gruyter, 1980.

Shroyer, Montgomery J. "Alexandrian Jewish Literalists," *JBL* 55 (1936) 261–284.

Siegert, Folker. "Gottesfürchtige und Sympathisanten," *JSJ* 4 (1973) 109–164.

Signer, Michael A. "Barmherzigkeit III. Judentum," *TRE* 5 (1980) 228–232.

Skehan, Patrick W. *Studies in Israelite Wisdom and Poetry*. CBQMS 1. Washington D.C.: Catholic Biblical Association, 1971.

–. "Structures in Poems on Wisdom: Proverbs 8 and Sirach 24," *CBQ* 41 (1979) 365–379.

Skladny, Udo. *Die ältesten Spruchsammlungen in Israel*. Göttingen: Vandenhoeck & Ruprecht, 1962.

Skutsch, Otto. "Dicta Catonis," *PW* 5.1 (1903) 358–370.

Sly, Dorothy I. "Philo's Practical Application of Δικαιοσύνη," *SBLSP* 30. ed. Eugene H. Lovering. Atlanta: Scholars Press, 1991. 298–308.

Sorabji, Richard. "Aristotle on the Role of Intellect in Virtue," in Rorty, *Essays*, 201–219.

Spanneut, Michael. "Geduld," *RAC* 9 (1976) 243–294.

Speyer, Wolfgang. *Die literarische Fälschung im heidnischen und christlichen Altertum: Ein Versuch ihrer Deutung*. HAW 1.2. München: C. H. Beck, 1971.

Spicq, Ceslaus. *Les Epitres Pastorales*. 4th ed. EBib. 2 vols. Paris: J. Gabalda, 1969.

–. *Notes de Lexicographie Neó-testamentaire*. OBO 22. 3 vols. Fribourg: Editions Universitaires; Göttingen: Vandenhoeck & Ruprecht, 1978–1982.

Spoerri, W. "Gnome," *KP* 2 (1967) 822–829.

Staats, Reinhard. "Hauptsünden," *RAC* 13 (1985) 734–770.

Staudinger, Ferdinand. "ἔλεος," *EDNT* 1 (1990) 429–431.

Stein, Edmund. *Die allegorische Exegese des Philo aus Alexandria*. BZAW 51. Giessen: Töpelmann, 1929.

Sterling, Gregory E. "Philo and the Logic of Apologetics: An Analysis of the Hypothetica," *SBLSP* 29. ed. David J. Lull. Atlanta: Scholars Press, 1990. 412–430.

Stewart, Zeph. "Democritus and the Cynics," *HSCP* 63 (1958) 179–191.

Stork, Traudel. *Nil Igitur Mors est ad Nos: Der Schlussteil des dritten Lukrezbuchs und sein Verhältnis zur Konsolationsliteratur*. Habelts Dissertationsdrucke, Reihe klassische Philologie 9. Bonn: Rudolf Habelt, 1970.

Stowers, Stanley K. *Letter Writing in Greco-Roman Antiquity*. LEC 5. Philadelphia: Westminster, 1986.

Straub, Johannes A. *Vom Herrscherideal in der Spätantike*. FKGG 18. Stuttgart: W. Kohlhammer, 1939.

Sykes, D. A. "The Poemata Arcana of St. Gregory Nazianzen: Some Literary Questions," *Byzantinische Zeitschrift* 72 (1979) 6–15.

–. "Gregory Nazianzen as Didactic Poet," *Studia Patristica* 16 (1985) 433–437.

Tannehill, Robert C. "Types and Functions of Apophthegms in the Synoptic Gospels," *ANRW* II.25.2 (1984) 1792–1829.

Taubenschlag, Rafael. *The Law of Greco-Roman Egypt in the Light of the Papyri*. 2nd ed. New York: Herald Square, 1955.

Taureck, Bernhard. "Gerechtigkeit VIII. Philosophisch," *TRE* 12 (1984) 443–448.

Taylor, Archer. *The Proverb and an Index to the Proverb*. 2nd ed. Hatboro, PA: Folklore Associates; Copenhagen: Rosenkilde and Bagger, 1962.

Thackeray, H. J. "The Poetry of the Greek Book of Proverbs," *JTS* 13 (1911–12) 46–66.

Thillet, Pierre. "Jamblique et les Mystères d'Egypte," *REG* 81 (1968) 172–195.

Thissen, Heinz-Josef. "Lehre des Anch-Scheschonqi," *LÄ* 3 (1980) 974–975.

Thom, Johan C. *The Golden Verses of Pythagoras: A Critical Investigation of its Literary Composition and Religio-historical Significance*. Ph.D. Dissertation, University of Chicago, 1989.

–. "The Semantic Universe of the Pythagorean Akousmata," *AARSBLA*. ed. Eugene H. Lovering and Barbara S. Yoshioka. Atlanta: Scholars Press, 1991. 21.

Thomas, Johannes. "παρακαλέω, παράκλησις," *EWNT* 3 (1983) 54–64.

–. *Der jüdische Phokylides: Formgeschichtliche Zugänge zu Pseudo-Phokylides und Vergleich mit der neutestamentlichen Paränese.* NTOA 23. Freiburg (Schweiz): Universitätsverlag; Göttingen: Vandenhoeck & Ruprecht, 1992.

Thraede, Klaus. *Grundzüge griechisch-römischer Brieftopik.* Zetemata 48. München: C. H. Beck, 1970.

Tov, Emanuel. "Jewish Greek Scriptures," in Kraft and Nickelsburg, *Early Judaism and its Modern Interpreters,* 221–237.

–. "The Septuagint," in Mulder, *Mikra,* 159–188.

Triantaphyllopoulos, Johannes. *Das Rechtsdenken der Griechen.* MBPF 78. München: Beck, 1985.

Turcan, Robert. *Mithras Platonicus: Recherches sur l'Hellénisation Philosophique de Mithra.* EPRO 47. Leiden: E.J. Brill, 1975.

Turck, André. *Evangélisation et Catéchèse aux Deux Premiers Siècles.* Paris: Cerf, 1962.

–. "Catéchein et Catéchesis chez les Premiers Pères," *RSPT* 47 (1963) 361–372.

Umphrey, Stewart. "Plato's Laches on Courage," *Apeiron* 10 (1976) 14–22.

van den Hoek, Annewies. *Clement of Alexandria and his Use of Philo in the Stromateis: An Early Christian Reshaping of a Jewish Model.* VCSup 3. Leiden: E.J. Brill, 1988.

van der Horst, P. C. *Les Vers D'Or Pythagoriciens: Etudes avec une Introduction et un Commentaire.* Leiden: E.J. Brill, 1932.

van der Horst, Pieter W. "Pseudo-Phocylides and the New Testament," *ZNW* 69 (1978) 187–202.

–. "Pseudo-Phocylides Revisited," *JSP* 3 (1988) 3–30.

–. "Phocylides, Pseudo-," *ABD* 5 (1992) 347–348.

van de Sandt, H. "Didache 3.1–6: A Transformation of an Existing Jewish Hortatory Pattern," *JSJ* 23 (1992) 21–41.

van Geytenbeek, A. C. *Musonius Rufus and Greek Diatribe.* Wijsgerige Teksten en Studies 8. Assen: van Gorcum, 1962.

van Otterlo, W. A. A. "Beitrage zur Kenntnis der griechischen Priamel," *Mnemosyne* 8 (1940) 145–176.

van Straaten, F. T. "Gifts for the Gods," *Faith, Hope and Worship: Aspects of Religious Mentality in the Ancient World.* ed. H. S. Versnel. Studies in Greek and Roman Religion 2. Leiden: E.J. Brill, 1981. 65–151.

van Veldhuizen, M. D. "Moses: A Model of Hellenistic Philanthropia," *Reformed Review* 38 (1985) 215–224.

Vatin, Claude. *Recherches sur le Mariage et la Condition de la Femme Mariée à l'Epoque Hellénistique.* BEFAR 216. Paris: E. de Boccard, 1970.

Verbeke, Gerard. *Moral Education in Aristotle.* Washington, D.C.: University Press of America, 1990.

Vermaseren, Maarten J. *Cybele and Attis: The Myth and the Cult.* New York and London: Thames and Hudson, 1977.

Vermes, Geza. "A Summary of the Law by Flavius Josephus," *NovT* 24 (1982) 289–303.

Vetschera, Rudolf. *Zur griechischen Paränese.* Programm des Staatsgymnasiums zu Smichow. Smichow: Rohlicek & Sievers, 1912.

Vokes, F. E. "The Ten Commandments in the New Testament and in First Century Judaism," *Studia Evangelica 5.* ed. F. L. Cross. TU 103. Berlin: Akademie-Verlag, 1968. 146–154.

Volz, Paul. *Jüdische Eschatologie von Daniel bis Akiba.* Tübingen and Leipzig: J.C.B. Mohr (Paul Siebeck), 1903.

von Albrecht, Michael. "Das Menschenbild in Iamblichs Darstellung der pythagoreischen Lebensformen," *Antike und Abendland* 12 (1966) 51–63.

–. "Didaktische Poesie," *KP* 2 (1967) 4–6.

von Fritz, Kurt. "Periktione," *PW* 19.1 (1937) 794–795.

von Geisau, Hans. "Buzyges," *KP* 1 (1964) 977.

–. "Hybris," *KP* 2 (1967) 1257–1258.

von Lips, Hermann. *Weisheitliche Traditionen im Neuen Testament.* WMANT 64. Neukirchen-Vluyn: Neukirchener Verlag, 1990.

von Lyden, Wolfgang. *Aristotle on Equality and Justice: His Political Argument.* New York: St. Martin's Press, 1985.

von Rad, Gerhard. *Wisdom in Israel.* trans. James D. Martin. London: SCM, 1972.

von Wölfflin, Eduard. "Epitome," *Archiv für lateinische Lexikographie und Grammatik* 12 (1902) 333–344.

Wachsmuth, Kurt. *Studien zu den griechischen Florilegien.* Berlin: Weidmann, 1882.

Wagner, Walter H. "Philo and Paideia," *Cithara* 10 (1971) 53–64.

Walcot, Peter. *Envy and the Greeks: A Study of Human Behavior.* Warminster: Aris & Phillips, 1978.

Wallach, Barbara P. *Lucretius and the Diatribe Against the Fear of Death: De Rerum Natura 3, 830–1094.* Mnemosyne Sup. 40. Leiden: E.J. Brill, 1976.

Walter, Nikolaus. *Der Thoraausleger Aristobulos.* TU 86. Berlin: Akademie-Verlag, 1964.

–. "Jewish-Greek Literature of the Greek Period," *The Cambridge History of Judaism,* Volume Two: *The Hellenistic Age.* ed. W. D. Davies and Louis Finkelstein. Cambridge: Cambridge University Press, 1989. 385–408.

Waszink, J. H. "Abtreibung," *RAC* 1 (1950) 55–60.

–. "Aether," *RAC* 1 (1950) 150–158.

Wedderburn, A. J. M. *Baptism and Resurrection: Studies in Pauline Theology against its Graeco-Roman Background.* WUNT 44. Tübingen: J.C.B. Mohr (Paul Siebeck), 1987.

Wefelmeier, Carl. *Die Sentenzensammlung der Demonicea.* Athens: Rossolatos, 1962.

Wendland, Paul. "Die Therapeuten und die philonische Schrift vom beschaulichen Leben," *JCPhSup* 22 (1896) 693–772.

–. *Anaximenes von Lampsakos: Studien zur ältesten Geschichte der Rhetorik.* Berlin: Weidmann, 1905.

Wengst, Klaus. *Tradition und Theologie des Barnabasbriefes.* AKG 42. Berlin and New York: de Gruyter, 1971.

West, Martin L. *Studies in Greek Elegy and Iambus.* Berlin and New York: de Gruyter, 1974.

–. *The Orphic Poems.* Oxford: Clarendon, 1983.

Westermann, Claus. *Wurzeln der Weisheit: Die ältesten Sprüche Israels und anderer Völker.* Göttingen: Vandenhoeck & Ruprecht, 1990.

White, Stephen A. *Sovereign Virtue: Aristotle on the Relation Between Happiness and Prosperity.* Stanford Series in Philosophy. Stanford: Stanford University Press, 1992.

Whybray, R. N. "Proverbs 8.22–31 and its Supposed Prototypes," *VT* 15 (1965) 504–514. Reprint, Crenshaw, *Studies,* 390–400.

–. *Wisdom in Proverbs: The Concept of Wisdom in Proverbs 1–9.* SBT 45. Naperville: Allenson; London: SCM, 1965.

Wicker, Kathleen O. "Mulierum Virtutes (Moralia 242E–263C)," in Betz, *Plutarch's Ethical Writings,* 106–134.

Wiens, Devon H. "Mystery Concepts in Primitive Christianity and its Environment," *ANRW* II.23.2 (1980) 1248–1284.

Wiggens, David. "Weakness of Will, Commensurability, and the Objects of Deliberation and Desire," in Rorty, *Essays,* 241–265.

Wilckens, Ulrich. *Weisheit und Torheit: Eine exegetisch-religionsgeschichtliche Untersuchung zu 1 Kor. 1 und 2.* BHT 26. Tübingen: J.C.B. Mohr (Paul Siebeck), 1959.

–. "ὑποκρίνομαι, κτλ.," *TDNT* 8 (1972) 559–571.

Wilckens, Ulrich, and Georg Fohrer. "σοφία, σοφός, σοφίζω," *TDNT* 7 (1971) 465–528.

Wilckens, Ulrich, with Alois Kehl and Karl Hoheisel, "Heuchelei," *RAC* 14 (1988) 1205–1231.

Wilken, Robert L., ed. *Aspects of Wisdom in Judaism and Early Christianity*. University of Notre Dame Center for the Study of Judaism and Christianity in Antiquity 1. Notre Dame and London: University of Notre Dame Press, 1975.

Williams, Bernard. "Justice as a Virtue," in Rorty, *Essays,* 189–199.

Wilson, Walter T. *Love Without Pretense: Romans 12.9–21 and Hellenistic-Jewish Wisdom Literature*. WUNT 2.46. Tübingen: J.C.B. Mohr (Paul Siebeck), 1991.

Wimbush, Vincent L. "Sophrosyne: Greco-Roman Origins of a Type of Ascetic Behavior," *Gnosticism and the Early Christian World: In Honor of James M. Robinson*. ed. James E. Goehring, Charles W. Hedrick, Jack T. Sanders, with Hans Dieter Betz. FF 2. Sonoma, CA: Polebridge, 1990. 89–102.

Winston, David. "Was Philo a Mystic?" *Studies in Jewish Mysticism: Proceedings of Regional Conferences Held at the University of California, Los Angeles and McGill University in April, 1978*. ed. Joseph Dan and Frank Talmage. Cambridge, MA: Association for Jewish Studies, 1982. 15–39.

–. "Philo's Ethical Theory," *ANRW* II.21.1 (1984) 372–416.

–. "The Sage as Mystic in the Wisdom of Solomon," *The Sage in Israel and the Ancient Near East*. ed. John G. Gammie and Leo G. Perdue. Winona Lake: Eisenbrauns, 1990. 383–397.

Winter, Martin. *Pneumatiker und Psychiker in Korinth: Zum religionsgeschichtlichen Hintergrund von 1. Kor. 2,6 – 3,4*. Marburger Theologische Studien 12. Marburg: Elwert, 1975.

Winton, Alan P. *The Proverbs of Jesus: Issues of History and Rhetoric*. JSNTSup 35. Sheffield: JSOT, 1990.

Wisse, Frederik. "Die Sextus-Sprüche und das Problem der gnostischen Ethik," *Zum Hellenismus in den Schriften von Nag Hammadi*. ed. Alexander Böhlig and Frederick Wisse. Göttinger Orientforschungen 6.2. Wiesbaden: Otto Harrassowitz, 1975. 55–86.

Wolf, Erik. *Griechisches Rechtsdenken*. 4 vols. Frankfurt: Klostermann, 1950–1970.

Wolfson, Harry A. *Philo: Foundations of Religious Philosophy in Judaism, Christianity, and Islam*. 2 vols. Cambridge: Harvard University Press, 1947.

Woodbury, L. "The Seal of Theognis," *Studies in Honor of Gilbert Norwood*. ed. Mary E. White. Phoenix Sup. 1. Toronto: University of Toronto Press, 1952. 20–41.

Wyß, Bernhard. "Gregor II (Gregor von Nazianz)," *RAC* 12 (1983) 793–863.

Zandee, Jan. "The Teachings of Silvanus (NHC VII,4) and Jewish Christianity," *Studies in Gnosticism and Hellenistic Religions Presented to Gilles Quispel on the Occasion of his 65th Birthday*. ed. R. van den Broek and Maarten J. Vermaseren. EPRO 91. Leiden: E.J. Brill, 1981. 498–584.

Zauzich, Karl-Theodor. "Pap. Dem. Insinger," *LÄ* 4 (1982) 898–899.

Zeller, Dieter. *Die weisheitlichen Mahnsprüche bei den Synoptikern*. FB 17. 2nd ed. Würzburg: Echter Verlag, 1983.

–. "σωφροσύνη, κτλ.," *EWNT* 3 (1983) 790–792.

Ziegler, Konrat. "Tyche," *PW* 7A.2 (1948) 1643–1696.

Zimmerli, Walther. "Das Buch Kohelet- –Traktat oder Sentenzensammlung?" *VT* 24 (1974) 221–230.

Zucchelli, Bruno. *ΥΠΟΚΡΙΤΗΣ: Origine e Storia del Termine*. Brescia: Paideia, 1963.

Zuntz, Günther. "Zum Kleanthes-Hymnus," *HSCP* 63 (1958) 289–308.

Index of Passages

Old Testament

Old Testament Apocrypha

New Testament

Old Testament Pseudepigrapha

Philo

Dead Sea Scrolls, Rabbinic Literature, and Josephus

Patristic Literature and Nag Hammadi Tractates

Greco-Roman Literature

Near-Eastern Instructional Texts

Index of Modern Authors

Index of Subjects

Texte und Studien zum Antiken Judentum

Alphabetical Index

Schäfer, Peter, Gottfried Reeg, Klaus Herrmann, Claudia Rohrbacher-Sticker, Guido Weyer (Ed.): Konkordanz zur Hekhalot-Literatur. Volume 1. 1986. *Volume 12.*

Schäfer, Peter, Rina Otterbach, Gottfried Reeg, Klaus Herrmann, Claudia Rohrbacher-Sticker, Guido Weyer (Ed.): Konkordanz zur Hekhalot-Literatur. Volume 2. 1988. *Volume 13.*

Schäfer, Peter, Hans-Jürgen Becker, Anja Engel, Kerstin Ipta, Uta Lohmann, Martina Urban, Gert Wildensee (Ed.): Synopse zum Talmud Yerushalmi. I/1 Ordnung Zeraᶜim – Traktate Berakhot und Peʾa. 1991. *Volume 31.*

–: I/3–5 Ordnung Zeraᶜim – Traktate Demai, Kilʾayim und Sheviʾit. 1992. *Volume 33.*

–: I/6–11 Ordnung Zeraᶜim – Traktate Terumot bis Bikkurim. 1992. *Volume 35.*

Schäfer, Peter, Margarete Schlüter, Hans Georg von Mutins (Ed.): Synopse zur Hekhalot-Literatur. 1981. *Volume 2.*

Schäfer, Peter, Hans-Jürgen Becker, Klaus Herrmann, Claudia Rohrbacher-Sticker, Stefan Siebers (Ed.): Übersetzung der Hekhalot-Literatur. Volume 2: §§ 81–334. 1987. *Volume 17.*

Schäfer, Peter, Hans-Jürgen Becker, Klaus Herrmann, Lucie Renner, Claudia Rohrbacher-Sticker, Stefan Siebers (Ed.): Übersetzung der Hekhalot-Literatur. Volume 3: §§ 335–597. 1989. *Volume 22.*

Schäfer, Peter, Hans-Jürgen Becker, Klaus Herrmann, Lucie Renner, Claudia Rohrbacher-Sticker, Stefan Siebers, (Ed.): Übersetzung der Hekhalot-Literatur. Volume 4: §§ 598–985. 1991. *Volume 29.*

Schlüter, Margarete: see Schäfer, Peter

Schmidt, Francis: Le Testament Grec d'Abraham. 1986. *Volume 11.*

Schwartz, Daniel R.: Agrippa I. 1990. *Volume 23*

Shatzman, Israel: The Armies of the Hasmonaeans and Herod. 1991. *Volume 25.*

Siebers, Stefan: see Schäfer, Peter

Swartz, Michael D.: Mystical Prayer in Ancient Judaism. 1992. *Volume 28.*

Urban, Martina: see Schäfer, Peter

van Loopik, Marcus (Übers. u. Komm.): The Ways of the Sages and the Way of the World. 1991. *Volume 26.*

Veltri, Giuseppe: Eine Tora für den König Talmai. 1994. *Volume 41.*

Wewers, Gerd A.: Probleme der Bavot-Traktate. 1984. *Volume 5.*

Weyer, Guido: see Schäfer, Peter

Wildensee, Gert: see Schäfer, Peter

Wilson, Walter T.: The Mysteries of Righteousness. 1994. *Volume 40.*

For a complete catalogue please write to
J. C. B. Mohr (Paul Siebeck) · P. O. Box 2040 · D-72010 Tübingen